INTRODUCTION BEHAVIORAL ECONOMY

JOHN LOK

Made with ♥ on the Notion Press Platform
www.notionpress.com

Contents

Preface

Introduction

Behavioral economics combines elements of economics and psychology to understand how and why people behave the way they do in the real world. It differs from neoclassical economics, which assumes that most people have well-defined preferences and make well-informed, self-interested decisions based on those preferences. Behavioral economics is a field of study aimed at understanding why people make economically irrational decisions. Rational choice theory holds that consumers make choices that maximize their utility. In reality, people can be swayed or distracted from doing so.

Behavioral economics is primarily concerned with the bounds of rationality of economic agents. Behavioral models typically integrate insights from psychology, neuroscience and microeconomic theory. The study of behavioral economics includes how market decisions are made and the mechanisms that drive public opinion. Behavioral economics is a field of study aimed at understanding why people make economically irrational decisions. Rational choice theory holds that consumers make choices that maximize their utility.

Behavioral economics combines elements of economics and psychology to understand how and why people behave the way they do in the real world. It differs from neoclassical economics, which assumes that most people have well-defined preferences and make well-informed, self-interested decisions based on those preferences. Behavioral economics (BE) uses psychological experimentation to develop theories about human decision making and has identified a range of biases as a result of the way people think and feel. BE is trying to change the way economists think about people's perceptions of value and expressed preferences. We need behavioural economics to understand the daily life decisions of customers and anyone else. It is used in the health sector, insurance sector, corporates, multi-national companies etc. In all sectors, it has a significant role to play. Companies are inhabiting behavioural economics to rising their sales. How transport may help economic development in possible?

In my this book, I shall indicate our daily fun human behavior to explain how and why our daily lives any matters, may have relationship to behavioral economy to let readers understand.

Prologue

Tablc of contcnt

Why has any individual country have many people invest share behavior which can influence the country's macro consumption desire?

Can technology influence human shopping behavioral change?

Why and how human behavior may influence the country's economic growth or recession?

Technology how impacts human behavior changing?

How and why employees behaviors may influence economy development?

Robots invention whether they can help organizations to raise efficiencies or inefficiencies?

Why social behavior may influence organizational strategy needs to be changed ?

How and why human behavior may influence economic growth or recession?

CHAPTER ONE

Factors influences fuel price change

Market economy theory is an economic system and distribution are guide by the price signals created by the force of supply and demand. So , the concept of market economy is an economic system in which economic decisions, and the pricing of goods and services are guided by the interactions of a country's individual citizens and businesses.

The both principles of market economy indicated that producers and sellers of goods and services with offer that at the highest possible price that consumers are willing to pay for goods and services . When the level of supply needs to level of demand a natural economic equilibrium is achieved. Hong Kong, Singapore, New Zealand, Switerland, United States , Ireland united Kingdom, these countries are applying market economy principle to dominate themselves countries business activities. However, it is difficult to free market economy, because market economy depends on supply and demand regulate the economy, but a time free market economy is an economy in what all resources are owned by individuals.

The advantages of a market economy may include : Innovation, variety, and individual choices, but it is distribution of wealth, poor work condition and environmental degradation. However, a pure market economy development is difficult because people will always have incentives to use to choose what kinds of product in preference. The characteristics of a market economy, they may include that it is unplanned free enterprise, private property, economic freedom, consumer competition incentive profit pursue, voluntary exchange,, limited government involvement, freedom of enterprise and choice, the role of self interest, market and price, the reliance on technology and capital goods, specialization, use of monetary ad to active, but limited role of government.

So, market economies work using the forces of supply and demand to determine the appropriate prices and quantities for most goods and services in the economy. Hence, one country needs to develop market economy, it needs have a good market environment, such as one commodity needs have advertisement to let consumers to know its existence, in economics, market does not refer why to a fixed location, on enough number balance of buyers and sellers, perfect competition, perfect competition, building good relationship between buyers and sellers, one price (no change) price to any product easily, sound monetary system. Then, when the country can have good market environment, it can develop or implement its market economy strategy more easily.

The free market economy may be the best economic strategy choice because it contributes to economic growth . It ensures competitive markets, supply and demand create competition, which also help ensure that this best goods or services are provided to consumers at a lower price (reasonable price). It can compare the best among perfect competition imperfect competition, oligopoly, monopoly. Hence, market economy encourages market force occurrence, e.g. when the price of crude oil increases, when there are shortages in the supply , when the shortages occur, they become market forces. The demand is more supply, which causes the prices to rise as the crude oil is less available and therefore consumers will be willing to pay more.

The market economy is decides, when the wants of the consumers and the profit motive of the producers will decide what will be produced and management (the owners) together will determine how goods will be produced in a market economy. So, such as oil sale case, when the country has many oil manufactures hope to change oil price, they won't manufacture more oil to supply to oil users, e.g. car drivers, public transport service organizations, the aim to bring oil shortage supply in order to rise oil price more easily.
So, free market economy may bring product unfair sale price to any consumers in the country. Because free market economy is too free for manufacturers / producers to make unreasonable product manufacturing decision whether their products manufacturing number (supply number) is more ore less in order to achieve the highest sale price.It won't bring consumer benefit, when they need to pay high price to buy the product in long time. For oil product case example, when the country all oil suppliers, they make decision to manufacture less number oil product in order to reduce oil supply number. They aim to cause oil shortage challenge, when the oil need, e.g. when the country has many air planes need gas to private energy to fly frequently, but gas supply is less to airlines to pay higher gas price to buy, or the country has many people need to catch buses, but gas supply number is less. So, bus companies also need to pay higher gas price to buy even the country has many people own cars. They often need to drive cars to go to work or relax. So, many country car owners , they need to pay higher gas price to drive themselves cars.

In fact, in the country implements free market economy strategy, so it causes many product manufacturers attempt to cooperate to reduce products manufacturing number. They aim to reduce product supply , but when consumers number is still increasing. Their demand to the product increases, when the product's demand number is more than supply number, it will cause supply shortage challenge. Consequently, the kind of product price may be reasonable to increase. Hence, in consumer behavior view, the country's consumers still accept to pay higher price to buy the product, because they believe the kind of product supply is decreasing.

Hence, it has relationship between how many product choice and consumer payment desire, if the market has many difficult kinds of product to let consumers to choose, then the kind of product's price can not be increased easily. Such as oil product case, when the country has less number oil manufacturing number. Then, oil buyers feel there are not many oil suppliers to let them to choose and in general these several oil suppliers' oil prices are increasing together . So, oil consumers number will not be influenced to reduce easily, because they have no many oil suppliers choice in the country.

Positive , Negative and social change and Terrorisms attack influence to fuel price

What situation is negative social change. I shall indicate globalization society example. We are entering globalization society. For example, air tickets can be bought from internet, so travellers won't need to go to travel agent to buy conveniently. It is due to the global travel industry is increasingly competition. Thus, global travel industry competition will bring negative social change to influences fuel price rising because it will increase traveller numbers and airline flight times to fly. When, traveller's travelling desire demand numbers will be grown up fast, then their online electronic-ticket buying or consumption behaviors will be rise. Thus, it will also cause online e-ticket price is decreased to attract many travellers to choose to buy e-ticket from online channel more than paper-ticket visiting travel agent channel. Thus, it is negative social change influences to cause fuel price rising due to plane flight flying times will increase and airline company will increase demand to buy many fuel to prepare to fly often. When fuel demand will rise, then the fuel sellers will rise fuel price in possible. Thus, airline industry global competition will being negative social change to influence fuel price raising up and air ticket price falling down to attract many traveller numbers to choose to buy among different travel agents.

Negative social change influence

What situation is positive social change. I shall indicate economic growth example. When one country has better economic development in the year. Then, employers will have more effort to do businesses. Then, they will create many jobs to provide to the country citizen to do. When, these unemployed people have jobs to do, they will have extra income to save. They can spend extra to prepare to spend to enjoy their entertainment every year, such as travelling. Thus, the positive social change will influence traveller number increasing, then the plane flight flying times will also increase, it will cause planes need to use much fuel to fly. The result, it will also increase fuel demand, but the fuel natural resource number will decrease , so fuel supply will also decrease. Finally, it will also cause fuel price to be risen.

Also, I shall indicate the financial risk of airline industry evidence from Cathay Pacific airways and China airlines against key determinants of which include interest rate, exchange rate and fuel price risk for the period of January 1996 year to December 2011 year. During this period, these key external factors which were the most serious influence to cause these two airlines choose to change their strategic behaviors.

Due to any these financial risks is difficult to predict and it was also changing often, these factors will also affect any airlines stock returns which arise from changing economic conditions, e.g. fuel price movements and fluctuations in exchange rates. These external unpredicted changing factors will attribute to the air tickets cyclical demand, capital investment, fixed costs of labor and landing rights to this global airline industry.

However, the relationship between fuel price and stock prices varies across economies. The effects of oil price changes in sub-sector indices, such as wood, paper and printing, insurance and electricity. In the past, on global stock exchange market was positively significant in 2011 year. Otherwise, with respect to the U.S.A. aviation industry, some economists suggested that global airlines stock returns were negatively to percentage change in fuel prices related to any airline firm value, e.g. Qantas and Air New Zealand were negatively share price growth to fuel price risk in the short term in the 2011 year.

Thus, it brings this question. Whether positive or negative social change will be one important factor to impact fuel price rising. I feel positive social or negative social change will be one important factor to impact fuel price rising. The reason is such as below:

Nowadays, airline transportation demands are increasing, due to many travelers need to catch planes to travel as well as many cargoes need to be carried to planes to transport to different countries to sell. It seems aviation transportation industry is important to influence the health of the global economy growth nowadays. However, ignorance of internal or external market dynamics, catching travelers business can be detrimental to airline profitability more than carrying cargoes business. Because the demands of travelling different countries' travelers' consumption are still more than the demands of businessmen carrying cargoes in any countries every year. Thus, the travel industry will increase demand to human travelling business more than cargo transportation business. However, the cargo flying transportation demand will rise, due to many global fast speed post businesses are growing. Base on both global cargo flying transportation demand and travellers' flying travelling demand are increasing. Thus, the fuel demand will increase, but the fuel supply will be shortage. So, it will cause fuel price rising consequently.

How can positive or negative social change influence any airlines' air ticket prices to be risen or fallen? In fact, the increase in petroleum price can have chance to affect airlines in a negative manner because increased oil prices have resulted in the reduction of services operations, the number of airline schedules flights, even airline bankruptcies.

Thus, it seems that plan travellers and air flying cargo transportation both demand have been increasing. This social increasing demand change factor, it will be the most influential cause the bad effects to cause airline industry share price reducing or reducing air ticket price or decreasing traveler numbers more than the other factors influence, such as inflation, terrorism, oil shortage, bank interest rate etc. unpredictable external situation factors.

To support this hypotheses, this are my research questions, such as : Does a combination of terrorism and price of petroleum significantly influence airline profit changing mostly? The alternative hypothesis was base on a significant relationship exists between terrorism, price of petroleum and airline profitability more than other factors, such as inflation, bank interest rate or air ticket price changing of these factors influence. I shall indicate that the first assumption was that terrorism has a negative effect on airline profitability and another assumption was that only external factors as oil prices or terrorism affect airline profitability.

Terrorisms attack influence

Whether terrorisms attack will influence fuel price rises up or falls down. I feel terrorisms attack to any country, which will cause plan fuel price falls down. Because travellers will feel dangerous and worry about their life safety when they catch the plan to enter the country if the country has serious terrorisms attack risk to cause plan crash accidently.

However the effects of oil price and terrorism on airline profitability was limited to a regional perspective, e.g. the terrorism attack of plane crash event to USA on 11 Sept. After the terrorism attack happened on USA 11 Sept. incident of terrorism attack was restricted to events of skyjacking, attacks on oil production, refinery and distribution. Thus, USA on 11 Sept. terrorism attack will cause oil price falls down , due to it will influence travellers fear death , so who will reduce times to travel to USA after 11 Sept. date terrorism attack occurrence at the year. The oil sellers will reduce oil sale price to attract many airline companies to buy more supply, due to airlines will decrease demand to buy fuel to provide planes to fly when the traveller numbers has decreasing and flying times will be decrease also. Thus, the fuel price will be decreased consequently after the terrorism attacks to any country.

Other types of terrorist activities, such as attacks on financial targets or senior government officials could have an adverse effect on the petroleum and airline industry. I think the disruption of the production or distribution of petroleum because of incidents of terrorism was costly in terms of loss of business and the inflationary effect on fuel dependent products or services.

In fact, some airlines have adopted more fuel saving technology, so whose fuel consumption would not use more than other non fuel saving technology airlines. So, the owned fuel saving technology airlines which will buy less fuel to use. It means that they won't need fear fuel rising to increase their expenditure because they only need to buy less fuel to use and their fuel demand won't fall , even fuel price has risen.

However, it seems fuel price increasing will not be the only factor to influence the airline industry's traveler numbers decreasing, due it is possible that the airlines need to rise air ticket price to riase their profit, sue to their fuel cost has risen. However, due to some airlines which have fuel saving technology, so which can avoid to use more fuel to provide planes to use and which fuel costs will be reduced, then which can provide cheaper air ticket fare prices to compare the non fuel saving technology airlines. The result will cause some non owned fuel save technological airlines will lose travelling customers in this global airline travelling market, also the non fuel saving technology airlines need to renew their fuel technology if which want to keep their competitive abilities to avoid to close down their businesses.

Can airline fuel self-organization avoid
fuel price rising cost

I feel one airline fuel self-organization can avoid fuel price rising to influence cost rising because it doesn't often buy any fuel from fuel suppliers. However, there are some airlines which are the characteristic of airline fuel self organization and they are present in that both of oil fuel production and providing flights service in airline industry. So, these airline fuel self organizations can control the oil fuel price by themselves. However, one airline fuel self organization is also evident in efforts by businesses acts of terrorism against economic targets by adopting proactive steps, such as airline and airport security. So, it seems airline fuel self organization can reduce the risk to avoid oil price raising and terrorism attacks to raise cost in airline industry risk management sector.

Beside, these airline fuel self organizations which have high technology of fuel efficient aircrafts, the use of one aircraft model, the adoption of direct routes versus customer loyalty programs and other operational cost reductions are strategies for increased profitability. It seems these airline fuel self organizations can solve oil price, terrorism etc. external factor influences to raise cost.

Instead of high technology of fuel efficient aircrafts and airline fuel self organization methods can solve terrorism attacks and oil price rising risks. However, I believe that there are other risks are caused to these airline fuel self organizations to raise their airline cost possibly. The risks include such as user factor, such as culture, tradition, education ; economic factor, such as costs, human resources and macro economic factor, such as political stability, economic development, educational policy, health policy, environmental policy. However, these risks occurrences are resulting in the relationship of cause and effect events. These events are not directly observable. Such as, the complexity of relationship between terrorism and airline profitability. Hence, if global airline industry can predict when those risks occur to do protective strategic behavior. It is possible that which can understand when these risk events will occur and to adopt their protective strategic behaviors to influence their outcomes to be positive to avoid any external risk threats on the long term. However, I think hierarchy, airlines fuel self organization efficiency methods which are as possible predictors of user preferences to avoid risk threat events to cause whose airline businesses cost rising to cause failure occurrences in airline industry.

● Is fuel price rising only factor to
cause airline risk in short term

In my study, I suppose terrorism and the price of petroleum both factors which had properties of distinct and interrelated close relationship to raise airline cost. Moreover, these variables (terrorism and the price of petroleum) displayed differentiation, self replication, efficiency and hierarchy which can cause risk events to airline industry. However, I also think the other internal and external threat factors of airline industry, such as inflation, bank interest rate, business model, service quality, airline fuel or plane engine technology, air ticket pricing, brand loyalty, airline strategic management, government policy and fuel hedging of these factors which can also raise the risks to threaten any airlines existence in airline industry.

There are two basic business models in tourism industry. They are network (full service) and low cost (discount) carriers. The network carrier model employs diversification strategy by increased domestic destinations, serving international routes, providing diverse seating arrangements (business, economy and first class), maintaining a complex system of offering high quality service. Otherwise, low cost (discount) airlines focus on lower air fares. To keep operating costs down, discount airlines offer shorter routes and provide point-to-point destinations rather than through sophisticated flights are primarily in domestic destinations. So, discount airlines operate a common model aircraft fleet, offer a single seating arrangement and cheaper flight services offered to compare network airlines. However, these two basic business models have their unique competitive abilities to provide any airlines existence in tourism industry nowadays.

In fact, natural resource of oil is decreasing in our earth. But as the same time, human demand is increasing and oil supply is decreasing, so it also causes the oil fuel price is increasing to supply to airline industry. It influences not only to airline industry, it also impacts of higher oil fuel price to tourism, such as expansion of airports are made based on expected demand increase.

Tourism has been proven to many adverse events, including terrorism, flight disruptions. Beside, the bad natural climate change influences, such as the volcanic ash cloud event occurred in April 2010 year. So, airline industry need to concern climate change because it will cause high fuel prices indirectly. For example, the event occurred the extreme increase in operating costs for airlines in 2008 year, due to unprecedented prices for aviation fuel also meant, that despite the introduction of fuel charges, so this event causes the global tourism industry recorded losses seriously. Even if alternative fuels become commercially available for airlines which are still likely to be more expensive than present aviation fuel.

Higher airfares in the future are likely to lead to reduction in travel and cause tourists to shift from more distant to closer destination. When some of the economic responses to higher oil prices are obvious assessing the overall economic impacts on tourism is difficult. However, long term changes in global oil price rises will be similar to global changes in other commodity prices, exchange rates and income. It is therefore important to consider the impact of high oil prices on tourism from a general equilibrium perspective rather than relying only on bottom partial equilibrium approaches.

However, I believe tourism and airline industries have close relationship, such as tourism and airline industries are likely to suffer in an environment of high oil prices. Given that tourism destinations receive tourists from a range of origins, it would be useful to understand of some countries are increasing oil prices than others. Such as the net oil importing countries are selling higher oil prices than oil exporting countries generally. For example, New Zealand is an oil import country to provide planes for international visitor arrivals, so its oil fuel price is usually higher to charge to NZ airlines because any NZ airlines need to pay to foreign countries to buy any oil more expensive price. So, NZ airlines usually charge higher airfares to its visitors to compare the other exporting oil countries' airlines. It will impact NZ has negative influence to domestic tourism industry as well as planes need will also be decreased , due to NZ charge high fuel price to cause air ticket price to be raised.

In economic theory, on income effects indicate negative impacts on tourism demand, the exact effects of higher oil fuel prices for specific destinations are far from clear. However, airline industry's different market segments show different sensitivities to air ticket fares changes.
On the first hand, if the visitors are long destinations generally wealthier than average and therefore potentially less affected, as energy costs would be a smaller proportion of their income compared will be those from less wealthy groups. Thus, the more wealthier travelers who won't decrease travelling desire, even the fuel price raises to case the air ticket price to be increased.
On the second hand, oil prices don't translate into higher transport costs especially not on air routes that are highly competitive and that are maintained for strategic reasons. So, non air transportation industry won't influence customer number to be decreased easily.

On the third hand, many other factors shape tourists' decision making, including emotion drivers or those related to images, fashions and perceptions. Increasing environmental protection awareness of tourists could also be an important factor to influence tourism consumption, instead of oil fuel price raising causes air ticket fares raising factor to reduce traveler numbers. However, oil price raising reason causes also due to high use of cars, vans and domestic air transport in some countries, e.g. Hong Kong, China countries, there are many people like to buy cars to drive. So, the private driver numbers are increasing demand to cause these countries' oil fuel prices raise in the short time suddenly. It implies airlines need to consider their country car number whether is increasing or decreasing. If their country car number is increasing, it is possible to cause fuel price to be risen up because car demand is increasing to need to use more fuel and it has less supply of fuel in the year. Otherwise, if their country car number is decreasing, it is possible to cause fuel price to be fallen down because car demand is decreasing to need to use less fuel and it has more supply of fuel in the year.

Is fuel price rising only factor to cause airline risk
in short term

In long run, fuel raising price will not cause risk to airline, due to implications of changes to supply and demand side conditions of oil fuel energy may differ qualitatively. For example, due to investment responses of producers, consumers and governments in alternative energy sources and more energy efficient plants, vehicles are supplied in order to achieve oil fuel price can't be risen seriously.
However, I believe oil fuel rising charge will be an important factor to influence global airline ticket fares to be

increased in the short term to cause risk because oil fuel rising charge will be influenced to raise any airlines pressure from other unpredicted factor risk influences.

Firstly, on the bank interest changing factor, e.g. bank interest rate rising which only attract more bank saving. But it can not influence the bank savers who choose to reduce relax time to go to other countries travelling. Otherwise, when the bank savers can save more money to earn higher interest in banks, who will prefer to choose to use their saving to consume travelling. Due to who can earn higher interest rate after a period of saving time. So, I believe who behavioral travelling consumption will be raised when the banks will raise interest rate, then the bank savers won't choose to save more money in banks. So it is possible that who will withdraw more money to consume to go to travelling from banks. It seems bank interest rate changing won't influence bank savers' behavioral travelling consumption to be reduced.

Secondly, on the exchange rate changing factor, although any country's exchange changing will cause other countries' money value to be fallen down or risen up. However, it won't influence any travelers' behavioral consumption to be reduced seriously. Although, it is possible that the traveler won't spend too much to go to shopping when who travel to the another country and arrive the country. But, it is not possible to influence the traveler decides to reduce consumption to buy any air ticket to go to travelling in short time.

Thirdly, any country inflation also can not reduce travelers' travelling consumption easily because inflation can influence consumers who choose to buy cheaper foods and clothing and reduce entertainments in their every day life. But, one country's inflation can not influence it's citizen do not spend much travelling expenditure because travelers only spend one time or two times of travelling every year usually. So, the travelling expenditure rate of any households is not too much to compare daily essential expenditure.

So, it seems that bank interest rate and exchange rate changing and inflation won't influence any travelers' travelling consumption of decisions to be reduced easily in short time. Otherwise, if the oil fuel price raises too much, then global airlines' cost will be raised in long term. So, the airlines only choose to increase their air fare prices to aim to avoid loss possibly in long term. It seems that oil fuel raising price and bank interest rate and exchange rate changing and inflation factors will have direct influence airline income in long term.

Biofuels energy increases supply

I suggest these methods how to avoid the oil raising price factor to cause airline air fare prices to be risen to lead the risk of traveler numbers to be reduced as below:

The first method: Whether aviation fuel markets will have what benefits from biofuels supply to planes. I shall refer the scope includes trends in jet fuel price, airline response to fuel price, increases and volatility and environmental goals for aviation. The aviation fuel supply industry includes production, distribution and consumption of aviation fuel and it outlines players in the aviation fuel supply chain. For example, at each airport, fuel supply chain organization and fuel sourcing could differ with regard to the role of oil companies, airlines, airport owners and operators and airport service companies. However, major jet fuel purchasers are airlines, general aviation operators, corporate aviation and the military, with most of the jet fuel in global different countries demanders being used for domestic commercial and civilian flights carrying passengers, cargos or both.

Commercial aviation fuel efficiency has improved dramatically over time, largely due to aircraft and engine upgrades and operational and air traffic control improvements. So, it seems that fuel supply factor can influence airline fare prices majorly. However, jet fuel prices generally correlate with prices of crude oil and other refined petroleum products, such as diesel. So, increasing prices and the persistent price volatility of jet fuel markets import airline industry finances in any countries.
However, airlines use various strategies to manage aviation fuel price certainty, including financial hedges, increased vertical integration and adjustments in aircraft utilization and size to avoid the jet fuel raising price risk.

Investments in alternative aviation fuel could be a mechanism to diversity expose to the price of petroleum. It seems the use of alternative aviation fuel would serve to diversify the fuel mix to reduce the risk of jet fuel monopoly raising price threat. If a diversified fuel mix were to avoid either fuel raising price in short term or to avoid fuel raising price in long term. Potential benefits include reduced actual fuel costs from only choice of jet fuel supply increased price certainty and lessened fuel costs. This diversify could allow airlines to become more consistently profitable and to make other investments in their businesses.
So, biofuels have potential to meet aviation industry needs, possibly including managing risks of upward fuel price trends and fuel price volatility and avoid risks with greenhouse gas emissions. So, the aviation fuels market could use biofuels to reduce greenhouse gas emission and mitigate long-term upward price trends, fuel price volatility or both.

What are the challenges of high priced oil for aviation? In fact, nowadays not the resources of oil as such, but much more the insecurity of supply, due to geopolitical instability in combination with a tight oil market makes a scenario with much higher oil prices than the world is currently experiencing not unlikely.
Aviation is completely dependent upon oil as its fuel source. Since no practical energy substitute is readily available for commercial aviation, a scarcity of petroleum relative to demand will present a major aviation policy. In addition, efficiency gains, due to operational measures and new aircraft medium term. In particular, it has been demonstrated that the annual reduction rate in fuel consumption traffic unit is not a constant, but is itself also falling, in contrast to past estimates.

So, a high-priced oil scenario will have severe consequences for demand, airline revenues, the competitive position of airports and eventually airline networks, strategies and fleet development. In particular, transfer demand, short-haul and leisure traffic can be expected to be heavily affected by high oil prices, due to their relative high price sensitivity. Also, different countries' governments or/and airlines are valuable to research another new and potential biofuel energy to substitute oil energy to supply our planes to reduce the threat of oil monopoly supply to influence the cause of air fare raising prices. Because the elasticity is very high to travelers, when the travelers feel air fares are rising high or even low level to influence travelers who will choose not to buy the air tickets to go to travel easily.

Whether will the fuel (oil based inputs) risk be high to compare other costs, e.g. engineering maintenance, employees salaries, general cleaning, security office expenses etc. expenditures to airlines? If the probability-weighted upside effect on firm value when a risk is resolved favorably is greater the risk than the probability-weighted downside effect if the risk is resolved badly, then expected value work not be enhanced by hedging. So, the risk will be resolved badly to any commercial airlines.

Airlines are an interesting case because the direct effect of source of risk resides squarely within the no offset in revenue functions (unlike for oil producers, for example), so value effects from costs feed directly into equity value. Most directly, the risk source is fuel costs to commercial airlines. Jet fuel is of course, a mix product of crude oil, so airlines indirectly face oil price risk. There are reasons to expect that airlines' fuel costs might to convex in oil price (i.e. absent any hedging). For example, oil prices, being generally pro-cyclical in recent times, tend to be highest when airline demand is strong.

In conclusion, airlines are therefore apt to use more high priced fuel than low-priced fuel over time. Airlines can raise air fare benefit is limited by the elasticity of demand. Also, cost functions could be influenced from fuel cost corresponds to upturns in economic activity overall (due to demand pressures on oil related prices), so it causes that airline's capacity delivers their services given their level of fixed capital. The essence of airlines basis risk in the case of jet fuel is essentially the time profile of the refining margin between crude and jet fuel, or the time profile of the price differential between other refined distillates and jet fuel. Thus, it is far from clear that risk management with oil is sure to add value to any airlines. It seems the impact of airline energy and any countries' domestic or foreign airline passenger travel numbers which have direct close relationship.

Reducing terrorism occurrence

Can reduce terrorism occur to reduce airline failure risk? It needs to judge to determine if a combination of terrorism and the price of petroleum significantly predicted airline profitability and which variable whether the further period was the most significant between the terrorism occurrence and the price of petroleum influence.

I suggest that different countries' governments or airlines need to collect samples of financial records from which country's any airline commercial passengers and cargo airlines on costs of fuel and any airline profitability. Also, gathering the terrorism data were comparison of terrorist attacks on petroleum in oil-producing nations, and incidents of high jacking aboard any country's aircraft.

When any countries' airlines or governments can judge whether the impact of airline energy and terrorism risk level is high or middle or low level. Then, which can use this sample data to measure how to do positive social change to decide either ought rise or reduce employment in commercial aviation industry, or ought need to invest other higher commercial activity in tourist and other travel related service businesses and when is the most right time to adopt of green technologies by the civil aviation manufacturing industry after the terrorism attacks occurrence to any country. It seems that any countries' governments or airlines which ought concern that the event of when the terrorism attacks will occur and gather past sample data to predict when the next time terrorism attacks event will be occurred and the risk will be high or middle or low level to influence global airline industry development.

● Methods to solve rising air fare
prices to decrease travellers'demand
Will airline industry's ticket price elasticity be influenced by demand and supply factor
In fact, the airline industry is largely dependent on the supply of the oil industry. Otherwise, the oil industry is inelastic. However, the increase or decrease of the price of airfare is directly related to the increase or decrease of the oil's price to fuel the aircrafts because there has no any new energy which can be substituted to oil fuel to airline industry.

So, it seems oil fuel producers are monopolies to control its sale price to be raised easily. Another factor that can affect airline industry to be directly targeted by a tragedy brought about by terrorism. The past four years, from 2001 year to 2005 year, there had been at least $40 billion worth of losses in the airline industry because of the September 11 date terrorism attacks in 2000 year. There had been an expected and significant decrease in the demand for the airline industry services because of the attacks that involved planes hijacking and crashing into key locations like the World Trade Center and the Pentagon in USA. Although, terrorism attacks can bring risk to influence fuel price rising in airline industry. However, this risk occurrence to airline industry is only that after the terrorism attacks occurred. It is possible that terrorism attacks won't occur again in the future.

Otherwise, our concerning ought be the greenhouse emissions and how it affects global warming. The air quality would be better once this new regulations are adopted. However, it would affect large airlines. So, it would increase the price of airfares because of economic fees that airline companies have to cover. Air pollution can give a negative impact on the domestic or oversea owned airline companies for long term. If airlines' planes can use clean fuel to fly, e.g. biofuel, then it will bring benefits to global airlines for long term.

On the positive side, the environment would be healthier as the earth's temperature would rise, and greenhouse effect would be dramatically reduced. This positive effect can come at a cost that is greater than most people perceive. On the psychology view point on travelers, who will be more preferable to catch planes to go to different countries to travel, due to the chance of air pollution and global environmental warm issues will be reduced to low risk to influence our health if planes can use biofuel to be energy to fly in the future one day.

It seems that spending expenditure to research other non polluted biofuel new energy is one solvable method to global airline industry in the future. To solve, any airlines or countries' governments or oil producers ought choose to spend more time to research new biofuel. Otherwise, the predicting when terrorism attacks event will be occurred, it is more difficult to predict the time more than researching to produce new biofuel energy method in the future. So, I recommend that researching the new biofuel energy or other kinds of energy to substitute the oil energy is the urgent behavioral economy which the airlines or oil producers or different countries' governments which need to concern nowadays.

Global energy is facing shortage problem. It is possible that secondary energy or human -made energy can be popular to replace to primary energy to use for global householders at home. How to apply micro economic method to predict this kind of secondary energy will be accepted to consume much than primary energy for global householders energy users in the future?

Global householder energy users and energy manufacturers are considering when earth's primary energy will be all used or energy shortage problem, keeping environment has not been polluted, plays a major role in weather and climate around the world. Several key facts are evident if we follow the flow of energy from the sun through the Earth system. Energy, like sound, travels as invisible waves of different sizes. Essentially, the energy absorbed by the land and oceans is what drives atmospheric and oceanic circulations. Hence, environment pollution issue influences global energy consumers, such as householders and business energy users , they hope to use secondary energy to replace primary energy because they fail primary energy will be used all in future one day. It seems that secondary energy need or demand will increase for global energy users.

Why do energy users and energy manufacturers need to consider earth's energy budget? Because we need to know about how much different kinds of energy can supply enough to us to use for our next generation. If some kinds of energy that we waste to use, then we shall face shortage of supply of the kinds of energy crisis to our next generation

- Global warming and energy shortage challenge influences energy users raising secondary energy need desires

We are facing global warmth and natural resource and energy shortage challenges. Due to our Earth have limited natural resource numbers to supply to us to manufacture energy, but global population has been increasing every year. Thus, it is possible that we have energy shortage crisis. Also, manufactures are spending too much energy to waste to manufacture any products, the energy will cause air or water pollution in manufacturing process or drivers are driving their vehicles to pollute air on the roads. Then it will cause global warmth crisis. Hence, it explains that why householder energy users and business energy users begin to consider whether second energy (man-made energy) can replace primary energy to be used for driving energy, home electrical energy, office electric energy or any property energy used aim. It implies that second energy need or demand ought increase rapidly as well as primary energy need or demand will decrease , due energy consumers are fear primary energy shortage problem and they feel to use less primary energy, their useful behaviors can reduce the energy shortage speed.

- Greenhouse primary gas energy householder users demand number increases

Have you ever seen a greenhouse? A greenhouse can trap heat in the sunlight and keeps the air inside the greenhouse warm enough for plants to grow. The glass roof and walls of a greenhouse let in sunlight but prevent heat from escape, this makes the greenhouse warm inside. Similarly, some gases in the Earth's atmosphere can trap heat from the sun and keep the Earth warm. This is called the greenhouse effect. The gases energy that can trap heat from the sun are called greenhouse gases. It is future one kind of potential primary energy to reduce environmental pollution new energy products for human consuming.

● Underwater primary water energy householder users demand number increases

The world's underwater meeting took place around a table about five meters underwater. Many scientists believe that due to melting of ice caused by global warming, the sea level will rise by as much as 1 m by the end of this century. If the level of the sea rises in the future, most regions of the country will be underwater.

Questions

What impact of global warming is mentioned by underground water?

Can human apply underwater water technology to explore natural underground water energy to avoid global warming threat?

Why do safety in using fuel and handle gas leaks factor can influence fuel energy users' demand number to be decreased? Why can town gas smell influence town gas energy buyers‘ demand number to be decreased ? How is electricity located at electric station far away from town area? How to solve problems caused by the use of fossil fuels? How to reduce the use of fossil fuels? All of these fuel related matters which will bring poor emotion to influence fuel energy users's demand to be decreased if second energy (man-made energy) can be invented to replace this kind of fuel energy to use in future one day.

This fuel energy consumers will feel how to solve the problems, the best way is to reduce their used of fossil fuel. This helps prevent fossil fuels form being used up too quickly. Also, it helps us to reduce environmental problems because fewer pollutants are given out when less fossil fuels are used. Can human help to reduce the use of fossil fuels? Fossil fuels are mainly in power station. Although we use some fossil fuels for our gas cooker and car, it won't make much difference if I use less. So, if fuel manufacturers can not solve any one of above bad emotion feeling to any one fuel users, I believe that fuel energy users number will decrease, if one day second energy (man-made energy) is invented to replace any one kind of primary energy to use in success.

● Why does fossil fuel will not be one kind of popular energy to be used by householders?

Fossil fuel is not used renew primary energy. Most of energy we use come from fossil fuels, for example, the electricity we use is generated in power stations by burning fossil fuels. The buses we ride use diesel oil. Therefore, we can help reduce the use of fossil fuels by saving energy in our daily lives. The actions that we can take such as: setting the air-conditioner to a higher temperature, walking instead of using lift, taking a short shower instead of a bath. This reduces the use of the hot water and thus the energy needed to heat the water. Thus, many people can help a lot to reduce our use of fossil fuels to avoid fossil fuel shortage risk occurrence.

For Hong Kong people energy consumption case, how much energy is used when a person travels from Hong Kong to Beijing by airplane? (The distance between Hong Kong and Beijing is about 2000 km). How much energy is used when Hong Kong people take a bus form Tai PO city to Central city? How much energy is used if Hong Kong people drive a car instead? (The driving distance between Tai Po city and Central city is 10Km).

Science explorer, we can visit the England website. Find ways to reduce energy usage from UK people energy using methods. Energy is very important to us. We need energy to walk and carry on any actions. We need energy to grow. We also need energy from food to survive. Without energy, we will die. All machines we use need energy. Without energy the electrical appliances in our homes won't work, the machines in factories will stop.

There are different forms of energy, e.g. light, heat, sound, wind, water, electrical kinetic, chemical and potential energy. Some form energy is primary energy and it can not renew to use, e.g. light, sound, wind, water, fossil fuel etc. Some form energy is secondary energy and it can renew to use in possible, e.g. nuclear, electric charge battery etc. Why does human need to concern how to manufacture secondary energy? Because it is possible that our natural resource will be consumed all, thus we will face primary energy shortage risk. If human can invent any new form of man-made secondary energy to renew to use in order to avoid primary energy shortage to supply to use to use, then human won't only depend on our Earth natural resource energy supply numbers. Hence, energy manufacturers can invent any new secondary energy to renew to use again either replaces primary energy or instead of primary energy limit number supply.

What is energy change? For television energy change power case. Firstly, electrical energy changes to television power to be used by television itself, then it changes to light power, next it changes to light power. How to choose fuel form to use? Due to energy can change to different form of powers to supply different form of power advantages to supply to human to use, so it is possible that we can also invent any secondary man made renew used energy to change different form powers to supply us to use, e.g. nuclear energy changes to light or sound or heat form of powers ; electrical charge batteries changes to light or sound or heat form powers to satisfy our daily life needs. For primary natural resource fuel energy example, different fuel has different feature, e.g. easy to burn, safe to use, gives out a lot of energy, inexpensive, produces little air pollution, easy to transport and store. How can we use in different channels, such as heating food, hot pat, driving vehicles. For example, although coal is not expensive to cause electricity energy for past transportation tool, e.g. traditional coal energy train or our daily home cooking, but it has negative influence to environment air pollution. Hence, we ought to follow the primary natural resource energy's feature to decide how to apply what aspects of our life needs. For example, if the country's people hope to reduce pollution when who use any kind of energy, e.g. US , Europe energy markets. The energy entrepreneur ought concentrate on manufacturing the kind of energy which can reduce environment pollution to be the least level to supply the country people to use, e.g. electric charge battery supplies to these countries' drivers to drive their vehicles on the roads, wind energy or water energy to manufacture electricity power supply to reduce air or water pollution ; or if the country people hope to buy the inexpensive energy to use, even the energy's quality and performance is worse, e.g. China, India, Hong Kong markets. The energy entrepreneur ought concentrate on manufacturing the lowest cost and enough supply of natural resource to manufacture the kind of energy to sell cheap price to these countries to use, e.g. China, Africa can accept to use e.g. gas, coal, fuel energy to use to compare developed countries people, e.g. UK, US; or if the countries people who hope to use energy which can easy to transport and store, e.g. light coal. The energy entrepreneur can choose to concentrate on manufacturing much coal to supply to the countries people to use, e.g. China, Arica Thus, to choose to manufacture which kinds of energy supply to the countries market people to use, the energy entrepreneur how decides to manufacture which kind of energy, it depends on which kinds of fuel advantages of the countries people most concerning.

Hence, when human feel energy shortage will come soon, energy users will reduce to use more energy to avoid energy shortage occurs in possible. It means that energy consumption number will be influenced to reduced or energy consumption buyers will reduce much expenditure to buy energy products for driving use or home use or office , warehouse working places to use. Energy needs or demand will reduce, due to environment pollution problem and energy shortage problem can influence global energy consumers' useful behaviors to be reduced in the future.

Why does secondary energy demand increase?

What is energy meaning? It is defined a dynamic quality, it is a fundamental entity of nature that is transferred between parts of a system in the production of physical change within the system, and it is usually regarded as the capacity for doing work, and it is usable power (such as heat or electricity) or the resources for producing such power. Why does secondary energy own investment worth? Because the different forms of primary natural resource energy will have supply shortage crisis, such as natural resources coal, gas, solar, wind, water, geothermal, biomass(organic material) etc. However, human can attempt to explore any undiscovered Earth or Space resource to manufacture any kinds of secondary energies, e.g. nuclear energy, electric recharge battery energy to supply to electric vehicle or space robots transportation tools to use or satisfy our daily life needs in future one day. So any kind of undiscovered secondary man-made renewed used energy resources have potential commercial worth to any energy entrepreneurs, it is possible that they can replace traditional primary energy to supply to human to use for our different aspects of life needs. In the future, the secondary energy demand will increase, when primary energy supply number has decreased form natural exploration. So, it will cause the effect of any demand of secondary energy product to be raised and prices to be increased in possible. Due to global population has been growing up, considerably China and India both countries populations have been increasing rapidly. Scientists predict there are more than 1.2 billion people worldwide will lack access to electricity, and more than 2.5 billion still use wood, charcoal to cook and heat in the future when primary energy has no enough number to supply to us to use. Hence, the fact that demand is this much greater than supply to make energy a prime market for further growth.

- Secondary energy can reduce investment risks

Although, secondary energy will have much investment worth, but energy like all other investments will carry risks. The internal and external risk factors include such as: policy is always changing to prohibit which do energy trading more easily between the energy exporting and importing countries, the secondary energy manufacturer itself own abilities to invent and to manufacture any kinds of secondary energy, improved technology can quickly make an technology obsolete, geopolitical rifts can happen overnight, the country's energy consumer (user)'s preferable choice to use which either kinds of secondary energy or secondary energy. So, it seems that (man-made) renewed used secondary energy industry can provide above-average returns, but it can also bring high risk commercial investment.

● Second energy solves energy exploration challenge

Traditionally, energy supply companies will apply those methods to operate energy providing businesses. For Shell,. Exxon examples, which had own gas stations, explore and drill for gas on their own. Other companies specialize in a part of the energy market, e.g. leasing oil rigs for example, or operating a pipeline. Energy supplying companies can choose to manufacture any kinds of energy to supply, e.g. trade oil, gas, coal, uranium, electricity etc. Any energy price and supply is demanded on the countries energy users' which kinds of energy most choice need or certain energy commodities to be chose to use popularly. For example, if US most people prefer to use secondary man-made renew used energy more than primary energy. Then, US energy manufacturers ought concentrate on manufacturing much different kinds of secondary man-made renew used energy to prepare to supply to its domestic US market in order to raise secondary energy price to sell in its country. So, the energy manufacturer's energy manufacturing choice, it is depend on which the country's people prefer to use which kinds of energy for their daily life needs.

However, scientists predict secondary energy market will have large market share, due to primary energy will have shortage to explore to supply in our earth and future energy consumers(users) prefer to choose to use more efficiency, less energy consumption, none environment pollution cause, cost effectiveness, renew to use of any kinds of energy. For example, the electricity recharge battery secondary man-made renew used energy is one kind of reducing air pollution power to push any electric battery vehicles to be driven to compare gas energy during drivers are driving their cars on the roads. They can reduce noise and air pollution and drivers can drive safely, who only need to buy one electric recharge battery to recharge in any electric recharge battery stations on streets when the electric recharge battery has no enough power to push their cars and they need to recharge their electric recharge battery drive when they had driven between one to two days. Due to primary energy, e.g. fuel , gas, the kinds of primary energies will have shortage to supply to global drivers to drive their traditional cars. Thus, the electric recharge battery or any undiscovered secondary energy will be future driving market needs. So, man-made renew used secondary energy, e.g. biofuel, hydro-electric, nuclear, will be one kind of efficient, clean, less pollution cause, cost-effective of energy to supply to our global vehicle market, even any other undiscovered new markets. Supposing they are popular to be used for electric vehicle market globally in future one day, then their prices will be decreased and constructed to average car requires up to 1,700 gallons of oil. Also supposing that making average computer requires more than ten times or weight to fossil fuels, every calories of food eaten in the US requires roughly then calories of fossil fuels. Hence, cheap energy will be one successful factor to influence future potential energy consumer (user) individual choice needs. Conversely, ion good economic times, people are more willing to travel, to buy products, and all of which success demand and low process for energy.

- Food production industry needs secondary energy useful number increasing

In the future, secondary energy will be the best choice to food production market. The modern food production system is essentially a success of changing fossil fuels into food. So, raising energy prices are almost higher food costs and even shortage for fossil fuels energy. If one day, one kind of discovered secondary man-made renew used energy can supply to any restaurants or homes to be used to cook at the cheap price, then the profit is very high for this kind of food production energy. Thus, future food production secondary energy consumption market is large and because the primary energy inputs for agriculture are higher than the energy outputs of the food. However, future secondary man-made renew used energy for food production system is only one part of whole energy consumer in food industry. The food production is related to whole food consumption market which includes: household cooking energy market, agriculture or vegetable, rice, fruit etc. foods farming machines energy market, food manufacturing factories market, food machine package market, transportation food delivery market, supermarket or fruit/food sale stores market. They must need any energy inputs to achieve the food production or food transportation or warehouse / stores electricity supply or cooking energy needs. Hence, these food suppliers relate to any whole food factory manufacturers, food retailers, food wholesalers, farmers and home/restaurant cookers, all of them must need to use energy to carry on their food producing or food cooking or food transportation activities every day in overall food industry. Thus, it seems that undiscovered any second energy demand will be increased, when the primary energy supply number is decreasing. Also, when people can accept to use secondary energy to replace primary energy to be used for any cooking, transporting food, manufacturing food, food retail stores or warehouse food delivery energy need activities. Then, the secondary energy price will be fall down to attract many food energy consumers.

Nowadays, the food industry energy may includes primary nature resource gas energy or electricity energy for house families or restaurants cooking needs, food delivering lorry drivers driving needs usually. If future second man made renew used energy is invented successful popular to be used, e.g. hydrogen, electric recharged battery energy for electric vehicles or restaurant/home families cooking needs or food factories machine manufacture energy needs. Then, the secondary energy will have possible to replace primary energy to be food industry energy market.

Wiley, composition services graphics indicated that global primary energy consumption had been increasing 30 billion tons from 1830 year to 510 billion tons in 2010 year as well as global population size had been increasing from 70 billion 1830 year to 510 billion in 2010 year. Thus, it seems that global primary energy consumption will be needed largely after 2010 year. If future global nature resource primary energy is explored full number and it had not enough energy number to supply global human to use. Then, it will being many people feel uncomfortable and inconvenience ,e.g. Some countries won't have enough energy to supply transportation tools to be driven, some homes and restaurants won't have enough energy to supply to cook to eat or to provide restaurant clients to eat etc.

daily activities, due to human's much activities which are needs energy supply. Thus, it seems that global primary energy consumption will be needed largely after 2010 year.

● Primary energy faces shortage challenge influences energy users' useful desires to be reduced

Wiley, composition services graphics also explains that why the primary energy consumption demand can be needed to achieve the same level to the global population size increasing in 2010 year. The graph showed these reasons why cause the same level of global population size and global primary energy consumption demand which may include: The graph showed that after a nation is developed, its per-person energy use high to level off. In North America and Europe, where energy demand has remained flat, or fallen sight, in each of the past few years. But the 1.3 billion people on those two continents are far out weighted by the 5 billion people in Asia and Africa, e.g. Chinese and Indian. who currently have more energy need to compare average per man to North America and Europe per man, ensuring that overall energy demand will rise for years to come.

Wiley, composition services graphics also predicted that the growth in primary energy demand. China will have 4,500 million tons in 2035 year. India will have 3,000 million tons in 2035 year. Other developing Asia will have 2,000 million tons in 2035 year. Russia will have 1,500 million tons in 2035, Middle East will have 1,300 million tons in 2035, other rest of world will have 1,000 million tons in 2035. Hence, it implied that China will be the largest primary energy need country in the future.

China will be future the primary potential energy consumer market. The primary energy includes water, coal, wind, fossil oil, gas ,solar, geothermal energy, biomass (organiz material) etc. different natural resource primary energy. Otherwise, US, UK, Europe will be secondary energy potential need market. For example, electrical recharge battery energy will be raised demand to supply to any future new design electrical charge battery vehicles in US, Europe, UK markets.

Due to US, Europe, UK people concern environment protection, so they will invent many electric charge battery vehicles to consume electrical charge battery to replace polluted gas energy to avoid air pollution when the drivers are driving cars on themselves countries' roads. For example, second man-made renew used nuclear energy can be applied to rockets to push them to leave our earth to fly to other space far away and consuming nuclear energy will be cost efficient, and nuclear energy saving will be more when nuclear to spend long time to be used in any long time space journey. Hence, nuclear energy and electric charge battery secondary energy will be popular to be applied to vehicles and rockets energy needs in US, Europe, potential markets, even our daily energy needs in global second energy market.

● Law and policies in energy supply industry influences primary energy price rises and energy users' useful desires to be reduced both effect. They have cause effect relationship.

Every energy entrepreneur needs to consider how whose government implement law and policies to prohibit whose energy consumption, energy distribution and energy production behavior in order to protect energy consumers can have fair price energy purchase from the country's energy suppliers between themselves. For US energy law and policy example, the energy independence and security Act of 2007 year. It's major provisions include: Accelerated research of clean energy technologies Act, energy savings in building and industry Act, improved standards for appliances and lighting Act, improved vehicle fuel economy Act and increased production of biofuel Act. It aims to prohibit any US energy manufacturing suppliers do any unfair energy trading transaction behavior to its domestic or foreign energy consumers immortally.

● Energy entrepreneur's business strategy influences different kinds of energy users' demand desire to be controlled to increase or decrease

Before you decide to operate either any kinds of secondary energy or primary energy supply business or both kinds of energy supply business. I recommend that you need to consider how to solve these questions before choosing which kind of energy product to manufacture. The questions may include as below:

Who are your energy business's competitors (peers)? How do they compare? How have your energy business company performed cyclically? How to choose to manufacture to sell which kinds of primary or secondary energy product(s), either manufactures only primary energy product(s) or manufactures only secondary energy products or both? Which countries do you plan to sell your energy product?

Illustration by Wilsey, composition services graphs showed that these natural resources to energy product the world's electricity percentage, such as below:

41% of coal, 5% of oil, 21% of gas, 13% of nuclear, 16% of Hydro, 3% other renewable secondary man-made energy.

Hence, coal will be future the major natural resource to produce electricity. The energy entrepreneur ought attempt to explore any coal resources, when who choose to supply electricity power to consumers for future energy consumption country markets.

Wiley, composition services also predicted that the expectation is that North America coal will supply the expectation is that North America coal will supply Asian demand, Us export terminals have a total capacity of 173 million ton output. China will drive 16% of the nations total output. China will drive the sea-born demand for coal over for the predictive future. Chinese energy consumption will grow more than 12 % between 1980 and 2009 years. Though, China heads global demand, India is growing faster in terms of coal imports. Much of the global coal demand will be supplied by Indonesia and Australia. Colombia, Russia, South Africa and Mongolia are also players in global export coal energy resources.

Consequently, I believe that secondary energy will be one kind of new energy product to replace traditional primary energy product for human energy consumption market global needs. Hence, it is right time any energy entrepreneur needs to research how to explore any undiscovered man-made renew used secondary energy products to avoid primary energy shortage crisis occurrence.

● Solar energy efficient useful characteristics raises secondary energy (human -made energy) needs or useful desires to be raised.

What is solar energy? Every day, the sun radiates (send out) and enormous amount of energy, called solar energy. It radiates more energy in one day. Then, the world uses in one year. This energy comes from within the sun itself. The sun makes energy in its inner core in a process called nuclear fusion.

Only a small part of the visible radiant energy (light) that the sun emits into space ever reaches the earth enough to supply all our energy needs. Every hour enough solar energy reaches the earth to supply our nation's energy is considered a renewable energy source due to this fact. Today, people use solar energy to heat buildings and water t generate electricity. Solar energy accounts for a very small percentage of U.S. energy less than one percent. Solar energy is used by residences and to generate mostly electricity.

Method to gather solar: A solar collector is one way to capture sunlight and change it into usable clean energy. A closed car on a sunny day is like a solar collector. As sunlight passes through the car's windows, is it absorbed by the seat covers, walls, and floor of the car. The absorbed light changed into heat. The car's windows let light in, but they don't let all the heat out. A closed car can get very hot!

Which is space heating? It means heating the space inside a building. Today, many homes use solar energy for space heating. A passive solar home is designed to let in as much sunlight as possible. It is like a big solar collector. For example, a passive solar home doesn't depend on mechanical equipment, such as pumps and blowers to heat the house, whereas active solar homes do. It seems that future human can attempt to apply solar energy to use in home conveniently.

How can apply solar energy? Solar energy can be used to heat water. Heating water for bathing, dishwashing and clothes washing is the second largest have energy cost. Installing a solar water heater can reduce home water heating bill be as much as 50 percent. A solar water heater works a lot like solar space heating. For example, installing a solar collector on a house roof where it can capture sunlight. The sunlight heats water in a tank. The hot water is piped to faucets throughout a house, as it would be with an ordinary water heater.

Solar energy can also be used to produce electricity. Two ways to make electricity from solar energy are photovoltaics and solar thermal systems both. However, compared to other ways of making electricity photo voltic systems are expensive. It can cost to 30 cents per kilo hour to produce efficient from solar cells. Similar to solar cells, solar systems also celled solar power, use solar energy to produce electricity, but in a different way, most solar thermal systems use a solar collector with a mirrored surface to focus sunlight onto a receiver that heats a liquid. However, solar energy has great potential for the future. Solar energy is free, and its supplies are unlimited. It doesn't pollute or otherwise damage the environment. It can't be controlled by any one nation or industry. IF we can improve the

technology to harness the sun's power, we may never face energy shortages again.
For active solar home example, passive homes can get 30 to 80 percent of the heat, they need from the sun. They store their heat energy by using think walls and building materials that retain heat well like concrete, stone and even water. For sole water heating another example, solar energy can also be used to heat water for household use. Heating water for bathing and washing is the second largest home energy cost. Installing a solar water heater can cut that cost in half. A solar water heater works a lot like solar space heating. The sunlight heats water and stores it in tank. The hot water is piped to faucets throughout a house, such as it would be with an ordinary water heater. Finally radiant energy to electricity example, solar energy can be used to produce electricity, e.g. solar-powered toys, calculators, many lighted roadside signs all use solar cells to covert sunlight into electricity.

Next kind of solar electricity manufacturing method is solar power tower. At full peak, estimated electricity generation each year is 155,000 megawatt-hours, enough to power 11,000 homes. This makes the Martin Next generation solar energy center the largest solar thermals power plant in the Eastern United States.
In conclusion, human can earn benefits of solar energy include: Solar electric systems are safe, clean and quiet to operate. Solar systems are highly reliable, solar systems are cost-effective in remote areas and for some residential and commercial applications, solar systems are flexible and can be expanded to meet increasing electrical needs for homes and businesses, solar systems can provide independence from the grid on backing during outages, the fuel is renewable and free and domestically produced, harnessing solar energy spurs economic development, using solar energy to generate electricity produces no greenhouse gases. Hence, future solar energy will be a kind of renewable and reused and recycled natural resource energy to be provided to human to use.

- Water energy efficient useful characteristics raises

energy users' demand number increases

The efforts to improve water and efficiency from both the supply and the demand sides would allow countries to reduce resource scarcity and maximize water energy benefits. However, water efficiency is a concept, it means " doing more and better with less by obtaining more value with the available resources by reducing the resource consumption and reducing the pollution and environmental impact of water use for the stage of the value chain and of water service provision."
Improving water efficiency means increasing water productivity, reducing the intensity of water use for, and pollution from socio-economic activities through maximizing. The value of the uses of water, improving the allocation of water greater socio-economic value per drop of water in order to achieve aim to ensure environmental flows, and improving technical efficiency of water services and the management efficiency of their provision over the complete life cycles.
How to enable water and energy efficiency? Water thirsty energy demonstrates the importance of combined energy and water management approaches through demand-based work in several countries. In order to ensure water

energy users to earn water energy efficient benefits.
How to make the right choice among water resource efficient technologies? These include recycling and reuse of water, low water using appliances, efficient irrigation systems, decentralized sewerage systems, information and communication technologies, rainwater cater and reclamation of nutrients and creating new opportunities to water renewable energy potential and the need of innovation and development and serves to solve energy shortage from water renewable and reused resource energy invention.

Water energy efficient production method includes, it will allow differentiating between water withdrawal, water consumption and net water consumption and calculating different kinds of interactions between the activity and its water environment. With an annual investment of US$198 billion on average over the next forty years, water use can be made more efficient, enabling increased agricultural, biofuels, and industrial production (UNEP, 2011).
Investing US$170 billion annual in energy efficiency worldwide could produce energy savings of up to US$900 billion per year (SE4ALL, 2012) and each additional US$1 spent on energy efficiency in electrical equipment, appliances and buildings avoids more than US$2 on average in energy supply investments (IEA, 2012).

How can water energy distribution solution? The facilitate greater operational efficiency including energy-efficient water supply operation systems and water distribution control systems that help in ways that include reducing electricity costs as well as the load on the environment. For one example to water distribution solution for more efficient operation of water supply and individual technologies. The water distribution system will consist first stage is component technology to (linear programming and modeling). Second stage is solution: water supply, it is operation and planning techniques that works with electronic power demand response. The final stage is water source, water will be in taken to adequate them to deliver water treatment plant. Next step, the water treatment plant water will be delivered to main water pipe. Final stage, water will be delivered to water distribution network from water distribution network to this whole water distribution process. It depends on the time of day. Incentive schemes, such as load control programs request users to reduce their power use at times when the supply of electric power is constrained and pay them for doing so in the form of a bonus from water power station suppliers. So, nowadays, some countries' water power station supplies have developed a water supply operation technique that reduces electricity costs by earning these incentives.

What is water supply operation technique? The water supply operation technique consists of operation mode that seeks to smooth electric power use in ways that cut the basic tariff by smoothing demand across the course of day and a demand response operation mood that earns incentives by reducing demand in response to requests. Water supply surplus uses a large number of distribution reservoirs to buffer the gap between demand for water and the supply from the water treatment plants.
Furthermore, falling demand in recent years means there are a significant number of distribution reservoirs with

excess capacity. This means that peaks in electricity demand can be shifted or cut by taking advantage of this unused water storage capacity to shift the timing of conveying pump operation. Minimizing electric power consumption as far as possible during demand peaks or during time periods specific in demand response requires. But, it also requires risk management to ensure that the water levels in distribution reservoirs don't full below their lower limits. Consequently, water supply will be another kind of reused energy resource to provide to human to use.

● What is future household energy consumption trend?

In general, household energy consumption includes , i.e. for lighting, cooking, heating etc. The household sector is responsible for about 15 to 25 percent of primary energy use for a higher share in many developing countries. Average per capita household energy use in developed countries is about nine time higher than in developing countries, even though in developing countries a large share of household energy is provided by non-commercial fuels are historical trends in per capita household energy consumption by these kinds of energy, i.e. fuel, coal, petroleum, natural gas and electricity etc. energy.

Some scientists indicate Asia and South America have consequently lower energy efficiency. However, the major factors contributing to countries which lower and higher energy efficiency differences include, such as levels of urbanization, economic development and living standards. Other factors are country or region specific, such as climate or cultural practices. However, energy efficiency depends both in the types of fuel used and on the characteristics of particular appliances.

Consequently, future trend of energy will be renewable, reused, cheap more efficient and productive secondary energy for human to use.

● The reasons why water and solar energy users number will increase

In our earth, we own much natural resource supply, some natural resource has shortage crisis, e.g. gas, coal, fuel etc. But, some natural resource which still have unlimited supply and we shall have enough energy supply to solve our energy shortage crisis if we can invent them to change to electricity or any power successfully, e.g. wind, solar, water natural resource.

However, I believe that wind and water and solar nature resource will be another kind of potential energy supply to solve our energy shortage crisis. I shall indicate the reasons as below:

First, on wind nature energy supply aspect, human can apply wind power to change to be electricity energy. So, I recommend human can seek any places which can have much wind natural resource to attempt to produce wind energy. For New Zealand country, Auckland and Wellington cities which own much wind natural resource power. Hence, this countries are suitable to invent any wind electricity manufacturing factories to manufacture wind electricity to solve our electricity shortage crisis.

Second, on water natural energy supply aspect, New Zealand is one country which own clean water place. It's water can even to be driven and it does not need to heat to supply to us to drink fresh water. So, New Zealand own much clean water supply, we can attempt to use this country extra water natural resource to manufacture water electricity when New Zealand has many water manufacturing factories, then we shall have much water electricity to prepare our future use.

Third, on solar natural energy supply aspect, our sun will have unlimited natural heat supply. Hence, solar natural resource will be our future one kind of energy supply source. I shall recommend Africa country will be one good location choice to build solar factories because Africa is one hot and much sun natural resource country. Hence, if scientists can attempt to build solar power factories to manufacture solar energy. Then, we shall have one country which can concentrate on manufacturing solar energy to supply to us to use.

Consequently, New Zealand and Africa will be the suitable countries to build solar, wind and water factories to manufacture solar, wind and water energy to prepare to us to use as well as natural resource solar and wind and water will be our future reused and recycle energy to solve our electricity needs for our next generation. So, nowadays, it is right time that energy scientists ought attempt to build energy factories on these both countries to invent any one kind of these three kinds of natural resources to solve energy shortage crisis.

CHAPTER TWO

Environment pollution how influence human live cost rises

Can economic environment influences householder electricity energy consumption or useful activities to be more or less? In general, house owners have both intentions for whose property. One intention is living the house by householder himself or herself or householder with families themselves. Another intention is that renting to others to receive rent income (landlord). So, in the housing market, the housing consumer includes either the property owner intents to rent to others to live for rent income aim or the property buyers intents to buy the house to be house owner to live. Does these both different property purchase intentions, which will influence the householder's attitude to use electricity energy consumption desire to be more or less, due to the householder's demand to whose house quality factor influence? This is one interesting question concerns the householder electricity energy consumption desire change to the householder, due to house's investment or house's living intention influences to house quality factor.

How does house quality factor influence to householder electricity energy consumption desire to be more or less? Has it relationship between house quality and house investment or living intention to cause house quality demand to influence the householder electricity energy consumption desire change or demand to be more or less? Has it relationship between regional housing market living or rent investment intentions, housing quality and electricity energy consumption more or less desire? I suppose that the determinants of the residential electricity energy demand form space-heating and cooking, due to the property quality demand influence and the householder's living or rent investment intention influence both, which will influence the householder's electricity energy consumption or useful behavior when he/she/they is/are living in the house.

I argue that rent properties are not only consumer goods, but it also constitute financial market assets. It is therefore reasonable to assume that rational (rent income investment intention) investors choose to raise housing quality (e.g. thermal insulation technological installing at home, heating or cooling technology or artificial intelligent window, lighting, door opening or closing) in order to attract many people choose to rent whose house to live. The

householder's aim is to achieve an acceptable return on investment (ROI) or raising rent income aim when he/she rents whose house to anyone, it is easy to attract many people to choose to pay higher rent his/her house to live in the property rent market. Moreover, the another important factor is that rents and future house sale prices of properties differ regionally (or even locally), and largely depend on housing market fundamentals, such as either the house living buyer's income levels or the house rent buyer's income levels, vacancy rates, and/or householder investor's expectations.
Thus, if the householder expects to rent whose house and raises rent to attract many people choose to rent whose house to live, who will attempt to install many new technology in order to satisfy their high quality of life need when they can pay higher rent to rent to choose to rent whose houses to live. Their aim only achieves to raise housing quality, but any new technology will lead to increase electricity energy consumption or use in the house.

Hence, any high quality of houses will influence the householder to use or consume more electricity energy at home. It means that the householder will choose to consume or use more electricity energy at home, if he/she or the family householder demands to live more comfortable house and he/she/they can have high quality of living life at home. This comfortable living demand to the householder (property renter or property buyer) view point can explain why the better quality of house factor will influence the electricity energy consumption desire to the householder also to be more daily.

I shall indicate one home electricity energy consumption experiment, it indicated that utilizing aggregate data on regional space-heating energy consumption form over 300,000 apartment buildings in 97 German planning regions. The study applies structural equation modelling to estimate the influence of housing market fundamentals on the level of housing quality, and subsequently on regional electricity energy consumption. Consequently, it suggests that housing market fundamental explain regional differences in the housing quality.

In particular, findings show that the level of per capita income, investor' expectations about future housing market development as well as vacancy all explain regional differences in housing quality has a significant impact on electricity energy consumption.

In the way, this experiment can indicate evidence that regional housing market fundamental have a substantial influence on regional levels of housing quality and energy consumption desires to the German regional householders.

This Germany regional householder experiment found important implications for high or low housing quality of the regional property building and householders either property living or property rent intention of comfortable living feeling need factor which will influence the regional property householder electricity energy consumption desire to be raised or reduced. These factors will influence the consequence of electricity energy demand to be increased or decreased needs every day for the regional householder as well as the country's electricity energy supplier(s) can gather the regional properties whether they are high or low quality to predict the regional properties householders' electricity energy consumption supply budget more accurate. It implies that an important determinant of residential housing quality will have possible to influence electricity energy demand to be more or less for long term. IN particular, this Germany regional residential experiment can explain and find an important role in formulating assumptions about the quality factor has chance to influence the regional residential future levels of electricity energy efficiency and consumption in the country. Hence, housing developments and electricity energy firms can follow this regional residential housing quality factor to evaluate whether the regional housing market is the corresponding investment patterns as well as the energy researchers can follow the regional residential housing quality whether it is high or low housing quality factor to evaluate the more accurate models of regional electricity energy demand to any regional residential householders' houses in the country.

In consumer behavioral view point, it explains that if the country government expected many householders feel to need to spend much electricity energy or have much electricity energy useful demand or desire at home. The country government ought to encourage the country residential property or house developers choose to build many houses which have technological product installed to satisfy the regional householders' residential comfortable living need when they choose the regions to build the high quality houses to let them to live. Then, the regional householders will be influenced to consume or use much electricity energy at homes, due to they feel that they are living at high quality and comfortable and high building technological installed apartments in the country's regions. Then, the country's government and electricity energy provider(s) may be raise much electricity energy efficiency and supply and profit , due to the regional residential householders' electricity energy consumption or useful desire need is therefore influenced to be more by the regional high quality of residential houses factor. So, the regional high quality of residential house factor will have relationship to the regional electricity energy consumption and efficiency to the regional householder's houses.

Otherwise, if the country government felt electricity energy is shortage, it ought encourage the property developers build many low quality and low building technological houses to let householders to live themselves or rent to others to live in the country's different regional residential development market. Due to the low quality of properties and low technological installed to properties factor which will influence any these different regional residential householders to choose method to solve shortage of electricity energy challenge to the country.

In conclusion, to apply consumer behavioral economic theory to property development market, if property quality factor can really influence the householder's electricity energy consumption desire to be used more or less at home daily. The country's property developers can apply this factor to predict property consumer individual property buying consumption behaviors more accurate. For example, if the US property developer planned to build low quality and low technological design buildings and lesser comfortable residential houses in the region in US. Then, its residential householder target will be trended the less acceptable of electricity energy consumption property buyers to choose to buy these regional properties to live in the US region because they can only accept to spend less electricity energy to use when they are living in the houses in order to save money daily. SO, the low quality , less comfortable and low technological installed design residential houses will satisfy their living needs.

Otherwise, if the US property developer planned to build high quality and high technological installed design buildings and more comfortable residential houses in the region in US. Then, its residential householder target will be trended to the more acceptable of electricity energy consumption property buyers to choose to buy these regional properties to live in the US region because they can accept to spend more electricity energy to use when they are living in the houses in order to improve their living of quality. So, they wont's consider to spend more expenditure to use electricity energy for any technological products are installed in their properties in order to satisfy their comfortable living needs at their homes every day.

Consequently, property developers can attempt to gather marketing research concerns whether how many people who accept to use more electricity energy or use less electricity energy in order to predict they ought build how many high quality or low quality houses number in different regions more accurate in themselves countries or overseas countries property development market.

- Environmental impacts of householder greenhouse gas electricity energy consumption activities

Has environment factor relationship to influence householder electricity energy consumption behaviors? Socially, householder electricity energy consumption provides us with sources of living satisfaction , but if any sudden environment factor changes, whether it will influence householder consume or use more or less electricity energy decision at home. However, I assume householder electricity energy consumption will have a considerable proportion of the environmental impacts be influenced by our way of life and our economic decision of electricity energy consumption behavior.

What different environmental factors will influence householder electricity energy consumption decision? The external environmental factors include, for example, the country's electricity firms or government changes to electricity energy regulations, electricity energy production technologies change and business practices and government policies changing etc. different external environmental factors will influence any country's electricity energy consumption to householders' consumption desire to be more or less. It will also require changes to influence the householders to consume which kinds of electric products which are needed to be used in different electricity energy natural manufacturing resources.

Why does these external environmental factors impact householders' any behaviors to influence them to concern to use more or less electricity energy power or which kinds of electricity energy products choice at homes. How

any why environmental factors impact will influence householder activities at home, such as electricity energy consumption and choice? What are the key components of external environmental factors influence householders' electricity energy consumption behaviors. I shall explain as below:
Firstly, we need to know whether what external environments are which can influence why and how householders need to change their activities to choose more or less or which kinds of energy power to be provided to them to use at home. Who is householder? Householder is an individual, family, or group of individuals living together as unit in a home. Consumption of electricity energy at home may be cooking food needs, needing have colder feeling to turn on fan or air condition at home in summer or needing have warm feeling to turn on heater at home in winter, watching television programs or listening music , playing computer games or used computers activities , reading activities and applying artificial intelligent technological tools to help householders to open or close homes' windows, doors etc. different home equipment which need to use electricity energy provisions. SO, their home activities need to turn on lighting electric tools , televisions, music machines, radios etc. different equipment which need to use electricity energy provision at home. SO, the purpose of householder consumption means consumption by individuals living in a household and it includes consumption both in and outside the home. Why does environmental impacts link to householders' electricity energy consumption? I shall focus on discussing of greenhouse gases (GHGS) energy product how any why it can influenced to householders to use.
The environmental impacts will influence this kind of greenhouse gases (GHGS) energy in the product lifecycle or delivery of the service to link the householder's energy consumption at home such as these several aspects:

Extraction and greenhouse gases production (supply number), physical distribution (delivery far long or close near short distance between the greenhouse gases manufacturing factory and the greenhouse gases supplier), resources consumed by marketing and retail activities (householder's needs to use the quantity of the greenhouse gases energy product), the greenhouse gases consumers search and purchasing activities(e.g. travel to shops, internet purchasing channel, , finding the which kinds of greenhouse gases products from internet, magazines, newspapers, radio advertisements etc. different medias,) , post-use greenhouse gases energy disposal (resale, reused or rubbish). The householder's physical behavioral impact environmental factor will influence how and why he/she chooses to consume greenhouse gases energy daily , e.g. impacts of a housing development, or a wind –farm that supplies greenhouse gases with power. So, the householder's greenhouse gases energy consumption behavior which will depend upon individual personal and subjective perspectives and value.

So, the householder's useful behavior or attitude of greenhouse gases energy product which will influence how he/she/ the family use or consume greenhouse gases energy, such as the householder individual environmental protection attitude which can impact how he/she/the family spends the quantity of greenhouse gases energy every day at home, if the householder does not expect our air or water or land is polluted , due to extraction of any natural gas resources to be manufactured any kinds of greenhouse gases products. Then, this environmental pollution issue will influence some householders choose to reduce to use more quantity of greenhouse gases products every day. Another environmental factors include the bio relates the (unsustainable) use of resources to avoid wasting much greenhouse gases energy to cause greenhouse gases energy supply shortage, avoiding the cause negative impacts of quality life , e.g. noise causing when the extraction of any natural resource from lands to the householder's house is near to the natural resource extraction land and health impacts, e.g. when the greenhouse gas householder user who often use the kind of greenhouse gas product when it is used to cook or heat any equipment to cause they to breathe dirty air at home often. These impacts can be measured in different ways include: monetary costs or loss, physical quantities of resources used or waste or pollution produced and the burden the greenhouse gases energy place on environmental resources. All of these external environment factors will impact the householder individual attitude or behavior how to use or consume greenhouse gases energy product at home.

All these environmental factors concern householder greenhouse gases energy consumer individual consumption attitude is influenced by environment pollution, greenhouse resource supply shortage challenge, greenhouse gases influence the householder's negative quality of life, negative health impacts, noise, waste money , raising economic cost to the householder which will impact whether how the householder choose to use the quantity of greenhouse gases product or the kinds of greenhouse gases products or other kinds of electricity energy products.

However, these are other external environmental factors which can impact how the householder decides to use greenhouse gas product at home. They include: the changes of energy regulation, e.g. the country government has quota number implementation to prohibit to import above the limited quantities of any kinds of greenhouse gas products to any countries. So, when the greenhouse gas energy supplying quantity is decreased, but if the country has may householders who need to buy different kinds of greenhouse gases products to be used at home. Then, the different kinds of import greenhouse gases energy products prices will be raised in possible, due to demand is more than supply in the country's greenhouse gas energy product market. Consequently, if the greenhouse gas energy price us risen above the general social acceptable level to the home greenhouse gas energy product householder consumers. Finally, it will influence them to choose to buy other kinds of gas energy products to replace the greenhouse gas energy product to use at home.

Another side, if the country's greenhouse gas energy manufacturing supplier sudden changes its greenhouse gas energy production technologies to choose to concentrate on manufacturing other kinds of energy products. Then, the greenhouse gas energy supply quantities will be only decreased, even future one day , it will cause greenhouse gas supply shortage challenge to let the country's home greenhouse gas householder consumers who can not buy enough quantity of any kinds of greenhouse gas energy products to satisfy their electricity needs at home every day. Consequently, when future on day , the country greenhouse gas energy manufacturer has none any quantity of greenhouse energy products to supply to the country's greenhouse energy householders to use at home. The, they must only choose other kinds of new energy products to replace the traditional useful greenhouse gas energy products to be used at homes.

In conclusions, these non-controlled external environmental factors can impact and influence the country's every householder consumer individual attitude or consumption behavioral change to how any why the country's householders either choose to buy much or less quantity of greenhouse gas products to use at home.

- The effect of house space occupancy and building characteristics influences householder electricity energy use

Can economic factors measure how much space occupancy is the suitable size as well as what the most suitable building characteristics influence each householder electricity energy useful activities or behaviours? In general, society believes large space size occupancy house building characteristics factor which will influence householder use more energy at home, e.g. in summer, when the householder is living at the large space size occupancy house, who ought turn on all air conditions or fans at sleeping rooms or eating room or studying room. So, if the householder's house has two to three or more sleeping rooms. Then, he / she needs to buy more air conditions or fans in order to let all rooms' temperature to be fallen down to let he /she feel more cool comfortable feeling when the temperature is above 30 degree or more extreme hot in summer weather. Otherwise, when the temperature is low, e.g. between 0 degree to 10 degree or below 0 degree in winter weather. When the householder is living in one large space size occupancy apartment, which has thee to five sleeping rooms , even more and two studying rooms and one eating room, even more as well as every room has one heater. Then, he / she must turn on all heaters to let who to feel warm feeling when he / she is staying in the house. It brings these interesting questions.

Will large or small size space occupancy housing characteristics influence any householder often turn on heater or air condition or fan in whole house space occupancy area in order to the householder feels warmer or cooler feeling when he /she is staying in the house?

Has any space occupancy housing characteristics relationship to influence any householder to turn on heater or air condition or fan in whole house space occupancy area in order to the householder feels warmer or cooler feeling when he /she is staying in the house?

Does it bring positive relationship between turning on long time fan or air condition or heater and the house occupancy space characteristics is large or small size?

I shall attempt to give psychological evidences to explain the householder's house space occupancy area large or small size factor whether it can influence the householder choose to do long time or short time turning on heater or air condition or fan behavior in order to let he/she/the family to feel more cooler or warmer comfortable feeling when he/she/the family is staying in the house in summer or winter weather.

Does the house occupancy space size characteristics factor is the only one or important factor to influence the householder choose to turn on long or short time fan or air condition or heater in the house to let him/her/the family

to feel more cooler or warmer comfortable feeling in summer or winter weather?
I feel that it is not exact right , due to the householder's house space occupancy size whether it is large or small characteristics to influence the householder choose to turn on long time or short time fan or air condition or heater time to let him /her/ the family to feel more cooler or warmer when he / she / the family is staying at home in summer or winter weather. The reason is because that the lifestyle of living quality need is different between developed countries and developing countries. The lifestyle of living quality factor will change the country's householder's expectation about the quality of living life. For example, for Africa, Korea, China , Japan, Hong Kong etc. developing countries. On the lifestyle of living quality need to these developing countries' householders aspect, that will cause a high environmental burden when they need to often turn on air conditions to satisfy more cooler feeling when they are staying at homes in summer or they need often to turn on heaters to satisfy more warmer feeling when they are staying at home in winter. Due to if their houses are large size space occupancy characteristics and they have more than at least two sleeping rooms and studying rooms and eating rooms and toilets number. Then, these householders who are developing countries‘ large space occupancy size characteristics houses, they won't like often turn on heaters long time to keep more warmer in their indoor whole space area in winter or they won't like often turn on air conditions or fans long time to keep more cooler in the their indoor whole space area house environment in summer .

The reason is possible because that the developing countries' householder chooses often to turn on their heaters or air conditions or fans long time in their houses when they are staying long time in their houses and their houses space occupancy sizes are very large, it will bring the electricity energy to be used more to these developing countries‘ householders' large space occupancy size characteristic houses. It means that the electricity fee will be also increased due to they often turn on heaters or air conditions or fans long time to keep their indoor temperature to be more cooler in summer or more warmer in winter. So, it seems that the developing countries‘ householders are living in the house whose space occupancy have very large size characteristics and more than two rooms house characteristics in the developing countries as above. Then, they won't often choose to turn on heaters or air conditions or fans long time to keep more cooler or warmer feeling in their house whole indoor space occupancy environment when they are often staying at home long time.

Their lifestyle of living comfortable feeling are lesser than the developed countries householders. Consequently, their lesser cooling or warming comfortable demand of living lifestyle factor will change their attitudes to use air conditions or fans or heaters turning on time in order to limit heaters or air conditions or fans turning on time to be shorter than the developed countries householders' heaters or air conditions or fans turning on time at homes. Due to the long time turn on air conditions, fans , heaters at the developing countries‘ householders' homes, it will cause to spend much electricity energy to lead electricity fee charges to be raised to the developing countries‘ householders ' homes when they are often staying at homes in summer or winter weather. Hence, the house space occupancy large size characteristics ought not influence the developing countries householders choose to turn on air conditions , fans or heaters long time in order to let them to feel more cooler or warmer at homes in summer or winter weather.

So, the developing countries‘ house space occupancy large size characteristics householders won't be more acceptable to pay higher electricity energy fee when they are staying at homes at summer or winter weather. Due to they do not often choose to turn on heaters, air conditions or fans long time during they are staying at homes. Otherwise, the developed countries, e.g. UK, UK , France, Germany, Swiss, Singapore, Italy etc. countries. In general, these developed countries' householders‘ living lifestyle quality needs are higher than the developing countries. So, when the summer or winter weather is coming, if the temperature is extreme cold, e.g. below than 0 degree or it is extreme hot, e.g. higher than 30 degree.
Then these developed countries' householders will easy accept to turn on air conditions or fans or heaters long time at home in order to keep their apartment in door temperature to be more cooler in extreme hot in door environment or more warmer in extreme cold in door environment when these developed countries‘ householders are often staying at homes long time at night after their day time working time or schooling time. Because these developed counties' householders‘ quality of living lifestyle needs or demands are higher than the developing countries' householders. So, they won't consider that they will pay more electricity fee , due to they often turn on air conditions, fans or heaters long time to let them to feel more comfortable in cooler or warmer indoor large size space occupancy environment. So, it seems that the electricity energy efficiency will be raised to the developed countries‘ householders who are living in the house space occupancy large size characteristics and they will be possible to pay more electricity fees during they are often staying at home in extreme hot summer or extreme cold winter weather.

In conclusion, due to the living lifestyle quality need (demand) is different between the developed countries' householders and the developing countries‘ householders. It will influence the householders' long time or short time spending time on air conditions or fans or heaters indoor space occupancy size characteristics environment in order to achieve more cooler or more warmer feeling in their houses. Consequently, the long or short time of turning on air conditions, fans, heaters for the developed or developing countries householders‘ activities factor will be more influential to compare the house space occupancy large or small size characteristics factor to influence their cooler or warmer feeling in their houses. SO, the house indoor environment electricity energy consumption efficiency degree to the developing or developed countries' every householder house in summer or winter to the developing or developed householders in summer or winter weather , which is more influenced by the living lifestyle qualty factor to the either developed countries or developing countries householders. Hence, any developed or developing countries‘ electricity suppliers need to consider the building areas of property development market buyers their living style quality demands (needs) whether their living style quality demands are higher or lesser than the other building areas of property development market, they ought not consider whether the building locations of the houses' space occupation sizes whether they are large or small sizes in order to evaluate the householders will live at the building areas of property development locations ,whose electricity energy spending efficiency more accurate.

- How economic factor influences low income household earners to reduce not essential electricity energy expenditure spending at homes

Has it relationship between the householder income and the electricity energy needs? How to evaluate the subsidies and social tariffs to assist lower income earners to analyze household energy consumption more accurate?

Electricity energy is essential needs for every householder at home, e.g. lighting, cooking power, healthcare, sanitation, cooler or warmer temperature indoor control at home. However, for lower income household earners, it its burden when they need often to use electricity energy to supply power to any home electricity tools to do any activities at homes. If any these countries‘ lower income householder earner target can not get the reasonable subsidies to assist them to solve any electricity energy tools' electricity energy needs. Due to their lower income level, it is possible that to influence them have enough electricity supply to help them to use to cook rice and food and vegetables to eat, boil water to drink, turning on light tools to help them to read, watch TV, listen radio, music any entertainment or essential needs at homes at night or morning afternoon time. These lower income household earners will be easy to sick , due to they have no enough electricity supply to help them to use electric bottles to boil water or cook food to eat. Then they only drink not boiled water or not cooked food to eat at homes in possible, due to they have no enough income to pay electricity fees every month.

Hence, how to evaluate the lower income household earners‘ electricity fee need (demand) level in order to provide the reasonable subsidies amount to assist every country's low income household earner to help them to pay the reasonable electricity fee which is one important issue to every country's government today. It brings this question: How to evaluate or analyze or predict every lower income household individual or family earner's every month electricity energy demand (need) more accurate?

It is one essential issue to be value to consider to every country's government. Moreover, to the extent that energy subsidies must be essential to be provided by public sources to all low income household earners or that a social tariff may be designed for improving access to energy for certain low income social earner groups. Hence, how to structure the energy subsidies between energy and income levels to be better target, such public mechanisms, and to avoid regressive subsidies unfairly. For example, India and China these both countries ' income poverty and energy poverty population are the large number. So , these both countries‘ governments need to focus on more aggregated effects and analyze the effects of rural electrification at the local level on the decrease in energy poverty in rural low income poverty and energy poverty householders. Therefore, every country government needs to point regressive of the subsidy for electricity. There is room to analyze to what extent low income household earners along the income distribution demand some forms of energy, and to suggest better and fair low income targeting household earners energy subsidies supply policies.

Each government does not only consider energy issues from a social point of view, it also needs have a manner to consider a possible link between energy, hunger reduction, and food security for each country's low income household earners group. So, every government has responsibility to calculate the determinants of different sources of energy consumption at the low income household earner level for urban and rural both populations in order to evaluate the electricity subsidies and to test whether every low income householder earner characteristics plays a role in determining energy consumption.
In general, in the use of energy measured as that for cooking, such as LPG reduces the exposure of households to hazardous, increases the consumption of different types of foods and medicines, improves the distribution of time between household members, enables studies with more light, reduces the use of digital computer entertainment tools at home, and moderates the use of wood as fuel, preventing deforestation. These methods are the best suggestions to help low income householder earner groups to reduce time to use electricity at homes. When they spend less time to use electricity to do any not essential activities, e.g. watching television, playing electric games from home computers, listening music. They only use electricity to turn on light read, to turn on rice cooker to cook, when they feel hungry to eat. Then, I believe that these social low income household earner groups will reduce to pay much not essential electricity energy expenditure at homes. Hence, every country government ought need to persuade low income household earners to avoid to use electricity to do any not essential activities in order to raise electricity energy consumption in long term time.

It will bring less amount of energy subsidies expenditure benefits to every country's government. Hence, the success to persuade any countries' low income household earners to reduce to spend much time to do any electric entertainment activities of consumption behaviors at homes often. This is the most efficient and the most successful energy subsidiary method to help them to reduce electricity energy expenditure when they are staying at homes. Hence, if any country government expected the low income household earners can continue really reduce electricity energy expenditure, they need to learn to do the meaning essential activities which are needed to use electricity at home in habit. Then, they can change their electricity useful entertainment living habit, e.g. using computers to play games, listening music, watching television entertainment habits at homes to cause essential daily needs of electricity useful living habit, e.g. using cookers to cook rice or cook food to eat, turning on lights to read , turning on heaters to bath, turning on air conditions to keep cool temperature or turning on heaters to keep warm temperature at homes. Consequently, they won't need to pay much electricity expenditure at home, due to their waste useful electricity entertainment living habits have changed to do any essential useful electricity activities at homes.

Another kind of method to reduce the determinants of energy demand to the low income householder earners. The governments can persuade them to consider the variation factor can influence their electricity energy expenditure are increased or decreased at homes. It is not the electricity or gas price is increased from the electricity suppliers.

It is that their bad living habits of waste electricity or gas to do any not essential activities at homes. e.g. the householder often turn on light tools to read or listen music or watch television in whole night, he/she ought need to sleep at night, but he/she does not go to bed to sleep in whole night. He/she chooses to turn on light to do these activities. Then, he/she will waste much electricity at whole night. Also, some householders like to bath more than half hour, even one hour, when it is winter, they need to turn on heaters to provide electricity to cause the bath room has warm water to provide to them to bath, Their long time bathing behaviors will be also waste electricity or gas energy from long time heating in bath rooms. So, they need to change their waste electricity consumption living behaviors at homes.

So, I suggest that some low income household earners will need to be taught to change their bad using electricity energy living habits from governments' public relation promotion in order to change the low income household earners' bad or incorrected useful electricity or gas living attitude to achieve and to avoid them often to do electricity or gas energy waste behaviors at homes. So, different countries' governments need to teach them how to do the correct or right electricity or gas useful activities (living habits) or let them know or feel how to use their electricity or gas which can help them to reduce to waste the not essential extra electricity or gas energy. Consequently, they must reduce electricity or gas expenditure as well as electricity or gas shortage challenge won't be caused by their electricity or gas useful waste behaviors (activities) at homes.

In conclusion, energy subsidies method is not the best solution to help low income household earners to reduce to use electricity or gas energy. Because it is only short term benefit to reduce their electricity or gas expenditure at homes. The best solution is that to let them to know or feel why and how they have responsibilities to change their incorrent or wrong electricity or gas consumption bad habits in order to avoid global electricity or gas energy is waste to be used, even it is caused shortage from householders' energy waste behaviors.

● Factors influence householder energy efficient consumption behaviors at homes

What factors can influence householders how to use energy in efficient way at homes? It depends on different countries householders' living habits to cause their choices to use energy efficiently at homes. In general, global householders energy every day consumption or use aims include cooking, heating, and cooling or warming rooms, lighting , water-boiled use and computer playing games entertainment etc. activities at homes every day. Some activities are often essential at homes, e.g. cooking, cooling or warming temperature in rooms, lighting , water-boiled use. So, their activities must not avoid to use energy at homes often. Otherwise, some activities are not essential at homes, e.g. playing entertainment games from computers, cooling rooms in summer, listening music, watching television etc. these activities. The householder can choose either to use energy to turn on these equipment tools or not to do these non essential activities at homes often. In general, householders rely on energy to make ourselves lives comfortable, productive and enjoyable. However, global householders need to learn how we can use energy resources wisely because global every householder has responsibility to manage resources includes: reducing total energy use and using energy more efficiently in order to avoid energy shortage crisis occurrence. The choices are make about how we use energy, e.g. turning machines off when not in use of choosing to buy energy efficient appliances will have increasing impacts on the quality of our environment and lives.

Energy conservation includes any behavior that results in the use of less energy. Energy efficiency involves the use of technology that requires less energy to perform the same function. For example, a compact fluorescent light build that uses less energy to produce the same amount of light as an incandescent light bulb is an example of energy efficiency. So, a householder's decision to place an incanadescent light bulb with compact fluorescent is an example of energy conservation. So, as individuals, every countries' householder choices and actions can result in a significant reduction in the amount of energy used in each sector of the economy.

So, I bring this interesting question: What factors can influence householder to choose to do any efficient energy consumption or useful behaviors at homes? I believe every countries' householders will have their different living attitudes and their living attitudes can influence their behaviors or activities to choose how to use energy at home. I shall indicate some countries' householders' living attitudes to explain the factors can influence them to use energy efficiency at homes as below:

- Is the low income and rising price of modern fuels both factors best to influence Nigeria householders choose to use energy efficiently?

Firstly, for Nigeria householders energy consumption habit at homes example, it is richly with natural resources, modern energy resources which provide many householders with biomass (mostly firewood) and some other householders modern energy sources, such as kevosene, liquefied, petroleum, gas and electricity for their use. So, it is one country which can manufacture to provide energy for itself to use. It doesn't need to depend on other countries to import any kinds of energy to householders to buy to use at homes. But, it has social challenge, the poverty problem in Nigeria goes beyond low income, savings and growth rate, due to its low level of education, poor governance, high level of unemployment factors influence.

It is important to know how Nigeria householders meet their basic energy needs between poverty and energy can be described in terms of quality and quantity of energy used. Generally, most poor householders use biomass fuels because of affordability and they (householders) do not have energy equipment (such as, gas cookers, electric cookers etc.) . So, it seems Nigeria householders won't demand their living quality to be improved. It implies that they will use any kinds of energy efficiently at homes, e.g. gas, electricity, due to they find themselves in energy poverty. Although, this country has enough nature resources to manufacture energy to provide to householders to use, but due to many people are low income group, so they won't spend too much expenditure to buy much energy to use at homes. So, the rising prices of modern fuels, such as liquefied, petroleum , gas (LPG) and electricity and their erratic supply have made many householders revert to the use of traditional fuel, such as firewood and charcoal. It brings this questions: Is the low income and rising price of modern fuels both factors best to influence Nigeria householders choose to use energy efficiently?

The hypothesis is predicated on the economic theory of consumer behavior. However, when income increases, householders not only consume more of the same goods, they also need higher quality . So, it applies economic theory to householder's energy consumption behavior at home. It explains why low living standards induce greater dependence on firewood and other biomass fuels owing to a combination of income and substitution effects, such as Nigeria low income household energy home users case. it explains why Nigeria householders can accept to use firewood and charaval traditional energy to replace liquefied, petroleum , gas (LPG) and electricity modern energy . So, economic theory explains the Nigeria household energy users why they can accept to use traditional energy to replace modern energy and their energy useful or consumption behaviors are efficient at homes. Although, Nigeria has enough natural resource to manufacture modern energy to supply to householders to use at homes. But, due to these modern energy products prices are raised to the price level of householders who can not accept. it causes to Nigeria householders only choose to buy the cheap biomass, fire woods to replace high price of modern energy products to use at home often. So, they can accept their quality of living to be fallen down. So, expensive modern energy product price is one factor to influence some countries' householders to choose to buy cheap traditional poor quality of nature energy, e.g. firewood or biomass, to use at homes. Hence, they can raise energy efficiency to use when they choose to use traditional nature energy to replace modern nature energy at homes.

● Does season factor influence New Zealand householders' energy consumption behaviors at homes?
Secondly, for New Zealand householders energy consumption habits at homes , for example, their living quality needs are general comfortable need feeling. Their countries' houses of space heating was found to average 34% of total householder energy use. The relation to space heating includes low indirect temperature are associated with persistent under-heating , whether some space heating sources tend to be higher or lower in winter indoor temperature than others and winter indoor temperatures are compared to international benchmarks and established healthy temperature ranges. So, New Zealand occupant's perceptions of winter indoor temperature conditions are presented and explored in relation to heating patterns and household energy consumption. So, it seems that NZ winter temperature is low. Moreover, it will influence householders need to turn on heaters to keep more warmer feeling indoor. Then, they will use more electricity energy. In special, if the householders' houses spaces are large sizes . Hence, their heaters need long time to keep whole houses' areas or spaces or rooms temperature to be risen up in order to let they do not feel very cold in winter. So, NZ's winter extreme cold weather will influence householders' energy use or consumption to be increased in winter.

The electricity efficiency to every NZ householder is very high in winter to compare spring, summer, autumn

seasons. Hence, if NZ electricity suppliers expected to forecast electricity consumption more accurate in NZ. In order to ease the life for both electric net designers and electricity suppliers, it was decided to find out, how the NZ weather conditions and every householder's house space size factors to influence the power consumption to NZ householders. If there is a clear trend observed , then this relation can be used for power consumption forecasts to NZ householders.
Why does NZ weather condition factor and householder's house space size factor can predict householders' electricity consumption at homes. Due to geographic location on the global the lowest south sets specific conditions for weather, such as NZ's south island geographic location is near to south ocean in our earth. It is a country where average annual temperatures are well between 10 degree to below 10 degree at NZ south island special geographic location to near to the South ocean in our earth at the same time.

However, large part of mankind is living in the conditions where there are four different seasons in NZ geographic location, dark winter, which is cold and snowy, spring with rising temperature and high precipitation, sunny , dry and rather hot summer, and windy and wet autumn. These conditions lead to different patterns in electric appliances use in NZ householders, in special, in NZ south island householders. If trends in electric energy use have substantial correlation with weather conditions, this can help NZ electric energy suppliers and producers to forecast electricity consumption and thus organize and manage production of electric energy.

Consequently, it will lead to much more stability in energy supply to NZ every householder. For example, when the NZ energy supplier gathers data concerns every householder's house space size data, e.g. the house has how many sleeping rooms, toilets, bath rooms, eating rooms and reading rooms number, even the house has how many family members are living in every NZ geographical location. Then if it can follow different location of NZ houses spaces sizes whether they are large or small space size as well as whether every house has how many family members are living to evaluate whether how much electricity efficiency can satisfy their comfortable living needs in winter. Then, it can evaluate whether they will use how much electricity efficiency for their needs in different seasons. If in winter, many householders are living in the large space size house in the geographic location. Then, it is possible that the geographic location is householders will use much electricity efficiency and where geographic location householder who will be possible to pay the most highest electricity fee to compare the other geographic location of small space size of house householders. Hence, weather factor is the most influential to change NZ householders ' electricity energy consumption behaviors at homes.

● Urbanization level and income per capita both tangible factors as well as temperature (weather variation factor) will have close relationship to influence China householder energy consumption or useful needs at home every day For China householder energy consumption habit example, what factors can determine to impact this country's householders energy useful behavior at homes? Can the impacts of these factors be quantified? What are China householder energy consumption trends and characteristics? I shall explain as below:

I believe the influential factors include these three aspects to China householder energy users: Income per capita, urbanization level an annual average temperature (weather). These factors will influence any China householder energy useful or consumption behavior at homes.
Temperature (weather variation factor) is intangible from eastern region to western region of Chin, variances largely depend upon economic level and the provincial level. So, some regions were warmer and cooler temperature will influence the regional China householder how to use electricity. In addition, the influence of urbanization level varies according to income level as well as the urbanization level has more significant impact on the structure and efficiency of China householder energy consumption that on its quantity. So, the urbanization level and income per capita both tangible factors will have close relationship to influence China householder energy consumption or useful needs at home every day. Moreover, these two tangible factors (urbanization level and income per capita both factors) have the more influential to impact China any one of household family energy consumption or useful habit to compare temperature factor at home. Because temperature can only influence than to choose to turn on heaters to keep more cooler in summer or turn on air conditions (fans) to keep more warmer in winter.

The electricity energy needs for these equipment tools which will be influenced less. Otherwise, the urbanization level and income per family householder how to choose to spend more or less electricity or gas etc. energy at homes. Because in behavioral economy view point, when individual householder has more income and the urban in the China geographic location is rising many high income and high household families members to every house. Then, the urbanization household energy household energy useful or consumption level will be raised. Such as China household electricity users case, e.g. large cities have many high income and many houses have more than four families members to live on one house together. Then, the electricity or gas energy efficiency will be influenced to rise. The city urbanization and per capita income level is high to these large cities have high to income population, who are living in these cities in China.

Moreover, the impact of lifestyle on energy use mainly reflects types and purposes of fuels are chosen by different China households factor which will influence the urbanization level of energy choice use. China is a country with typical binary economics and social diversity and these is significant difference in the consumption pattern between urban and rural regions. Urban residents consume high-quality energy, such as electricity, natural gas , heating power, solar energy and gasoline. For rural residents, usually use coal, and biomass energy because they are cheaper price energy products which requires much time and labor and are heavy indoor pollutants . The difference in energy consumption pattern between urban and rural China residents is closely related to living of quality needs, building structure, e.g. steel or stone etc. different materials, manufacture, easily access clean and effective feels through the electric grid, natural gas network and district heating systems.

Therefore, it explains why urbanization level is as an integrated variable reflecting social progress situation to influence urban and rural regions, such as large cities , small cities and rural countryside regions' household energy consumption or useful behaviors which have different kinds of fuel useful demands and energy efficiencies qualify and quantity demand, or needs at homes. Consequently, it explains, urbanization level and income per capital level both factors are more influential to China household energy consumption at home to compare temperature (weather , seasonal) factor.

● Employment rates or gross domestic product macro economic variation factor, residential space size factor, and the government's implementation of energy labeling schemes provide significant impacts on Taiwan residential electricity consumption .

For Taiwan householder electricity consumption characteristics in the residential sector, which has different factors and pattern to compare China householder electricity householder electricity consumption habit at home. Although, they are the same Asia country. I shall explain these reasons as below:

For Taiwan electricity householder factors influence their energy useful or consumption behaviors at homes. The main factors can influence their electricity energy useful patterns include: employment rates or gross domestic product macro economic variation factor, residential space size factor, and the government's implementation of energy labeling schemes provide significant impacts on Taiwan residential electricity consumption . However, the impacts of electricity raising price and the energy supply reducing shortage efficiency standards do not significant to influence the Taiwan residential electricity consumption behavior at sources.

It means that it won't influence Taiwan householders to use electricity or gas or any kinds of energy number to be reduced, even the Taiwan government energy suppliers sudden raise, any kinds of energy price and reduce to supply energy to satisfy Taiwan householders daily essential needs at homes.

In fact, Taiwan had improved gross domestic product (GDP) and it had raised employment rates recently. So, many Taiwanese has jobs to work, due to Taiwan economy had improved to be better. So, growth had also raised. The economy improvement causes many Taiwanese had enough jobs to work, due to new businesses are set up. Many consumers excite any kinds of businesses are invested to Taiwan from overseas or local investors. So, consumption is grown, the electricity consuming appliance are selected, as the household consumer focus group number if also influenced to be increased. So, Taiwan economy had improved to be better, it will encourage many electricity consuming appliances products are encouraged to excited to be selected to sell in Taiwan. Due to many different kinds of electricity consuming appliances are supplied to attract Taiwanese to choose to buy to bring to their homes for cooking, boiling water, or keeping rooms to be cooler or warmer temperature comfortable feeling intention in winter or summer seasons. So, these electricity consuming appliances, e.g. rice cookers, heaters, air conditions, fans, bathing gas heaters etc. different home electricity consuming appliances will be increased to supply to satisfy Taiwan householders' needs. When they decide to buy any news electricity consuming appliances to bring to homes to use.

● Environment scientists' education message how to influence Greece householders home energy consumption behaviors from primary energy to change secondary energy
Finally , I shall indicate Greece, this western which will influence this country's householders have desires to do household energy conservation patterns or conservation energy consumption behaviors or energy conservation activities at homes. I shall explain the social economic variable, such as consumers' income and family size variation factor which can influence the different Greece family household members differences towards energy conservation preferences. IN addition, the variable, such as environmental information feedback and consciousness of energy problems are characteristics of the energy saver consumer.

Why and how can environmental pollution , environmental protection, energy conservation information message can influence Greece householders to choose to do energy use consumption conservation or less energy useful behaviors at homes. It is one interesting energy efficient use behaviors , due to Greece householders are influenced by energy conservation or environmental protection message.
In fact, scientists agree overconsumption of natural resources is a major threat to our lives in earth. Environmental problems like greenhouse effect, ozone layer depletion, and acid rain effect are not any more problems of a specific region or environmental problem. Also, economic theory is indicated that in order to gain comfort and time households are becoming excessive energy users, neglecting the environmental impact of their choices.

Environment scientists bring these environment pollution message to influence Greeks (Greece householders) to change their energy consumption behaviors at homes. The environment scientists' message indicate that we are facing global warmth and natural resource and energy shortage challenges. Due to our Earth have limited natural resource numbers to supply to us to manufacture energy, but global population has been increasing every year. Thus, it is possible that we have energy shortage crisis. Also, manufactures are spending too much energy to waste to manufacture any products, the energy will cause air or water pollution in manufacturing process or drivers are driving their vehicles to pollute air on the roads.

Hence, environment scientists' message influence Greece householders began to consider these questions concern to reduce fossil fuel energy. Why do we need to Safety in using fuel and handle gas leaks? Why do we feel town gas smell? How is electricity located at electric station far away from town area? How to solve problems caused by the use of fossil fuels? How to reduce the use of fossil fuels?
Greece householders consider to solve the problems, the best way is to reduce their used of fossil fuel. This helps prevent fossil fuels form being used up too quickly. Also, it helps them to reduce environmental problems because

fewer pollutants are given out when less fossil fuels are used. Can human help to reduce the use of fossil fuels? Fossil fuels are mainly in power station. Although they use some fossil fuels for our gas cooker and car, it won't make much difference if I use less. Fossil fuel is not used renew primary energy. Most of energy Greece householders use come from fossil fuels, for example, the electricity we use is generated in power stations by burning fossil fuels. The buses they ride use diesel oil. Therefore, they can help reduce the use of fossil fuels by saving energy in Greece daily lives.

The actions that Greece householders can take such as: setting the air-conditioner to a higher temperature, walking instead of using lift, taking a short shower instead of a bath. This reduces the use of the hot water and thus the energy needed to heat the water. Thus, many people can help a lot to reduce our use of fossil fuels to avoid fossil fuel shortage risk occurrence.

Greeks (Greece householders) had been beginning to concern that they will face energy shortage challenge if they can not adopt more energy conservation actions. Because the Greece government began to bring negative environmental pollution and energy shortage challenge message if they often waste to use any kinds of energy, e.g. electricity , gas excessive number efficiency at homes. Then, they will be possible to face energy shortage and environmental pollution challenge to their country in future one day. So, this energy shortage and environment pollution message has bring predictive negative worries to influence many Greece householder energy home users choose to reduce to avoid the waste of any kinds of energy use at homes.

So, their reducing energy use actions that had encouraged them to cause habits to avoid to waste excess energy to do any non essential electric appliances useful or consumption activities at homes often. Moreover, the environment protection and energy conservation message has changed many Greece householder to make decision and activities to change their lifestyle to b low living quality from high living quality. So, the environment protection and energy conservation message factor has much influential to change Greece household energy users' daily energy conservation or less energy use consumption activities at homes.

Greeks feel greenhouse energy can be environmental protection energy. A greenhouse can trap heat in the sunlight and keeps the air inside the greenhouse warm enough for plants to grow. The glass roof and walls of a greenhouse let in sunlight but prevent heat from escape, this makes the greenhouse warm inside. Similarly, some gases in the Earth's atmosphere can trap heat from the sun and keep the Earth warm. This is called the greenhouse effect. The gases energy that can trap heat from the sun are called greenhouse gases. It is future one kind of potential primary energy to reduce environmental pollution new energy products for human consuming. So, environmental protection message influence them to consume greenhouse energy at homes.
So, environment scientists' environment pollution message had influence Greece householders concern to apply secondary energy (environment protection) to replace electricity energy to use at home. They will change energy to use at home. The scientists' messages have more influential Greece householders energy change consumption behaviors at homes. The messages are as below:

There are different forms of energy, e.g. light, heat, sound, wind, water, electrical kinetic, chemical and potential energy. Some form energy is primary energy and it can not renew to use, e.g. light, sound, wind, water, fossil fuel etc. Some form energy is secondary energy and it can renew to use in possible, e.g. nuclear, electric charge battery etc. Why does human need to concern how to manufacture secondary energy? Because it is possible that our natural resource will be consumed all, thus we will face primary energy shortage risk. If human can invent any new form of man-made secondary energy to renew to use in order to avoid primary energy shortage to supply to use to use, then human won't only depend on our Earth natural resource energy supply numbers. We can invent any new secondary energy to renew to use again either replaces primary energy or instead of primary energy limit number supply.

What is energy change? For television energy change power case. Firstly, electrical energy changes to television power to be used by television itself, then it changes to light power, next it changes to light power. How to choose fuel form to use? Due to energy can change to different form of powers to supply different form of power advantages to supply to human to use, so it is possible that we can also invent any secondary man made renew used energy to change different form powers to supply us to use, e.g. nuclear energy changes to light or sound or heat form of powers ; electrical charge batteries changes to light or sound or heat form powers to satisfy our daily life needs.

The environment scientists' energy consumption education influence Greece householders concern how to change to use secondary energy to replace primary energy at homes as below:

For primary natural resource fuel energy example, different fuel has different feature, e.g. easy to burn, safe to use, gives out a lot of energy, inexpensive, produces little air pollution, easy to transport and store. How can we use in different channels, such as heating food, hot pat, driving vehicles.

For example, although coal is not expensive to cause electricity energy for past transportation tool, e.g. traditional coal energy train or our daily home cooking, but it has negative influence to environment air pollution. Hence, we ought to follow the primary natural resource energy's feature to decide how to apply what aspects of our life needs.

For example, if the country's people hope to reduce pollution when who use any kind of energy, e.g. US , Europe energy markets. The energy entrepreneur ought concentrate on manufacturing the kind of energy which can reduce environment pollution to be the least level to supply the country people to use, e.g. electric charge battery supplies to these countries' drivers to drive their vehicles on the roads, wind energy or water energy to manufacture electricity power supply to reduce air or water pollution ; or if the country people hope to buy the inexpensive energy to use, even the energy's quality and performance is worse, e.g. China, India, Hong Kong markets. The energy entrepreneur ought concentrate on manufacturing the lowest cost and enough supply of natural resource to manufacture the kind of energy to sell cheap price to these countries to use, e.g. China, Africa can accept to use e.g. gas, coal, fuel energy to use to compare developed countries people, e.g. UK, US; or if the countries people who hope to use energy which can easy to transport and store, e.g. light coal. The energy entrepreneur can choose to concentrate on manufacturing much coal to supply to the countries people to use, e.g. China, Arica Thus, to choose to manufacture which kinds of energy supply to the countries market people to use, the energy entrepreneur how decides to manufacture which kind of energy, it depends on which kinds of fuel advantages of the countries people most concerning.

What is energy meaning? It is defined a dynamic quality, it is a fundamental entity of nature that is transferred between parts of a system in the production of physical change within the system, and it is usually regarded as the capacity for doing work, and it is usable power (such as heat or electricity) or the resources for producing such power.

Why does secondary energy own investment worth? Because the different forms of primary natural resource energy will have supply shortage crisis, such as natural resources coal, gas, solar, wind, water, geothermal, biomass(organic material) etc. However, human can attempt to explore any undiscovered Earth or Space resource to manufacture any kinds of secondary energies, e.g. nuclear energy, electric recharge battery energy to supply to electric vehicle or space robots transportation tools to use or satisfy our daily life needs in future one day. So any kind of undiscovered secondary man-made renewed used energy resources have potential commercial worth to any energy entrepreneurs, it is possible that they can replace traditional primary energy to supply to human to use for our different aspects of life needs. In the future, the secondary energy demand will increase, when primary energy supply number has decreased form natural exploration. So, it will cause the effect of any demand of secondary energy product to be raised and prices to be increased in possible. Due to global population has been growing up, considerably China and India both countries populations have been increasing rapidly. Scientists predict there are more than 1.2 billion people worldwide will lack access to electricity, and more than 2.5 billion still use wood, charcoal to cook and heat in the future when primary energy has no enough number to supply to us to use. Hence, the fact that demand is this much greater than supply to make energy a prime market for further growth.

Although, secondary energy will have much investment worth, but energy like all other investments will carry risks. The internal and external risk factors include such as: policy is always changing to prohibit which do energy trading more easily between the energy exporting and importing countries, the secondary energy manufacturer itself own abilities to invent and to manufacture any kinds of secondary energy, improved technology can quickly make an technology obsolete, geopolitical rifts can happen overnight, the country's energy consumer (user)'s preferable choice to use which either kinds of secondary energy or secondary energy. So, it seems that (man-made) renewed used secondary energy industry can provide above-average returns, but it can also bring high risk commercial investment.

Traditionally, energy supply companies will apply those methods to operate energy providing businesses. For Shell,. Exxon examples, which had own gas stations, explore and drill for gas on their own. Other companies specialize in a part of the energy market, e.g. leasing oil rigs for example, or operating a pipeline. Energy supplying companies can choose to manufacture any kinds of energy to supply, e.g. trade oil, gas, coal, uranium, electricity etc. Any energy price and supply is demanded on the countries energy users' which kinds of energy most choice need or certain energy commodities to be chose to use popularly. For example, if US most people prefer to use secondary man-made renew used energy more than primary energy. Then, US energy manufacturers ought concentrate on manufacturing much different kinds of secondary man-made renew used energy to prepare to supply to its domestic

US market in order to raise secondary energy price to sell in its country. So, the energy manufacturer's energy manufacturing choice, it is depend on which the country's people prefer to use which kinds of energy for their daily life needs.

However, scientists predict secondary energy market will have large market share, due to primary energy will have shortage to explore to supply in our earth and future energy consumers(users) prefer to choose to use more efficiency, less energy consumption, none environment pollution cause, cost effectiveness, renew to use of any kinds of energy. For example, the electricity recharge battery secondary man-made renew used energy is one kind of reducing air pollution power to push any electric battery vehicles to be driven to compare gas energy during drivers are driving their cars on the roads. They can reduce noise and air pollution and drivers can drive safely, who only need to buy one electric recharge battery to recharge in any electric recharge battery stations on streets when the electric recharge battery has no enough power to push their cars and they need to recharge their electric recharge battery drive when they had driven between one to two days. Due to primary energy, e.g. fuel , gas, the kinds of primary energies will have shortage to supply to global drivers to drive their traditional cars. Thus, the electric recharge battery or any undiscovered secondary energy will be future driving market needs. So, man-made renew used secondary energy, e.g. biofuel, hydro-electric, nuclear, will be one kind of efficient, clean, less pollution cause, cost-effective of energy to supply to our global vehicle market, even any other undiscovered new markets. Supposing they are popular to be used for electric vehicle market globally in future one day, then their prices will be decreased and constructed to average car requires up to 1,700 gallons of oil. Also supposing that making average computer requires more than ten times or weight to fossil fuels, every calories of food eaten in the US requires roughly then calories of fossil fuels. Hence, cheap energy will be one successful factor to influence future potential energy consumer (user) individual choice needs. Conversely, ion good economic times, people are more willing to travel, to buy products, and all of which success demand and low process for energy.

In the future, secondary energy will be the best choice to food production market. The modern food production system is essentially a success of changing fossil fuels into food. So, raising energy prices are almost higher food costs and even shortage for fossil fuels energy. If one day, one kind of discovered secondary man-made renew used energy can supply to any restaurants or homes to be used to cook at the cheap price, then the profit is very high for this kind of food production energy. Thus, future food production secondary energy consumption market is large and because the primary energy inputs for agriculture are higher than the energy outputs of the food. However, future secondary man-made renew used energy for food production system is only one part of whole energy consumer in food industry. The food production is related to whole food consumption market which includes: household cooking energy market, agriculture or vegetable, rice, fruit etc. foods farming machines energy market, food manufacturing factories market, food machine package market, transportation food delivery market, supermarket or fruit/food sale stores market. They must need any energy inputs to achieve the food production or food transportation or warehouse / stores electricity supply or cooking energy needs. Hence, these food suppliers relate to any whole food factory manufacturers, food retailers, food wholesalers, farmers and home/restaurant cookers, all of them must need to use energy to carry on their food producing or food cooking or food transportation activities every day in overall food industry. Thus, it seems that undiscovered any second energy demand will be increased, when the primary energy supply number is decreasing. Also, when people can accept to use secondary energy to replace primary energy to be used for any cooking, transporting food, manufacturing food, food retail stores or warehouse food delivery energy need activities. Then, the secondary energy price will be fall down to attract many food energy consumers.

Nowadays, the food industry energy may includes primary nature resource gas energy or electricity energy for house families or restaurants cooking needs, food delivering lorry drivers driving needs usually. If future second man made renew used energy is invented successful popular to be used, e.g. hydrogen, electric recharged battery energy for electric vehicles or restaurant/home families cooking needs or food factories machine manufacture energy needs. Then, the secondary energy will have possible to replace primary energy to be food industry energy market.

Wiley, composition services graphics indicated that global primary energy consumption had been increasing 30 billion tons from 1830 year to 510 billion tons in 2010 year as well as global population size had been increasing from 70 billion 1830 year to 510 billion in 2010 year. Thus, it seems that global primary energy consumption will be needed largely after 2010 year. If future global nature resource primary energy is explored full number and it had not enough energy number to supply global human to use. Then, it will being many people feel uncomfortable and inconvenient ,e.g. Some countries won't have enough energy to supply transportation tools to be driven, some homes and restaurants won't have enough energy to supply to cook to eat or to provide restaurant clients to eat etc. daily activities, due to human's much activities which are needs energy supply. Thus, it seems that global primary energy consumption will be needed largely after 2010 year.

Wiley, composition services graphics also explained that why the primary energy consumption demand can be needed to achieve the same level to the global population size increasing in 2010 year. The graph showed these reasons why cause the same level of global population size and global primary energy consumption demand which may include: The graph showed that after a nation is developed, its per-person energy use begins to level off. In North America and Europe, where energy demand has remained flat, or fallen, in each of the past few years. But the 1.3 billion people on those two continents are far outweighed by the 5 billion people in Asia and Africa, e.g. Chinese and Indian. who currently have more energy need to compare average per man to North America and Europe per man, ensuring that overall energy demand will rise for years to come.

Wiley, composition services graphics also predicted that the growth in primary energy demand. China will have 4,500 million tons in 2035 year. India will have 3,000 million tons in 2035 year. Other developing Asia will have 2,000 million tons in 2035 year. Russia will have 1,500 million tons in 2035, Middle East will have 1,300 million tons in 2035, other rest of world will have 1,000 million tons in 2035. Hence, it implied that China will be the largest primary energy need country in the future.

China will be future the primary potential energy consumer market. The primary energy includes water, coal, wind, fossil oil, gas ,solar, geothermal energy, biomass (organize material) etc. different natural resource primary energy. Otherwise, US, UK, Europe will be secondary energy potential need market. For example, electrical recharge battery energy will be raised demand to supply to any future new design electrical charge battery vehicles in US, Europe, UK markets.

Due to US, Europe, UK people concern environment protection, so they will invent many electric charge battery vehicles to consume electrical charge battery to replace polluted gas energy to avoid air pollution when the drivers are driving cars on themselves countries' roads. For example, second man-made renew used nuclear energy can be applied to rockets to push them to leave our earth to fly to other space far away and consuming nuclear energy will be cost efficient, and nuclear energy saving will be more when nuclear to spend long time to be used in any long time space journey. Hence, nuclear energy and electric charge battery secondary energy will be popular to be applied to vehicles and rockets energy needs in US, Europe, potential markets, even our daily energy needs in global second energy market.

Who are your energy business's competitors (peers)? How do they compare? How have your energy business company performed cyclically? How to choose to manufacture to sell which kinds of primary or secondary energy product(s), either manufactures only primary energy product(s) or manufactures only secondary energy products or both? Which countries do you plan to sell your energy product?
Illustration by Wilsey, composition services graph showed that these natural resources to energy product the world's electricity percentage, such as below:

41% of coal, 5% of oil, 21% of gas, 13% of nuclear, 16% of Hydro, 3% other renewable secondary man-made energy.
Hence, coal will be future the major natural resource to produce electricity. The energy entrepreneur ought attempt to explore any coal resources, when who choose to supply electricity power to consumers for future energy consumption country markets.
Wiley, composition services also predicted that the expectation is that North America coal will supply the expectation is that North America coal will supply Asian demand, Us export terminals have a total capacity of 173 million tomes output. China will drive 16% of the nations total output. China will drive the sea-born demand for coal over for the future. Chinese energy consumption will grow more than 12 % between 1980 and 2009 years. Though, China heads global demand, India is growing faster in terms of coal imports. Much of the global coal demand will be supplied by Indonesia and Australia. Colombia, Russia, South Africa and Mongolia are also players in global export coal energy resources.
Hence, environment scientists' education messages influence Greece householders believe that secondary energy will be one kind of new energy product to replace traditional primary energy product for human energy

consumption market global needs. Hence, it is right time any energy entrepreneur needs to research how to explore any undiscovered man-made renew used secondary energy products to avoid primary energy shortage crisis occurrence. Greece householders will be the highest population number to choose secondary energy to replace primary energy to use at homes. it means that environment scientists had changed Greece householders' energy consumption behaviors at homes.

In conclusion, different countries will have different factors influence how the country's householders energy consumption behavioral changes. Hence, it seems that any country's householders‘ energy use of consumption behaviors will be possible influenced by exteral environment factors influence. Also, every country's energy providers can attempt to find whether the country has what kinds of unique factors to influence its householders' energy consumption efficiency to increase or decrease in order to find the methods to solve the energy efficiency demand reducing challenges successfully.

Why does environment changing impact our living model change? Does they have close relationship between environment and living? How and why environment influences our living model needs to be changed in order to adapt any sudden economic environment changes. In macro view, economic environment and our living environment which have direct relationship. When our social economic environment changes significantly suddenly, then our society needs to find the best methods in order to let us to feel adapt to the sudden economic environment changes to threaten the least living negative effects. I shall indicate the reasons as below:

Any countries must have themselves methods to adapt any time sudden economic environment changes. Such as China and US, China is one non -freedom country, but US is one freedom country. Hence, the relationship of how to adjustment policies, poverty and the environment was complex and different between them. Due to these are different, so they will influence themselves citizen decide how to do behaviors in order to adapt their living when they are living in themselves countries. It seems that any countries citizen need to find the best methods in order to adopt to live in themselves countries easily. Otherwise, some people feel difficult to adapt to live in themselves countries. Then, they will

choose emmigrate to other countries to live because they feel that they cannot adapt to live themselves countries more easily.

Some countries feel macroeconomic stability is one good method to keep their countries can have long term economic growth. But, it is not absolute right because it is not sufficient

to ensure long-term environmental sustainability. For example, lower inflation rates, increased savings, lower budget deficits, and improved trade balances were central to creating conditions for increased investment, a higher growth rate, employment creation, and poverty reduction. However, macroeconomic stability and increased economic efficiency would not and could not solve other basic development issues, such as income inequality and cost internalization, which directly threatened the sustainability of the countries‘ development strategies. Such as Mexico and Thailand that bring the shortcomings in addressing specific environmental impacts of the price corrections and government failure to implement complementary policy reforms to bring Mexico and Thailand people often immigrate to US illegal because they feel living difficulty to live in their countries. So, in long term, poor economic development will bring the number of immigrants increases effect to any country in possible. Also, it seems that the immigrants number is more or less, it has close relationship to the country's people how feel their country is suitable to them to live forever.

Why does environment can impact liberalized trade regimes and influence consumers' consumption desires change ? Many criticisms of the impacts of structural adjustment on the environment focus on the negative environmental consequences of liberalized trade regimes. These concern on these aspects: The fact is that liberalized trade discourages internalization of environment costs. IN the logic of competitive advantage , countries that lower the production costs for private enterprises can enjoy an advantage over competing nations by failing to internalize environment costs associated with production and disposal of commodities and manufactured goods. Such as the General Agreement on Tariffs and Trade (GATT), which prevails trade practices that encourage the externalization of environment cost. For example, GATT rules do not allow countries to distinguish between production processes that internalize environment costs and those that pass such costs to present and future generations. However, this policy failure of trade regimes thereby grants competitive advantage to those who do not internalize environment costs. In fact, environmental standards can be attacked as nontariff barriers to trade that run contrary
to the principles of enhanced international trade. Hence, it creates the difficult international trade co-operation relationship between environment protective countries and non-environment protective countries. For example in agricultural farm industry aspect, it will bring agricultural export difficulty to in Latin America, the trade-offs between short-term economic growth benefits and the long term environment costs of promoting non traditoinal agricultural exports in Latin America. When Latin America evaluates it will bring less and short term benefits to export any agricultural food to environment protective countries. Then, it will reduce export to them, even forever without any agricultural exports to them again. Then, these environment protection countries people won't eat any Latin America agricultural food easily. Shortage of Latin America agricultural food will be shortage to supply these environment protection countries, then Latin America agricultural food price may raise, if these environment protection countries agricultural food consumers still need to eat much Latin America agricultural food

Consequently, the shortage of Latin America agricultural food issue will bring long term inflation to any Latin America agricultural food. It will influence these environment protection countries‘ Latin America agricultural food consumers their eating needs to be reduced and they will decide to change their taste to eat other countries' agricultural food to replace Latin America agricultural food. Finally, any Latin America's agricultural food to these environment protection countries‘ people, they won't have any higher market worth or higher price or lose any worth to compare other
countries' agricultural food because they will like to eat other countries‘ agricultural food more than Latin America agricultural food. Hence, environment protection environment will influence
some countries' export reduces as well as the import countries‘ consumers' choices will also changed and their consumption desires will also change in long term.

I shall explain why environment pollution will influence consumer behaviors to be changed also.The findings of behavior analysts on resource conservation and pollution control are interpreted in terms of the classification of consumer behaviors and contingencies

proposed by the model. These environmentally-impacting consumer behaviors are elucidated through discussion of both their consequences and the nature of intervention to a
meliorate them. An appropriate social marketing mix for each class of consumer behavior is suggested. Why does the country some consumers reduce to use some products or reduce to buy some products, e.g. riding bicycle to replace driving car; reducing to use plastic and paper bags at homes or going supermarket shopping; reducing to catch air planes to fly to travel because avoiding air plane's gas pollutes air on sky; reducing to catch ferry on sea number because avoiding gas pollutes on sea. Their living
behaviors changing reaon aimed at environmental preservation. So, these environmentally-impacting consumer behaviors issue will be one good example to explain how and why environment changing and consumer behaviors changing have close relationship.

Applied behavior analysis has contributed substantially to knowledge of economic consumption as it adversely affects the physical and social environment (Cone and Hayes 1980; Geller, Winett and Everett 1982). Skinner's (1953) behavior theory which stresses
that the causes of behavior are found in its environmental consequences. They indicate how environment protection attitude can change consumer behavior, such consumer behaviors as excessive use of private transportation, over-consumption of domestic energy, littering and waste generation, and consumption of scarce resources such as water.

Social advertising from television, radio, newspapers, magazine which is one good example to encourage environment protection behavior to consumers e.g. not purchase cars to drive on road to avoid air pollution from gas. Further, the effectiveness of campaigns intended to change behavior by modifying attitudes has been questioned. To the extent that environment protection aware consumers rely heavily on the use of persuasive communications to change pre-behavioral attitudes and values, social information campaigns have had little impact on consumers' conservation behavior.

Despite vast general public knowledge about the potentially catastrophic consequences of failing to conserve energy, researchers report an inability to identify the required relationship
between attitudes toward energy use and conservation; even those maximally informed are no more likely to save energy; nor does specifically informing people about
the personal costs of current energy use and the benefits of reducing consumption affect behavior (Costanzo, Archer, Aronson and Pettigrew 1986).

However, applied behavior analysis indicates that simply informing people of the consequences of their actions is unlikely to modify their behavior unless they have been systematically exposed to those consequences in the past. Social de marketing based on applied behavior analysis can be systematically related to marketing mix management

by a model founded on the behavior theory that underpins that analysis, the nature of both environmentally-impacting
consumer behavior and its deleterious ecological effects. The major consumers target whose useful behaviors can be changed when they aware the
environment protection , they include transportation, energy consumption, waste disposal, water use consumers.

At the theoretical level, the purpose of the model and its developmental research program is not to supplant these or other structural approaches but to further understanding of the role of contextual influences and consumers' learning histories on their current actions as buyers and users of economic resources. The central explanatory mechanism of the model is the synomorphic consumer situation,
the meeting place of the consumer's history of reinforcement and punishment (representing the personal variables responsible for current behavior) and the setting in which purchase and consumption occur (representing the contextual influences on behavior). The former incorporates the consumer's prior experience of purchase and consumption and the effects of the consequences of these acts on the probability of their performing similar consumer behaviors in the present and future.So, when one person who is living in one environment protection awarerness is strong country, he will be influenced by its country's environment protection message to avoid to do any environment pollution behavior in every day.

Environment pollution is Social and public costs accrue to the community as a whole and not specifically to the individual consumer who is responsible for their being incurred. Consumer behaviors frequently take the form of behaviors that are damaging to the environment: e.g., seeking ever-greater accomplishments that provide rewards and show forth one's status may result in the consumption of scarce and irreplaceable resources. Beyond a point, pleasure-seeking may also have a deleterious effect on the environment through energy consumption. Accumulation brings with it the need to dispose of packaging and, in societies marked by ever-shortening product life-cycles, the products themselves. And, finally,the consumption of the basic commodities of life themselves, such as water, now threatens further consumption by depleting stocks.

Whereas the environmentally deleterious results of the behavior are encountered, if at all, indirectly and only after a period of time has elapsed. The immediate reinforcement of behavior with ultimately deleterious effects is so great, and the aversive outcomes so remote, that the longer-term consequences can sometimes only be reduced or prevented through active self-management. The relatively open settings
in which these behaviors typically take place and their maintenance by strongly hedonic reinforcers mean that some closure of the setting has been advocated in of self-management in order to compel a degree of prosocial behavior.

Private Transportation Environment Protection awareness

Of the environmentally-impacting consumer behaviors with which applied behavior analysts have been concerned, the use of private automobiles, often carrying a single individual to or from work, falls into this category. Such behavior is apparently maintained by
the fun of driving, control of one's journey - and informational reinforcement - speed, low and flexible journey times.

In addition to these immediate sources of reinforcement, personal driving is powerfully maintained by apparently available on a variable ratio schedule: social approval, personal safety, simplification of journey planning routines, all of which are contingent on the performance of a number of responses that varies among situations.

In environment protection high awareness countries, private drivers attempt to modify consumers‘ private transportation behavior which has been intended to reduce fuel consumption, urban congestion, and pollution by discouraging unilateral use of private cars and promoting public transportation. The most successful interventions have offered in the form of financial incentives: provision of small monetary rewards for riding the bus has, for example, increased the number of users of public travel services by 50-180% . Riding the bus and other strategies which avoid private transportation (such as walking, car pooling and cycling) are at best minimally reinforced by social contact and, eventually, feelings of fitness, and informationally by cost savings. But they are punished by aversive consequences: slowness, discomfort, danger, exposure, crowding, noise, inflexibility, unpredictability, and lack of control.

Discouragement of car travel has reduced mileage travelled by between 10 and 50% (Cone and Hayes 1980). The provision of informational plays a strong role in reducing driving.While feedback alone (on the number of miles travelled, operating costs, depreciation, social costs, etc.) had no effect on mileage travelled, performance feedback influences behavior by allowing the driver to monitor his or her behavior in order to achieve the incentives.

In the marketing of alternatives to private car use, notably transportation by bus which for many drivers is likely to prove highly disruptive of their journey routines, Domestic Energy Consumption as ’Pleasure‘. Among environmentally-impacting consumer behaviors, pleasure is exemplified by the over-consumption of domestic energy derived from fossil fuels, notably electricity for heating and lighting. The hedonic reinforcements are high and closely related temporally to the responses that produce them - convenience, comfort. While informational reinforcement is less obvious, social approval may follow generous use of these resources in the company of others (meanness will certainly lead to social disapproval and loss of status). The long term consequences are remote: e.g. depletion of resources, social disapproval. Consumption behaviors are apparently controlled by a variable interval schedule: comfort and satisfaction depend upon employing the source of heat or light for a time that varies from occasion to occasion with the individual’s task requirements and state variables (e.g. cold, hunger).

Social demarketing should concentrate on making the behavior (including avoidance)
more involving, encouraging the avoidance of high bills and a feeling of self-gratification at saving energy and reducing pollution.By increasing the costs of energy. Support for the classification of domestic energy use as pleasure and for the efficacy of this strategy comes from the attempted modification of consumers’ domestic energy consumption which has used prompting, feedback, and incentives, separately and in combination. Alone, information relating to the environmental effects of pollution caused by high consumption of electricity at peak periods had little if any effect on peak usage. Greater effect was achieved by consumer self-monitoring of current energy usage: peak consumption reduced by up to 30% of mean baseline levels. Overall energy usage (i.e. peak and non-peak consumption) has also proved sensitive to informational feedback, even at times of steep increases in

the price of energy. Combined feedback and monetary incentives have reduced peaking by about 65% of baseline, confirming the efficacy of combined consequences.

Waste Disposal will reduce for environment protection consumers

Waste generation is a consequence of accumulation but it is actually a problem manifested in the opposite of accumulation: disposal. Indiscriminate waste disposal has relatively few hedonic benefits other than convenience but its informational outcomes are extensive if subtle: it confers status through the assumption that someone else will clear up, and it may also imply conspicuous consumption. Such behaviors are maintained seemingly on fixed ratio schedules. Their long term consequences are also remote: gradual spoliation of the physical environment, accruing social disapproval.

The findings of applied behavior analysis in this area do indeed confirm the analysis and classification. Attempts at reducing littering have relied heavily on the use of prompts. The results have been generally disappointing unless the prompts were accompanied by positive reinforcement, usually hedonic. Exhortations, lectures, and relevant general education have proved largely ineffective in this sphere. Even the attempt to reduce littering among children in a theatre by manipulating the physical environment (providing bags for waste) had little effect. Combined with messages pointing out the disadvantages of litter, the provision of bags had a moderate effect. However, when a reward was given for each bag of rubbish, the decrease in littering was massive. Another form of hedonic reward in the form of a ticket for a movie had a similarly substantial negative effect on littering. Similar results have been found in experimental studies of the reduction of littering in streets, and around and within buildings.

Success is also apparent in the closure of the behavior setting, e.g. providing more litter bins and devising trash cans that are fun to use, and by ensuring the initial cleanliness and attractiveness of the environment; all of these strategies have had some effect by bringing behavior under stimulus control, but only the presentation of positive reinforcers in the form of payments has any dramatic effect on behavior. Prompts, used alone, have little if any effect, perhaps because of their reliance on punishment for unapproved behavior: the individual who litters nevertheless and avoids immediate punishment is actually likely to be reinforced for his or her littering.

The relative effectiveness of prompts and incentives indicated by litter studies has been confirmed by experiments aimed at increasing consumers‘ willingness to conserve irreplaceable materials through recycling. Attempts at increasing consumers’ purchases of returnable bottles are a typical example. The use of prompts informing customers of the savings to which such behavior would lead and that they would be contributing to the fight against pollution have had mixed effects . Giving consumers small financial rewards for the reuse of such items as egg cartons, milk containers and grocery bags, accompanied by in-store prompts and a pleasant and enthusiastic reaction by salespersons, has led to increases in custom.

Some attempts at increasing consumers‘ recycling behavior have had significant punishing consequences. The Bottle Laws enacted first in Oregon and subsequently adopted by several other states impose considerable transaction, inventory and time costs on retailers who pass them on to their customers (Guerts 1986).

Both are penalized for their participation in the waste reduction campaign and, even though distributors are legally bound to comply, their consumers are in general unlikely to incur the costs involved in prepaying deposits and returning glass bottles unless they are adequately compensated for the punishing consequences of these prosocial endeavours. Experimental attempts to encourage the recovery of waste materials such as paper which can be recycled also indicate that prompts have minimal effects on behavior while the provision of hedonic and, to a smaller extent, informational reinforcers has a substantial reinforcing effect. Hence students offered prizes in contests and raffles are more likely to reduce wastage than those who are only exposed to educative prompting. The provision of convenient containers for the collection of recyclable waste is also significantly more effective than prompting on the promotion of appropriate prosocial behaviors perhaps because it achieves a degree of closure of the setting and the combination of prompts and suitable receptacles for the collection of waste has produced a combined
effect on behavior greater than that expected from their individual contributions.

Domestic Water Consumption is encouraged to households useful behaviors at homes

Maintenance is exemplified as an environmentally-impacting consumer behavior by the domestic over consumption of water. The luxury and status of having water
continuously available on tap are easily taken for granted but being able to drink, clean, bathe and water the garden are indicative of comparative wealth and power; they
are informational benefits directly related to the consumer's state of deprivation. The consumption behaviors in question are apparently maintained on fixed interval ratios, most of the uses of water taking place at some time or other on most days or most weeks.

These methods can threaten householders abuse water useful behaviors. They include punishment, especially involving price would be especially efficacious in reducing consumption; metering, to provide general association between behavior and its contingent consequences and to provide accurate and quick feedback on the outcomes of consumption would be especially effective ; closing the setting by reducing the time and place during which water can be consumed would be effective.

A study of the conservation of metered water in Perth, Australia (Geller et al. 1982) indicates that water consumption decreased by over 30% in both an experimental group provided with daily feedback on water use and a rebate proportionate to demand reduction, and a control group provided only with feedback,
though change in climatic conditions may also have affected the results. The low elasticity of demand for water makes financial rebates less appropriate than for other classes
of consumer behavior.

Modification of accomplishment behaviors, exemplified here by private motoring, requires the development of a radically more attractive product with strongly reinforcing informational attributes: this may even necessitate the creation of a different product. Price may be important too, but only when the new or thoroughly revamped product has been successfully launched and established:

the price of the original might then be raised to punish its use. Until this point is reached, however, such a price rise would have little overall effect on demand for the original product given the abundant hedonic and informational reinforcers it provides.

Indeed, to the extent that private transportation is a good, maintained by informational reinforcement that derives from conspicuous consumption, an increase in the costs associated with it might be counter-productive, encouraging rather than discouraging consumption. During the introductory phases of the new product, its price might be subsidized to ensure that consumers switched to its use: whether the price reduction has to be maintained indefinitely depends upon the effectiveness of the primary hedonic and informational reinforcers provided by the novel product. As far as promotion is concerned, prompts are unlikely to have a strong effect on demand, though coupled with effective consequential stimuli they provide a necessary informative and persuasive role. However, advertisements containing modelling of the prosocial behaviors advocated would probably both increase awareness of the campaign
and encourage imitative responses. Finally, as far as place is concerned, the behavior setting should be opened further by increasing competition and making the new product
widely and flexibly available.

Consumer behavior modification in the case of pleasure is more changed through the provision of increased, relatively rapid and regular information on consumption. This information can be seen as part of the product provided by the utilities companies. Since the overall goal of the campaign is a reduction in energy use, this must be accomplished by the encouragement of personal and domestic arrangements
which promote thermal savings (e.g. better insulation, the wearing of more heat-efficient clothing and the elimination of useless energy consumption such as the illumination
of unoccupied rooms). These factors, which might be considered part of the place element of the marketing mix since they determine the location of consumption, contribute to the closure of the behavior setting. Price might also be used to deter over use of resources but, given the highly hedonic consequences of energy consumption, it is unlikely to have a strong independent effect on usage.

The single most cost-effective means of reducing littering is probably the closure of the behavior setting. Since litter is itself a discriminative stimulus for further littering, the provision of bins, bags and other containers that encourage disposal is likely to have a cumulative effect on behavior. Prompting alone also has some effect on litter disposal if it is directly related to the means of acting prosocially, e.g. by pointing out what to put, where to put it and when. The behavior setting for recycling can be closed by the provision of containers for bottles, plastics, papers, and so on in convenient positions for consumers to use.

Competitions and variable person schedules appear to be the most effective means of changing behavior, especially if coupled with promotional campaigns emphasizing modelled prosocial behavior. The costs involved in some prosocial

behaviors presently punish the consumer -
e.g. in the case of returning bottles and other packaging; either these costs must be reduced through the collection of waste materials or the financial recompense for their return must be expanded until behavior is economically controlled.

Finally, in the case of household water consumption and conservation, it is important to control the behavior setting by installing water-conserving methods (e.g. smaller cisterns), by encouraging the use of rainwater for garden watering, and the opportunity to use water less expensive than fully-purified drinking water for some domestic purposes such as flushing toilets. The alternative place strategies (rationing, standpipes, etc.) are politically unacceptable and usually unnecessary except during
emergencies, though metering is probably an essential prerequisite of most systems of behavior modification based on consequential stimuli whether informational or hedonic.
Price might be used to overcome overuse, though again this would be politically acceptable only within close bounds.

- Why environment and human's qualify of life and economic growth has close relationship.

I shall explain how this study confirms the invested correlation between economic growth and environmental degradation of hypothesis that is at the early stage economic growth which increases environmental degradation, then environmental degradation decreases after reaching a certain level of average income per capita. Moreover, I shall explain how other factors, such as trade openness, industrial extension also cause an increase in environmental degradation. This study also has been investigated the between environmental pollution and per capita income when have close relationship to influence economic falling down in long term.

The key indicators are used to capture the changes in environmental conditions have been developed and used in many countries. A high rate of economic growth has been a primary and permanent goal of government and society, particularly in developing countries. The increase in economic growth is related to an increase in the production and consumption of products and services. Consequently, it may lead to an increase in the multiplied products of the people and income per capita consumption. However, economic growth may produce negative impacts on the environment pollution, overexploitation of natural resources, degradation and loss of wildlife habitat and climate change. Hence, many countries have been facing the decline in environmental quality issue when which neglect to reduce environmental pollution challenge in long term.

I believe that the impact of economic growth on environment quality is categorized through three different channels: The first is the scale effect, the second is the composition and the end is the technique effect. The scale effect means to happen as pollution increases with the size of the economy, the explanation being that even of the structure of the economy and the technology doesn't change, it is assumed that an increase in the scale of economic activity leads to an increase in pollution and environmental degradation, when the composition effect refers to the change in production structure of an economy from agriculture-based to industry and service. The last effect is the technique effect, which captures improvement in the technique of production and adaption of cleaner technologies and hence a reduction in pollution

● Explaining why the Environmental Kuznets Curve key indicator method is measured to any country's economic growth and environmental pollution relationship commonly

Generally, evidence shows that some environmental pressures have diminished in developed countries, the hypothesis could generalized to the global relationship between economy and environment at all. The hypothesis is called the Environmental Kuznets Curve (EKC) hypothesis because of its similarity with the relationship between the level of inequality and per capita income is posited by Kuznet. According to the EKC hypothesis, it indicated that "at the first stage of economic development environmental pressures increase as per capita income increases, but after a critical turning point these pressures diminish along with higher income levels(Beckerman,1992)". In its most optimistic view, the hypothesis suggests that economic growth is itself the solution to environmental problems, because environmental improvement will be an almost unavoidable.

In fact, energy consumption, environmental protection and economic growth belong to an organic whole. The development of industry plays an important part in the development of the national economy. Meanwhile the development of industry spends lots of energy and makes serious pollution. Energy is a important material basis of human survival, economic development and social progress. Instance, China is promoting energy production and sustainable economic growth. We know that the environmental pollution should be the cost of economic development. Energy consumption and environmental pollution in-depth has a great practical significance for guiding the healthy development of China's economy.

The sustainable economic growth, urbanization and environmental protection in China. China has developed to become the second largest economy in the world next to USA. With fact economic growth , cities in China have been expanding and it is through urbanization to cause serious environmental problems, such as pollution of air, water and solid waste, which have imposed huge challenges to economic growth. In fact, urbanization has led to damage to the environment. So, the China environmental pollution is caused from the relationship between economic development and urbanization and then urbanization is driving economic growth. Also, the major environmental pollution is driving to China's economic growth and the major environmental problems of China are caused by urbanization in China and urbanization will cause negative consequences. However, China industrialization demands are increasing and China economic growth is also increasing, but the environment pollution is also increasing at the same time. Another environmental pollution of country, such as Australia, its economy has grown an average of 3.3 % gross domestic product (GDP) annually the past 40 years, corresponding to an average annual GDP per capita growth rate of 1.3% (ABS, 2014). There are concerns that growth has been accompanied by excessive natural resource use and declines in environmental quality. However, economic growth can also stimulate demand for environmental quality and thus environmental policy has been enabling the development and adoption of new technologies. Whether income growth is associated with increasing or decreasing environmental quality issue for long term, which is a question that varies across environmental quality measures and economies growth.

The fact is as the scale of Australia economic activity increase, environmental degradation, including increasing resource use and negative externalities tends to increase as well. On the one hand, econometricians indicated that "starting in the early 1990 year highlights the possibility that for some environmental pollutants there tends to be an inverted "U" shaped development path with respect to income, as measured by GDP, such that pollution tends to after some switching point (Grossman and Krueger, 1991)." This relationship could arise from demand side pressures (environmental quality is a normal product) or supply side pressures (technological and structural changes) . It is possible to bring the relationship between environmental quality and economic growth. On the other hand, nowadays, the conflict between economic growth and biodiversity conservation is concerned from many countries' governments. A more compelling response to the conflict is that may be resolved with technological progress. However, I review the conflict between economic growth and biodiversity conservation in the absence of technological progress. The conflict between economic growth and biodiversity conservation is based principle of ecology, such as trophic levels and competitive exclusion, the human economy grows at the competitive exclusion of nonhuman species in the aggregate. However, the conflict via technological progress has not occurred and is infeasible because of the linkage between technological progress and economic growth at current levels of technology.

My supportive reason is that surplus production in existing economic sectors is requires for conducting the research and development necessary for bringing new technologies to market. Technologies also reflect macroeconomic goals, and if the goal is economic growth, technologies are less likely to be developed. As the economy grow, the loss of biodiversity may be partly mitigated with end use innovation that increases technical efficiency, but this type of technological progress requires policies that are unlikely if the conflict between economic growth and biodiversity conservation and other aspects of environmental protection is not acknowledged.

In my discussion concerns that environmental damage has not only created obstacles to economic development, but it is also posing great threats to human health and life, to ecological systems and natural world, and to the socio-cultural environments in which human beings lead their daily lives. Hence, I suggest that different countries' governments need to concern mobilization of political risk and socio-economic resources. The concept of "sustainability" was formulated as a result of the linkage between pesticide use and widespread pollution, of the effects of pollution on the health of humans and other animals and plants, and through proposal for managing resources in a way which doesn't destroy supplies of resources needed in the future.

A country is considered "developing" when it is experiencing expansion of its productive capacity, the indicator is used, such as gross national product (GNP), and/or GNP per capita. The well being of all people depends largely on economic growth. However, when a country, such as developing countries Hong Kong and India both countries which populations are increasing, indeed it is difficult to imagine development without economic growth. As a result, however, nature has been scarified in the name of economic development. The pursuit of wealth and exploitation of the planet had taken place on an individualistic basic or collectivist basic, environment problems are began to cause increasing concern in growing segments of societies, mainly in the developed countries, such as India and China. We emphasizes quality of life, but the bio centric view, gives greater recognition to the planet, regarding the pursuit of wealth through industrial expansion and economic growth as incompatible with the earth's resource base. This view also takes the position that economic growth at the expense of natural represents consumption of what belongs rightly to future generations.

However, becomes human kind is seen to be living within ecological constraints, economies will have zero growth in quantitative terms. Instead growth should be measured in qualitative terms, such as clean and healthy natural environment level, in other words, on the basis of quality of living rather than standard of living. Quantitative growth may occur only in certain areas, for example, in developing countries, such as China or India and poor areas of developed countries, such as USA, but there must also be negative growth in areas which are already highly developed.

In General, the economy growth is always the attention focal point to every country. The economy growth impacts the protecting environment, on the contrary, the protecting environment also impacts the economy growth whether the environment is a factor considering the economic growth. In fact, environment not only provides the substance foundation and activity space for human, but also is responsible for production. Economic development not only enhances the integration national power and improves the people's life quality, but brings number of environmental problems, soil degradation, desertification etc.

Concerning how to reduce environment pollution and to raise economic growth at the same time. I shall have these questions to be needed to answer in order to give suggestion to solve this challenge. These questions are such as below:

- Whether does economic growth affect the environment?
- On the contrary, whether also does the protecting environment affect the growth economy?
- Whether is protecting economy and protecting environment a pair of contradiction or not what creates the environment problem?
- Is economic development incompatible with environmental quality?
- What is the effect of an increase in employment or wages on the environment in a particular industry?
- How do environmental conditions or regulations influence firm location and expansion decisions and thus economic growth in a community?

However, I feel that poverty is another factor to cause environmental pollution. Instead of factory manufacturing industry, such as India has many poor people neglect to keep natural river, ocean, hill, farming, and any public places environment to be clean and not direct to use these natural places. Solving this problem is that developing countries'

economy how to increase economy under the protecting environment. Analyzing poverty and environmental pollution relationship is the focal point. We need to concern problem formulation, such as what the conflict is between developing economic and protecting environment. For example, the problem is concerned the traffic point problem, such as the environment impact of transportation has now become a global issue. Otherwise, environment impacts from transportation in the developed world are now equalized or exceeded by those in developing countries. It is given the relatively high level of car ownership and use in developing countries, such as developed country Hong Kong, which is a small Asia city, but there are many Hong Kong people who like to buy cars to drive to go to office on the roads every day. Hence, it causes much traffic jam transportation problems to Hong Kong roads every day. Otherwise, developing country, Africa. Because people are poor commonly, so there are less many own cars. The air pollution will be reduced also. However, Hong Kong has higher level of pollution to have a negative impact on employment growth due to the following reasons:
Better environmental quality attracts more skilled workers at lower wages and firms have access to whose more easily in regions where environmental quality is higher. Hong Kong has high level of pollution because Hong Kong firms attracts more skilled works to work in high technological manufacturing industry to case air or water pollution.

Production costs may be lower in regions with higher environmental quality if cleaner air and water result in lower rates of sick leaves and higher worker productivity. Hong Kong firms aim to raise worker productivity, so which uses high technological machines to raise whose productivity, but it also brings oil energy pollution to air or water.

I give a hypothesis is that higher earnings and lower employment growth rates contribute to decrease in pollution growth rates, resulting in better environmental conditions in a country. The usual hypothesis is that earnings and environmental quality are positively correlated. Since as earnings rise, the demand for environmental quality increases through an income effect, as do the public and private resources available for environmental improvement. Otherwise, increase in employment might increase pollution activities in the region, due to a scale effect. The scale effect reflects the increase in the level of economic activity in the relevant constant techniques of production and composition of final product. Hence, it seems Hong Kong income growth associated with decreasing environment quality nowadays. Because Hong Kong is lower earnings and high employment growth rates contribute to increase in pollution growth rates, resulting in worse environmental conditions in Hong Kong.

Why countries need to pollute environment to develop economy, such a need for industrialization related environmental degradation in the course of economic development. A country needs and chooses to achieve industry production it can raise technological advancement and adopt technologies, which are substantially less polluting than the technologies used by countries which industry in the past. The environmental development trade off might have existed historically. But it is not bad to developing countries to scarce environment quality for industry development. Nowadays, different countries' governments need to concern how to reduce environmental pollution and to raise economic growth at the same time. In fact, human are facing these challenges, such as energy crisis is from 1970 year is precipitated by oil price jumps, market failure in allocation of environmental resources. At the same time, human are also facing economic development that meets the needs of the present without compromising the ability of the future generations to meet our own needs. Due to natural resource is limited to be supplied in the future, industry needs manufactured, human and natural is left undiminished, so this needs restricting consumption to save natural resources for asset creation and conservation and protection of the natural environment. Efforts and indicators for monitoring sustainability indicates the environmentally adjusted national income or Green Domestic Product (GNP)=NDP less depletion of natural capital-environmental damage and green national accounts indicates degradation of environmental capital is like depreciation of man -made capital. Hence, it implies environmental pollution is a damage cost to any countries. Hence, if the country can reduce or avoid the environmental pollution, then its environmental damage cost will not influence its GDP (Green Domestic Product) income amount indicator to be reduced for the country's national income in the year. Then, it's economic growth will be better in the year. Due to GDP is the country whole year income financial performance indicator. It will concern the country's economic growth level in the year.

Environmental pollution is an important issue in the process of economic growth. Instance, China has obtained remarkable economic growth with an average annual growth rate of 9.6% in gross domestic product (GDP) from 1979 year to 2004 year. Despite the impressive economic performance, the environment qualities have become worse during the past two decades. China government began to concern about to following these questions: will the high economic growth be able to sustain within environmental constraints or without exceeding ecological system? What is the effect of economic growth on environment quality? Are there any tradeoff between attaining high economic growth and protecting environment? And will the environment conditions become improved automatically at higher income level? What should the government do to the environmental degradation? When environmental sustainability, due to the increasing scarcity or overuse of renewable natural resources, arisen non renewable commodities, such as fossil fuels or industrial metals which cause problems, such as water and air pollution, atmosphere or the ozone layer. Thus these bad happening(result) have cause-effect relationship between pollution and public health.

Environmental policy aims at putting environmental resources, such as land, water, air, the atmosphere regime, with clear and enforceable rules. The tools various forms of restriction on activity: access to these resources may be limited, for example, by placing limit values on emissions or their use may be limited (by restricting the kind of activities allowed in natural habitats or drinking water reservoirs) or make subject to specific conditions (such as paying a tax or an environmental levy or the obligation to clean and recycle them after use). Rising incomes and rising pollution have brought with them a rising demand for environmental protection of policies. Market forces themselves have led to a reduction in the pollution in intensity of economic activity of the dynamic growth of the " cleaner" rates of return for local and regional pollution are closer to social rates, then for global commons. However, policy action has nevertheless been strong needed to decouple economic activity and emission levels. In fact, environmental policies cause an adjustment of economic structures. The price of using environmental resources and of exposing the public to health risks should be brought closer with social cost, with consequence that pollution and risks to public health should decline and GDP becomes less pollution intensive. Besides, polluting industries will be held in check when cleaner industries will be boosted and net effects on welfare though not necessarily on economic activity as measured in national accounts statistics. This adjustment comes at th price of fiction between regulated industries, their supplies and customers which could offset potential welfare gains. A cost effective environmental policy should aim to minimize costs incurred in achieving an environmental objective by dynamic character of adjustment needs and cost and benefit can be estimates in the absence of well functioning markets. In this way, it could contribute to significantly relaxing potential trade off between environmental protection and economic growth aim and supporting welfare enhancing structural adjustment.

In conclusion, in the future, environmental behavior change will be limited by unclear solutions and low political profile, but models of human behavior can help in understanding how to support change. I shall recommend three methods to solve environment pollution challenge to influence economic growth for long term at the same time.

The first point, it is practical for example, governments need to promote teaching behavior to let their countries' citizen to know the corrective attitude to putting rubbish to rubbish boxes in streets and to promote recycling schemes to achieve more environmentally friendly products. For example, Hong Kong have 7 million people are living in one small city. If HK citizen put their rubbish to any streets, gardens etc. public places. It will influence natural environment to be worse, then it will influence the flowers, trees plants and bees, butterflies, ants etc. insects which can not be alive, due to their natural environment has been polluted by HK citizen. Hence, human have responsibility to protect their natural environment to let any animals and plants can be alive safely and healthy. If our world could have health and good natural environment which can let human and animals and plants to be alive, then pollution can also be reduced, even our countries' economy can grow fast because product manufacturers can have good and beautiful places to let them to build their plants to manufacture their products every day, due to good natural environment will provide good places to let manufacturers to build their plants, then their workers will also have good health to do their jobs in their plants to raise their productivity and work efficiency. Hence, good natural environment and good places provision to be built plants, then workers will have good health to work, so which has cause and effect relationship closely. Manufacturers need to know their workers should not raise their productivity and work efficiency, even they will reduce their productivity and work inefficiency if their work places are polluted.

The second point, economic and legislative need, for example, fines and incentives, making the polluter pays and international action, for example, debt relief international pollution control. Air pollution is the discharge of waste products into air and main sources are cargo or airplanes exhausts, power stations and industrial process as well as water pollution is the discharge of waste products into river or ocean and main sources are ferry, cargo shipping exhausts and industrial process. Thus, governments ought have legislative force to threaten the product manufacturers pollute air or water during their industrial process in their plants.

The third point, involving and empowering people, for example, local decisions and resources of allocation, such as economic decisions about the uses which should be made of land, labor and capital leading to an overall of resources, which generally matches the pattern of consumer demand. Consumer demand creates profitable opportunities for entrepreneurs to organize inputs of factors of production so as to meet that demand. In this way, the allocation of resources responds to the pattern of demand exhibited by consumers. However, the idea and the allocation of resources can be applied much more widely to a range of decision which may be taken by individual or by governments. Such as, people decide how to allocate their own resources when they choose between work and leisure or whether to save more or consume more. Also, governments make resource allocation decisions when they consider making changes to different categories of spending: they may consider whether to allocate more towards defense or education or towards health care or environment protection or unemployment benefit.

However, it is not always which the allocation of resources conforms to the pattern of consumer demand. The manufacturing firms and governments can sometimes control certain aspects of the allocation of manufacture raw material resources through monopoly power or through administrative decisions. It aims to reduce natural resource waste and reduce air and water pollution issues occurrence to any oceans, rivers, lands etc. places.

The final point, different countries' governments can achieve agricultural stabilization policies, such as many governments intervene in some way in agricultural markets. In developed countries, the objective is to raise farm incomes, usually by keeping prices above the world market price, and perhaps to keep out cheap imports. This tends to raise food prices to consumers. Within the EU, most policy decisions are embodies in the Common Agricultural Policy. These policies are unpopular with food exporting countries, especially those that are also developing countries. Some developed countries sell subsidized food to very poor countries, which useful if these is a famine. But it is counter-productive when it reduces farm prices and thus poor local farmers' incomes and their incentive to increase output and productivity. So, this developing countries, governments, such as China, India etc. can allocate the limited land natural resources to give to the farmers to use to help their to grow a lot of rice, potatoes, tomatoes, vegetables or to feed many pigs, cows to keep themselves countries' farming sector long term development to earn overseas or local both GDP income and per capita farmer income for long term. Beside, they do not need concentrate on developing manufacturing industry sector income and their environmental pollution will also reduce, due to there are less lands are supplied to manufacturers to build factories to use for long term.

In conclusion, every country needs to concern how to keep economic growth and to avoid to cause environment pollution challenge at the same time. Because, which economy will not be grown, even will be fallen if their environment is polluted seriously for long term, although which economic growth will be raised for short term.

CHAPTER THREE

How does economics contribute to organizational Behavior

How organizational behavior influences organizational performance ?

In macro economic view, when one country has many different kinds of businesses, whether these different kinds of organizational behavior may influence the country overall economic environment changes to be better or worse?

How does Organisational Behaviour affect change? In micro economic view, I believe that any kinds of organizations , themselves business activities may influence their staffs performance, efficiency and productivity, even customer number can be influenced to increase or reduce by the organizational behavior.

Organizational behavior means that culture, and attitudes can affect change management initiatives in many ways. A few examples include: Increased Efficiency – Better attitudes and behaviors will result in greater cooperation and less resistance to change. Otherwise, I believe that the physical environment of an organization has a significant influence on employee behavior. A good work environment, including factors such as office layout, lighting, furniture, and equipment, can enhance employees‘ well-being and satisfaction, leading to higher levels of commitment and performance.

How does economics contribute to organizational Behaviour? In OB, economics helps understand how incentives, rewards, and decision-making processes affect employee behaviour and performance. Economic principles are used in OB to design compensation systems, incentive plans, and cost-effective HR policies. However, I believe that the economic factors that influence employee behavior in an Organisation because economic factors that influence employee performance and productivity include competence, compensation, leadership, motivation, working environment, and work discipline. Studies have shown that these factors have a significant impact on how well employees perform their jobs.

How does organizational behavior impact the growth of an organization? Understanding organizational behavior can help companies and businesses create and cultivate a positive culture and work environment that will ultimately improve the organization as a whole. Benefits of organizational behavior have been shown to include: Increased employee satisfaction. Increased customer satisfaction. So, it seems that any kinds of organizational behavior may bring positive or negative impact to employee performance, even the organization's customer number can increase or decrease in possible. Consequently, when the country can have many organizations can increase customer number, they ought help the country to grow GDP. Or when the county can not have many organizations can increase customer number, they ought not help the country to grow GDP in possible. Hence, it seems that organizational behavior can bring indirect impact to influence the country;s GDP in possible in behavioral economic view.

What methods can develop economy ?

Can encourage consumption develop economy? Can new technology products develop economy? Can creating new jobs develop economy? Can human behaviour influence economic development? Can encouraging new energy education knowledge development economy? I shall attempt to answer these questions as below:

How consumption can develop economy? Economists explain that if a resource used in production, such as labour or equipment, becomes more expensive,, firms have an incentive to find new methods of production that economize on that resource. When economists study the behaviour of people or firms , they look at the incentive being faced. So, I feel that when new technology resource is needed to apply to manufacture any kinds of products, it can help the kind of product to bring consumer purchase desire increases to choose to make purchase decision more easily and quickly. Hence, new technology is one factor to bring new incentive to manufacture the kind of product, when the kind of product can be manufactured by the kind of new resource. Consequently, it can attract many consumers to choose to buy the kind of new product, e.g. smart mobile. This kind of smart mobile product is invented and is applied to manufacture by new resource, e.g. manufacturing phone equipment, labour smart phone inventors, and phone designers. They can bring new incentive to find new methods of production that encourage on that resource to help new smart mobile products to develop to global phone market.

SO, any kinds smart mobile products can be increased to phone product sale market and they can replace traditional mobile product products. Due to different kinds of smart mobiles need increases. They bring new incentive to global mobile products users accept to use smart mobile popularly as well as their smart phone use needs increase their smart mobile using desire.

IN behavioural economic view, new method of production technology need can bring new technique products market development, then when new technological products can be popular to be accepted by global general users. They can feel more satisfactory to use this kind of new technological product to replace old technological product, such as innovative smart mobile phone products can be accepted to use to replace traditional mobile phone or home telephone products.

ON consequence, global smart mobile demand needs will be influenced to increase by cost of production reducing factor. It explains that when new production of technological resource needs increase, it can influence the new kind of technological products demand and supply number also be influenced to increase. Consequently, these both of factors can encourage consumption desire increases to consumers as well as the country's economic growth GDP is also influenced to climb up rapidly in possible. So, I believe that " new production technological resource is main factor to cause consumption desire increases and economic growth effect in nowadays society.

Can creating new jobs develop economy?

Some economist believe that cost of production determines supply, supply determines final degree of utility, final degree of utility determines value. They bring this question: If all of these factors have concern to any kinds of products need increases or decreases , when the cost of production increases, then the kind of product supply will be influenced to decrease.

Due to the kind of product supply decreases , but consumers demand to the kind of product increases. SO, the kind of product utility increases, when the kind of product utility increases, it can increase the kind of product sale value. When the kind of product sale value increases, it will bring creating new jobs need increases. Can this kind of new creating jobs of increasing need develop economic growth?

For laptop new style of computer product example, if any kinds of laptop cost of production decreases, then laptop manufacturers can decrease expenditure to any kinds of laptop cost of production. Consequently, laptop supply of manufacture number may be influenced to increase, they must need many laptop labours help to manufacture many laptops to satisfy global laptop computer users need.

So, laptop is popular to be accepted to use to global computer users, due to their utilities values are also influenced to increase. Laptop sale value must be influenced to increase by raising laptop utility factor. SO, global laptop computer manufacturers must need to increase labour number in order to manufacture many different kinds of laptop products to satisfy global laptop users needs. Consequently, in behaviour economic view, due to laptop cost of production decreasing factor, which can bring laptop manufacturing number needs increase and creating new jobs need for laptop market development. On conclusion, laptop market development can create new jobs chance to help the country economic growth in possible. So, creating new jobs chance can help the country to bring economic growth in possible.

Can human behaviour influence economic development?

Can ourselves daily behaviour help economic growth? Some economists believe that unemployment causes become real wage were too high. In other words,, workers were looking for too much money, relative to the rate of inflation and output in the economy. To reduce the number and of work, therefore it was just a case of " lowering salary demand".

In behaviour economic view, if one country has many workers can accept lowering salary demand, whether they can influence the country will develop economy rapidly or slowly, or whether they have cause and effect relationship in behaviour economic view.

I assume that when the country can have many labours accept low salary demand, their daily working behaviour and working attitude may influence the country develop economy speed slowly. For China example, nowadays, China has many labours or workers, their salaries level are very low to compare developed countries, e.g. US , UK due to in general China labours their salaries. SO, low salaries demand factor may influence China laze labours number increases. When China has many labours number are laze more than hard labours number. Their working behaviours and performance may influence any kinds of products manufacture number reduces to compare US, UK labours. Consequently, the same kind of products manufacture number will be influenced to reduce by low inefficiency factor in China as well as China will have many businesses will earn less sale income from global consumers. When these China's products their sale number decreases, it will influence China economic growth speed slowly in possible in macro economic environment.

SO, it seems that labour behaviour and their working performance may bring indirect negative influence to the country's economic growth speed to be sloe. I mean that human behaviour may influence the country's economic growth speed rapidly or slowly.

It explains that how human behaviour influences an economy grows to the country. It depends on " each country has how many workers , natural resource (may be coal or metals) or non natural resource e.g. machine, equipment and capital and land which all bound together by technology. Using those in the right combination will make the country's economy grows rapidly or slowly.

For another case example, it explains how huma behaviour may influence economy grows. I shall indicate the circular flow income theory to explain. It indicates that when one person (working people) who earns wages, he/ she makes decision either saves to bank or investment aspect or spends on cash purchase goods aspect. In the year, for US country example, if the year US faces economic recession, US has high unemployment rates, it will have many workers loss jobs or US has many workers reduce wages.

ON consequence, reducing wages or lose jobs both factors which will influence many US people reduce much living expenditure spending , e.g. shopping or leisure expenditure. They will prefer to make decision to save money to bank or invest, e.g. buying shares. To finance aspect. SO, in the year, US will have many businesses reduce products sale number. In behavior economic view, due to US has many people make decision to save money to bank or invest to shares market more than spending to buy any kinds of products or leisure activities aspect. So, in the year, US's economic growth speed will be influenced to be slow by reducing spending behaviour on human behavior factor aspect.SO, it explains why human behaviors may bring positive or negative influence to the country's economic growth speed, whether it's economic growth speed is either rapid or slow.

Can encouraging education help economic growth?

DO education and economic development have close relationship? I shall attempt to apply behavioral economic theory to explain this question as below:

Some economists explain human development is depended on education, also education can help our global social economic growth. I shall indicate energy education development example to answer this question.

In fact, cheap energy development , it is one constraint to influence any country economic growth speed whether it can develop rapidly or slowly. IN human energy technological education development history, prior to industrial revolution, the energy needed for life and industry was provided by human and animals, and bio-mass fuels like woods, water and wind. In the 19th century, the use of fossil fuels commenced. So, it seems that human energy education knowledge had been developed rapidly, such as below development progress.

IN the first age of fossil fuel exploration, coal driven stream engines powered industry, ships and railroads , as well as generating electricity pollution from burning coals, over time, encouraged the use of oil and gas energy , coal remains an important source of electricity , special in China and India, where poor air quality and illnesses are serious of 19th century UK.

The second age of fossil fuel exploitation focuses on hydrocarbons beginning in 1859 with commence , oil production in the US . After world war II, it became the predominant energy source because of superior energy intensity. The rising use of oil with the development of the internal combustion engine, crucial to modern transportation in the form of cars, trucks, trains, ferries and airplanes. Oil also became important in agriculture, chemical processes and manufacture of synthetic , material and fibers.

Increased oil and use was facilities by discoveries of large fields in the Middle East, US, Canada, Mexico progressively from the 1920s. It was supported by energy investment , such as pipelines, tankers and improved refining technology.

IN the 20 th century, natural gas invested as a major fuel, driven by improved transportability using high pressive pipelines and the process of liquefaction and re-gasfication.

So, when US, UK developed countries even India China Korea developing countries can concentrate and focus on energy education technological development, they can bring energy businesses development chance and allow natural gas to be used to electricity generation, heating and cooking as well as raw material from the manufacture of new energy resource industry development.

In fact, nowadays coal, oil and gas provide 80 to 90 percent of all energy. They have allowed the development of modern economies, facilitating the production of food, goods, and services efficiency , transportation and improving living standards.

Decoupling economic growth from the availability of cheap and efficiency energy is difficult. So , any countries need to invest time and money to new energy educational development if they hope to help economic growth to themselves countries.

However, if the country can encourage scientists learn new kinds of energy education knowledge. Their any kinds of possible new energy invention will help the country to bring huge new kind of energy sale income chance, even the country's new kind of possible energy invention will help the country grow economy rapidly, if the country can develop education on new energy invention aspect.

I ASSUME ON THESE REASONs:

Nowadays energy consumption is driven by changes in population, urbanization, industrialization, economic growth and energy efficiency, the amount of energy needed per unit of GDPs. Since 1990, energy consumption in developed economic has grown slowly. A significant factor , this lower growth was the economic slowdown in 2008 . In the US and Europe , energy consumption ha increased by 20 percent and 7 percent respectively. But it is growing strongly in developing countries. In China, it has increased by 146 percent, India by 90 percent, in Africa by 70 percent, and in the Middle East by 170 percent.Since 1990, the average energy use per person globally has increase by around 10 percent.

Moreover, the information and communication driven digital energy consumers increasing amount of energy. AN lot of computers, laptops, notebooks, desktops and smart phones, in aggregate, consumer significant amounts of energy in both manufacture and use. The data centers , digital warehouses and server farms that lie a the internet and cloud computing that run the global economy and households are also heavy power users. The digital economy consumers around 10 percent of the world's electricity, which is the equivalent of the amount that was used to high in the planet in 1985.

Hence, it seems that energy education can help the country's economic growth, due to human needs to use energy to either on manufacture or consume both aspects, if the country can educate itself energy scientists to invent any kinds of new energy to replace old energy. They will help the country's economy development in possible.

Can organizational behavior influence economic environment ?

What is Organisation behaviour in economics? Organisational behaviour is a study which involves examining and analysing the human behaviour in an organisation. An organisation may be divided into top-level(owners), middle level(management) and low level(employees).

How does organizational behavior affect the company?

Organizational behavior is used to develop strategies to improve employee engagement and motivation. These strategies can include recognition and rewards programs, employee involvement initiatives, and career development opportunities.

How does human behaviour affect economics?

Human behaviour in the economics arena decides many statistics in the market, both domestic as well as international markets. The economic model of human behaviour tries to explain the reason behind the rational economic decisions individuals make.

What is economic pressure in organizational behavior?

Economic pressure refers to the various economic factors that affect a business's growth and profitability. In OB, it can present different challenges like affecting employee morale, destabilising the organisation, and forcing tough decisions regarding resource allocation.

I assume that economic environment change which can influence any kinds of organizational behavioral change because organizations need to implement the best strategy to adapt any change of environment .How does economics affect organizational behavior? Organizations are also heavily influenced by economic factors.A market crash or a recession will directly impact the sales of an organization. When people are no longer able to afford a product or choose to spend their money elsewhere, companies are directly impacted.

Why do we study organisational behaviour in economics?

This branch of applied economics is most useful in the aspect of firm structure, developing company policies, making management decisions, assessing business risks, implementing incentives and rewards and the overall structure of the firm.

How does behavioral economics play a role in our lives and in the economy? Behavioral economics sheds light on most every day activities and why we consume goods and services the way we do, why we make certain choices about ourselves or others, and how we decide courses of action. It is an incredible lens that exposes our inner biases and approaches to decision-making.

Four Organizational Behavior Models for Performance

- Understanding Organizational Behavior Models.
- The Autocratic Model.
- The Custodial Model.
- The Supportive Model.

Any one of these 4 models of OB which may influence organizational performance, even the country;s economic environment change when the country have many organizations make decision to implement which model of organizational behaviors as below:

Understanding Organizational Behavior Models

Organizational behavior is a fascinating field that seeks to understand how individuals, groups, and organizations interact within the workplace to achieve common goals. It is a complex and dynamic field that requires a deep understanding of human behavior, psychology, and sociology. Organizational behavior models are based on theories and concepts that seek to explain how people behave in the workplace.

The Importance of Organizational Behavior in Performance

The importance of organizational behavior in determining an organization's performance cannot be overstated. Organizational behavior affects how employees interact with each other, how they carry out their duties, and how they handle challenges. It is a critical factor in determining an organization's success or failure. By understanding organizational behavior models, organizations can identify the best practices to improve performance and achieve their goals.

Essentially, organizational behavior models help organizations identify the factors that contribute to high performance. These models provide a framework for understanding how different components of an organization interact with each other and how they can be optimized to achieve better results.

Key Components of Organizational Behavior Models

Organizational behavior models consist of several interconnected components that work together to achieve organizational goals. A change in one component can significantly impact the entire model.

- Structure: The way that tasks, roles, and responsibilities are organized within the organization. A well-designed structure can improve efficiency, reduce conflicts, and enhance communication.
- Leadership: Inspire and motivate employees to achieve their goals and create a positive culture that encourages innovation and collaboration.
- Communication: Improve collaboration, reduce conflicts, and enhance productivity. It involves the exchange of information, ideas, and feedback between employees and departments.
- Motivation: Factors that drive employees to perform at their best. Motivated employees are more productive, creative, and committed to achieving organizational goals.
- Culture: Shared values, beliefs, and practices that shape an organization's behavior. A positive culture can create a sense of belonging, improve employee morale, and enhance organizational performance.

The Autocratic Model

The Autocratic Model is a leadership model where all power is concentrated at the top of the organization. Characterized by a strict hierarchy, low employee involvement, and little to no delegation of tasks, this model has been used in many organizations throughout history, from military organizations to large corporations. It is often seen as a way to ensure that decisions are made quickly and efficiently without the need for extensive consultation and debate. This can be beneficial in situations where time is of the essence, such as during a crisis or emergency. However, this approach can also have significant drawbacks, as it can lead to low employee motivation and poor morale. Employees have little to no input in the decision-making process and tend to fear speaking up or offering suggestions for fear of reprisals.

Implementing the Autocratic Model for Performance Improvement

The Autocratic Model may be implemented where decisions need to be made quickly, and the input of employees is not necessary. However, it is crucial to find a balance between autocratic and democratic management styles to ensure employee engagement and trust.

Try communicating the decision-making process to employees and explain why it is necessary to take an autocratic approach. When employees understand the reasons behind the decision, they may be more willing to accept it and work towards its implementation.

Another suggestion is to provide opportunities for employee feedback and input in other areas of the organization. For example, team members may be given the opportunity to provide feedback on new products or services, or to suggest improvements to existing processes.

The Custodial Model

The Custodial Model is a management approach characterized by a paternalistic leadership style. The emphasis is on job security, good working conditions, fair compensation, and benefits as primary motivators for employees. Communication flows from management to employees, with little to no input from employees in decision-making processes. Moreover, this model is based on the belief that employees are more likely to be productive and satisfied when they feel secure in their jobs and have access to benefits such as health insurance and retirement plans.

While the custodial model can be effective in retaining employees that are loyal and feel supported via higher rates of job satisfaction, it can also create a culture of complacency, where employees are not challenged or motivated to perform better. Additionally, this model can be expensive, and companies may not be able to afford to offer all the benefits associated with a custodial model. The lack of employee input in decision-making processes can lead to a lack of innovation and creativity in the workplace.

Implementing the Custodial Model for Performance Improvement

The Custodial Model can be implemented by organizations that are committed to investing in their employees' well-being, such as healthcare and retirement benefits. To ensure its success, it is essential to create a culture of appreciation and trust and to communicate effectively with employees. Also, this model should be complemented with career development opportunities to challenge and motivate employees to perform at their best.

Consider offering a comprehensive benefits package that includes health insurance, retirement plans, and paid time off. This lets employees feel secure in their jobs and reduce turnover rates. Additionally, organizations can create a positive work environment by offering perks such as free snacks, flexible work hours, and team-building activities.

The Supportive Model

The Supportive Model is a management approach that emphasizes the role of management in providing support and guidance to employees. This approach is based on the belief that employees are the key to achieving organizational goals and that management should focus on creating a supportive work environment that fosters employee engagement, innovation, and productivity.

The Supportive Model is characterized by a participative management style, where employees are involved in decision-making processes. This technique encourages communication and collaboration between management and employees, and emphasizes the importance of providing employees with the resources, training, and support they need to achieve their goals.

One of the key benefits of the supportive model is that it fosters employee engagement and morale, which sets the foundation for a culture of innovation and creativity, with improved productivity and performance.

However, implementing the supportive model can be time-consuming, and decision-making processes may take longer. Additionally, organizations must be willing to invest in resources and training to ensure that employees have the skills and knowledge they need to be successful.

Implementing the Supportive Model for Performance Improvement

The Supportive Model can be implemented effectively by organizations that value employee input, encourage innovation, and seek to create a positive work environment. To ensure success, it is essential to provide employees with the resources, training, and support they need to achieve their goals effectively. It is crucial to build trust and effective communication channels between management and employees.

Consider creating cross-functional teams that include employees from different departments and levels of the organization. By involving employees from different areas of the organization, organizations can tap into a diverse range of perspectives and ideas that can lead to improved decision-making and innovation.

Another effective strategy is to provide employees with regular feedback and recognition. By recognizing and rewarding employees for their contributions, organizations can create a culture of positivity and motivation that leads to improved performance and productivity.

On conclusion, it seems that any kinds of organizations need to implement these any one model of organizational behavior to achieve the satisfactory performance, when the country can have many organizations can achieve satisfactory performance, their customer number can increase, then GDP can also grow rapidly.

CHAPTER FOUR

The relationship between human behavior and society and economic change

Explaining supply and demand economic theory

The difference between past and nowadays economists their demand and supply economic theory explanation?

The law of supply and demand defines the relationship between the price of a given good or product and the willingness of people to either buy or sell it. Generally, as the price of a good increases, people are willing to supply more and demand less. These economists had explained economic demand and supply theory as below:

Philosopher John Locke is credited with one of the earliest written descriptions of this economic principle in his 1691 publication, Some Considerations of the Consequences of the Lowering of Interest and the Raising of the Value of Money. Locke addressed the concept of supply and demand as part of a discussion about interest rates in 17th-century England. Many merchants wanted the government to lower the cap on interest rates charged by private lenders so that people could borrow more money and thus purchase more goods. Locke argued that the free-market economy should set rates because government regulation could have unintended consequences. If the lending industry were left alone, interest rates would regulate themselves, Locke wrote: "The price of any commodity rises or falls by the proportion of the number of buyers and sellers."

Sir James Steuart's Inquiry into the Principles of Political Economy, published in 1796, was the first known printed use of the term "supply and demand." When Steuart wrote his treatise on political economy, one of his main concerns was the impact of supply and demand on laborers.

Adam Smith dealt extensively with the topic in his 1776 epic economic work, The Wealth of Nations. Often referred to as the Father of Economics, Smith explained the concept of supply and demand as an "invisible hand" that naturally guides the economy. According to Smith, the invisible hand is the automatic pricing and distribution mechanisms in the economy. Smith described a society in which bakers and butchers provide products that individuals need and want, providing a supply that meets demand and developing an economy that benefits everyone. It is important to note that Smith's ideas haven't gone without critique over the years since his ideas were first published, though. Over time, his ideas have been added to in order to represent the changing times and include concepts such as marginal utility, comparative advantage, entrepreneurship, the time-preference theory of interest, and monetary theory.

One of Marshall's most important contributions to microeconomics was his introduction of the concept of price elasticity of demand, which examines how price changes affect demand. In theory, people buy less of a particular product if the price increases, but Marshall noted that in real life, this behavior was not always true. The prices of some goods can increase without reducing demand, which means their prices are inelastic. Inelastic goods tend to include items such as medication or food that consumers deem crucial to daily life. Marshall argued that supply and demand, costs of production, and price elasticity all work together.

Nowadays economists they explain demand and supply economic theory, they have some different to past economists whose explanation as below:

How Does Supply and Demand Work? The law of supply and demand is a theory that explains the interaction between the sellers of a resource and the buyers of that resource. Generally, as price increases, people are willing to supply more and demand less and vice versa when the price falls. What does the bottom line mean. Despite the origins of the law of supply and demand beginning hundreds of years ago, it's still a topic frequently referenced and utilized today in economic theory and discussions. The theory has developed over time to accommodate recent technological and economical advancements, but the basic ideas of the theory remain largely the same.

Does demand depend on supply?

Supply and Demand Determine the Price of Goods and Quantities Produced and Consumed. Consumers may exhaust the available supply of a good by purchasing a given good or service at a high volume. This leads to an increase in demand. As demand increases, the available supply also decreases.

What does market demand depend on?

Market factors affecting demand of consumer goods. The demand for a good increases or decreases depending on several factors. This includes the product's price, perceived quality, advertising spend, consumer income, consumer confidence, and changes in taste and fashion.

Who controls the demand in supply and demand?

Supply and demand are in turn determined by technology and the conditions under which people operate. At one extreme, the market could be populated by a large number of virtually identical sellers and buyers (for example, the market for ballpoint pens).

What are the two laws of demand and supply?

The law of demand holds that the demand level for a product or a resource will decline as its price rises, and rise as the price drops. Conversely, the law of supply says higher prices boost supply of an economic good while lower ones tend to diminish it.

What factors affect demand and supply?

Price fluctuations are a strong factor affecting supply and demand. When a product gets expensive enough that the average consumer no longer feels it is worth it to buy the product, then the demand declines. This leads to cuts in production that will hopefully stabilize the product's value.

What factors affect demand and demand?

Demand may be defined as the quantity of a commodity that a consumer is able and willing to buy, at each possible price, over a given period of time. • Essential elements of demand are quantity, ability, willingness, prices, and period of time.

Which factors affect supply?

Generally, the supply of a product depends on its price and other variables such as the cost of production.

a. Price. Price can be understood as what the consumer is willing to pay to receive a good or service. ...

b. Cost of production. ...

c. Technology. ...

d. Governments' policies. ...

e. Transportation condition.

How does supply and demand work together?

It's a fundamental economic principle that when supply exceeds demand for a good or service, prices fall. When demand exceeds supply, prices tend to rise. There is an inverse relationship between the supply and prices of goods and services when demand is unchanged.

What happens to supply when demand increases?

An increase in demand, all other things unchanged, will cause the equilibrium price to rise; quantity supplied will increase. A decrease in demand will cause the equilibrium price to fall; quantity supplied will decrease.

What is the theory of demand?

Demand theory describes the way that changes in the quantity of a good or service demanded by consumers affects its price in the market, The theory states that the higher the price of a product is, all else equal, the less of it will be demanded, inferring a downward sloping demand curve.

What are the 4 basic laws of supply and demand?

1) If the supply increases and demand stays the same, the price will go down. 2) If the supply decreases and demand stays the same, the price will go up. 3) If the supply stays the same and demand increases, the price will go up. 4) If the supply stays the same and demand decreases, the price will go down.

The different types of demand are as follows:

i. Individual and Market Demand: ...

ii. Organization and Industry Demand: ...

iii. Autonomous and Derived Demand: ...

iv. Demand for Perishable and Durable Goods: ...

v. Short-term and Long-term Demand:

What creates demand for a product?

You can create demand for a unique product if you can manage to solve a persistent problem for the consumer. People are always running away from pain, and providing them with an outlet is a sure-fire way to create massive demand for your goods.

What are the 7 factors that affect supply?

The seven factors which affect the changes of supply are as follows: (i) Natural Conditions (ii) Technical Progress (iii) Change in Factor Prices (iv) Transport Improvements (v) Calamities (vi) Monopolies (vii) Fiscal Policy.

What can affect demand?

Factors Affecting Demand

Price of the Product. ...

The Consumer's Income. ...

The Price of Related Goods. ...

The Tastes and Preferences of Consumers. ...

The Consumer's Expectations. ...

The Number of Consumers in the Market.

What are the three factors affecting demand?

The demand for a product will be influenced by several factors:

Price. Usually viewed as the most important factor that affects demand. ...

Income levels. ...

Consumer tastes and preferences. ...

Competition. ...

Fashions.

What are the 4 factors of supply?

The four factors that can shift the supply curve include natural conditions, input prices, technology, and government.

What causes increase in supply?

If the cost of production is lower, the profits available at a given price will increase, and producers will produce more. With more produced at every price, the supply curve will shift to the right, meaning an increase in supply.

What causes supply changes?

A change in supply is an economic term that describes when the suppliers of a given good or service alter production or output. A change in supply can occur as a result of new technologies, such as more efficient or less expensive production processes, or a change in the number of competitors in the market.

Is supply and demand a good strategy?

When it comes to profit placement, supply and demand zones can be a great tool as well. Always place your profit target ahead of a zone so that you don't risk giving back all your profits when the open interest in that zone is filled.

How is demand created?

Demand creation is a process that fuels the revenue pipeline so the sales team can meet or exceed their quotas. In other words, it takes your big idea — the creative appeal of your brand and turns it into sales. That sounds a lot like demand generation, which often gets confused with lead generation.

What are the two parts of demand?

Economists define demand as the quantity of a good or service that buyers are willing and able to buy at all possible prices during a certain time period. Notice that there are two components to demand: willingness to purchase and ability to pay.

Can we control demand?

If you're willing to think and act strategically, you can easily manipulate the laws of supply and demand. It should be surprising to learn, however, that by manipulating the laws of supply and demand, you can make more profit in less time and with far fewer headaches

How do you control demand?

Here are five short-term actions to improve your demand variability management plans in this time of uncertainty:

Maintain transparent, proactive relationships with your suppliers. ...

Activate alternate sources of supply. ...

Reduce lead times. ...

Update inventory policy and planning. ...

Align supply and demand management.

What are the 8 types of demand?

There are 8 states of demand: negative demand, no demand, latent demand, falling demand, irregular demand, full demand, overfull demand and unwholesome demand.

What is Demand?

Types of Determinants of Demand. Every factor has a unique impact on demand. ...

Price of the Product. ...

The Income of the Consumers. ...

Number of Buyers in the Market. ...

Consumer's Expectations. ...

Tastes and Preferences of The Consumers. ...

Complement Goods. ...

Substitute Product.

What is theory of supply?

The law of supply is a fundamental principle of economic theory which states that, keeping other factors constant, an increase in price results in an increase in quantity supplied. In other words, there is a direct relationship between price and quantity: quantities respond in the same direction as price changes.

What are the types of supply?

There are five types of supply—market supply, short-term supply, long-term supply, joint supply, and composite supply.

Which comes first supply or demand?

Demand comes first and it's followed by the corresponding supplies. Supply and demand are both very important to economic activity. Supply is the total amount of a particular good or service available at a given time to consumers at a given price. Demand is a representation of a consumer's desire to purchase goods and services; it acts as a measurement of a consumer's willingness to purchase a specific good or service at a given price. These two economic forces influence each other; they are both important for the economy because they impact the prices of consumer goods and services within an economy and the quantities produced and consumed. Supply and demand are both keys to understanding the economy because they reflect the prices and quantities of consumer goods and services within an economy.

What are the relationship between demand and supply?

According to market economy theory, the relationship between supply and demand balances out at a point in the future; this point is called the equilibrium price.

Economists and companies analyze the relationship between supply and demand when making strategic product decisions. Both economists and companies analyze the relationship between supply and demand when making strategic product decisions. The assumption behind a market economy is that supply and demand are the best determinants for an economy's growth and health.

Consumer Behavior Influences Demand

One way that companies or economists might analyze this relationship is to create graphs that chart the equilibrium price of certain goods and services in order to determine product development and their production schedule. Consumer behavior dictates which products are produced and sold because consumers create the demand that companies attempt to meet. As a result, companies may study consumer behavior in an attempt to understand the current demand and predict future demand. It is vital that companies maintain the capacity to produce enough of a good or service that they can satisfy consumer demands.

Supply and demand are two sides of the same market coin. Generally, supply is how much of something is available or will be produced at a certain price. Demand is how much of something people want to purchase or consume at a certain price. One way to develop a more precise relationship between the two is to consider how the price of something affects its supply and its demand. Generally when the price of a good goes up, so does the supply, since firms are willing to create more when they can sell at higher prices. But when the price of a good goes up consumers will, at the same time, generally demand less. It is the interaction of supply and demand that determines how much will be produced and consumed and at what price, converging to a state known as equilibrium.

Human Behavioral network job brings social economic benefits

Whether human social job change it depends on social job demand more or job supply more? What does human network job mean ? Why may human network job be popular? Why human network job behavior may influence economy ?

Nowadays internet is popular to use. We can apply internet to find data , search any new things, even earn money. Why does internet may become human network job source. For example, e-publish may be one kind of new human network job. Any authors may apply internet channel to help them to sell electronic or paper books from e-publisher web store. They may apply facebook, you tub etc. any online channel to promote themselves new books to let new readers to know whether when they may buy themselves favorable new topic books to read from electronic publisher web store.

Thus, future electronic publisher industry may help any authors to build internet network platform to help them to sell and promote to advertise their any one new electronic or paper book topic to let global any one reader to choose to buy their any new topic books from electronic publisher web store easily and conveniently. However, it implies that electronic network platform author may be one kind of future new human network job in our societies.

How electronic network platform author job may bring economy benefit in macro economy view? A person can have few friends, contacts and still be very influential if these few friends and contacts are themselves highly influential, e.g. one author must not need to know any one reader in global society. When they like to choose any electronic books from electronic internet network platform. They may become the author's any one topic book buyer, when they feel the author's any one topic book is fun and attract they make decision to both the strange author whose the topic book from electronic book publisher's platform web store convenience in short time. Although, they are strangers, they do not know themselves , but the reader can understand what it way that made Google from writing platform to create new creative mind and typing network job method to replace traditional hand writing book method for global authors. It will be one kind of new human network writing job.

Hence, global any one reader can apply an innovative search engine , such as google.com to find whether whom author personal new topic books are value to read from internet. Then, the electronic publisher's web store may be new book store platform sale network to help the author to sell many electronic or paper books from electronic network platform in short time. So, internet may be future new network platform to help global any one author to create network writing job absolutely. Furthermore, internet may be popular social media to help any one author to build good relationship between his/her readers. It is one kind of new network, human network job. New authors do not need to buy many paper books to prepare to put in any one book shop warehouse. Their every book can print on demand to reduce out of book stock in any one book shop. They may choose to sell either electronic books or paper books both from any one book publisher web store. So, electronic network platform may be one kind of good writing channel to help human authors to create income and it can also help authors to bring new creative mind and new topic fun content books to let readers to know and buy to read from electronic publisher network platform.

Why does human behavior may be one kind of new human network job to bring global economic advantages. Although, it may be free income or without income, but the person does the network behavior, his/her behavior may be bring advantages to influence many other people's health. For this case, when a worker in a coffee shop in an airport gets a vaccination aganist the flu, it does not only helps him or her stay healthy, but also helps the many travellers who might otherwise have been inflected if that workers caught the flu. So, the externality , the result implies the vaccination of even a part of a community conveys benefits to the whole community. For example, governments pay special attention to the vaccinations of school children, teachers, health mothers, and the elderly, categories of people particularly susceptible not only to catching, but also to transmitting a disease.

It is not accidential that governments are heavily involved with vaccination . When there are externalities, free market, fail to persuade individual incentives with society's their the worker's decision of whether to get a vaccine ends up attracting whether other people get sick. The workers might not fully take all these other people's potential suffering into account when making her or his vaccination decision.

As Stanford University does many suggestions, understand this and tries to help them make the right decisions and so providers free flu vaccines for its staff and students.

Small pockets of unvaccinated individuals can allow a disease to gain a spread more widely well-being. For example, parent weighing the costs and benefits of a vaccine for their child is not always thinking of the consequences of that vaccination to other people. These are markets in which subsidizing or regulating behavior can make everyone better off. Because the reason for requiring that a child be vaccinated before enrolling in school is not just to protect that child, because each child's vaccination affects others via potential contagions.

On conclusion, it seems that many traditional paper book publish business begin to change to electronic book publish business. Due, to online technology existence, it influences many readers choose to buy electronic books to read. Hence, due to readers reading demand change which is from paper book reading habit to electronic book reading habit.Then,it explains that electronic book supply number depends on electronic book reader reading demand in economic view.

Robot job behavior brings economy influences

Whether robot labor needs are depended on employer labor demand more or robot labor number supply more? If one day robots can replace human to do simple, even complex jobs. They will bring what influences to our global societal economy.The popular economic refrain declares that the

global middle class is dying and robots will soon take our jobs, e.g. shopping center customer service jobs, library service jobs, cinema ticket sale jobs, restaurant kitchen cooker jobs,

even, bus drivers, taxi drivers etc. public transport driving jobs, accountant, doctors etc. professional jobs. Whether it is beautiful or petty matter if our future societies have many human jobs can be replaced to do from robots. Businessman must may reduce to employ employees and reduce to pay salary or wage, when robots can be replaced to do their employees tasks. But, societies must bring unemployment rate rises , due to societies will have many people loss jobs when their employers choose to buy robots to serve their clients or do any office tasks or customer service or cleaning etc. tasks.

In micro economy view, employers may save money in long term, but in macro economy view, it will cause unemployment ratio rises , even crime rate rises when there are many people lose jobs in societies. These models of doom, though, fail to account for the hundreds of businesses riding the waves of change in their industries when robots may be invented to replace human to do many simple , even complex tasks in our future societies.

WE may image that one small factory needs to manufacture fishes canes to sell to supermarket, the small , cheaper stuff and higher margin parts of the fishes manufacture industry. Before, this factory needs to employ many human factory workers need to help every fresh customer making the perfect fishing gear, designed for performance, durability, and cost in order to achieve to manufacture every fish cane in whole fished processing manufacturing stages. Every worker needs to spend about 15 to twenty minutes to finish every fish cane , till to delivery to any supermarket to sell. If this fish canes manufacturing factory can apply manufacturing robots to help them to finish any one working tasks , every robot can only spend five minutes to finish whole fresh fish cane manufacturing process. Thus, every robot can

help this factory save 10 to 15 minutes time to finish every fish cane manufacturing process. IN fact, time is money, because when every robot can help this factory to reduce 10 to 15 minutes time to compare human worker. Then, this factory can finish about 20 fish canes in one hour if it can use robot to help it to manufacture fish canes. Otherwise, if this factory still use human workers to help it to manufacture fish canes, then it can finish about 3 to 4 fish canes in one hour. SO, the manufacturing efficiency ensures that robots must help this fish manufacturing factory to raise fish canes number more than human workers. So, in robotic behavioral economy view, manufacturing robots must help this fish canes manufacturing factory to raise fish canes manufacturing number and deliver increasing number to supermarkets to prepare to sell every day. Robots can help this fish canes manufacturing factory bring manufacturing time saving, rising manufacturing efficiency, improving performance and reducing wages expenditure long time advantages in micro economy view. However, manufacturing robots can also bring disadvantages to society, e.g. increasing unemployment ratio, increasing crime rate, this factory workers will lose jobs and income, they need earn social welfare from government and increasing government finance pressure in short time, even long time in macro economic view.

Stanford University graduate program in economics, Scott lecturer explained that "in demand and supply economic theory for robots supply and demand case, robots supply number increasing may influence human workers demand number decrease. It sometimes calls " the efficient frontier".

No specific human beings were mentioned in any of economics classes. As robots supply and demand in market case, They (robots) may be purely theoretical " agents" who reached to the most reasonable sale prices in order to persuade any one businessman buyer to make manufacturing robot buying decision whether robots can help him / her to bring how much saving time , saving money, saving cost, improving performance, efficiency economic benefit before he/she plans to reduce workers number when he/she decides to apply robots to replace human workers in his/her factory or office or any service department, e.g. cinema ticket sale service, shopping center customer service, shopping center cleaning , supermarket customer service etc. service or sale tasks. When robots can replace human to do any one of these tasks in any organizations. So, robots may be human worker agents who reached to prices the way robots would react to a software

command. There was nothing that explained why some people thrived and others did n't or why truly brilliant, hardworking people could fail when much lazier folks succeeded." Having been admitted to the Stanford University graduate program in economics, Scott lecturer hoped to get his answers there.

How robots influence our future social changing? Using the right technology can be a boon to your business in this economy. For internet example, it is easier than ever to find well-matched customers all around the world, to stay in contact with them, and to more quickly design the products they want. If you focus solely on being cutting -edge, though you risk letting the technology

take over what should be very robust relationships with your customers , employees, and colleagues. IN nowadays society, technological advances and automation, personal

relationships in business are more crucial than ever. I mean that robots can not replace human to serve clients to let them to feel more comfortable and passion more easily. For shoe shop case example, if the shoe shop apply one robot to serve its clients to replace human shoe salesperson to serve its shoe customers. Robots ensure that they can not persuade every shoe potential buyer to make shoe buying decision more easily when robots need to contact every shoe potential buyer. The reason is simple, because robots can not touch any one shoe buyer individual emotion very easier.

If the shoe buyer needs the robots to help him/her to choose any right shoe styles when he/she can not feel himself / herself can make the most right shoe style choice decision. The robots can not replace human shoe salesperson to make shoe style choice judgment more easily. They must need longer time to analyze whether which shoe style may be the most suitable to the shoe buyer. Otherwise, human shoe salesperson may attempt to make the most right shoe style choice decision to help any one shoe buyer to choose the most right style shoe because he/she owns shoe style sale experience, shoe style knowledge, the most important reason is that they can feel every shoe customer individual emotion to touch whether he/she will feel comfortable or happy when they attempt to help every shoe customer to seek the most right shoe style in every shoe customer whole shoe searching processing. Otherwise, serving robots are only one machine, they can not touch or feel every shoe customer individual emotion whether he/she feel comfortable or unhappy or happy when they need to contact them in whole shoe searching processing. Hence, I believe that some tasks robots can not replace human staff to do very easily. Otherwise, robots may bring disadvantages to let any one businessman to loss his/her customers, due to robots can not touch every customer emotion to compare human staff in service tasks more easily. Robots serving customer behaviors may cause money lose and customers number lose to the shop in micro economic view.

On conclusion, in demand and supply economic theory for robots supply and demand case, robots supply number increasing may influence human workers demand number decrease. So, it seems that robots number supply will be depended on global robots supply number more than robots demand number because when human began to accept robots to replace human to do general simple jobs in global labor market. Then, it means that global robots labor number must need to be increased in order to satisfy global businessmen workers number need. If any kinds of robot workers manufacture number is not enough to be supplied to let global future businessmen to buy, then robot supply will be shortage and they can not provide to satisfy global businessmen robots labour purchase need. So, future robot number will be depended on supply more than demand.

Human intellectual demand and supply behavior relationship

Intellectual human economic behaviors

What does intellectual human economic behaviors mean ? Human foolish behavior is depended on social enjoyment need more or material social supply more? I believe that when we choose or decide to do intellectual behaviors, then our societies will be influenced to bring economic growth in consequence.I shall attempt to indicate pollution case to explain how and why eithet our intellectual or foolish behaviors may bring economic growth or recession in consequence as below:

On one hand, for air pollution social case aspect example, if we only consider to buy cars to drive for working aim or holiday leisure aim. Then, our societies air will be polluted. Our health will be influenced to bad. Our car driving behaviors may cause global environment air pollution seriously. In long time, global air pollution will bring our bodies health to be bad. Although, ourselves car driving behaviors may bring our driving travelling leisure enjoyment and comfortable feeling in short time, also we so not need to pay public transport fare often, but we need to compensate ourselves health economic intangible loss due to air pollution , when cars number increases, dirty air will cause ourselves health to become bad.

In the result, we will need to pay more medical expenditure when we are old age, due to ourselves bodies will become bad, due to we breathe global dirty air every day, due to ourselves cars pollute air in long time, e.g. 10 to 20 years, even 30 more without limited air pollution environment. So, driving cars behavior may be one kind of human foolish behavior and our foolish behavior may bring ourselves future long time medical expenditure absolutely.

One the other hand, water pollution social aspect, if we often keep much rubbish to pollute sea, oil exploration processing pollute ocean , ships gas pollute ocean, then fishes will eat polluted food and drive dirty water, due to global ocean is polluted.

In fact, because human only to consider how to buy boats to carry on leisure enjoyment activities, or catch cruises to travel on the sea. Also, oil manufacturers only consider researching anywhere to find new oil exploration places to manufacture oil product, when their oil exploration processes pollute ocarn . Consequently, global fishes drink polluted warer or eat polluted food. They will have poison. SO, human will have high chance to eat poison polluted fishes, due to fishes are poison or are polluted.

So, human is doing foolish activities, we only hope to find oil exploration places to pollute ocean or we only spend money to buy ticket to catch ships to travel anywhere in global ocean. All of these human foolish behaviors will bring pollution to global ocean. On consequently, we will need to compensate to eat polluted or dirty or poision fishes, ourselves bodies health will be bad. In long time, we need have high chance to pay medical expenditure when we are old. So, pollution case may be one good example to explain how and why human foolish behavior may influence ourselves future need to compensate serious medical loss.

All of these human foolish behavior will bring pollution to global ocean. On consequently, we will need to compensate to eat polluted or dirty or poison fished , ourselves bodies health will be bad. In long time, we will have high chance to pay medical expenditure, when we are old. So, pollution case may be one good example to explain how and why human ourselves intellectual or foolish behaviors may influence future long time economic loss or economic growth or recession in micro and micro economic view.

On another water pollution aspect hand, if we often keep rubbish to sea, oil exploration processing pollutes ocean and ships' gas pollute ocean, then fishes will eat polluted food and drink dirty water, due to fishes will eat polluted food and drink dirty sea water because the global ocean is polluted seriously.

In fact, because human only consider how to buy boats to carry on any leisure water activities, or catches cruises to travel on the sea. Also, oil manufacturers only consider any where to find oil exploration places to manufacture oil products from ocean, when their pol exploration processes can plloute ocean. Consequently, global fishes drink polluted water or eat direty food. They will have poison. So, human will have high chance to eat poison fishes.

Otherwise, such as pollution case, it can influence inflation or deflation. Consequently, the reason indicates supply and demand theory. If air pollution is serious, then we will consider health issue, global cars demand number may be influenced to reduce, when global cars number demand will reduce, global car prices and supply number will need to change to fall down in order to attract or persuade global car consumers choose to make car purchase decision.

Hence, global car manufacture number and car price will be influenced to reduce, due to global air pollution issue. Consequently, deflation will occur because when the country citizen usually does not spend much extra saving money to buy car expensive goods. Money value will be low. Otherwise, if global car pollution is not serious, human considers to buy cars to enjoy driving leisure lives. So, global car demand is influenced to increase , also global car price will also influenced to increase.

Consequently, global human will choose to buy cars to drive. Due to we accept to spend extra saving to buy expensive car goods. Car sale price and supply may be influenced to rise up. Money value is influenced to reduce. Inflation may be influenced, due to global car consumers number increases, we would not have extra money to spend easily. Car expensive goods expenditure influences our spending habit to avoid to make car purchase decision more easily. So, human intellectual or foolish activities may bring inflation or deflation consequence in possible indirectly in macro economic view.

On conclusion, above pollution case explain that how and why human intellectual or foolish economic behaviors may bring inflation or deflation consequence as well as economic growth or recession consequence as well as any goods demand and supply increasing or decreasing consequence. It implies that human behavior may have indirect relationship to influence any goods demand and supply number to either increase or decrease result as well as any goods price will be influenced to increase or decrease in micro and macro economic view. Hence, Human foolish behavior is depended on social enjoyment need more or material social supply more because human needs to raise enjoyment feel , so we will choose to do foolish behavior, e.g. air pollution, when many people choose to buy cars to drive to replace catch public transport. So, such as car market, it depends on car demand number more than car supply number absolutely in demand and supply view.

The relationship between social change and human behavior

Why does economic changes may influence human individual behavioral change? I shall attempt to indicate shopping behavior and staying at home behavior to explain their case and effect relationship as below:

Human behavior can be influenced by economic change or economic change can be influenced by human behavior? Why does recession may influence consumers reduce shopping desire? In social recession situation, it is possible that many people lose jobs suddenly, due to businessmen lose many customers. They need to make decision to reduce employees number in order to continue to keep businesses. Consequently, many firms (organizations) their employees may lose jobs. When they have much time, due to lose jobs, they will feel to avoid to spend too much time and money to go to shopping often. Many losing jobs people, they will often stay at homes.

So, they will reduce time to go to shopping, then non essential products won't their preferable choice purchase products. Hence, recession will change many losing jobs people their shopping or consumption desires to avoid to buy non essential products often . Usually when economic boom, many people have jobs to do because consumers number must increase when many people have jobs to do. Then, many people can accept to spend money to buy non essential products often. Many people feel spend time to go to shopping can satisfy their purchase of any kinds of new products useful psychology or desire. So, recession is one good example to explain it can influence many people do not like often to leave homes to go to shopping easily. Many people like to stay at homes, because they feel worry about spending too much shopping time when they leave homes. Their staying home time is one good negative shopping behavior example. So, economic change may influence human individual behavior changes , they have direct cause and effect relationship in behavioral economic view.

May human behavior influence economic change? Is it possible that human behavior may bring the country social economic change in macro economic or micro behavioral economic view ? I shall indicate publishing industry example. Do you feel that if there are many students feel learning is very important when they read many books or many of students feel interesting to read or they have reading new books in habit, then it is possible that the country will have many students like to spend time to go to any book shops to choose the books, they feel that they can help they learn new knowledge. Then the country will increase students number, they often spend time to visit any one book shop every week. Their visiting book shops behavior which may become their habits. So, the country will increase students number, they often spend time to visit book shops. Also, it implies that visiting book shops behaviors may be their behavioral habits.

So, when the country has many students often spend time to visit book shops , their visiting book shops behaviors may help any one book shop to raise books sale chance. So, the country's student individual often visiting book shop behaviors, their habitual visiting book shops behaviors must may assist help any one book shop to increase books sale number absolutely.

Consequently, any one book shop , its books sale number must be influenced to increase to increase because the country will have many students like or feel need visit book shops habit in order to choose any suitable books to buy to read at home in order to raise themselves learning effort. When the country has many bok shops often have many students visit their book shops, then their books sale number may be influenced to increase. It explain why student individual visiting book shop behavior may help any one book shop sale number increases also. So, visiting shops products sale number is depended on online products supply number, if online products supply number increases, then it may cause many customers choose to buy the kind of products from online webstore. So, any shop products sale number will depend on online products supply number in supply and demand view.

Technology or human behavior whether may influence economic growth or recession

What does human network job mean ? Why may human network job be popular? Why human network job behavior may influence economy ? Nowadays internet is popular to use. We can apply internet to find data , search any new things, even earn money. Why does internet may become human network job source. For example, e-publish may be one kind of new human network job. Any authors may apply internet channel to help them to sell electronic or paper books from e-publisher web store. They may apply facebook, you tub etc. any online channel to promote themselves new books to let new readers to know whether when they may buy themselves favourable new topic books to read from electronic publisher web store.

Thus, future electronic publisher industry may help any authors to build internet network platform to help them to sell and promote ot advertise their any one new electronic or paper book topic to let global any one reader to choose to buy their any new topic books from electronic publisher web store easily and conveniently. However, it implies that electronic network platform author may be one kind of future new human network job in our societies.

ow electronic network platform author job may bring economy benefit in macro economy view? A person can have few friends, contacts and still be very influential if these few

friends and contacts are themselves highly influential, e.g. one author must not need to know any one reader in global society. When they like to choose any electronic books from electronic internet network platform. They may become the author's any one topic book buyer, when they feel the author's any one topic book is fun and attract they make decision to both the strange author whose the topic book from electronic book publisher's platform web store convenience in short time. Although, they are strangers, they do not know themselves , but the reader can understand what it way that made Google from writing platform to create new creative mind and typing network job method to replace traditional hand writing book method for global authors. It will be one kind of new human network writing job.

Hence, global any one reader can apply an innovative search engine , such as google.com to find whether whom author personal new topic books are value to read from internet. Then, the electronic publisher's web store may be new book store platform sale network to help the author to sell many electronic or paper books from electronic network platform in short time. So, internet may be future new network platform to help global any one author to create network writing job absolutely. Furthermore, internet may be popular social media to help any one author to build good relationship between his/her readers. It is one kind of new network, human network job. New authors do not need to buy many paper books to prepare to put in any one book shop warehouse. Their every book can print on demand to reduce out of book stock in any one book shop. They may choose to sell either electronic books or paper books both from any one book publisher web store. So, electronic network platform may be one kind of good writing channel to help human authors to create income and it can also help authors to bring new creative mind and new topic fun content books to let readers to know and buy to read from electronic publisher network platform.

Why does human behavior may be one kind of new human network job to bring global economic advantages. Although, it may be free income or without income, but the person does the network behavior, his/her behavior may be bring advantages to influence many other people's health. For this case, when a worker in a coffee shop in an airport gets a vaccination against the flu, it does not only helps him or her stay healthy, but also helps the many travellers who might otherwise have been inflected if that workers caught the flu. So, the externality , the result implies the vaccination of even a part of a community conveys benefits to the whole community. For example, governments pay special attention to the vaccinations of school children, teachers, health mothers, and the elderly, categories of people particularly susceptible not only to catching, but also to transmitting a disease.

It is not accidential that governments are heavily involved with vaccination . When there are externalities, free market, fail to persuade individual incentives with society's

their the worker's decision of whether to get a vaccine ends up attracting whether other people get sick. The workers might not fully take all these other people's potential suffering into account when making her or his vaccination decision.

As Stanford University does many suggestions, understand this and tries to help them make the right decisions and so providers free flu vaccines for its staff and students. Small pockets of unvaccinated individuals can allow a disease to gain a spread more widely well-being. For example, parent weighing the costs and benefits of a vaccine for their child is not always thinking of the consequences of that vaccination to other people. THese are markets in which subsidizing or regulating behavior can make everyone better off. Because the reason for requiring that a child be vaccinated before enrolling in school is not just to protect that child, because each child's vaccination affects others via potential contagions.

Robot job behavior brings economy influences

If one day robots can replace human to do simple, even complex jobs. They will bring what influences to our global societial economy.The popular economic refrain declares that the

global middle class is dying and robots will soon take our jobs, e.g. shopping center customer service jobs, library service jobs, cinema ticket sale jobs, restaurant kitchen cooker jobs,

even, bus drivers, taxi drivers etc. public transport driving jobs, accountant, doctors etc. professional jobs. Whether it is beautiful or petty matter if our future societies have many human jobs can be replaced to do from robots. Businessman must may reduce to employ employees and reduce to pay salary or wage, when robots can be replaced to do their employees tasks. But, societies must bring unemployement rate rises , due to societies will have many people loss jobs when their employers choose to buy robots to serve their clients or do any office tasks or customer service or cleaning etc. tasks.

In micro economy view, employers may save money in long term, but in macro economy view, it will cause unemployment ratio rises , even crime rate rises when there are many people lose jobs in societies. These models of doom, though, fail to account for the hundreds of businesses riding the waves of change in their industries when robots may be invented to replace human to do many simple , even complex tasks in our future societies.

WE may image that one small factory needs to manufacture fishes canes to sell to supermarket, the small , cheaper stuff and higher margin parts of the fishes manufacture industry. Before, this factory needs to employe many human factory workers need to help every fresh customer makeing the perfect fishing gear, designed for performance, durability, and cost in order to achieve to manufacture every fish cane in whole fished processing manufacturing stages. Every worker needs to spend about 15 to twenty minutes to finish every fish cane , till to delivery to any supermarket to sell. If this fish canes manufacturing factory can apply manufacturing robots to help them to finish any one working tasks , every robot can only spend five minutes to finish whole fresh fish cane manufacturing process. Thus, every robot can

help this factory save 10 to 15 minutes time to finsh every fish cane manufacturing process. IN fact, time is money, because when every robot can help this factory to reduce 10 to 15 minutes time to compare human worker. Then, this factory can finish about 20 fish canes in one hour if it can use robot to help it to manufacture fish canes. Otherwise, if this factory still use human workers to help it to manufacture fish canes, then it can finsh about 3 to 4 fish canes in one hour. SO, the manufacturing efficiency ensures that robots must help this fish manufacturing factory to raise fish canes number more than human workers. So, in robotic behavioral economy view, manufacturing robots must help this fish canes manufacturing factory to raise fish canes manufacturing number and deliver increasing number to supermarkets to prepare to sell every day. Robots can help this fish canes manufacturing factory bring manufacturing time saving, rising manufacturing efficiency, improving performance and reducing wages expenditure long time advantages in micro economy view. However, manufacturing robots can also bring disadvanages to society, e.g. increasing unemployment ratio, increasing crime rate, this factory workers will lose jobs and income, they need earn social welfare from government and increasing government finance pressure in short time, even long time in macro economic view.

Stanford University graduate program in economics, Scott lecturer explained that "in demand and supply economic theory for robots supply and demand case, robots supply number increasing may influence human workers demand number decrease. It sometimes calls " the efficient frontier".

No specific human beings were mentioned in any of economics classes. As robots supply and demand in market case, They (robots) may be purely theoretical " agents" who reached to the most reasonable sale prices in order to persuade any one businessman buyer to make manufacturing robot buying decision whether robots can help him / her to bring how much saving time , saving money, saving cost, improving performance, efficiency economic benefit before he/she plans to reduce workers number when he/she decides to apply robots to replace human workers in his/her factory or office or any service department, e.g. cinema ticket sale service, shopping center customer service, shopping center cleaning , supermarket customer service etc. service or sale tasks. When robots can replace human to do any one of these tasks in any organizations. So, robots may be human worker agents who reached to prices the way robots would react to a software command. There was nothing that explained why some people thrived and others did n't or why truly brilliant, hardworking people could fail when much lazier folks succeeded." Having been admitted to the Stanford University graduate program in economics, Scott lecturer hoped to get his answers there.

How robots influence our future social changing? Using the right technology can be a boon to your business in this economy. For internet example, it is easier than ever to find well-matched customers all around the world, to stay in contact with them, and to more quickly design the products they want. If you focus solely on being cutting -edge, though you risk letting the technology take over what should be very robust relationships with your customers , employees, and colleagues. IN nowaddays society, technoligical advances and cutomation, personal relationships in business are more crucial than ever. I mean that robots can not replace human to serve clients to let them to feel more comfortable and passion more easily. For shoe shop case example, if the shoe shop apply one robot to serve its clients to replace human shoe salesperson to serve its shoe customers. Robots ensure that they can not persuade every shoe potential buyer to make shoe buying decision more easily when robots need to contact every shoe potential buyer. The reason is simple, because robots can not touch any one shoe buyer individual emotion very easier.

If the shoe buyer needs the robots to help him/her to choose any right shoe styles when he/she can not feel himself / herself can make the most right shoe style choice decision. The robots can not replace human shoe salesperson to make shoe style choice judgement more easily. They must need longer time to analyze whether which shoe style may be the most suitable to the shoe buyer. Otherwise, human shoe salesperson may attempt to make the most right shoe style choice decision to help any one shoe buyer to choose the most right style shoe because he/she owns shoe style sale experience, shoe style knowledge, the most important reason is that they can feel every shoe customer individual emotion to touch whether he/she will feel comfortable or happy when they attempt to help every shoe customer to seek the most right shoe style in every shoe customer whole shoe searching processing. Otherwise, serving robots are only one machine, they can not touch or feel every shoe customer individual emotion whether he/she feel comfortable or unhappy or happy when they need to contact them in whole shoe searching processing. Hence, I believe that some tasks robots can not replace human staff to do very easily. Otherwise, robots may bring disadvanages to let any one businessman to loss his/her customers, due to robots can not touch every customer emotion to compare human staff in service tasks more easily. Robots serving customer behaviors may cause money lose and customers number lose to the shop in micro economic view.

Intellectual human economic behaviors

What does intellectual human economic behaviors mean ? I believe that when we choose or decide to do intellectual behaviors, then our societies will be influenced to bring economic growth in consequence.I shall attempt to indicate pollution case to explain how and why eithet our intellectual or foolish behaviors may bring economic growth or recession in consequence as below:

On one hand, for air pollution social case aspect example, if we only consider to buy cars to drive for working aim or holiday leisure aim. Then, our societies air will be polluted. Our health will be influenced to bad. Our car driving behaviors may cause global environment air pollution seriously. In long time, global air pollution will bring our bodies health to be bad. Although, ourselves car driving behaviors may bring our driving travelling leisure enjoyment and comfortable feeling in short time, also we so not need to pay public transport fare often, but we need to compensate ourselves health economic intangible loss due to air pollution , when cars number increases, dirty air will cause ourselves health to become bad.

In the result, we will need to pay more medical expenditure when we are old age, due to ourselves bodies will become bad, due to we breathe global dirty air every day, due to ourselves cars pollute air in long time, e.g. 10 to 20 years, even 30 more without limited air pollution environment. So, driving cars behavior may be one kind of human foolish behavior and our foolish behavior may bring ourselves future long time medical expenditure absolutely.

One the other hand, water pollution social aspect, if we often keep much rubbish to pollute sea, oil exploration processing pollute ocean , ships gas pollute ocean, then fishes will eat polluted food and drive dirty water, due to global ocean is polluted.

In fact, because human only to consider how to buy boats to carry on leisure enjoyment activities, or catch cruises to travel on the sea. Also, oil manufacturers only consider researching anywhere to find new oil exploration places to manufacture oil product, when their oil exploration processes pollute ocarn . Consequently, global fishes drink polluted warer or eat polluted food. They will have poison. SO, human will have high chance to eat poison polluted fishes, due to fishes are poison or are polluted.

So, human is doing foolish activities, we only hope to find oil exploration places to pollute ocean or we only spend money to buy ticket to catch ships to travel anywhere in global ocean. All of these human foolish behaviors will bring pollution to global ocean. On consequently, we will need to compensate to eat polluted or dirty or poision fishes, ourselves bodies health will be bad. In long time, we need have high chance to pay medical expenditure when we are old. So, pollution case may be one good example to explain how and why human foolish behavior may influence ourselves future need to compensate serious medical loss.

All of these human foolish behavior will bring pollution to global ocean. On consequently, we will need to compensate to eat polluted or dirty or poison fished , ourselves bodies health will be bad. In long time, we will have high chance to pay medical expenditure, when we are old. So, pollution case may be one good example to explain how and why human ourselves intellectual or foolish behaviors may influence future long time economic loss or economic growth or recession in micro and micro economic view.

On another water pollution aspect hand, if we often keep rubbish to sea, oil exploration processing pollutes ocean and ships' gas pollute ocean, then fishes will eat polluted food and drink dirty water, due to fishes will eat polluted food and drink dirty sea water because the global ocean is polluted seriously.

In fact, because human only consider how to buy boats to carry on any leisure water activities, or catches cruises to travel on the sea. Also, oil manufacturers only consider any where to find oil exploration places to manufacture oil products from ocean, when their pol exploration processes can pottute ocean. Consequently, global fishes drink polluted water or eat direty food. They will have poison. So, human will have high chance to eat poison fishes.

Otherwise, such as pollution case, it can influence inflation or deflation. Consequently, the reason indicates supply and demand theory. If air pollution is serious, then we will consider health issue, global cars demand number may be influenced to reduce, when global cars number demand will reduce, global car prices and supply number will need to change to fall down in order to attract or persuade global car consumers choose to make car purchase decision.

Hence, global car manufacture number and car price will be influenced to reduce, due to global air pollution issue. Consequently, deflation will occur because when the country citizen usually does not spend much extra saving money to buy car expensive goods. Money value will be low. Otherwise, if global car pollution is not serious, human considers to buy cars to enjoy driving leisure lives. So, global car demand is influenced to increase , also global car price will also influenced to increase.

Consequently, global human will choose to buy cars to drive. Due to we accept to spend extra saving to buy expensive car goods. Car sale price and supply may be influenced to rise up. Money value is influenced to reduce. Inflation may be influenced, due to global car consumers number increases, we would not have extra money to spend easily. Car expensive goods expenditure influences our spending habit to avoid to make car purchase decision more easily. So, human intellectual or foolish activities may bring inflation or deflation consequency in possible indirectly in macro economic view.

On conclusion, above pollution case explain that how and why human intellectual or foolish economic behaviors may bring inflation or deflation consequency as wll as economic growth or recession consequency as well as any goods demand and supply increasing or decreasing consequency. It implies that human behavior may have indirect relationship to influence any goods demand and supply number to either increase or decrease result as well as any goods price will be influenced to increase or decrease in micro and macro economic view.

The relationship between social change and human behavior

Why does economic changes may influence human individual behavioral change? I shall attempt to indicate shopping behavior and staying at home behavior to explain their case and effect relationsip as below:

Human behavior can be influenced by economic change or economic change can be influenced by human behavior? Why does recession may influence consumers reduce shopping desire? In social recession suitation, it is possible that many people lose jobs suddenly, due to businessmen lose many customers. They need to make decision to reduce employees number in order to continue to keep businesses. Consequently, many firms (organizations) their employees may lose jobs. When they have much time, due to lose jobs, they will feel to avoid to spend too much time and money to go to shopping often. Many losing jobs people, they will often stay at homes.

So, they will reduce time to go to shopping, then non essential products won't their preferable choice purchase products. Hence, recession will change many losing jobs people their shopping or consumption desires to avoid to buy non essential products often . Usually when economic boom, many people have jobs to do because consumers number must increase when many people have jobs to do. Then, many people can accept to spend money to buy non essential products often. Many people feel spend time to go to shopping can satisfy their purchase of any kinds of new products useful psychology or desire. So, recession is one good example to explain it can influence many people do not like often to leave homes to go to shopping easily. Many people like to stay at homes, becaue they feel worry about spending too much shopping time when they leave homes. Their staying home time is one good negative shopping behavior example. So, economic change may influence human individual behavior changes , they have direct cause and efect relationship in behavioral economic view.

May human behavior influence economic change? Is it possible that human behavior may bring the country social economic change in macro economic or micro behavioral economic view ? I shall indicate publishing industry example. Do you feel that if there are many students feel learning is very important when they read many books or many of students feel interesting to read or they have reading new books in habit, then it is possible that the country will have many students like to spend time to go to any book shops to choose the books, they feel that they can help they learn new knowledge. Then the country will increase students number, they often spend time to visit any one book shop every week. Their visiting book shops behavior which may become their habits. So, the country will increase students number, they often spend time to visit book shops. Also, it implies that visiting book shops behaviors may be their behavioral habits.

So, when the country has many students often spend time to visit book shops , their visiting book shops behaviors may help any one book shop to raise books sale chance. So, the country's student individual often visiting book shop behaviors, their habitual visiting book shops behaviors must may assist help any one book shop to increase books sale number absolutely.

Consequently, any one book shop , its books sale bumber must be influenced to increase to increase because the country will have many students like or feel need visit book shops habit in order to choose any suitable books to buy to read at home in order to raise themselves learning effort. When the country has many bok shops often have many students visit their book shops, then their books sale number may be influenced to increase. It explain why student individual visiting book shop behavior may help any one book shop sale number increases also.

How human productive behavior may influence economic development

May any country which citizen behavior assist themselves country development? It is one cause and effect economic question. I mean that if the country itself citicen can not concentrate mind or energy to choose to do one kind of industry in order to let themselves country can bring the most benefit, then whether the counry itself economy can bring the most serious economic benefit. I shall attempt to indicate these countries themselves indistry choice to explain whether these countries themselves citizen productive behavior may help themselves countries to achieve the largest economic benefits. I shall indicate as below:

New Zealand farmer individual wine productive behavior

For New Zealand country example, this country concerns itself effort is foucs on farming agricultural aspect. So, this country has many farmers concentrate on farming agricultural aspect. May New Zealanders choose to spend time to produce different kinds of wines, e.g. wine or red grape wine is for the people are eating meat, or they are eating dinner.

When these New Zealanders their behaviors choose to do farming or agriculture to grow and produce different kinds of taste of white or red grape wine drinking products job. Themselves grape agriculture behavior will influence these New Zealanders themselves, they can learn how to improve different kinds of grape wine drinking products in order to achieve every kinds of white or read grape wines taste improving aim during their white or red grape producing process.

Why can New Zealander every individual white or read grape wine producers improve their white or read grape wine taste more easily? In behavioral economic view, it can explain that why any one New Zealander white or read grape wine producer can be encouraged or excited or persuaded to concentrate nervous and energy and effort to learn how to improve their white or red grape wine products easily.

In fact, New Zealand is one agricultural food export country. It has good natural environment resource , e.g. land, seed to provide any one farmer to produce themselves any kinds of agricultrual food products, e.g. fruit, or wine food products. Because New Zealanders know themselves country has enough natural resource . So, in common, many New Zealanders choose to attempt to do farming agricultural jobs in order to export themselves any kinds of fruit or meat or wine products to overseas or sell to domestic in order to earn profit.

So, when these New Zealand farmers number has been increasing every year. This country farmers will feel themsleves competition between this New Zealand farmers themselves are serious due to they may feel New Zealanders choose to do agriculture businesses in order to export themselves different kinds of farming food to overseas or sell to local to earn profit.

Hence, when many New Zealand farmers feel that farmers number has been increasing every year. They will feel themselves competition is serious. They must need to spend much time and nervous and effort to research what method is the best how to produce the best taste of white or red grape wine products in order to let local or overseas wine buyers to choose to buy his/her producing white or read grpae products to drink.

Hence, in competition psychological view, may influence many New Zealand white or reaad wine producers had been beginning to change their learning behavior on researching what method is the best in order to produce the best quality of taste red or white wine products to sell in order to attract overseas or local white or read grape wine drinkers to choose to buy his/her wine products. Their behavior will focus on learning how to raising or improving white or read grape wine taste method more than only focus on producing a large number white or red grape wine products. They believe wine quality is more important to compare wine producing number. So, New Zealand wine producers themselves wine producers behaviors have been changing on concentrating on researching wine quality method aspect more then wine producing number aspect in behavioral economic view.

America high technological productive behavior

For America example, US is one high technological country, it owns many high technological knowledge talent inventors, e.g. computer science inventors. Hence, US must attract many diferent countries owning high technological computer inventors choose to go to US to develop their computer science profession career. Also, it seems that when many computer science inventors or professions choose to go to US to develop themselves computer science new career. In behavioral economic view, due to their leaving themselves countries choice, which may bring influence themselve country job behaviors need to be changed. They must need to adapt US new live. Because they will forgive their past computer science job. These computer science professionals need to spend time to adapt US new lives. They " past computer science job behaviors" will need to be changed to their new US any computer employer's new computer science job model.

Because their traditional computer science jobs needed to be forgot in their themselves countries. They will feel their old computer science job knowledge and behavior needed to change in order to let their US any one new of computer company employer feels satisfactory to accept their new working behavior in any one US computer organization.

So, on the other hand, many US computer company employer will feel that they must need time to accept any one new overseas computer science professions their working behaviors, their working attitude daily, because these foreign comouter science professional, their past computer working behaviors and working attitude must be different to US domestic computer science professions.

In behavioral economic view, these overseas computer science professions, their working behaviors and attitude must be needed to change in order to adapt any one US new computer company itself domestic or local computer science professional stafs themselves daily working behaviors and attitude because these overseas and local computer science professionals must need to team work together.

In behavioral economic view, it is only one way that foreign computer science professionals must need to change themselves past country traditiona daily working behaviors and attitude in order to cooperate with these US local computer science professionals in teams more easily.

Consequently, if these foreign compute science professionals can change their past working behaviors and attitude to let any one US local computer science professional feels to cooperate with them easily in short time.

Then, the US computer company itself whole computer professional teams themselves efficiencies will be influenced to raised or improved by the changing past working attitude and working behaviors of these foreign computer science professionals. So, in behavioral economic view, only if US any one computer company hopes itself computer teams themselves efficiency can be raised or improved when it decides to employ foreign computer science professionals and US domestic computer science professionals. They need to work in teams together. They must need to let these foreign computer science professionals to know how to change their working behaviors and attitude to let their domestic computer science professionals feel easy to work together. Then, the US computer company itself whole team efficiency must be rasied or improved easily in short time.

China share market investing behavior

For China share market example, economic development depends on financial market. Because if many Chinese have interest to invest to carry on shares buying and selling activities in orde to learn how to earn shares interest and share profit when the China shareholder can make decision to sell himself/herself shares in the the high price, then he/she can earn money when he/she can sell the China company's shares in the high sale share price position.

If China has many Chinese like to spend time to carry on investing shares activities. Themselves shares buying and selling behaviors will influence China has many companies can increase fund from many Chinese shareholders in order to have enough money to expand or develop themselves businesses in China in long term.

Consequently, when China can have many Chinese like to attempt to carry on buying and selling shares investing behaviors in China share market. Themselves buying and selling shares behaviors can help many Chinese companies have effort to increase enough money or capital in order to continue to do their businesses in long term absolutely. So, it explains why when many Chinese become shareholders , they can assist China will have many companies continue to develop their businesses if many Chinese like to carry on shares buying and selling investing behaviors in long time in China financial investment market nowadays in behavioral economic view.

Why has any individual country have many people invest share behavior which can influence the country's macro consumption desire?

I shall apply shares market buying and selling investment behavior to explaiin why shares investment behavior which may impact the country's overal consumption desire as below:

In behavioral economic view, I assume that when the coutry has many people have interest to attempt to carry on shares buying and selling investment behavior, then their frequent shares buying and selling behaviors which may bring negactive consumption desire or shopping desire of these shares investors their consumer behavior.

The reason is simple, when the country has many share buyers number suddenly been increasing rapidly. Consequently, these large group share investors must need to spend much time to research any kinds of company shares variations, whether when their share prices will rise up of fall down in order to achieve buying the company's shares in the lowest price and selling the company's shares in the highest price level in order to earn profit.

Basic on this reason, they must need to spend much extra time to research share prices changing behavior every day, e.g. one working person will wait to leave his/her job, after he/she can spend time to gather data to research the day's share price changing behavior after dinner. So, the working person's right time may be his/her share price market research behavior. Before he/she may spend his/her night time to go to shopping after dinner, but nowadays, he/she will fogive to do his/her shopping behavior before dinner or after dinner at hight sometime. He/she will make decision to spend much night time to turn on computer to click on share market website to research his/her share purchase choice to investigate whether his/her share price whether it rises up or falls down at the moment in order to make his/her share buying or selling decision at ever night time.

I mean the when the country has many people are share investors, their shares investment behavioral spenging time which will influence many shops lose customers at might often because the country will have many people feel need to spend night time to turn on computer or watch television to investigate share price variation. So, the country will have many people / share investors choose to stay at home in order to carry on share price variation investigation behavior, they need to listen share market update news from radios or watch the share market update news from computer or TV at home every night. Consequenly, they must reduce times to leave themselves homes at night. So, their shopping behavior also will be reduced. Because these share investors feel need to spend time to investigate share price variation news at homes which can bring economic benefits (high opportunity benefits) when they choose to forgive to leave homes to go to shopping times (opportunity cost) every night.

On conclusion, it seems that when the country has many people are share investors, then their share price investigating behavior may bring negative shopping emotion at night. Consequently, the country's any one shop may lose many customers from this share investor consumer group in behavioral economic view. Hence, when the country's share investors number had been increasing rapidly, it will influence any shops lose many customers from this share investing customer group at night frequenly in short time, even long time in behavioral economic view, because their shopping desires or shopping emotion will be brought negative feeling when they make decisions to spend much time to listen radios or watch TV or computers share price update nes at night. Hence, share market will bring negative impact to influence consumer shopping desire or negative shopping emotion in behavioral economic view.

Can technology influence human shopping behavioral change?

Nowadays, technological development has reached mature stage, whether technological mature stage may bring positive or negative shopping emotion influence to global consumers. I shall aplly internet inventin or ecommerce shopping channel tool to explain whether internet technology can bring postive or negative influence to global consumer behavior in behavioral economic view.

Internet is a good technological tool, it brings e-commerce business chance. In fact, commonly, global has have many businessmen choose to use internet channel to carry on their products transactions between global online-buyers and their electronic websites. So, global many shoppers had begun to feel online shopping is more convenient to compare visiting shops shopping. Their shopping behaviors have been changed from internet technological tool. Global has many shoppers choose to buy any products from any overseas or local businessmen their web stores. They only need to spend time to find any businessmen their webstores to choose the most suitable products to pay visa to buy from their webstores. at homes. So, in general, global had have may shoppers had changed their shopping behaviors from visiting shops to visiting webstores at homes often.

So, it seems that internet technological tool had influenced global many shops disappear, but internet webstores will be replaced their actual shops on streets. Some of businessmen either they choose webstores to replace shops or choose websotes and shops both or still keep shops only. Hence, internet tool influences global businessmen have three kinds of products sale channels to let globa local and overseas consumers to choose how to buy their products.

However, in fact, many of global shoppers, youngers and olders had begun to accept to buy any products from webstores. They feel to spend time to leave homes to visit shops , their shopping behaviors will be wasted time to not essential part to their daily lives. Hence, since internet technological invention, it had changed many consumers their traditional visiting shops shopping habit to change to buying products from webstores channel.

However, on the one hand, internet creates webstores ecommerce shopping channel to let global many consumers do not need to leave homes to go to shopping. It brings negative visiting shops shopping emotion to global general consumers nowadays. But on the other hand, it also brings positive visiting internet webstores shopping emotion to global general consumer nowadays. So, it seems that global many consumers feel that they often do not need to spend much time to go out shopping. Many global consumers feel convenient and enjoy to choose any products to buy from different internet webstores, when the online buyer chooses the most suitable product, he she only needs to pay visa card to buy the product from the online seller's webstore conveniently at home.

Hence, online shopping can bring economic benefit to online buyers, e.g. avoiding walking time or spending transport fare to visit the shop to go to shopping, shortening or reducing shopping time to do another important matter.

On conclusion, global many consumers began feel online shopping can bring more economic benefits on shortening shopping time, avoiding transport fare spending aspect. So, online shopping will be popular shopping behavior for future long time. It may encourage global many shoppers can make rapid shopping decision in short time in order to carry on any products buying transaction to global any one online shopper in short time easily in behavioral economic view. So, global many businessmen had begun to build themselves one attraction webstore in order to persuade different countries consumers to choose to click themselves webstores from internet channel to buy any kinds of products in short time easily.

So, internet technology had changed consumers traditional shopping behaviors to build positive online shopping emotion as well as raise online sellers' any products sale chance easily in behavioral economic view.

Why and how human behavior may influence the country's economic growth or recession?

When one country has many people choose to do the same matter for one period, whether their behavior may influence the country's pvera; economic growth or recession . I shall attempt to indicate cases toexplain their relationship as below:

For flowing rubblish behavioral case example, do you feel that when the country has many people often flow rubblish on the streets, instead of their flowing rubblish behavior may bring streets dirty? But, their flowing rubblish behavior may explain that this country has people may have enough money to buy food to ear, or enough cloths to wear, enough bottles of water to drink, even they may have enough money to buy new television, radio, refrigeraters , washing machines, desktops or laptops electronic home products from old to new to use in order to satisfy their living needs. So, when they flow old electronic home products, their flowing old home electronic products behaviors may seem that they have enough money to buy other new home electronic products to replace old home electronic products to use at homes.

However, it seems thaat this country ought have many people have jobs to do. So, many of them, they can easy to make purchase decison to flow any old home electronic products and buy any new home electronic products to use . Because this country has many people have jobs to do. So, they can often not use old home electonic products to become rubblishs to flow on streets after they had bought any kinds of new home electronic homes.

In fact, it also implies that this country's economy grows rapidly. So, many businesses can glow up rapdly. When they expanded their businesses, they must need to increase employees number in order to let they help themselves to raise productivity or serve their clients absolutely. So, when the country has many businesses can grow up, it seems that its economy must be better or it is improved to compare past. Due to many different kinds of home electronic products had been often bought to use by this country people in this period. So, this country's any streets can be observed that expensive electronic home products were flowed on streets anywhere. then, this country will have many electronic home products sellers can sell their home electronic products very easily. When this country has many people can find any kinds of jobs to do easily. So, due to unemploymen rate had been decreasing.

In behavioral economic view, as this many electronic home products rubblish country case, we can observe this country may have many people have jobs to do. So, consumption number has been increased long time. So, cheap food, or expensive home electronic products may be rubblish on any streets. This country's people , their flowing rubblish behaviors may be explained that many of people have enough jobs to do, so they have ability to buy any good taste food to eat or buy any kinds of expensive electronic home products to use. So, this country's economy may be improved for this long period. So, in behavioral economic view, when this country can have many electronic home products rubblishs are flowed on anywherer in streets frequently. It seems that this country will have many people have jobs to do, so it causes they often change old home electronic products or replaced them easily, when they have enough income to spend to buy any kinds of new home electronic products to use at homes easily. Moreover, their flowing old electronic home products behaviors also indicate that this country has many people their salaries may be increased in possible from their emplyers. When this country can have many different kinds of home electornic products are sold. It means that this country's electronic home products needs or demand had been increasing, due to many people have jobs to do and income increases to excite their living of needs also improve. Consequently, this country may seem have better economic improvement. We can observe from this country's electronic home products rubblish increasing income in theis period.

On conclusion, this country ought experience economic growth at this period. So, " flowing expensive electronic home rubblish increasing number " may seem that this country's economic growth is rapidly in this period, due to many people have jobs to do as well as salaries increase in this period.

Technology how impacts human behavior changing?

Technology how influences human behavior to bring changing? For example, online share purchase and sale transaction from smart phone brings share investor can do share buying or selling transation in any where and any time conveniently, non manual driving auto vehicle, bring car owner feels comfortable and spends free time to do other matter, e.g. reading, listening mucis in himself or herself car freely. electrical energy vehicle can help car owner to reduce air polluton and it can brings the drivers do not feel drive long time in any journeys in order to avoid air pollution for environmental protection responsible car drivers in our societies. Thus, they will drive long time in any journeys when they can drive electronic energy cars to replace oil energy cars.

However, online technology can also bring consumers can choose to stay at homes to buy any things from seller individual online webstore conveniently. Such as online technology can bring shoppers do not need to spend much time to visit shops to buy any things. They can choose any kinds of products from any online sellers individual online webstores conveniently at homes. Online technology excite busy consumers can make purchase decision easily as well as it can help online sellers sell any kinds of products from internet easily.

In behavioral economic view, technology can change human behavior to be improved, it can let human feels comfortable, more free time ro use, rapid making any decisions, such as apply smart phones to make share purchase or sale transaction decision, online shopping decision, even travelling any where decision in short time, when the traveller finds the most cheap hotel accommodation room price and air ticket price frm any travel agent online tourism webstore, then the potential travel customer can follow the online hotel accommodation price and air ticket price data to make decision when to buy the air ticket from the airline travel agent or make decision when to prebook which hotel accommodation room to go to the country to travel from online travel agent tourism webstores. So, technology can encourage global any country travelers to make anywhere to trvel rapidly. If the traveler can find the country's general hotel rooms and airline tickets prices had been decreasing more sightly. The traveler may make travel decision to choose the country to travel in short time, then he/she can prebook the country;s any hotel room and airline ticket to pay by visa fraom the country's any hotel and airline travel agent webstores., before one week, even one month or more easily. Hence, online technology can also encourage traveler individual frequent travel times to be increased, due to global travelers can find any hotel rooms and airline tickets prices from internet conveniently at homes. They do not need to spend time to visit any airline travel agent to enquire travel choice country's hotel rooms prices and airline ticket prices. They can compare global travel of countries choices ' all hotels rooms and airline agents air tickets prices to make prebook airline seat and hotel room decision before one week, one month even six months early.

On conclusion, online technology can encourage global travelers can make travelling any where and when traveling time desicions easily. It can excite tourism industry develops in long time. Also, such as electricity cars invention can encourage environment protection car owners do car purchase decision easily, because they can choose to drive electronic energy cars to replace oil energy cars in order to avoid air pollution occurs easily. So, electronic cars can increase electronic car purchasrs number, due to many of environmental protection attitude of car owners can choose to drive electricity cars to bring air cleans, even non -manual driving cars can encourage lazy driving and free time driving car owners to choose to buy non-manual (artificial intelligent) cars to drive , because they can spend much free time to read, listen music or do any matters in themselves cars, they do not need to drive cars, robotic (AI) auto driving machine is such one non-manual driver to help them to drive themselves cars confidently. So, non-manual driving cars can attract lazy and enjoying free time driving car owners to choose to buy to replace traditional manual cars to drive easily. Moreover, online share transaction can help any share investors to make share buying and selling decision in short time easily. When they can apply smart phones technological tool to carry on share buying and selling activities easily. They can observe any share rising or falling price suitation from smart phones in any where any any time easily. So, smart phone technology can help global any shareholders to make share purchase and sale transaction easily. So, technology can encourage human makes decision in short time rapidly.

How and why employees behaviors may influence economy development?

In behavioral economy view,I believe the country's any organizational employees behavior may bring indirect relationship to influence the country's long term economic development. I shall indicate past manufacture industry social development period to explain their relationship. For many countries' past business activities had belonged to manufacturing industry, such as US, UK past before 1980 year, it focused on steel manufacturing and steel manufacturing related machine products. So, US, Uk developed countries manufacturing industries may be past main country's economic income sources. I assume US , UK past had one million number different kinds of industries. They ought had about seven houndred thousand number organizational businesses were belonged to manufactured industry. They may include:

Steel manufacturing and steel related machine manufacturing, e.g. vehicle manufacturing, home appliances, e.g. washing machine, television, radio, refrigerate cooler, heater, air condition etc. different kinds of different kinds of steel -related manufacturing machine, they were manufactured from US, UK steel machine manufacturers. So, US, Uk the other three hundred thousand number industry may be general service industry, e.g. hotel service, restaurent, cinema, public transport service, tourism lesiure , wine bar, supermarket etc. different kinds of non-manufacturing industries business organizations were operated in UK, US past before 1980 year.

So, in UK, US developed countries industry development history, they ought have high percentage of businesses belonged to steel related manufacturing machine and steel products. Also, in the past before 1980 year, US, Uk business employers , they employed many workers are manufacturing workers. They needed to spend long time to work in factories. They were skillful workers, and they are trained to manufacturing cars, washing machine, television, heater, etc. even steel itself different kinds of steel related products to prepare to deliver to their shops to sell to US, Uk local or overseas clients.

So, I believe that past UK, US ought employ many employees, they belonged to skillful manufacturing workers, manufacture increasing steel machine or steel related machine number of products rapidly daily. So, if UK, US had had many of these manufacturing factories owned high skillful workers, then their manufacturing steel-related machine or steel both kinds of products number must be influenced to raise rapidly. Consequently, their steel machine manufacturing products would been exported to overseas or would been sold to local both markets , they may be influenced to raise sale number. They (these manufacturing workers) needed to be trained to know how to manufactur these different kinds of machine products in the efficient teams and they ought to be trained to raise their efficiencies in order to shorten time to manufacturing many kinds of steel related manufacturing machine or steel itself products rapidly. So , if their efficiencies and manufacturing performance was improved, these US, UK any one manufacturing worker and their teams ought achieve raising productivities significantly.

Hence, when past UK, US manufacturing industry development period, if these two countries‘ any manufacturing factories could have many manufacturing workers could be trained to be skillful and proficient manufacturing workers. Then, in past every day to these factories workers, they ought help their steel or steel related manufacturing employers to raise any kinds of machine or steel products number in every team. So, when past in the manufacturing industry development, US, UK could have many factories’ manufacturing workers themselves steel or steel related machine products manufacturing skill could be trained to to improve to any kinds of these machine or steel manufacuring products quality as well as their products number could be influenced to raise by themselves skillful improvement significantly every day.

Then, what would be influenced to occur to past UK, US manufacturing industry period? In behavioral economic view, when these two manufacturing industry developed countries, such as UK, US , if they had many factories workers can be trained to improve their skill in order to achieve any kinds of steel or steel-related machine products quality could be improved as well as products manufacturing number could be also increased absolutely.

In consequence, past UK and US both countries ought increase themselves any kinds of steel and steel related machine products number to be supplied to themselves local shops to let local clients to choose any one kind of machine manufacturing products to buy easily as well as they could also export to supply overseas any countries to buy their different kinds of steel or steel related machine products to let overseas steel or steel related manufacturing machine product buyers, they can have many of these different kinds of these steel or steel-related different kinds of manufacturing machine from UK and UK these both countries easily to compare other countries.

On conclusion, I believe that past US, and UK macro manufacturing industry income GDP would increase significantly. So, they would have good economic growth performance because when many of these manufacturing workers themselves manufacturing effort could be improved. So, it explained when employees manufacturing abilities can influence economic growth indirectly.

Robots invention whether they can help organizations to raise efficiencies or inefficiencies?

In behavioral economic view, in any organizations, when the organization hopes its worker teams can raise efficiencies , the organization may choose to increase more workers number and/or it can provide training to improve these workets themselves skills in order to raise their efficiencies. For one warehouse example, when the warehouse increases many goods , they are needed to delivered these goods from the shelves to the delivering destination locations. If this warehouse supervisors feel these workers themselves goods delivery speeds are slow, which is possible due to this warehouse's workers number is not enough. So, this warehouse supervisor ought increase workers number in order to increase their goods delivery speed in order to deliver goods from the shelves to every indicated goods delivery destination in order to let any one lorry driver can transport the right kinds of goods and ensure the accurate goods number to transport to any one client home rapidly.

However, if this warehouse supervisor planed to buy several warehouse goods delivery robots to assist these warehouse workers to find the right kinds of goods from shelves and then deliver to the right destination location in the warehouse. So, these warehouse orkers can concentrate on counting the accurate goods number and ensuring the right kinds of goods in order to prepare to let lorry drivers to transport these goods to these goods of buyers themselvers homes rapidly. Consequently, in the first step, robots can concentrate on finding th right goods from shelves and delivers them to the right goods transportation of location destination. Then, in the second step, these warehouse workers can concentrate on counting the accurate goods number and ensuring the right kinds of goods in order to prepare to put them to the lorry. Consequently, when warehouse robots and warehouse workers can cooperate to work together, the most important, robots, can deal on finding the right kinds of goods and deal on delivering the accurate number of goods of job duty as well as these warehouse workers can only concentrte on counting the right kinds of goods number in order to avoid it has none any mistake of wrong kinds of goods and inaccurate goods of delivery number to be transported to the lorry and to deliver to any one buyer's home.

So, it seems that warehouse robots ought help any one warehouse worker to raise himself efficiency and avoid goods delivery of mistake occurrence easily as well as their help to warehouse workers that can let any one goods buyer feels their goods can be delivered to their homes rapidly. Moreover, warehouse robots can also help these warehouse workers to raise efficiencies because warehouse robots can help them to shorten goods delivery time between any one shelf and any one goods delivery destination of location in the warehuse because robots may help them to find the right kinds of goods from the right shelf in the short time. So, any one worker does not need to spend long time to seek anywhere is the right shelf location for the kind of goods when the kind of goods are needed to deliver to the buyer's home from lorry. Warehouse robots can help them to do this aspect of " finding the goods from the right shelf in short time job duty". So, any one warehouse worker only needed tospend less time to do the counting of any right kind of goods number and ensuring the right kind of goods job duty. Consequently, this warehouse 's any one worker, his any one kind of goods delivery time may be reduced, because robots' assistance and they may have more confidence to avoid mistake to deliver the wrong number of goods and/or the wrong kind of goods to any one goods buyer's home.

On conclusion, it seems that warehouse robots ought may help any one warehouse worker to raise efficiency for any one team in the warehouse as well as the warehouse any one supervisor does not need to spend much time to observe any one worker individual performance for " goods delivery job duty aspect" because their goods delivery job duty that had been replaced to do by these several warehouse robots. Robots can achieve the more accurate of right kinds of goods and the right number of goods delviery job performance to compare any one of human warehouse worker themselves right kinds of goods of delivery and right number of goods of delivery job performance. So, when robots can participate to cooperate with this warehouse's any one worker to do their goods of delivery job duty in this warehouse every day. Then, robots can raies any one of supervisor individual confidence in order to let they do not need to spend time to observe any one of worker individual whose goods of delivery job performane. They can concentrate on supervising any one worker whose goods transport to lorry in the final step in order to avoid to deliver wrong goods number and / or wrong kind of goods to any one goods buyer's home every day. Consequently, this warehouse's overall teams of their delviery of goods performance many be improved by robotss' participatin to goods of delivery task as well as this warehouse's oveall teams themselves efficiencies may be influenced to raise by robots' goods of delivery task participation.

Why social behavior may influence organizational strategy needs to be changed ?

Why any organizations need to know whether nowadays social behaivor how has been changing in order to implement the kind of the most right strategy to achieve the profit aim pursue in possible. I shall indicate nowadays ecommerce or online, customer shopping behavior to explain above question concerns they ought have close relationship between social behavior and organizational strategic choice or organizational behavioral changing need.

On nowadays ecommerce business, or online shopping model, this kind of shopping model in global many young and old age consumers like to apply internet tool to choose any country sellers website stores in order to stay at home to buy any kinds of products from themselves webstores in global societies.

In fact, online shopping model had been popular for long time above to twenty years. Most of global sellers will make decision to design themselves webstores in order to attract global many online buyers to choose to buy their products from themselves webstores. So, it seems that social consumers purchase behaviors had been changed to online shopping from internet invention.

Hence, social consumers purchase behavioral changes may influence any organizations' strategies need to be changed from visiting shops purchase strategy model to online purchase strategy model, if the seller still concentrate on concentrate on considerate how to design itelf , but neglects to considerate how to design itself webstore, e.g. how to design attract product photos to put on itself webstore, how to arrange sale price information location to be putted on webstore and visa card payment location on itself webstore in order to let any one online buyer can feel very easier to buy itself any kinds of products from itself webstore. Then, its potential online buyers will be influenced to increase number when they can find this online seller itself any kinds of products photes and every kinds of product sale price information and visa card payment channel locations easily from itself webstore.

So, it implies that nowadays any one seller ought need to design one webstore to let any one online overseas and domestic consumers can have chance to click itself webstore to choose any one kind of product to buy conveniently when he/she does not hope to leave him/her home to go to shop, because nowadays social shopping behaviors had been influenced to change when internet invention, them it gives another online purchase method to replace visiting shops purchase method to global any one buyer in nowadays societies.

So, if nowadays any one seller still concentrate on how to design itself shop display in order to put any kinds of product on shelf in order to let any one visiting shop customer to find the kind of product to buy, but it neglects to change to choose to pursue another new technological shopping method, such as webstore purchase method in order to implement effective strategy to design the most right webstore as well as in order to attract global overseas and local consumers to find itself webstore easily from website and find its any one kind of product phots and sale price and visa card payment button in order to choose to buy itself any kinds of products in the short time. Consequently I believe that the seller will lose many customers from overseas and local when its other same or similar product sellers choose to design themselves webstores in order to let global any one product buyer can buy themselves any one kind of product when they can pay visa card to buy their products from them webstores conveniently when they stay at home habitly. Then, the seller will lose many global potential customers in long time.

On conclusion, in behavioral economic view, any consumer behavioral social changing, which will influence any in order to avoid customers number loses significantly . In future time, organizations need to make rapid decision in order to implement the most reasonable and the most useful strategy in order to avoid global potential customers number reduces or lose them in long time. So, social behavioral changing environment ought influence any global organizations need to decide how to change themselves strategies in order to avoid customers loses significantly in future time.

How and why human behavior may influence economic growth or recession?

May ourselves daily behaviors influence our global societial continue economic growth or recession? Do they have cause and effect close relationship between human behaviors and global economic growth or recession? I shall apply behavioral economic theory to analyze and explain whether ourselves daily behaviors and our global societial economic growth or recession which have close cause and effect relationship as below:

Every country itself economic development must depend on any business activities, otherwise, any kinds of business activities must need ourselves business activities or behaviors in order to achieve any business activities as well as achieve the country's overall economic development in macro view.

However, any country's overall business activites or behaviors which must depend on any kinds of individual businessmen, themselves employees daily working behavior or activity or performance in order to help them to attract or increase many clients number to acieve " earning profit" aim. So, it seems that any individual business, itself overall every department individual working behavior is one main factor to influence the company's overall business performance.

For agricultural fruit and meat food farming industry example, such as New Zealand is a farming main target industry country. It had had many New Zealanders were daily themselves own farming businesses for many years. Their farming businesses include growing fruit, sheep, cow, pig pork, meat etc. food sale business. If the New Zealand farmer owned a large size farming land, then he will choose either growing fruit or feeding sheeps, pigs, cows to be meat to to transport to New Zealand supermarkets to help them to sell to their farmers meet to New Zealanders in order to earn profit. Thus, if the New Zealand farmer owned large size of farming lands, then he needs to employ many farming employees (farming workers) to help him to carry on farming business daily tasks, e.g. picking up friuts, feeding pigs, cows, sheeps to eat food daily. These daily farming jobs are very important to influence this New Zealand farmer's meats or fruits sale number whether they can be easy or diffcult to sell in New Zealand supermarkets , if these farming workers can own encough farming knowledge or skill to know how to pick up fruits method and make judgement to know whether it is right time to pick up the kind of fruits from the trees , as well as know how feed this pigs, sheeps, cows to eat food in order to let they are better health. Consequently, their farming behaviors which can let these animals can provide the best taste and enough meat from these animals to let New Zealander to buy to eat from New Zealand any one supermarket. Even these New Zealand farming workers can know whether the kinds of fruits, e.g. oranges, apples, gapes etc. fruits whether they ought be picked up from the trees at the right time. Consequently, they can make judgement to decide to pick up any kinds of the best taste fruits to let any one New Zealander to buy to eat from any one supermarket in New Zealand. Otherwise, if they do not make judegement to know whether the kind of fruit ought not be picked up because they still need longer time to continue grow up to increase fruit size and better taste from the trees in order to let any one fruit buyer can feel better taste when they eat this kind of fruit later. If they can buy this kind of fruit to eat later, then this New Zealand farmer's his fruit buyers can buy the best taste of this kind of fruit to eat from an yone supermarket in New Zealand. Consequently, many New Zealand supermarkets will choose to buy any kinds of fruits from this farmer fruit supplier when they feel this farmer's fruits can provide more better taste fruits to compare other farmers' fruits.

Thus, due to New Zealand is one farming main income source country. It's any kinds of fruits and meats need to be export to overseas to sell , instead of local sale. It's GDP percent is very high to whole country 's overall income source. So, any one New Zealand farmer individual and any one farming worker individual working behavior will influence its economy whether it is influenced to grow or recession possible. Moreover, it also seems that farming workers' farming knowledge and skill will influence themselves farming daily activities to achieve the aim of the number of increase or decrease to any kinds of fruits whether they are better taste or the number of increase of decrease to any kinds of meats whether they are better taste to supply to any one New Zealand fruit or meat buyers to eat from any one New Zealand supermarket. So, it implies that any one New Zealand farming worker individual farming behavior may influence any kinds of fruits or any kinds of meat taste because they are transported to any one supermarket to sell in New Zealand.

Consequently, if New Zealans had many farmers can teach god farming knowledge and skill to let their any one farming workers know how to decide judgement to decide when it is right time to pick up any kinds of fruits from trees , or how to grow them on soil in order to let they can grow rapidly. Then, many different kinds of fruits can be provided to let any one New Zealanders can eat the best taste of fruits when their fruits are supplied to any one New Zealand supermarkets. Even, if they knew how to feed foods to pigs, cows, sheeps to eat daily. Then they can be more health and they can provide the best taste of meats to let any one New Zealanders can buy their meats from any one New Zealand supermarkets. Moreover, their fruits and meats can be transported to overseas to let any one country fruits or meats buyers can choose any kinds of New Zealand meats and fruits to buy to eat from themselves countries supermarkets. Then, many overseas fruit and meat buyers will perfer to choose New Zealand any kinds of fruits or meats to buy to compare other countries fruits or meats to buy when they go to any one local supermarkets.

On conclusion, it seems that New Zealand farming workers themselves farming behavior may influence their farming employers any kinds of fruits or meats sale number and income because their farming task behaviors must influence whether their fruits or meats taste are the better taste or worse taste to compare their other local farmers (the farmer competitors) whose fruits or meats taste. If tthe farmer's any one farming worker can be trained to learn how to know to feed animals skill and when is the most right time to pick up any kinds of fruits from trees or how to grow them on the soil methods. Due to these farming worker individual farming behavior may influence his different finds of fruits and meats sale number to be increase or decrease, so these any one New Zealand farmer must need to depend on any one farming worker whose farming working methods, if their farming working behaviors can be the best to influence any kinds of fruits to grow rapid or any kinds of pigs, cows, sheeps animals grow up rapidly , then their sale number may be increase significantly and their taste can be improved to let any New Zealand or overseas meat or fruit buyer to buy to eat to feel from any one New Zealand or overseas supermarkets, then New Zealand's agriculture industry must be influenced to increase. In the world, any one fruit or meat buyer must choose to buy New Zealand's fruit and meat to eat in prefer to compare other countries' fruits and meats. So, New Zealand's GDP may be influenced to raise from any one New Zealand farming worker individual farming working behaviors.

Reasons why human behavior may influence economic recession or growth?

Can ourselves daily behaviors or activies influence ourselves countries' economic growth or recession? I shall attempt to explain the reasons why they have direct or indirect relationship between human behavior and economy growth or recession as below:

I shall indicate environment pollition case to attempt to explain above question. Our societies had been experiencing servious environment pollution challenge. However, environment pollution , such as air pollution is caused by air planes and vehicles emission by air planes and vehicles emission as well as water pollution is caused by plastic rubblish, or dirty water or oil or gas chemical material, these both kinds of pollution ought may bring economic recession and this both kinds of pollution are caused by human ourselves daily foolish activities.

I believe human behavior and economy and pollution which have cause and effect relationship. I shall analyze this environment pollution case to explain why they have case and effect relationship between human foolish behavior and environment pollution and economic recession as below:

When global societies had many people like to buy cars to drive to bring emission to fresh air on the roads as well as many manufacturing factories will bring emission to pollute fresh air in their manufacturing processes. Factories and cars will bring air pollution , due to factories need to pollute fresh air in order to manufacture many products and car owners need to drive their cars to go to offices or leisure places. Their cars will also bring emisson to pollute fresh air. On consequence, car owners themselves frequent driving behaviors and factory workers themselves frequent manufacturing behaviors may bring environment pollution. Technology or human behavior whether may influence economic growth or recession. Moreover, air planes also brings emission to pollute air when they are flying in sky. Also, when ships bring oil pollution or sea plastic rubbish bring pollution to global oceans.

In fact, manufacturer and cars owners, such as factories workers manufacturing behaviour and car owners driving behaviors and pilots driving air planes flying behaviors and ships transport behaviors, which may cause plastic rubbish, oil or gas emission to sky or sea or on the road to cause ocean and air pollution is serious. However, human ourselves need to buy cars to drive to satisfy ourselves driving leisure or enjoyment, travelers need to catch air planes to travel to enjoy leisure needs, factories workers need help factories to manufacture many products to sell to customers to satisfy their using needs. oil exploration needs to find lands to explore new oil lands.

All of these business and leisure activities may bring serious air and water pollution. However, due to serious air and water pollution will bring earth warming challenge , such as some countries temperature will be influences to rise up to 40 degree or higher or earth warming. However, earth warming is caused by air and ocean pollution. Pollution must be caused by human ourselves, driving cars leisure and factories manufacturing business activities. Hence, if human decided to continue to do these foolish behaviors, we only pursue to manufacture different kinds of industrial products or drive cars to enjoy leisure aims, but we also neglect ourselves behaviors may bring environment pollution. Then, earth warming or earth temperature will be influenced to rise up absolutely in long term. Moreover, if our future earth will be influenced to bring serious high temperature effect by human ourselves these foolish behaviors.

On consequence, warmth warming will bring serious economic losses in possible because when ourselves earth temperature had been influenced to rise up to 40 degree or high. Ourselves health will be caused poor, due to we will feel difficult breath, we must need often tried and hard to work, due to our nervous and health will be influenced to poor by pollution and earth warming effect. Also, we need to pay more money to see doctors when we had long life. Then, our societies will lose may strong labors to help manufacturers to work, e.g. factories will reduce workers number to help manufacturers to produce more different kinds of products, due to workers health is general poor. Due to lacking enough workers to manufacture products, our societies will begin to reduce enough supply number of products to sell to global consumers to satisfy their use needs.

On conclusion, in behavioral economic view, our societies will lose many labors due to their bodies are not health by air and water pollution. Global economic and business activities will be influenced to worse by global workers reducing number reason. So, economic recession will begin to occur in possible when pollution reaches the serious level.

What factors influence future economic development ?

Our global societies had been continue developing, till to nowadays high technological society from farm industry stage. However, what are the influencing factors help our global social economic development in possible? Whether consumer behavioral market development to any kinds of industries factors, or technological development, such as robot invention factor, or human ourselves social behavioral factor, even leading country dominating trading factor, whether which factor may influence global social economic development in possible. I shall attempt to apply “ behavioral economic view” to answer whether which factors may bring direct or indirect influence to our future global social and economic development as below:

In fact, if we hope ourselves country can keep continue develop, we need to make assumption to analyze whether what different factors may bring positive or negative impact to influence ourselves country continue develop in possible.

Firstly, I shall explain whether marketing development factor , which may influence global economic development. I assume that if ourselves country's economic development in possible , for USA IBM computer manufacturer example, if IBM can manufacture many number of laptops to sell to nay countries, IBM laptop marketing development whether it can help USA economic development.

However, I fee that global laptops number had reached the absolute satisfactory need number to global laptop buyers. I mean that there are many laptop buyers do not want often change themselves old laptops or out-of -date laptops to new one. Because they feel need to spend much expenditure to buy any kinds of new laptops within 3 months or more months.

So, in general , global society had had many laptops users do not like often to change old laptops to new laptops . They won't have “ changing new laptops habit”. They like to use old laptops long time. So, although IBM likes to continue invent any kinds of new style of laptops in order to satisfy future laptops buyers individual using computer need, but any kinds of new style of laptops can not attract or persuade they buy easily.

So, global new laptops market development won't be one influencing factor to excite future laptops marketing development easily. New style of laptops need will be decreased. IBM ought not decide to concentrate on spending time and skill to manufacture any new kinds of style of laptops to sell in future global laptop market.

Otherwise, IBM ought concentrate on manufacturing more old style of laptops and keep old sale price in order to persuade many new laptops buyers to choose to buy any kinds of old style of laptops in order to keep IBM laptop marketing can continue develop to global computer market.So, it seems that marketing development won't be one essential influencing factor to let any country itself economy can continue develop in possible.

Moreover, IBM computer manufacturing case example, consumer behavior changing factor may be one influencing factor may be one influencing factor to influence any country itself economic development in possible. For IBM laptop example,

IBM laptop old users had begun to feel it is not essential to let them to change any kinds of new style of laptops often. Themselves traditional " frequent changing of new style of laptops consumer behavior" had changed to " avoiding changing of new style of laptops consumer behavior". So, such as BM laptop case, IBM laptops consumer behavior factor may influence whether future IBM laptop can keep sale increasing number, due to IBM laptops users, they do not like often change many new kinds of style of laptops , they like to use old style of laptops long time. Hence, IBM laptops need to find new method to decide how to excite old laptops users mind , they can accept to use new style of laptops often.

Consequently, it is only one way to change global IBM laptop users ' mind to accept "changing any kinds of new style of laptops " mind in order to make frequent purchase decision of future new style of laptops behavior easily. Then, when global IBM users' mind can be influenced to make purchase decision to frequent changing new style of laptops behavior. The, IBM laptops future any kinds of new style of laptops which sale number may be influenced to continue increase by " changing IBM laptops frequent changing new style of new laptops factor". So, consumer behavior may be one essential factor to influence future global economic development.

When we can learn behavioral economy, can our future societies can be influenced to change to be better or improve our future lives to be better or comfortable or reduce social cost etc. advantges?

Behavioral economists work to understand what consumers do and why they make the choices they make. Such economists also assist markets in helping consumers make those decisions. Behavioral economists may work for the government to shape public policy to protect consumers. Behavioral economics plays a vital role in diagnosing what's driving current behaviors and increasing our effectiveness in designing interventions to shift those behaviors. While behavioral insights alone aren't sufficient to solve most of the complex social issues we face, ignoring them is a sure way to limit our effectiveness. For exmaple,we spent a lot of energy, in many domains — technological, scientific, hard work, creativity, human ingenuity — to crack important social problems with technology solutions. That's been the discoveries of the last 2,000 years, that's mankind moving forward. When human learn behavioral eonomy, can our behavior can be influenced to spend lives expense, e.g. reducing driving time, or bath time in order to help global society to reduce social cost in behavioral economic view. Many times we (and our environments) are our own worst enemies. We know what we should do, but keep putting it off until tomorrow. Low and behold, tomorrow never comes.If you discover it's a problem of getting over these hurdles, it's a much different approach than if the intention isn't there. You might make the desired behavior the default choice so there's no hurdle. You might offer a small, immediate incentive to overcome the hurdle. You might get them to make a public commitment to take action. Or you may find ways to demonstrate that the desired behavior is the norm.If intention is there but action is lacking, look at their social network. Is there social pressure against the desired behavior? Is the dominant norm fighting your efforts? Is there competitive messaging pushing for a different behavior?

Behavioural economics is a useful tool to help influence (or 'Nudge') the decisions people make. It can potentially help them to do things which are better for themselves or for society as a whole. But it is just one of the tools available when planning and designing a social marketing programme. The economy also affects things like the cost of living, access to healthcare and education, and even things like crime rates. When people have more money, they are generally able to afford better healthcare and education, and are less likely to turn to crime as a way to make ends meet. Behavioral economics sheds light on most every day activities and why we consume goods and services the way we do, why we make certain choices about ourselves or others, and how we decide courses of action.

Reason invention may bring economic growth

Can human behavior may help economic growth? Why human behavior and economic growth have close relationship? I believe that productivity growth in different industries, how the shares of wages and profits, how taxation affects growth, how inventions which can bring global economic growth, create working chance, sale income chance, consumption chance, productivity chance, wealth chance. These factors may bring global short term or long term economic growth. All of these factors hace close relationship between human invention and economic growth. I shall explain as below:

For any kinds of things inventions example, are best regarded as a form of investments, and their volume depends in like manner, on their expected profitability. Investments opportunities are recreated by inventions investment. However, inventions may not be economig growth factor, but there is a high profitability that prior circumstances will bring them about, so learning from human past prior experience is important not just in scientific or engineering matters, but in other fields, such as business and social organization. So, research and development, such as human invention behavior which has chance to bring long term or short term economic growth.

I mean that human invention may be one kind of investment opportunity to bring global economic growth in possibility, because human new knowledge learning behavior may attribute to global new business invention chance to bring unlimited economic growth chance in nowadays society.

Hence, human can not neglect to create ourselves " invention mind or invention behavior" in order to help global economic growth more easily. SO, human invention may be one kind helping global economic growth new investment opportunuty, which is created from " human learning behavior". IN fact, an improvement in investmednt opportunity method may be created by human " any kinds of new inventions behavior". SO, nowadays society, any kinds of new inventions of product, whcih ought help global societies to bring economic growth chance.

The theory of economic growth may be based on income, labor and land which every one kknows and which are adequate. However, nowadays society had changed, such as scientific invention example, it can bring profit chance to business, creating job opportunities in global labor markets, such as smart phones, laptops, desktops, non-manual driving vehicles, electric energy cars invention etc. any kinds of new scientific invention products, they can bring new scientifical products businessess chance, they must need to employ may manufacture labour, salespeople, transport workers,logistic store workers, admin stafs, transport workers, product invention staffs , marketing promotion staffs etc. different job positions to let global human can have chance to find these jobs to do in order to earn income. Moreover, any kinds of scientific product inventions , which can bring many new jobs positions chance to let global unemployed people hace chance to work and earn incoime.Also, any kinds of new scientific products invention may create many new jobs chance to global and solve unequal wealth and income allocation problem to global human, even businesses have chance to sell these new scientific invention products to sell to global buyers to earn more profit.

I mean that " new products invention" may help global societies to reduce unemployment challenge and it can bring long term economic growth in global labour market view. Moreover, when any

kinds of new product inventions, such as battery energy vehicle, non-manual driving auto vehicle or public transport tools, home washing machines, televisions, radios, fans, smart phomnes, laptops, electronic book reading tools, internet invention etc, different kinds of new scientific product inventions, they can bring " consumption opportunity" to let global consumers have chance to buy any kinds of new scientific inventionw, which can also encourage global consumption rate raises in order to increase global wealth improvement rate speed rises up radidly.

So, global wealth rising rate whether which is rapid or slow, it depends on whether how many different kinds of new scientific products invention may be confirmed to scceed to sell in global business market. Hence, investment on invention, which may be tangible evidence to create economic growth in the distribution of income , wages and profits between global labor, scientific inventions of products sellers, and global scientific inventions of products consumers. They have close relationship to be influenced to increas economic growth speed whether they are rapid or slow from " global scientific new products inventions". If human product invention scientists can attempt to research how to invent any kinds of undiscovered new kinds of products inventions, for example, if global any kinds of scientific product invention scientistis can attempt to invest time to invent 100 kinds of new scientific products inventions in orde to provide global human have chance to buy to use. Then, these 100 different kinds of scientific invention products may help global new invention of scientific products sellers to provide many different kinds of new jobs vacancies to let global unemployed or job seekers have chance to work and earn income.

So, global unemployed rate will have chance to reduce in global societies. Moreover, they can also help these new scientific products sellers to bring " earning profit chance", even thes global

" new product invention scientists who have earn product invention royalty income chance after they can invent any kinds of products in success. Finally, global consumption market growth rate will be influenced to rise up, when in the year, there are 100 new kinds of nre scientific products invention have been already sold to let global consumers hacew chance to choose the kind of target of scientific product to buy to use. So, global new economic growth rate speed , it can rise up rapid up or slow down, it depends on whether the year, global has how many kinds of new invention of scientific products" have been invented to prepare to sell in global scientific products sale market

in macro economic view.

Hence, economic growth and human invention behavior, which have cloase relationship . The list of anti-growth factors could be extended perhaps however. Hartwell (1983) has pointed out that economies have always contained a mixture of three main systems for making production, consumption, and distribution decisions namely, administered and market free enterprise. It was the gradual freeing of man's entrepreneurial talents from the bonds of custom and command that finally resulted in the remarkable economic growth of the industrial revolution.

However, in the twrms of human history, sustained economic growth is rare, and this suggests that several conditions (Needham's Packet), rather than memely one or two , have had to be met before it earns occur. It is also the case, however, that its occurrence has at least in some respects made its survival more probable. HUman scientific investment has improved communications, such as smart phone, internet email and increased education (learning) chance, such as distancel learning, AI learning writing method, listening language learning method, , reading e-books from smart phone, laptop channel method, which can chance traditional classroom leanring method to new scientific channel learning method or which can change traditional telephone or post lewtter communication method to nowadays sending email, smart phone calling, whataps new scientific tool communication methos.

Reason invention may bring economic growth

Can human behavior may help economic growth? Why human behavior and economic growth have close relationship? I believe that productivity growth in different industries, how the shares of wages and profits, how taxation affects growth, how inventions which can bring global economic growth, create working chance, sale income chance, consumption chance, productivity chance, wealth chance. These factors may bring global short term or long term economic growth. All of these factors hace close relationship between human invention and economic growth. I shall explain as below:

For any kinds of things inventions example, are best regarded as a form of investments, and their volume depends in like manner, on their expected profitability. Investments opportunities are recreated by inventions investment. However, inventions may not be economig growth factor, but there is a high profitability that prior circumstances will bring them about, so learning from human past prior experience is important not just in scientific or engineering matters, but in other fields, such as business and social organization. So, research and development, such as human invention behavior which has chance to bring long term or short term economic growth.

I mean that human invention may be one kind of investment opportunity to bring global economic growth in possibility, because human new knowledge learning behavior may attribute to global new business invention chance to bring unlimited economic growth chance in nowadays society.

Hence, human can not neglect to create ourselves " invention mind or invention behavior" in order to help global economic growth more easily. SO, human invention may be one kind helping global economic growth new investment opportunuty, which is created from " human learning behavior". IN fact, an improvement in investmednt opportunity method may be created by human " any kinds of new inventions behavior". SO, nowadays society, any kinds of new inventions of product, whcih ought help global societies to bring economic growth chance.

The theory of economic growth may be based on income, labor and land which every one kknows and which are adequate. However, nowadays society had changed, such as scientific invention example, it can bring profit chance to business, creating job opportunities in global labor markets, such as smart phones, laptops, desktops, non-manual driving vehicles, electric energy cars invention etc. any kinds of new scientific invention products, they can bring new scientifical products businessess chance, they must need to employ may manufacture labour, salespeople, transport workers,logistic store workers, admin stafs, transport workers, product invention staffs , marketing promotion staffs etc. different job positions to let

global human can have chance to find these jobs to do in order to earn income. Moreover, any kinds of scientific product inventions , which can bring many new jobs positions chance to let global unemployed people hace chance to work and earn incoime.Also, any kinds of new scientific products invention may create many new jobs chance to global and solve unequal wealth and income allocation problem to global human, even businesses have chance to sell these new scientific invention products to sell to global buyers to earn more profit.

I mean that " new products invention" may help global societies to reduce unemployment challenge and it can bring long term economic growth in global labour market view. Moreover, when any

kinds of new product inventions, such as battery energy vehicle, non-manual driving auto vehicle or public transport tools, home washing machines, televisions, radios, fans, smart phomnes, laptops, electronic book reading tools, internet invention etc, different kinds of new scientific product inventions, they can bring " consumption opportunity" to let global consumers have chance to buy any kinds of new scientific inventionw, which can also encourage global consumption rate raises in order to increase global wealth improvement rate speed rises up radidly.

So, global wealth rising rate whether which is rapid or slow, it depends on whether how many different kinds of new scientific products invention may be confirmed to scceed to sell in global business market. Hence, investment on invention, which may be tangible evidence to create economic growth in the distribution of income , wages and profits between global labor, scientific inventions of products sellers, and global scientific inventions of products consumers. They have close relationship to be influenced to increas economic growth speed whether they are rapid or slow from " global scientific new products inventions". If human product invention scientists can attempt to research how to invent any kinds of undiscovered new kinds of products inventions, for example, if global any kinds of scientific product invention scientistis can attempt to invest time to invent 100 kinds of new scientific products inventions in orde to provide global human have chance to buy to use. Then, these 100 different kinds of scientific invention products may help global new invention of scientific products sellers to provide many different kinds of new jobs vacancies to let global unemployed or job seekers have chance to work and earn income.

So, global unemployed rate will have chance to reduce in global societies. Moreover, they can also help these new scientific products sellers to bring " earning profit chance", even thes global " new product invention scientists who have earn product invention royalty income chance after they can invent any kinds of products in success. Finally, global consumption market growth rate will be influenced to rise up, when in the year, there are 100 new kinds of nre scientific products invention have been already sold to let global consumers hacew chance to choose the kind of target of scientific product to buy to use. So, global new economic growth rate speed , it can rise up rapid up or slow down, it depends on whether the year, global has how many kinds of new invention of scientific products" have been invented to prepare to sell in global scientific products sale market in macro economic view.

Hence, economic growth and human invention behavior, which have cloase relationship . The list of anti-growth factors could be extended perhaps however. Hartwell (1983) has pointed out that economies have always contained a mixture of three main systems for making production, consumption, and distribution decisions namely, administered and market free enterprise. It was the gradual freeing of man's entrepreneurial talents from the bonds of custom and command that finally resulted in the remarkable economic growth of the industrial revolution.

However, in the twrms of human history, sustained economic growth is rare, and this suggests that several conditions (Needham's Packet), rather than memely one or two , have had to be met before it earns occur. It is also the case, however, that its occurrence has at least in some respects made its survival more probable. HUman scientific investment has improved communications, such as smart phone, internet email and increased education (learning) chance, such as distancel learning, AI learning writing method, listening language learning method, , reading e-books from smart phone, laptop channel method, which can chance traditional classroom leanring method to new scientific channel learning method or which can change traditional telephone or post lewtter communication method to nowadays sending email, smart phone calling, whataps new scientific tool communication methos.

ON conclusion, the free societies are influenced by any kinds of new scientific products inventions, Human had began to accept how attempted to buy any kinds of new scientific products inventions to use. New scientific inventions of products, which has bring more fashable of undiscovered new scientifical inventions of products choice to satisfy human ourselves daily new products invention using needs in our daily lives. SO, human scientists whose any kinds of new products inventions which will bring more chance to help global societies to create new social economic growth in global societies. Social change occurs due to various factors such as demographic, technological, cultural, political, economic and educational. These factors often act in concert resulting in changes either in a serial manner or something in parallel too. Among of technological invention, marketing development, consumer behavior factors, it is only consumer behavior factor , it can bring serious economic development to any countries in ourselves future societies.

Reference

Hartwell, R.M. (1983). The origins of capitalism. A Methodological Eassy. in Pejovich (1983).

Needham, J. (1963), Poverties and Triumphs of the Chinese scientific tradition, in Crombie (1963).

ReplyReply allForward

CHAPTER FIVE

Factors cause new products development

- Consumer leisure need whether it has what relationship between economy?

Consumer leisure need whether is more and less whether it has what relationship between economy? Also whether the country's economy recession or growth, can it influence consumer leisure need to increase or decrease ? I shall attempt to apply behavioral economy theory to explain whether they have cause and effect relationship as below:

In our societies, there are so many different kinds of leisure activities, also any kinds of leisure consumers can follow the kind of leisure activity's price factor, enjoyable feeling factor, satisfactory feeling factor, lesiure time need factor to influence the leisure consumer individual final choice to which kind of leisure activity among the different kinds of leisure needs. For example, travel leisure activity ought be the most experience, spending of leisure expense to compare general sport lesiure, e.g. swimming , playing basketballs , table tennis, tennis, football, purchae tickets seeing movies, purchase tickets listening music, purchase electronic playing games to stay at homes to play.

In simiarity, it uses only considers leisure price aspect, we shall do the comparable and reasonable decision is that travelling activity ought be the kind of leisure activity, any leisure consumers ought spend the least leisure times to enjoy this kind of leisure activity, e.g. one year has only one time or two-to-five times for overseas for overseas travel. But, in fact, in global there are many travellers, they can make many times of travelling frequent decision, e.g. they can spend one week at least time to go to overseas to travel per month. Hence, it means that global some travellers like to buy air ticket to go to overseas to travel, they spend average one month and one time overseas travel.

In fact, tourism agents hope to attract travellers to choose travelling leisure activity, they will attempt to decrease air ticket price in order to increase travellers number. However, some cheap travelling package price can persuade global some travellers accept to pay cheap price to bu air ticket to spend several days to go to the country to travel enjoy their holidays.

So, it seems that cheap air tcket price strategy, it can attract some countries travellers to accept to spend some time for their overseas holiday their overseas travelling leisure activity can explain why leisure price must be main element factor to influence leisure consumers to reduce spending amount to pay for the kind of leisure activity , such as travelling lesiure activity is one kind of good lesiure activity example.

Otherwise, some kinds of leisure activities, ever their lesiure prices are cheap, it must not influence them to like to spend much time to enjoy them, e.g. swimming, riding bicycles leisure activities, although those kinds of sport leisure activities prices must be very cheap to compare travelling activities , it can must influence many young people like to buy bicycles to ridem even they are proficient bicycle riders or they like to buy tickets to go public swimming pools to swin. The factors may include these both kinds of sports are tired sport leisures, any one must need more body energy to do these sports. Moreover, for student leisure consumers, although these both kinds sports prices, such as bicycles and swimming pool purchase tickets, they are cheap to students, but in fact, students must need to spend time to learn, if they often spend time to enjoy these both of sport activities, they will feel fear that they can not concentrate on spending learning time, if they spend on sport leisure time.

Hence, in behavioral economy view, it explains that lesiure price whether it is high or low, it is not main factor to influence any leisure consumers to do leisure kind of choice, such as sport case to student leisure consumers, they will not choose to spend much time on sport lesiure aspect, because the hard students must feel fear to influence their learning effort when they often spend time on sport leisure aspect. Otherwise, for a sport professonal, e.g. proficient riding bicycle sportman, he may accept to spend expensive price to buy one expensive bicycle , e.g. when he feels the US$3,000 bicycle, it can help him to improve riding speed skills, he won't choose to buy the another US$1,000 bicycle, when he feels that it can not help him to improve riding speed skill, hence, it also explains that the leisure produt high price , it must not influence lesisure consumers number to reduce, it depends on whether the leisure product function to the leisure consumer, e.g. for riding bicycle sport men , they may accept to pay higher price to buy more expensive bicycles , because the hope that the bicyces can help them to comprove their riding speed to more rapid. Otherwise, for student bicycle consumers, they won't compare different kinds of bicycles prices in order to decide whether which kind of bicycles are the most suitable to them to buy to ride.

Hence, behavioral economic theory can explain that price must not be the main factor to influence lesiure consumers' lesiure activities choices, their lesiure need psychological and leisure product individual function factors was also influence their lesiure activities choices.

What are main factors influence global product manufacturers and consumers feel to enjoy how to research new product manufacture and change any kinds of new products using needs? I shall attempt to apply consumer psychological and technological improvement (development) psychological factors to explain why human needs often to use products to replace old products needing mind in our future societies.

Our societies had been experiencing high population growth, special in China and India both countries, their population growth had risen rapidly as well as a climb up in the kind of transformative technological development, e.g. robots invention, non-manual auto driving vehicles, battery charge energy vehicles improvement, smart phones, laptops etc. technological products had been invented to replace old technological products. For example, telephones had been replaced from mobiles, till to smart phone products invention; gas energy vehicles may be replaced by electronic charge vehicles, battery charge vehicles, even non-manual auto driving vehicles, computers had been replaced by desktops, even laptops and notebooks etc. new technological products improvement. SO, in our future societies, many old technological products may be influenced to use and need to improve by human oursleves enjoying and using improved technological products needs. Old technological products are needed to innovate in order to satisfy future human ourselves new technological products using needs.

Moreover, when one technological product manufacturer feels need to innovate itself products, e.g. IBM computers are innovated to notebooks or laptops from desktops, to bring using satisfactory needs feeling : light weight and small size, convenient carrying on feeling. SO, IBM computer products are one kind of highly innovative capitalism driven , it can bring multiplies computer invention , job opportunity to create many new job positions to let global computer professional can earn income from IBM new computersproduct improvement pursue. SO, products improvement can help global job positions number increases and it can reduce unemployment number in global labour market.

However, internet invention had brought new using impact to our societies.

IN the past, telephones and typing machines communication products result of innovation in communication alone, people with the most minimal of internet connection today have unprecedented access to health-related information. The forward march of malaria, tuberculosis and HIV?AIDS had been slowed, even as antibiotic resistance is a new problem. There is no doubt that the interconnectivity between the Big data computer revoluation and medical research is transforming the medical field.

Monty transaction technology had been innovated by internet communication channel. Some call it the global Paypal, Payoneer online payments system, succeeded. This kind of new online payment transaction system, it can assist global purchase and sale transactions carry on transaction activities rapidly between sellers and buyers. It can replace traditional bank electronic payment transactions method. Many merchants began to accept to use online transaction payment system to replace bank electronic payment system. So, paypal and payoneer both onlne payment system can replace many bank electronic payment systems, they are their online transaction service competitors in global social money transaction business sector.

Among the residual factors left after differences in growth rates of the quantity of capital and labour had been allowed for new products innovation and quality differences, consumer using need changing differences , especially those resulting from technical progress and education, seemed to deserve much more attention. Human capital , and with it's education and transfer of technology and technical asistance, and manpower planning, they are assumed a new importance in thinking about future new technological product development increasing needs, such as distance learning had been influenced to develop by internet invnetion. It helps many university students can apply internet online technological learning channel to enrol any one overseas university learn. So, many overseas students do not need to spend renting rooms , foods, transport expenditure to leave themselves hometowns to arrive another country's university to study. So, distance learning , online learning learning method can satisfy many overseas students their reducing living expenditures needs when they decide to study in overseas. It is new kind of new educational and learning technological innovation to replace traditional classroom teaching method in global education sector.

Finally, one product invention brings funding need skill,the new and old skills of products improvement may help product manufacturers to make and raise money (creating new business chance). To generate funding in a new technological world, br it via revenues, investment capital, donation or loans to help product manufacturers to develop a freash set of skills, different from the ones needed to make things happen in the twentieth century. What are the differences between old power funding skills and new power funding skills.

In the past, old power funding skills include traditional salesman, proven credentials and technical experise, ability to development between consumers and manufacturers , capacity to navigate complex bureaucratic systems and creating a luxury ability. Otherwise, in ourselves future, new power funding skills include universally accessible stroytelling, a compelling personal or group discussion skill, ability to mobilize a crowd and key social influencers, capacity to navigate complex community dynamics, creating a participative proble.

Hence, when on product manufacturer decides to invent or improve one kind of old product to be new or fresh using experience to global consumers. They must need to learn how to raise money source from loans or shareholders increasing number or donation from old power funding skills to new power funding skills method. In this new funding skills learning stage, every department staffs can learn how to change or discuss themselves organizational behavior in order to achieving in raising funding aim to innovate themselves old products to new products dream. SO, their " needing raising funding" direction may excite them to continue to innovate themselves new products pursue in behavioral economy view.

On conclusion, product developement may encourage economic growth, due to global consumers began to accept to use new improvement products to satisfy consumers ourselves using and enjoying needs , when global new product improvement consumers number increases, new product manufacturers need to employ many workers and product inventors to manufacture many number of new products to satisfy global consumers using new product demands.

It can encourage global economic growth rapidly because workers and product researchers employees number will increase. So, unemployement rate will reduce when global had many people have jobs to do, spending desire will rise, global GDP growth may be influenced to rise up in long term. All of above factors may influence new product development pursue to global manufacturers.

CHAPTER SIX

DNA reproductive technology and social change relationship

Can DNA reproductive technology bring only positive impact to influence our social behavior change?
Human's medical technology had been continue developed to improve to satisfy our medical need, such as cancer patient medical different new drug research, it aims to help future cancer patients to avoid death. However, future human's new medical research will research on DNA biological medical improvement . So, future DNA biological medical technology may bring good or bad social impact, e.g. reproductive animal, such as pig, cow animals . So, when many pigs and cows can be reproduced. Then, pigs and cows number can increase. Consequently, porks beefs meats food number can be also been increased by DNA biological medical reproductive cell technology improvement.

It is good aspect to bring enough meats supply to global , when future DNA biological medical technology can be developed to the reprodctive many cows and pigs number stage in order to raise porks and beefs food number. However, DNA biological cell reproductive technology can also bring bad impact to our society, if one day human can apply DNA biological cell reprodutive technology to reproduce another ourselves, it means that reproductive human why is it bad new? if ne DNA scientist decides to help one country ambitious leader to reproduce himself, then when the country ambitious leader dies, but his another reproductive himself person can aontiue to bring war crisis to global, such as Japan's past leader, he was one ambitious leader to dominate global countries. If DNA reproductive technology is applied to help him to reproduce this Japan ambitious another himself . Then, the another new world war may be occurred easily. So, I also worry about future DNA reproductive technology may be applied to help the ambitous bad people to reproduce themselves to bring our societies safety and economic recession negative impact.
So, it brings this question: Can DNA reproductive technology bring only positive impact to influence our social behavior change? I shall attempt to explain as below:

Can DNA reproductive technology bring only positive impact to influence our social behavior change?
Human's medical technology had been continue developed to improve to satisfy our medical need, such as cancer patient medical different new drug research, it aims to help future cancer patients to avoid death. However, future

human's new medical research will research on DNA biological medical improvement . So, future DNA biological medical technology may bring good or bad social impact, e.g. reproductive animal, such as pig, cow animals . So, when many pigs and cows can be reproduced. Then, pigs and cows number can increase. Consequently, porks beefs meats food number can be also been increased by DNA biological medical reproductive cell technology improvement.

It is good aspect to bring enough meats supply to global , when future DNA biological medical technology can be developed to the reprodctive many cows and pigs number stage in order to raise porks and beefs food number. However, DNA biological cell reproductive technology can also bring bad impact to our society, if one day human can apply DNA biological cell reprodutive technology to reproduce another ourselves, it means that reproductive human why is it bad new? if ne DNA scientist decides to help one country ambitious leader to reproduce himself, then when the country ambitious leader dies, but his another reproductive himself person can aontiue to bring war crisis to global, such as Japan's past leader, he was one ambitious leader to dominate global countries. If DNA reproductive technology is applied to help him to reproduce this Japan ambitious another himself . Then, the another new world war may be occurred easily. So, I also worry about future DNA reproductive technology may be applied to help the ambitous bad people to reproduce themselves to bring our societies safety and economic recession negative impact. So, it brings this question: Can DNA reproductive technology bring only positive impact to influence our social behavior change? I shall attempt to explain as below:

How does DNA attract our behavior? In some situations, genes play a larger role in determining your behavior. How can genetic technologies impact society ? Although, genetic technology has a great potential to change the medical practice as we know it also has a potential to be misused , it also has a potential to be misused, and lead to further health disparities, discrimination and inequality in the human societies around the world.

However, I believe that those the ways that genetic engineering can help human society. Several works have been done on genetic engineering with major focus on its importance ranging from increasing plant and animal food productio, diagnosing disease condition, medical treatment improvement, as well as production of vaccines and other useful drugs.

● What is the focus of behavioral generics?

Behavioral genetics is the study of genetic and environmental influences on behaviors. By examining genetic influence, more information can be gleaned about how the environment operates to affect behavior. So, in behavioral economic view, gene DNA reproductive cell technology may seem to bring these benefits. Some benefits of genetic engineerinf in agricultures are increased crop yoelds, reduced need for food or drug production, reduced need for pesticides, enhanced nutrient composition and food quality , resistance to past and disease , greater food security, and medical benefits to the world's growing population . Also, the intangible , non economic measurement, possible

benefit of genetic engineering may include more nutritious food, tastier food, disease -and-drought resistant plants that require fewer environment resources , such as water and fertilizers, less use of pesticides, increased supply of food with reduced cost and larger shelf life, faster growing plants and animals.

All of these benefits, they can not measured by economic calculation, but they can be felt by us. So, in our social behevioral economic view to genetic engineering, it may bring both positive and negative impact to our societies. On negative impact, these are many risks involves in genetic engineering, the release of genetically altered organisms in the environment can increase human suffering, disease animal welfare, and lead to ecological disasters are positive impact aspect, it can help to defeat diseases, getting rid of all illnesses in young and unborn children potential to live longer, produce new foods, organisms can be tailor-made , faster growth in animals and plants, pests and diseases resistance. But genetic engineering can also bring risks to our societies, e.g. new allergens in the food supply, antibiotic reistance, production of new toxins, concentration of toxic metals, enhancement of the environment for toxic fungi, unknown harms, gene transfer to wild ot weedy relations, change in herbicide use patterns.

By knocking out genes repsonsible for certain conditions, it is possible to create animal model organism of " human disease" as well as producing hotmenes, vaccies and other drugs. So, if DNA can bring human diseases, it means that it can also bring economic loss to our societies, because human disease may bring illness to any one to cause low productivity to any industry development, if the factory has many people human disease from reproductive animal cell accident risk. Then, the ill worker number increases, low productivities and inefficiencies will cause to the factory. If global has many factory workers got human disease from reproductive animal cell accidently. Then, global factries products producing number must have been influenced to fallen down.

How does DNA attract our behavior? In some situations, genes play a larger role in determining your behavior. How can genetic technologies impact society ? Although, genetic technology has a great potential to change the medical practice as we know it also has a potential to be misused , it also has a potential to be misused, and lead to further health disparities, discrimination and inequality in the human societies around the world.

However, I believe that those the ways that genetic engineering can help human society. Several works have been done on genetic engineering with major focus on its importance ranging from increasing plant and animal food productio, diagnosing disease condition, medical treatment improvement, as well as production of vaccines and other useful drugs.

Consequently, global manufacturers will encountered serious loss, due to their products producing speed is slow and their different kinds of products supply number must decrease, if global will workers number increases, they are caused by reproductive animal cell disease. Hence, DNA genetic reproductive technology may also bring global economic loss crisis in possible.

CHAPTER SEVEN

How applying behavioral economic skill to organizations and societies

Behavioral economics is the study of the psychological, cognitive, emotional, cultural and social factors involved in the decisions of individuals or institutions, and how these decisions deviate from those implied by classical economic theory.

Behavioral economics is grounded in empirical observations of human behavior, which have demonstrated that people do not always make what neoclassical economists consider the "rational" or "optimal" decision, even if they have the information and the tools available to do so.

Behavioral economics combines elements of economics and psychology to understand how and why people behave the way they do in the real world. It differs from neoclassical economics, which assumes that most people have well-defined preferences and make well-informed, self-interested decisions based on those preferences.

Behavioral economics is often related with normative economics. It draws on psychology and economics to explore why people sometimes make irrational decisions, and why and how behavior diverges from the predictions of economic models. Behavioral economics is the study of psychology that analyzes the economic decisions people make. Moreover, behavioral economics explains that humans are not rational and are incapable of making good decisions.

How organizations need to learn behavioral economic skill to improve employees performance ?

A study on human behavior has revealed that 90% of the working population can be classified into four basic personality types: Optimistic, pessimistic, trusting. However, the latter of the four types. Envious is the most common, with 30% compared to 20% of each of the organization whole employee individual economic behavior, economic behavior occurs in a climate of formal and informal organizational rukes. These rules often act as incentives, e.g. appreciation, job promotion, increasing salary. These rules often act as incentives and influence the choices employees make , in general employees chooce to work desk jobs that do not keep to fit, and how they have to make more time to stay healthy.

In organizational behavioral economic view, whether they have cause and effect relationship between employees how to use resources behaviors and organizational resource excess use within organizations ?
In organizational behavioral economic view, whether they have cause and effect relationship between employees how to use resources behaviors and organizational resource excess use within organizations. For example, if the organization has many employees number, whether the organization will use its any internal tangible and intangible resources easily per day.

For construction organization example, one construction organization must need to buy different kinds of construction materials to prepare to let workers to help it to manufacture different kinds of properties or houses (products) in order to sell to property buyers. In its every building construction site, it will need more or less workers, they are needed to use different kinds of construction materials to build housess in different construction sites. I assume that construction site (A), it has 100 construction workers number, every day, construction site (A) 100 workers need to use different kinds of construction materials to help them to build 3 building floors wall at least floor number in the construction site (A).
I assume that these 100 construction workers , they include proficient workers and not proficient workers. For proficient construction workers group, they have 50 number, and not proficient construction workers group, they also have 50 number . Hence, the proficient construction workers only need to spend 3 hours maximum and use less number of constructoin materials, then they can finish to build 3 building floors wall per day.

I also assume that all constructoin material supply number is limited. It means that due to this construction firm needs to pre-booking to purchase this kind of the best quality of constructoin material from overseas before three worths. So, it must not have enough time to pre-booking to purchase this kind of best quality of constructoin materials when they are used rapaidly within one month, due to this one month is the final finishing time to this construction firm within one month. Hence, limited construction material supply number and limited finishing time to build this new 40 floors house within this final one month .

So , not proficient construction workers number , limit number of construction material and per day 8 hours which is its limited resources in behavioral eocnomy view. Moreover, total 50 proficient and not proficient 50 construction workers (human resource employees number) will cause this constructoin firm , it will possible need to build this new 40 floors house are more than one month, if these 50 proficient construction workers , they have more than 30 at least number, they are absent to cause their overall construction workers‘ efficiency to be fallen down, due to the other 50 not proficient constuction numbers must need their teaching how to cooperate ad how use less materials to build this new 40 floor hourse rapidly in order to raise overall constructon team efficiency and avoid to delay more than one month time to build this 40 floors new house successfully within this final one month time.

Hence, it explains that when one organization has more employees, it does not represent that this organization must need to use more resource to achieve its any mission, such as this construction firm case, although it has 50 not proficient construction workers, they need to use more construction materials to build this new 40 floors house in this construction site (A). But, in fact, it has other 50 proficient construction workers, they know how to reduce construction materials to build every building floor wall for this new 40 floors building house. So, they can teach the not proficient building workers to know hoe to avoid to use extra excess constructon material to finish to construct every building fllor wall. SO, although, it has 50 not proficient construction workers number, but they can be taught to learn how to reduce to use these limited the best quality of construction materials to build this 40 floors new house. It implies that if the construction workers number can increase, e.g. increases more 50 not proficient construction workers, this the best quality of construction material resource number must not need to increase demand, because this construction site (A) has 50 proficient construction workers , they can teach these 50 not proficient construction workers how to avoid to use extra excess this kind of high quality construction material to build this new 40 floor house efficiently and effectively within this one month.

Hence, if this construction firm won't have more than 30 proficient workers number is absent in this final one month, it will have enough proficient construction workers to teach these 50 not proficient construction workers to know how to use this high quality of construction materials to build this 40 floors new house building in order to avoid waste or construction material need shortage challenge occurs in this final one month time.

Consequently , it ought finish to build this 40 floors new house building within this month. Hence, it explains why its this kind of high quality of construction material resource need must not increase, because if its all proficient construction workers is absent and their absent number is less than 30, then they have enough proficient construction workers number , they can teach this 50 not proficient construction workers how to avoid to use extra excess construction materials resource number in order to have enough construction material resource supply to satisfy this new 40 floors building house to finish construction within one month finishing date need.

On conclusion, in organizational behavioral economic view, it explains that resource use need must not be influenced to increase when the organization's employees number increase. It depends on whether the organization has how many talent and proficient workers number in order to assist them and teach the not proficient employees how to use resource to manufacture any kinds of products in order to avoid to spend extra excess of resource need. Hence, organizational behavioral economic view, it can explain that any organization's increase to employees number, it does not mean that its resource number is also needed to increase. Moreover, in organizational behavioral economic view, it also explains that if the organization can have many proficient workers to help it to do any complex tasks, they will help it to bring avoiding waste or excess extra resource to use advantage, because they ought know whether how they work, they can help the organization to improve performance or raise efficiency e.g. car manufacture, computer manufacture, television manufcture etc. home electronic products or car leisure products. Due to that manufacturre processes are complex, if the organization can have more proficient high skillful workers to help it to manufacture their products. They ought help it to use lesser manufacturing time and less manufacturing resource to finish any above these products to compare not proficient or low skillful manufacture workers. So, in long time, the organization must may earn economic low cost benefits from proficient worker individual high manufacturing skillful knowledge behavior or performance. So, organizational behavioral economic theory explains why even the organization plans to increase employees number, it's resources number won't be influenced to increase rapidly because when the organization's proficient high skillful workers number is more 2 times at least than not proficient low skillful workers number. They ought have enough effort to train and teach and cooperate with the not proficient low skillful manufacture workers to improve their manufacture skills in order to raise manufacturing efficiency and reduce extra excess resources waste and avoid to bring long term resource waste economic loss.

So, any manufacturing organizations must need to increase proficient workers number to assist the not proficient low skillful workers to learn how to improve their skills and know how to reduce to use excess resources to keep to manufacture the highest number of products aim frequently. Consequently, the organization will bring long term low resource use manufacturing economic benefit.

So, behavioral economic theory explain any organization will need have behavioral skills to dominate employee individual performance to raise. Behavioral skills are interpersonal, self-regulatory, and task-related behaviors that connect to successful performance in education and workplace settings. The behavioral skills are designed to help individuals succeed thorough effecttive interactions, stress management and persistent effort in any organizations. for task-oriented behavioral skills examples, they may include: active always buy with something, ambitious, strongly wants to succeed, cautious, being very careful, conscientious, taking time to do things right and creative, someone who can make up things easily or think of new things. The six important employee behaviors in organizations are employee productivity, absenteeism, turnover, organizational citizenship behavior, job satisfaction and workplace misbehavior. So, managers need have good behavioral management skills. They are all about learnings appreciation and growth. Take the time to learn, try and grow oen strategies and leadership style.

Can organization apply behavioral economic demand to evaluate work performance for whole different departments?

Behavioral economies investigation may include evaluating demand for a commodity (such as drug experimentation and car manufacturing component material etc.) is given changes in price, using hypothetical purchase tasks, which are a reliable and efficient assessment method. Can behavior management examine work performance evaluation? The work performance evaluation target includes that employee individual and different department will performance evaluation in organization.

I believe high quality or low quality training , which can be evaluated whether the employee individual work performance or the department overall employees work performance can be improved after training. So, if the department employee individual or all employers work performance can be improved, e.g. work efficiency raises, client satisfactory feeling raises, product sale number . Then, the training is a high quality training to help the organization to earn future high economic benefit. Otherwise , if the organization can not earn above any one good result. Then, the training ia a low quality training.So, any organization can attempt to observe any department overall performance and employee individual performance in order to evaluate whether it can provide high or low quality of training to let employees to learn.
So, employee individual behavior can bring performance evidence to let the organization to evaluate whether its training is useful or not useful to achieve its training aim, e.g. when the car manufacturer provides money, time, effort training arrangement to teach all workers to learn how to manufacture car skill. After training provision, many of them, they do not need to work over time more than one hour to manufacture daily of least 10 cars per employee.Before, any one worker must need to spend more than one hour over time to manufacture daily 10 more cars.

So, when this car manufacture skillful improvement train is provided more than one hour more than one hour , none of them, they need work over time in order to manufacture more than at least 10 cars number per day. It seems that training improvement arrangement can be used to evaluate whether employee individual efficiency can be raised in organizational behavioral economic view.

Hence, any organization's internal training provision knowledge resource, it can be evaluated employees' behavioral performance can be improved, about being available to work, about role performance . It assumes that employees are likely to come to work and remain in the organization if they obtain satisfaction from their jobs, and that they are likely to put use effort and work more effectively if they are to be reward more for their effort and performance can be comfirmed to improved by management after they are taught by training. So, when the employee hopes to raise salary, he must hard to learn any new knowledge from the organizational training. Then, training can help the " expectation good reward employees" can improve performance in organizational behavioral economic view.

It is one important successful factor to help the organization to innovate and bring economic benefit, when the organization can implement any new useful training to improve any new useful training to imprve empllyee skills. It means that training is one long term economic organizational strategy, it depends on whether the training is useful or is ot useful in order to help any old employees to raise or improve their skills to achieve raising efficiency and satisfactory client service , sale product number, product manufacture increasing number aims.

How to apply behavioral eocnomic skill to help society to solve challenges ?
The three principles of social economics theory describes how the economy as a whole woks are (1) a country's standard of living depends on its ability to produce goods and services . (2) prices rise when the government prints too much money and (3) society faces a short-run tradeoff between inflation and unemployment. How to use behavioral economics for social impact. According to the American psychological association, social psychology is the study of how individuals affects and are affected by physical environment. Behavioral economics applies these concepts to the economic decisions that people make in addition to the ration thinking. It helps us understand how consumer participate in contest buy products and brand familiar choice in order to make the most rational purchase decison. Also, behavioral economists ask questions mostly about the way people make economic choices, judgements or the way particular financial purchase choice. Hence, behavioral economic is the study of psychology as it relates to the economic decision making processes of individuals and organizations. In general, our societies ask two important questions: Are economists' assumptions of utility of profit maximization good approximations of real people's behavior? So individuals maximize subjective expected utility?

IN our societies, we need to satisfy and earn the greatest benefit, in economics, rational choice theory, states that when humans are presented with various options under the conditions of scarcity, they would choose the option that maximizes their individual satisfaction. Behavioral economics draws on psychology and economics to explain why people sometimes make irrational decisions and why and how their behavior does not follow the predictions of economic models, e.g. decisions such as how much to pay for a cup of coffee, whether to go to graduate school, whether to pursue a healthy lifestyle , how much to contribute toward retirement. For example, humans are emotional and easily distracted beings, they make decisions that are not in their self interest. For companies are increasingly incorpoarting behavioral economics to incrase sales of their products case example, in 2007, the price of the 8 GB iphone was introduced for $600 and quickly reduced to $400, what if the intrinsic value of the phone was $400? If Apple introduced the iphone for $400, the initial reaction the price in the smartphone market might have been negative as the iphone might be thought to have too pricely. Buy by introdicing the phone at a hgh-pricing and bringing it down to $400, consumers believed they were getting a pretty iphone deal for Apple. So, Apple iphone began to understand tht its phone consumers are irrational, an effective way to behavioral economics in the Apple iphone's decision making policies to solve challenges.

What factors influence student makes subject choice decision ?
Behavioral economic on law and economy subject choice how to student individual subject learning choice behavior in universities economy and law subjects choice example, whether students will make subject either law or economt subject choice, it depends on future lawyer and economist salary whether which occupation can earn long term more salary comparision in order to decide wither law or economy degree learn.

Some university students make these two subjects either one learning choice, they will decide whether school fee is how much more than future salary earns, or personal interest psychological factor influences. So, if the student feels more interest to learn law degree , then he won't choose economy degree between these two degrees. Behavioral economy theory can be applied to explain this student individual economy and law degrees choice behavior because his subject choice decision is depended on personal psychological interest factor more than school fee or future salary possible earn economic salary reward factor influences. But, I assume that if the university can give scholorship for economic and law degree student when the student feels the law degree scholarship higher than economic degree. Then, he will decide to choose law degree to study more than economy degree. He chooses to study law degree because he hopes to earn higher scholarship.

IN behavioral economy principle , it can be applied to explain this student degree choice behavior. However, applying behavioral economy view, it assumes these principles to analyze whether how the student chooses to study the degree. The principles or factors may influence his degree choice may include: Cost and benevits, e.g. the student fee and future salary for the degree, when the student has interest to study law and economic degree. So, he needs to do degree choice. Then, he may compare whether how much law and economy degree school fee, it may be possible future earn salary, scholarship possible reward. All of these factors concern the price for law and economy degree (external cost) and future possible income (salary) for economist and lawyer occupation. It is behavioral law and economic factor to influence how the student chooses either law or economic degree to study in the university.

For example, when the (A) university on student enrolls to the (A) university before, he needs to choose wither law or economy degree to study. I assume that he only feels interest to study these two degrees. Then, he will compare school fees, if law degree school fee is per year US$5,000, 4 years is US$20,000 and economy degree school fee is per year US$3,000, 4 years is US$12,000. Although, it seems that economy 4 year school fee is more less US$8,000 to compare law degree 4 year, but this student also compare possible future salary for lawyer and economist occupation. He believes that future lawyer salary may pay more 4 times to compare economists salary after 5 years working experience. Although, if this student chooses economy degree to study, he may have chance to earn scholarship if his examination can be good, but it is one time short time economic researd and this scholarship reward is not sure that he must earn, if he can not get at least 5 (A) grade any one economic subject papers in this university economy degree structure. Otherwise, if he chooses to study law and get 5 (A) grade any one law subject papers in the university law degree structure, he can not get scholarship for this law degree. hence , he makes final choice to study law degree, although he can not get scholarship and school fee is more than economy degree. But he believes that he can earn higher salary when he can be one lawyer and he works after 5 years, his salary may be paid more than one economist salary.

In behavioral economic view, it can be applied to explain this university student his degree choice behavior, then he has interest to study law and economy degree. He must need to make one degree choice to graduate, then he may make degree choice decision by external economic cost (degree price) and future reward (possible income) behavioral economic factor . Then, he can judge whether which degree is more s

● How organization improvement may bring economic benefits ?
Can organizational economies, e.g. transaction cost economics, agency theory, organizational theory , e.g. models of formal organizational independent of the strategies, improve organizational behavior in order to bring economic benefit, e.g. development potentially valuable resources and capabilities, it can raise internal organizatonal strengths and avoid weaknesses in SWOT strategy in order to imporve performance and bring organizational internal economic benefit in organizational behavioral economic view.

For manufacturing industry example, if the car manufacturers can attempt to discover the most efficient steel, or different kinds of car components material, but they can help it to manufacture many high quality cars. Then, their manufactury cost reduce , but its any model of car quality does not caused to poor. Then, this car firm can apply the most efficient and the most high component materials to help it to manufacture high quality cars. Although, it must need to spend time to research how to invest the most efficient and high quality car manufacture components, but if it can apply the most efficient and the high quality components to help it to manufacture any new model of cars. Then, new components research spending time can bring long term low manufacturing cost and high quality of cars to achieve long time economic benefits.

So, on behavioral economic view, organization's spending time on different kind of cheap and high quality car manufacture manufacture components research and research expenditure spending on new kinds of different car manufacture components, it can help it to sell the high quality of different model of cars to satisfy car buyer comfortable needs. Moreover, it can earn high profit, when it 's any car manufacture component cost reduces. So, SWOT internal strengths (high quality and low cost) to this car manufacturer. It may help it to bring long term raising profit economic benefit, when its any new model of car prices do not need raise, but their compared material manufacture cost reduce, due to new kinds of car manufacture component materials can be invented in success.

Hence, high quality and low cost of car manufacture component invention researching on spending time and research experiment expenditure is value to this car manufacture company, because if high quality and low cost car manufacture component experience succeeds, it can help it to improve any new model of cars quality , but the most important factor is that its any new model of cars prices do not need increase. So, car buyer individual purchase desire won't be influenced to choose any brand of car seller to replace it more easily.

For one drug development process, case example ,I assume that this drug manufacture firm can attempt to spend 10 years time, but it can help it has possible to help it to invent one kind of new pharmaceutical drugs to kill cancer cells for global cancer patients. So, its spending time research on new drugs to kill any kinds of cancers cellers and experimentation expenditure is value, because it can help it to bring economic benefit when global will have many cancer patients believe its new discovery of cancer drugs , it may help them to kill cancer cells to get health or reduce death chance ratio raises after 10 years.

Consequently, in soon future, it's global cancer patients number may increase when they choose to buy its future new cancer drugs paroduct. It may bring high profit economic benefit. So, on organizational behavioral economic view, when the organization spends long time and experimentation expenditure to research new resources, if these new resources can be invented in success and it ensures help it to increase clients number to order to bring future economic benefit. The organization is value to spend time and expenditure to carry on new resources research.

- How organizational ethic influence employee behavior ?

Organizational ethic behavior concerns with explaining employee individual behavior in organization, e.g. ethical decision making, ethical conduct for example, when one marketing department manager does not attempt to carrying on any data research about new market research to sell the new model iphone to any country. He only depends on his personal judgement, he believes that this new invention of US iphone producs, they ought to be sell to Korean new iphone market, because he feels Korean must prefer to choose to buy US drand of new iphone products to compare other countries iphone product. However, this iphone marketing development manager lacks enough data research for different Korean iphone buyer age target, purchase experience, purchase desire to conclude Korean iphone buyers must like to buy any brand of US iphone products in preference.

His non ethical new iphone invention decision making to choice Korean ipohone buyers market will bring time waste rick to satisfy Korean iphone buyers' needs to replace other new model ipone users market, e.g. Hong KOng, China, ipone market. So, his ethical decision making to Korean iphone buyers ne iphone invention market may bring less economic benefit to this US iphone manufacture firm. So, this new model ipohone marketing development immoral judgement of this iphone marketing development manager individual decision making to Korean new model ipone invention to Korean ipone users, it can bring high economic loss to this US iphone firm.Otherwise, if this marketing department manager can spend time to carry on data gathering to make more accurate new model iphone invention decision making to choose which one country, then his ethical decision making may help his this US iphone firm to reduce new iphone invention loss risk. So, it explains that why ethic organizational behavior may influence the firm can earn more or less economic benefit. SO, ethic or moral behavior can influence the organization can earn how much economic benefit in long term significant.

- Can improve energy efficiency by organization building occupant's energy consumption relative behavior to bring economic benefit?

Reducing energy consumption in building , it must improve efficiency by building, but whether they have close cause and effect relationship between occupant's energy consumption behavior and improvement energy efficiency to the building? IN fact, high efficiency equipment is being developed, it can help any building to save energy and economic effectiveness, if building energy is subject to uncertainties, such as whether variations, human operations, human behavior changes and government policies. So, building technology equipment improvement may be one main factor to help buildings to save energy . But why occupant behavior may help building to save energy by their daily energy consumption behavior.

The occupant energy behavioral user inputs factor may include: Weather influences, internal heat gain, efficiencies, simplied/ normal occupant behaviors, e.g. a high efficiency chiller can save very limited energy in cold climates due to minimal cooling load, and a good designed natural ventilation building won't work if the occupants do not open windows when outdoor air favors cooling. So, it seems that if one living building hopes to reduce energy consumption, instead of building equipment technological change , e.g. air condition facilities, building occupants , artificial intelligent light, life, their daily energy consumption behaviors, they can influence the living building's energy consumption level in occupant energy consumption behavior and building energy saving economic benefit view.

In fact, when the occupant considers hot water, air condition, energy gas electricity expenditure, he won't use excess electricity, gas resources, because he needs to pay more energy expenditure , when gas and electricity energy consumption expenditure is applied to any business organization offices, warehouses , shops working facilities environment, such as offices, warehouses , shops can often use less electricity, gas energy far ther employees daily work . In long time, the organization must may reduce much electricity, gas energy expenditure for whole organizations business activities. In organizational behavior economic view, organizational energy consumption .

- Can Amazon e-commerce organization business activities bring economic benefit to global societies?

Amazon e-commerce is one online product sale e-commerce organization. Any one country e-buyer can use his/her home computer to click to Amazon webstores, when he/she saw the product phone and price, then he/she feels the product's price is reasonable and he/she believes that he/she can make the best choice to buy the product. Then, he/she can pay visa to buy the product from Amazon webstore.

Amazon can bring the most convenient online sale channel to global any one e-buyer. The e-buyer can buy the oveseas product from its e-webstores . He does not need to catch air plane to fly to the e-sellers' shop. he can pay visa to pay the product from Amazon e-webstores any time immediately. All Amazon e-webstores . He can open 24 hours, so all webstores have no close time. So , it can bring busy working people, they do not need to spend long time to visit any shops to make purchase decision. For busy working people example, time has important value to them, they do not want to waste time to make any purchase choice.

So, Amazon gives " economic purchase time benefit " to global any one full time working people. In their psychology, Amazon can help them to save much time to go to online shopping purchase chance at homes. They can stay at homes to shopping. Even, when they give their their address to Amazon to know, Amazon will deliver their products to their homes within several days rapidly. Also , they do not need to pay money to buy its products immediately. They can only pay visa to buy the product from Amazon webstores. So, they can save " consumption money" to use for another need in short time. So, one individual e-air ticket buyer, Amazon can bring economic benefit to him, he does not need to buy air ticket to fly to another country to buy the product. Amazon webstores are given more different kinds of similar brand products to let him to choose in order to pay the most reasonable price, working people do not need to spend much visiting shop time to choose any products in order to make the final purchase decision at home rapidly, any one has visa card , he/she can buy the product from Amazon webstores at homes.

Instead of individual e-buyer ecommerce time benefit, spending little time product choice, reducing catching air plane to visit another country seller shop to pay air ticket expense and travelling time spending activities to every e-buyer . Amazon also brings global economic benefits to any one country. When the e-buyer lives in one country to buy the product, it is saved in the overseas country's warehouse. Then, the product must need to deliver to his home by air plane. So, all of Amazon products can bring global goods air transport delivering service to any one overseas buyer, when the product is saved in the overseas seller's warehouse. Any one Amazon product overseas transpor delivery service activity, it can help air goods transport service need increases as well as their goods air transport service income will also increase. Amazon can bring global air goods transport service need increases. It can assist global GDP air goods transport industry grows, and economic benefit for the country's air plan goods delivery service industry development in long term. Hence, on behavioral economic view, Amazon online sale channel ,it can help global economic benefit to air plane goods delviery service industy as well as individual differeent country e-buyer individual time saving and short term money saving economic benefit by visa payment method.

Moreover, Amazon alsoo creates more high technology employment chance to any one country because Amazon owns many offices and warehouses in different countries, due to it is one high technological e-commerce online sale organization, It must need many high skillful website designers to help it to design different countries webstores in order to satisfy any one e-buyer online purchase need. So, it creates high technology job chance to any one country webstore designers . It can help them to raise competitive effort when any one graduate pursues website designer career. IN Amazon provides good employent chance for any one country computer ecommerce designers in order to let them to earn high salary. Also, Amazon public e-commerce organization provides good chance for any one country author to earn royalty income when he/she publishes any electronic or paper books to sell from Amazon publish. It gives good writing skillful authors have more writing chance to help them to sell electronic books and /or paper books from its different countries webbook stores to different countries' readers in short time. It can help them to increase book sale chance to let different countries book buyers can know whether new book topic to the author, he/she will publish soon. So, it brings author's new writing mind training chance when he/she needs to compare book sale rank from Amazon webstores.

Hence, Amazon can bring social employment benefit and author individual skillful training advantage and royalty income benefit to any on country author in nowadays online published industty. So, Amazon online business activities can increase global social employment chance, encourages global authors attempt to train writing skill, helps e-buyers to save visiting shops shopping time and air ticket expenditure for global overseas buyers.

● How and why Amazon e-commerce organization influence global consumee behavioral changes to bring ecommerce benefits to sellers?

In behavioral economic view, Amazon changes consumers behavior as well as product sellers sale method, such as global consumer sellers began to accept online purchase method to replace frequent visiting shop purchase method and global sellers began to accept to apply Amazon webstores to help them to sell products from its online sale channel to replace opening shops locate to the country sale channel.

The advantages to global sellers may include they do not need to pay rent or buy the shops, they can use Amazon webstores to show their different kinds of products photos and prices to let any one online buyer to know . The advantage to global buyers, they do not need to spend time to visit any countries shops to choose products in order to make purchase decision. They only need to spend some time to visit amazon any one country's webstore to see any brands of product photos and know their prices to different kinds of products to compare design and price and functions among of them in the online visiting short time when they stay at home to trun on themselves home computers . So, future home consumption behavior may replace visiting shop consumption behavior. Amazon 's online purchase method will encourage global many sellers have began to believe traditional visiting shop purchase model can not be accepted to global any one consumer more easily, when any one owns computer and internet service at home in common. Then, global shops number will reduce, due to different kinds of product websites purchase model needs number increases to global product sellers, they will close their shops and open themselves webstores or choose Amazon webstore to help them to sell their products conveniently. Consequently, global online purchase and sale transactions number will be influenced to increase by e-commerce organization development.

● Have they close relationship between consumer behavioral change and economic change?

● How does consumer behavioral change impact economic change?

● How does consumer behavior bring positive or negative influence to economic growth or economic recession to the country?

I shall attempt to apply behavioral economic theory to explain their cause and effect relationship why and hoe global economy growth or recession may be impacted by global consumer behavior change reasons ae below:

I shall indicate travellingleisure and goods air plane transport industries example, since air planes are invented, it is a kind rapid air transport tool, it can help human to do both kinds of transport asrvice, one is goods transport and another is human transport . So, any individual or business goods can be delivered to another country offices or homes by air planes transport tools rapidly. SO, air planes can create more overseas purchase and sale business activities chance between different countries nowadays. Moreover, internet invention, it also increase more e-coomerce online purchase and sale business acitivies to global any one online buyer, he/she only needs to apply computer tool to click to the online seller webstore, when he /she likes the product, he/she can pay visa to buy the product from the onlin seller webstore at home conveniently.

Hence, e-commerce encourages global consumers to choose to buy any products from internet channel, it also brings global goods are needed to transport by air planes between different countries, e.g. one US online buyer makes purchase decision from onlin channel, then he chooses the product from Korean one online seller webstore. After he pays visa to the Korean online seller webstore , then the Korea seller will follow his US address to send the product to the US buyer's home after several days rapidly.

Hence, it explains that if future global consumers like to buy any products from any one country's onine sell webstore. Then, the product must need to be delivered to the online buyer's home. When the seller's product is not located to the online buyer's country warehouse. It needs to be delivered by air plane. When, global there are man consumers, their traditional visiting shops purchase habits are influenced to change online visiting webstores habits. Then, when their purchase habits are influenced to change by rapid, convenient, visa card payment online purchase method at home, time online purchase technological new payment channel method.

In future new online purchase trend development, it may influence future global traditional visiting shops consumption model to change visiting webstores consumption model. Consequently, consumers will choose to pay visa online purchase at home in preference. Also, it encourages visa card purchase , consequently, online purchase may influence these industries development, airlines goods transport service needs increase, it can increase new visa cards number to the frequent online channel e-buyer number. So, online consumption encourages global households save long time money in banks, because we can pay money by visa card payment after we buy any products from online. Global bank may have more money to save longer time from global households, long time money save , because we do not need to withdraw money to buy any expensive products, immediately, e.g. computer , television, furniture etc. When global households begin to accept online purchase method is better to compare visiting shop purchase method. So, future global airline goods transport and bank saving businesses these two industries may have positive impact by future global online buyers raising number.

Hence, when global consumers behaviors began to change online purchase , their online purchase activities may influence global banks can have long time saving money and airlines goods transport need increase rapidly. However, online purcahse activies will bring negative consumers emotion impact to some businesses, e.g. property rent business, because when the country has high population of consumers, they choose online purchases, they won't often vitis shops to choose any kind of products frequently, they only like to stay at home and turn on themselves home computers to find whether global whom sellers, they have webstores to let global consumers to buy their products from online channel. Due to the cuntry willl not have many consumers like to spend time to visit any shops in the country. It means that the country will have many shops are needed to be close, because there are less number peple visit the businessmen shops every day. It will cause property rent service providers can not increase rent income, even decrease rent income, when there are many businessmen close their shops and change onine webstores to replace actual shops. Hence, it seems that online buyers number increases, it may also brings positive impact to influence shop rent service income decreases to the property rent developers.

On global macro economic changing environment, online buyers number increases, it can encourage any kinds of products, they can sell more more easily. So, global product sale number may be influenced to increase rapidly, when global online purchase and sale transactions number increase, GDP on any kinds of product income may be influenced to increase . So, online buyers number increases, it must may bring positive impact to influence global trading GDP high growth, but global shops rent income property developers may be influenced to reduce, due to there are many shops may be caused to close in possible.
How travellers' leisure need change, it may influence travelling leisure service industry development? I shall attempt to explain how COVID 19 disease influences global travellers lesiure need change and airpine and travelling service providers, e.g. hotels, travelling agents, their leisure service needs change. Nowadys, COVID 19 disease has caused global many travellers feel fear to catch airplanes, because air planes all windows are needed to close, he/she has COVID disease, then he/she can bring any one passegner to get this kind of disease by air plane close window air environment. So, when globa many travellers feel afreaid to catch air planes, this kind of COVID 9 air contact disease, it can cause global travellers number has began to reduce, many of travelles began to reduce travelling times per year, even 0 time travel per year. Consequently, it will bring negative impact to global travelling industry development.

Firstly, COVID 19 disease influences global traveller individual travelling desire decreases, every traveller began to avoid to catch air planes to travel. So, any country;s airlines air planes flying times began to reduce, because it is no full seats booking to any airlinees. It means that airlinee must decrease income, alsoo they need to pay parking airplanes rent to any countries airports. So, fixed rent expenditure will need to pay, and many airlines began to dismiss the excess extra number of airline front service staffs, e.g. airport front service staffs, air plane check in /out staffs, even pilots number began also decreased.

So, airline unemployment ratio increases , it causes pilots, airlines service staffs need to change jobsm even some coutnries pilots , choose to do simple goods delivery jobs in supermarkets or securities. Also, COVID 19 disease influences hotels, travelling agents income began to reduce, because there are none many travellers need to live hotels, and they do not need travelling agents to help them to arrange any travelling journeys. So , COVID 19 disease influences many different countries travellers began choose any leisure activities to replace travel, because they feel afraid to get COVID 19 disease when they need to sit in closed window air plane environment.

This kind of disease can influence any one travller individual leisure choice began to change, such as they began to forgive travel siure activities, they will spend holiday to do other leisure activities in themselves countries , e.g. climbing mountain, swimming, running, playing table tennis, tennis etc. different outdoor sports. all of these leisure sports have same features, global any one leisure needer, he does not catch air plane to fo to another country to carry on playing these any one sport and he/she does not need to pay more price to enjoy these sports. Otherwise m travelling leisure activity, it must need any one leisure needer to spend much expenditure to enjoy this kind of leisure activity . So, it explains why many travellers beagan to choose to do any kinds of sports to replace spending money to enjoy travel leisure in their holidays,

On conclusion,this COVID 19 disease had influenced global travel leisure businesses and travel related leisure service industries income and travellers number began to reduce and any countries GDP on travelling industry will have negative economic recession occurrence in this COVID 19 disease global envionment. Hence, it implies thaat consumers (travellers) behavior leisure activities need, it may influence global business activities increase or decrease , global economic growth or recession, they have close cause and effect relationship between consumer behavioral change and industries GDP changes in behavioral economic view.

CHAPTER EIGHT

E-service quality innovation successful factor

Globalization can bring China " one belt, one road strategy" global social economic advantages, such as China's 21 St. century " one belt , one road strategy. It aims to bring the different Asia countries, even Western countries' business cooperation more easily after it had built high speed railway to go to different countries which had road transport to link to China on land. So, in long term benefits, China businessmen can cooperate to these participative "one belt, one road strategy businessmen to carry on buying and selling their unique products from road transport conveniently. Even, e-commerce can bring important economic advantages to influence this " one belt, one road strategy " in success. I shall explain the reasons that why e-commerce can bring business advantages to them as below:

China's "one belt, one road strategy " aims to achieve the global world share GNP 55% , as well as global consumer number of 77% and global energy saves 75%. Instead of existing trading investment, China also compromises to provide US one hundred billion dollar of basic facility fund, central Asia one belt, one road strategy fund of forty billion US dollar to invest this "one belt, one road strategy" of long term business development. I believe that it seems that China only hopes to build railway facility and encourage the participative countries to build factories to invest to do businesses between China and these countries as well as create jobs to solve China unemployment ratio, but in fact, I believe that China will apply e-commerce technology to assist its businessmen to do online trading more easily. I shall indicate the reasons to explain that why e-commerce and China 's one belt, one road strategy , they have close economic growth of case and effect relationship.

China will be only one globalization main essential " one belt, one road strategy" country to control all participative countries' businessmen activities and China can help the excess of developing countries' economic development in the same tie. In fact, internet can assist China's future economic development. The reason is that I believe that when China's " one belt, one road strategy " can develop to succeed. It can encourage many " one belt, one road strategy" participative countries businessmen to be persuaded to apply internet technology to do e-commerce in the same time after the railway transport facilities are built to let all of these participative countries businessmen can transport their products to their cities from road transport more easily and rapidly. So, it can being short time product transport advantages when the participative country's consumers buy the product from the online platform as well as the product can be delivered to his home from railway transport rapidly. So, e-commerce and railway transport has close relationship to cause this business activities in success. For example, one Asia "one belt, one road strategy country's participative businessman , he can apply e-commerce technology to sell its products to Western countries , e.g. US, UK online clients in short time rapidly.

The participative countries may include India, Greece, Serbia, Hungary etc. 66 countries. So, these one belt, one road strategy participative countries can cooperate to do e-commerce business to sell themselves unique products to the non-participative "one belt, one road strategy" countries from e-commerce channel. When these non-participative " one belt, one road strategy " countries consumers have none of the kinds products to buy from themselves countries, but they click to these participative " one belt, one road strategy" countries participation businessmen themselves web stores to find the kinds of products which can buy from their web stores. Then, they can apply online to buy the products from these one belt, one road strategy countries' businessmen web stores more easily and conveniently in short time. The important factor is railway transport, when these products can be delivered from railway from China to these participative countries. For example, when one participative country businessman , he has none of this kind of product to sell to the US or US client, but he apply internet channel to click to the China businessman's web store to find the kind of product that he can sell. SO, he can apply internet channel to buy the Chins business's product after he pays visa. The China e-retailer can deliver the kind of product to his store by railway transport rapidly. Railway transport can reduce the transport cost , when the e-retailer (buyer) does not need to pays air freight fee. It is more cheap transport cost. Then, the participative " one belt, one road strategy " e-retailer can deliver the kind of product to the US, or UK buyer by air transport rapidly when he find the kind of product which can be provided from the China e-retailer from online channel immediately. So, railway building and e-commerce channel will influence the " one belt, one road strategy " in success.

The 21 St century sea transport considers different countries consumers' buying need when they feel that they can not buy the kinds of products from themselves countries easily. So, such as the participative " one belt, one road strategy" countries , they can transport their products between China and themselves countries by railway transport, then the sea transport will not be popular to help them to deliver their products because sea transport delivery speed must be slower than railway transport. Any consumers won't hope to receive their products in long transport time. So, railway transport must be one important transport factor to influence China 's "one belt, one road strategy" in success.
Moreover, e-commerce invention can help these participative " one belt, one road strategy" countries e-retailers to apply web stores sale channel to cooperate to sell their unique products between them. When one country e-retailer

can buy the another country retailer 's product from web store and it can be delivered to its country by railway transport , then it can still supply the kind of product to the e-consumer , even it has non any of this kind of product stock in its warehouse. Railway transport can help them to deliver their products from road in short time between China and these participative countries. So, they must have geographic advantage to deliver their products rapidly after railway transport facilities are built successfully between China and these countries. Moreover, web store can help them to advertise their products to let the non-participative "one belt, one road strategy" countries consumers to know whether which kinds of products these participative countries e-retailers , they can sell from themselves web stores when they click to their websites to see their product photos immediately.

So, China's " one belt, one road strategy" can influence to achieve global online ecommerce advantage for China and the participative " one belt, one road strategy 66 countries e-retailers and e-commerce can help them to promote their any products to Western countries to let they to know in short time rapidly.
ON currency gain benefit aspect, in fact, e-commerce can help this " one belt, one road strategy" participative countries earn exchange rate transaction more easily because when the non-participative " one belt, one road strategy " countries consumers pay visa to buy their products from their web stores. Usually, they need to pay US dollar to buy their products by visa card for every online transaction. So, when these participative "one belt, one road strategy" online e-retailers receive their US payment by visa. They have more currency earn chance when US dollar needs to exchange high local exchange to their dollar. So, the currency exchange earn will have possible to occur from e-commerce. For example, when one e-US consumer buys one product from the China's online e-retailer , when the e-US consumer pays US currency to buy it by visa. Then, the China E-RETAILER can receive the US currency sale profit and change to Chinese dollar to earn the foreign exchange income when it find decides to change the US currency to Chinese currency in the right time. So, e-commerce globalization can also raise foreign exchange earn chance between the countries' online consumers and the another e-retailers when they are carrying any e-commerce activities. Hence, e-commerce can assist the China's " one belt, one road strategy" development more success between Asia and Western countries.

However, the internet development can help China's 21 St century " one belt, one road strategy" to achieve these aspects of development, instead of e-commerce development. The five major achievements are such as , 1. Policy coordination, 2. Facilities connectivity, 3. Going out trade, 4. Financial integration, increased economic performance and productivity and 5. Encouraging people to people e-commerce transaction. Because internet development can help any countries consumers to search new products information as well as helping them to cooperate to analyze and achieving the best effective and efficient online shopping activities. So, it may reduce the incentives and opportunities for terrorist movement. Such as Beijing is becoming a top salesman city to promote the China made products and in big discount with some conditions when to achieve the global of made in China e-commerce in " one belt, one road strategy" 2025.

ON conclusion, internet invention can help China and the 66 participative one belt, one road strategy" countries to gather any new products information as well as discusses how they can operate do this global e-commerce in success. Nowadays, the world is focus on the China movement on the one belt, one road strategy, how impact of the international financial crisis keeps rapidly, the world economy is recovering slowly, and global development is uneven. So, internet development can encourage the international trade and investment for the participative one belt and one road strategy countries and even these countries still facing big challenges to their e-commerce development. So, internet can assist the one belt, one road strategy cooperative countries' information exchange to achieve success. Internet can help them to bring an economic area through building infrastructure, increasing culture exchange and broadening global e-commerce development. This innovative conceptual strategy will bring China to take a bigger role in global affairs and it is an easy way to let China to export China's reserve products in area of " over production" , such as electrical appliances, steel aluminum , railway equipment and building's material manufacturing between China and the participative countries by railway transport. Internet can help it to apply e-commerce channel to promote its material products to let overseas buyers to know from their web stores in short time. So, internet can bring successful advertisement promotion development to China and the 66 participative one belt, one road countries on overseas online e-commerce sale chance absolutely. Finally, internet can also bring further deepening and expanding beneficial cooperation in such areas as trade, investment, finance, transport and communication aspects to these participative one belt, one road strategy countries. For China example, it is the world's largest producer of gold and also major importer and consumer. It can apply e-commerce trading method to promote its gold products to global gold buyers from the gold sellers' web stores in short time. When the country's one gold buyer research the China's one gold online retailer web store to find its quality and appearance is more attractive to compare his country gold shops. Then, he will pay visa to buy the China gold e-retailer's gold from its web store by visa immediately. So, e-commerce can help China's gold e-retailers to promote their gold products to let global gold buyers to know from their web stores in the short time. Hence, global e-commerce activity can help China to promote products and increase sale chance in short time after its one, belt, one road strategy can implement to achieve successfully.

Socio-economic means that investigators had been addressing the key issues of mental life: Thinking, problem solving, the nature of consciousness. Their concept of human nature, human decision making in psychology. Economists understood utility in terms of conscious experience like pleasure or happiness. Utility arises from any commodity must be considered as measured by happiness. The some suitable quantitative measure of utility, or satisfaction, or desiredness.

However, economists research these questions concern consumer, such as : questions of motivation, preference formation and choice. In psychological view,human judgement and decision making and behavioral economics have always been concerned about psychological as well as sociological and variables as determinants of choice, which together , lend themselves to a better understanding choice behavior of consumption and production. The key points, critical to behavioral economics may indicate:

Assumptions are caused by causal and predictive analysis, be they of a psychological, sociological. It is important to understand why people behave the way they do, a critical component of behavioral economics is building models that better reflect actual behavior. Such behavior can be both rational and intelligent without being economy, related to this, behavioral economists and economic psychologists run experiments and engage to determine the choices people make and how these choices are made, and to asscertain to what extent from conventional economic wisedom.

Some important aspects on efficiency wages, efficient market hypothesis,social and personal captial, capabilities and soft, modification of economy theory does not suggest that relative
prices, opportunity costs and incomes play no role in affected behavior, material incentives matter, supply and demand analysis is enriched by the findings, and methodology of behavioral economics, introducing effort variability, non-material variables, capabilities and relative positioning enriches production theory.

In businessmen profit earn aik vire, they can also apply behavioral economic theory to seek rationally to maximize, their rxpected , returns and had full knowledge of the data needed to
succeed in this attempt, they knew the relevant cost and demand functions, calculated marginal cost and marginal revenue from all actions open to them, and pushed each line of action to the point at which the relevant marginal cost and marginal revenue were equal. Hence, for example, it is not by learning and applying appropriate mathematical formulas that one becomes and expert or decision maker, bur rather by developing the required skills. often learned in the pool hall and in the firm through learning -by-doing. A training program for firm decision making players, concentrating on math and engineering courses would by itself, not produce experts. Thus, behavioral assumptions should need to assume for optimal or rational intelligent choice behavior. Moreover, there exists a variety of non-profit maximizing behaviors that have a positive probability of never failing. In fact, it has shown that firms that maximize profits are the least likely to be the market survivors.

Hence, in different firms behavioral view, this sensitivity of outcomes to process can have important consequences for analysis at the level of market and economy, which assumes that consumer individual typically makes choices in their own best interest, " were best interest" is something that not incorporating into their calculations, the true costs and benefits of their choices.

Hence, behavioral economy theory can help product sellers to predict consumer individual choice , attitude in order to find what the important factors influence they choose to buy the seller's products in preference. Also, behavioral economic theory is an analytical predictions, how intelligent individuals actually behave. This approach to choice behavior does not assume that individuals are in any way irrational , even through such behavior is expected to deviate substantively. Hence, the behavioral economic theory assumes humans are rational and maximum their individual self interest.

In consumption view, in general , consumers choose to buy any products in preference, they will evaluate whether the product can bring the maximum economic or useful benefit to them in order to make the final purchase in our society. Such as organic food choice case, food consumers' choices , where people's may come from direct influence of other people's behavior and social norms on our behaviors. Then, theory assumes we independently know what we want and that our preferences are fixed. So, this standard theory is very good at explaining short -term decision-making. Suc as green vegatables and choose beans as they are on special offer, but can not explain longer-term changes in preferences. I now only choose organic foods. So, behavioral economy theory can predict short term consumers behavioral choice to decide what factors influence their choices change, but it can not predict long-term consumers behavioral choice to decide what factors influence their choices change, because it has much unpredictable factors are difficult to estimate , when they will influence now consumers behavioral change in our society.

Artificial intelligence is one good machine tool to predict consumer behavior in behavioral view, our social media, facebook, which is the most populat platform in the wourld. Any digital markets can apply webs, such as facebook to post message to communicate with their fans or followers (predicting online purchase behaviors , when they can occur). So, the applications of such method an be observed from data analysis in social media platforms to predict online consumers behaviors. Machine learning aims to maximize the efficiency of computer program using sample data or precedent experiences . A model is developed with designed in learning to perform computer program operation in order to enhance efficiency of the model using train data or post experiences. The model is developed to be capable of predicting or describing knowledge from the data or both. Hence, AI may be used to research consumer behavior probability from marketing communication by social medial web, face book online channel, on facebook using machine learning. Machine learning data classification to reseach consumer behavioral characteristicss to any kinds of product.

ON online purchase process research, online consumers must need to experience these five stages. They may include attention, interest, search, action adn share. In the beginning, working process starts when a consumer notices or sees a product, a service or an advertisement (attention). Then, the interest is stimulated in order to get more information about
such product or service (search). In this stage, a consumer will seek for the others' comments, reviews, posts from internet, comparison websites, formal webpages of organization or even from a conversation with family members or friends who have been using the product or service. After that, the consumer will express whose own opinion considering the others' opinions on that product or service. This stage leads to the decision of the consumer to buy (action). Finally, the consumer will act as a messager by word of mouth, conversation, or online posts of whose opinion and impression (sharing). Thus, it seems that facebook pages may influence upon consumer behavior. When marketers who posses Facebook account to test. The messages posted through Facebook pages are then collected so as too through Facebook pages are then collected so as to perform a study of online consumer behaviors.

In fact, Facebook comprises of two main functions , which are the posting of message brands wish to communicate to consumers and opinions and comments of consumers responding to brand communication. It is one social media analysis tool tends to carry out the studies and analysis of consumer opinion with data collected from comment. The results measure consumer sentiment towards the product or service in form of positive, negative and neutial opinion.

Why is Facebook social medial terchnology more efficient to predict consumer behavior? This is due to the fact of the differences in business operation pattern and communication methods of each page. For example, page a puts focus on interaction with customers by organizing activities that customers can join. On the other hand, page is emphasizes an awareness rising to promote product to be known and understood, whereas page (stimulates customers to make a decision to buy the products). It is one good technological social media method to gather online consumer behaviors in biuying decision. After verifying posted messages, consumers seek for information from various sources prior to buy products and services, and they evaluate and reflect their satisfaction after buying products and services. Online social media exercise greater influence that consumers can search for all concerned information , gather data from existing customers as much as possible before making a decision to buy. They do not need to meet the others and ask for their opinion towards product and service. IN addition, they can leave their opinion, impression and share information to others as well. This illustrates prefectly online consumer behavior in decision making process to buy.

How to apply behavioral economic theory to evaluate household electricity useful decision making ? How to evaluate and explain adoption of energy efficiency between environment protection electricity energy household users and non-environment protection electricity household users for household solar, electricity, solar hot water and in-house energy. Their energy useful behaviors are influenced whether by either climate changing factor or other factors? It aims to apply behavioral economic theory to test and

explain their differences between high and low adopters of energy efficiency by macro-level factors (e.g. technological , economic, demographic factors) and an individual's perceptions, preferences and abilities, and cold or hot climate changing factors.

ON conclusion, ON behavioral economy view, in general, it concludes that householders feel need to save energy. The main reason may include this, due to the environment protection

energy users feel the tend to occur in the future when they concern discounting investments over long periods of time, which makes it is difficult to bring financial costs with respect to energy efficiency investments, as when they feel electricity energy cost will increase. They feel the energy use into total consumption will have much share to allocate to their whole families expenditure consumption. So, their energy useful or consumption psychological pressure influence these householder decide to use less energy and become their energy useful habits. So, it is not the the householder's psychological factor,whether the family is environment protection or non-environment protection energy users. So, this would provide the environment protection or non-environment protection householder energy users have a better sense of what scale of energy efficiency is achievable,thereby enabling them to reduce much extra householder whole family expenditure. Hence, these expenditure factor will influence many householders electricity energy useful behaviors as well as it can cause their energy useful habits and staying short time at home because they hope to avoid to spend much time to use energy at home. So, behavioral economy theory explains that environment protection factor is not the main factor to influence hosueholders energy consumption behavioral change.

CHAPTER NINE

Can non-employees (Auto food sale machine) supermarkets bring reducing cost benefit

If one supermarket only choose to buy many auto food sale machines to let food customers to press food vending machines buttons to choose which kinds of food to buy after they pay visa to the any one auto vending machine. So, the supermarket does not need to employee cashiers, food shelf delivers, cleaners etc. different supermarket employees. Can food vending machines help the supermarket to reduce much cost? I shall apply behavioral economic principle to explain this question:

What are the key success factors in this supermarket food industry?

KSFs are the attributes or capabilities that are essential for a business to succeed in a given industry. They can be related to food quality to vending machines, innovation, cost efficiency, distribution, or any other aspect that gives a competitive edge.

There are these seven benefits of installing snack vending machines at work

Improve wellbeing. One of the most significant benefits of having vending machines for snacks in the workplace is that they can help improve the wellbeing of your employees. ...

24-hour access. ...

Save time. ...

Turn a profit. ...

Boost morale. ...

Take care of others. ...

Low maintenance.

Features of vending machines

Features

Identation required for access

RFID Pin code Barcode

Article withdrawal

Direct selection Select products on the display Scan product barcodes

Automated ordering

After every withdrawal Once a day

Transparency

Each withdrawal is documented Allocation to cost centres Reporting

What are the specifications needed for the vending machine?

Canteen Vending Snack

Machine Type

Dimensions

Electric

Machine holding 11.5 oz. and 12 oz. Cans

32"W 26"D 72"H

120V/11A

Machine holding 20 oz. Bottles

37"W 33"D 72"H

120V/11A

Machine holding 20 oz. Aquafina Bottles

37"W 35"D 72"H

120V/11A

What is the main purpose of a vending machine?

An automated machine which is intended to provide the users with a diverse range of products: snacks, beverages, pizzas, cupcakes, newspapers, tickets, etc. A vending machine dispenses a product to the users based on the amount of money inserted and selection of the product.

What are the key success factors of vending machines?

Listed below are these 3 crucial keys to success:

Find High Traffic Locations. Like everything in business, your number one key to success is the location. ...

Buy the Right Machine at the Right Price. In layman's Terms, this is called getting the biggest bang for your buck. ...

Provide the Right Service.

What are the competitive advantages of vending machines?

Low cost, 24/7 business operation

The vending machine is always operating, so it can sell at any time of the day. That means the machine operator can do business all day without having to worry about the cost of hiring staff.

What is the unique selling point of vending machines?

There's also strong advertising value because vending machines can be uniquely branded. In many vending locations, the products are more likely to get noticed than when hidden inside shops.

How does one supermarket describe a vending machine business?

An owner of one or multiple vending machines selects where to place them, what goods to sell, and collects money deposited by customers. Vending machine businesses sell a diverse range of goods, such as: Food (e.g., candy, chips, snacks) Beverages (e.g., soda, water, hot drinks).

What are the advantages of automatic vending?

The following are the advantages of vending machine:It is available to shop at any time of day or night. The buyer receives a constant supply of items at consistent weight and quality. There is no requirement for sales agents. So, when one supermarket can use many food vending machines to replace putting any kinds of food on shelves. The, it can operate 24 days to let any one food buyer to enter the supermarket to pay money or visa and press button from any one food vending machine in order to make different kinds of food purchase choice any time easily.

What are the classification of vending machines?

The vending machine can be categorized into product-oriented and service oriented machines . It distributes snacks, beverages, public transit tickets, jewelry, telephone facility, entertainment things, and etc.

How do supermarket choose a vending machine for the kind of food sale ?

Before you start looking for a vending machine, it's important to evaluate and assess your specific needs. Consider factors such as size, capacity, features, type, location, the technology used, etc. Evaluating your requirements can help narrow down your selection to the ideal machine for your business.

Factors to consider when buying a vending machine

Types of vending machines. There are a variety of vending machines serving products such as hot beverages, sweets, snacks, can and in cup. ...

Location. ...

Easy to use. ...

Safety. ...

Size. ...

Cost of vending machines. ...

Stock and maintenance. ...

Starting a Vending Machine business.

How vending machine is useful in retailing?

Even the retail organizations like malls and supermarkets have started keeping vending machines because the vending machines do not need staff. The training and basic pressure of salesman less. So this gives the option to connect to customers at their own end. The customers pay and collect the stocks.

What is the main technology used in vending machines?

Sensors: These can include cameras, weight sensors, and RFID readers, which can be used to detect when items are removed from the vending machine and to collect data on customer behaviour. Software: Smart vending machines may use software to manage inventory, track sales, and perform other tasks.

How do vending machines help any kinds of food buyers when they enter the supermarket?

Having a midday snack gives employees the fuel they need to keep going, and because vending machines function as an on-site source of food and drinks, employees don't have to waste time and leave the office to grab food. This allows them to be more efficient and spend more time in the office for improved productivity.

What are the benefits of a supermarket business using a vending machine approach to sales?

Generating additional revenue: Vending machines offer an additional source of revenue for businesses, as they can generate sales 24/7 without the need for additional staff.

Are vending machines a good supermarket business idea?

Benefits of a Vending Machine supermarket Business

Owning anywhere from a few to a few hundred vending machines can be a manageable, successful business for owners of any experience level. The cost to start a vending machine is basically just the cost of the machines and stocking them—you won't need an office space to house.

What are the disadvantages of vending machines to customers?

Vending machines do not stock healthy foods

Combined with the low prices and ability to place them just about anywhere, vending machines are an easily accessible source of unhealthy products. This is a major disadvantage as many countries worldwide face large-scale health problems.

What is the best thing to sell in vending machine?

Best Vending Machine Snacks

Popcorn – Act II, Pop Secret, Orville Redenbacher, Smartfood.

Pastries and doughnuts – Hostess, Little Debbie, Krispy Kreme, Dunkin' Donuts.

Fruit snacks and rolls – Fruit by the Foot, Fruit Roll-Ups, Welch's, Haribo.

Jerky and meat snacks -Slim Jim, Jack Link's, Perky Jerky, Oberto.

Hence, it seems that it is possible supermarkets can buy food vending machines to replace food are putting on shelves to sell in possible.

What do people buy most from vending machines when they enter the supermarket?

Snacks: Traditional snack items like chips, pretzels, cookies, candy bars, and popcorn are often in high demand and have a good profit margin. Beverages: Cold drinks such as soda, water, energy drinks, and sports drinks are popular choices. Consider offering a variety of options to cater to different preferences.

Is a vending machine a type of retailing? A non-store retailing refers to retailing in the market taking place outside a retail facility. A vending machine is a non-retail because it is placed outside the store enabling customers to buy different items without going inside the store.

Why should vending machines have healthy food?

In contrast, a vending machine filled with unhealthy choices, such as candy, potato chips, and cookies, can lead to sluggish employees who feel tired earlier in the day and lose focus easily. A sugary snack may energize an employee for 30 minutes, but it's not sustainable.

What kind of food vending machines are there?

Types of vending machines

Coffee vending machines. ...

Combo vending machines. ...

Snack vending machines. ...

Drink vending machines. ...

Frozen vending machines. ...

Smart vending machines. ...

Fresh food vending machines. ...

Cooked food vending machines.

What are the Different Types of Vending Machines?

Food Vending Machines. Vending machines that offer food or snacks have been around since the 1800s and started their humble beginnings by offering gum. ...

Beverage Vending Machine. ...

Combo Vending Machines.

What is the difference between vending machine and a vendor?

That's why the machines you buy things from are called vending machines and not selling machines, and some street sellers who sell small items from a tray around their neck etc may be called vendors or street vendors. The meaning is basically the same, but you should use "sell".

Where is the best place for a vending machine?

If a business has a break area, be sure to consider this as a location for your vending machine. Snack areas are a particularly great location if there is little nearby competition. Think about picnic areas, playgrounds, cafeterias, and other places where people normally take a break and eat at a business. So, it seems that supermarkets can attempt to put many food vending machines to sell different kinds food to let food buyers to choose to buy easily.

Listed below are these 3 crucial keys to success:

Find High Traffic Locations. Like everything in business, your number one key to success is the location. ...

Buy the Right Machine at the Right Price. In layman's Terms, this is called getting the biggest bang for your buck. ...

Provide the Right Service.

What are the advantages of using a vending machine?

Vending machines bring convenience to both consumers and investors. Consumers will be able to buy goods quickly and proactively without having to search for a place to buy or wait for staff to make payment.

How vending machine is useful in retailing?

Even the retail organizations like malls and supermarkets have started keeping vending machines because the vending machines do not need staff. The training and basic pressure of salesman less. So this gives the option to connect to customers at their own end. The customers pay and collect the stocks.

What is the main purpose of a vending machine?

An automated machine which is intended to聽provide the users with a diverse range of products: snacks, beverages, pizzas, cupcakes, newspapers, tickets, etc. A vending machine dispenses a product to the users based on the amount of money inserted and selection of the product.

How are vending machines convenient?

One of the prime reasons for the enduring popularity of vending machines is their user-friendliness. The process couldn't be more straightforward. No more queueing in long and unmoving lines. Vending machines offer a quick and hassle-free experience that saves your precious time and energy.

What kind of profit do vending machines make?

The gross margin on snack vending items ranges between 40% - 60%. On average, vending machine businesses can earn a profit of about$1000 - $1200 per machine each year. The average vending machine's monthly income from snack sales is about $125 per month. Candy vending machines typically earn less than $25 per month.

What are the advantages of vending machines in hotels?

Saves cost for hotel owners:

Vending machines are unmanned and any staff or visitor can use these machines without needing the help of anyone. It helps in reducing hotel expenses. Hotel customers who are pleased with their stay are more inclined to recommend you to others and come back to the same hotel again. So, it seems that supermarkets are similar to hotels , which can attempt to buy food vending machines to sell any kinds of food to their customers conveniently.

Where is the best place to put a vending machine?

Factors that Determine Best Locations

Apartment buildings. ...

Laundromats. ...

Hotels or lodging areas. ...

Office buildings. ...

Entryways and Exits. ...

Snack or break areas. ...

Nearby lines or queues. ...

Waiting areas. Similarly, waiting areas are one of the best locations for vending machines.

Even, any one locations in one supermarket, it can buy many vending machines to put on any locations to let customers to buy any kinds of food, e.g. Hot dogs, can be putted in the vending machine near the supermarket door or soft drinks can be putted in the vending machine to close to the hot dogs vending machine to let food buyers buy to buy hot dogs to eat and buy soft drink to drink easily in the supermarket.

So, it seems that any one supermarket may buy one vending machine, even many vending machines to replace to put food on shelves to sell different kinds of food to its customers conveniently.

What Are the Major Factors Affecting the Growth Of the Restaurant Industry?

Food waste.

Work overload.

Labor shortage.

High labor cost.

Market saturation.

High operating costs.

Who is most important in a restaurant?

The restaurant owner. You're the leader your restaurant needs. You work on budgets, marketing, developing your management team and holding them accountable.

What is the main factor affecting consumer choice to any kinds of
restaurant on behavioral economic view ?

Demographics are an important set of factors that marketers should not overlook when trying to understand and respond to consumers. Demographics include variables such as age, gender, income level, educational attainment, and marital status. Each of these can have a strong influence on consumer behavior.

Key Factors Affecting Customers' Experience At Your Restaurant

Food Quality. ...

Staff Behavior. ...

Value For Money. ...

Location Preference. ...

Restaurant Interiors and Ambience. ...

Unique Food in The Menu. ...

Convenience. ...

Customer Selection Behavior – Menu Innovation.

What are the factors affecting eating out?

As such, based on the reviewed literature, ambiance, quality of food, price, service, and friendliness of employees, value for money, cleanliness, location, portion size, speed of service, value-added deals, food presentation, and menu variety are factors that influence the selection of restaurant to cat out.

What are the 5 meal experience factors?

A meal experience, as a holistic event, includes the following dimensions: "the room," "the meeting," "the product," "the atmosphere/ambiance," and "the management control system," according to the Five Aspect Meal Model (FAMM) Gustafsson et al.

How can restaurants increase customer count?

How to increase restaurant sales by reaching new customers

Host a grand opening event to increase sales. ...

Establish and optimize a social media presence. ...

Focus on SEO to increase restaurant sales. ...

Optimize your Google My Business Listing. ...

Meet guests where they are. ...

Run digital ads to increase profits. ...

Run traditional ads.

What are the four factors influencing customer choice?

In general, there are four factors that influence consumer behaviour. These factors impact whether or not your target customer buys your product. They are cultural, social, personal and psychological.

What do people look for when choosing a restaurant?

People trust other's experiences, even if they are strangers. Often, when searching for a restaurant, after they search the menu and prices, potential clients will also have a look over your online reviews to see if your place is worth it. Therefore, make it a point to encourage past clients to leave a positive review.

What are three factors that influence how much restaurant customer eat?

Biological determinants such as hunger, appetite, and taste. Economic determinants such as cost, income, availability. Physical determinants such as access, education, skills (e.g. cooking) and time.

What is meal factor?

Factor is a prepared-foods meal delivery service specializing in nutritionally balanced meals. It's popular for its specialty menus that support dietary preferences including keto, low carb, and high protein. It also has a variety of other meal plans that will appeal to a broad spectrum of eaters.

What are six factors that influence meal planning?

Factors Influencing Restaurant eater Customer Meal Planning

Dietary Restrictions and Preferences.

Nutritional Requirements.

Time Constraints.
Budget.
Seasonal Availability of Ingredients.
Cooking Skills and Equipment.
Cultural and Regional Influences.
Meal Frequency and Portion Control.
Factors affecting menu planning. You need to be aware of the following factors when. ...
Environmental issues. The chef will need to think about environmental issues when planning a menu. ...
Skills of the chef. ...
Equipment available. ...
Time available. ...
Time of year. ...
Organoleptic properties.
What are the 7 factors to consider in planning meals?

These include meal occasion, who will be eating, whether the food will be eaten out or at home, dietary needs, religious, cultural or ethical beliefs, the cost and availability of ingredients; current healthy eating advice and/or personal preferences.

What are the 6 basic meal planning principles?
Though different, both strategies are based on key nutritional concepts and a comprehensive approach to diet:
Adequacy.
Balance.
Calorie (energy) control.
Nutritional density.
Moderation.
Variety.
What are the five factors that affect menu planning?
To plan a good menu you need to consider the following factors:
food cost and budgetary goals of the food service operation.
production capability, including available equipment and personnel.
type of service and food delivery system.
availability of foods.
the philosophy of the business and food service operation.
FACTORS AFFECTING MEAL PLANNING.
Nutritional Adequacy.
Age.

Sex.

Physical Activity.

Economic Considerations.

What factors influence the menu of a restaurant?

Lesson Summary. Seasonality, trends, emergency management, and product availability are all external factors that can influence a facility's menu. Seasonality refers to when food items are at peak quality for a geographical area.

What are the 8 factor that you need to consider in making a menu design?

8 Considerations for Your Menu Design

Design For Readability. Menus should be designed intuitively so customers can easily find what they are looking for. ...

Design for Persuasion. ...

Design For Durability. ...

Design For Uniqueness. ...

Design for Distribution. ...

Design for customization. ...

Design for Accessibility.

What are the 5 quality factors to be considered in serving quality meals?

These food quality attributes include:

Appearance (including size, shape, colour, gloss and consistency)

Texture.

Flavour.

Nutritional content.

Ethical and sustainable production.

How do you increase the number of customers?

Simple ways to increase your restaurant customer base

Offer a free newsletter. ...

Increase your customer base by asking for opinions. ...

Keep up and maintain excellent customer support and service. ...

Keep your website content fresh. ...

Promote your business on social media networks. ...

Encourage customer referrals.

How can I make my restaurant busy?

Enable table reservations. If you're wondering "how to make my restaurant busy," start by giving customers the option to reserve a table online. Many people don't want to call for a reservation, not to mention phone reservations can be unreliable.

How do you attract customers to food?

6 Ways to Attract More Customers to Your Restaurant

Offer Foods at Different Price Points. The competition for customers is fierce in the quick-service restaurant industry. ...

Sample Your Menu Items. ...

Renovate the Restaurant. ...

Build a Social Media Presence. ...

Optimize the Website for Local Searches. ...

Provide Online Ordering.

What are the six key factors in customer satisfaction?

Factors that affect customer satisfaction the most

Personalised services create happier customers. ...

An empathetic team. ...

Paying attention to customers' preferences and choices. ...

User-friendly websites and online platforms. ...

An active online community for your customers. ...

Customer appreciation and loyalty programs.

What are the factors that influence customer engagement to your restaurant ?

Customer engagement encompasses interest, loyalty, and commitment. All these factors are paramount to business growth. In short, an engaged customer is a happy and loyal customer, who is likely to stay on board and recommend your services to their friends, family, on public forums, and other word-of-mouth channels.

How do economic factors influence food choices to any kinds of restaurant ?

Economic decision factors such as food price and income do influence people's food choices. Moreover, food costs are a barrier for low income-families to healthier food choices. Several studies indicate that diet costs are associated with dietary quality and also food safety.

How do you increase the number of repeat customers?

How can I increase the number of customers in my restaurant?

Run promotions.

Allow online orders.

Take advantage of social media.

Offer free WiFi.

Offer email marketing incentives.

Ask for customer feedback and implement it.

Collaborate with local businesses.

Host major events.

7 effective ways to increase your repeat purchase rate

Segment your audience. ...

Send re-engagement emails. ...

Send personalised product recommendations. ...

Show off your reviews. ...

Send cart abandonment emails. ...

Start a rewards program. ...

Improve customer satisfaction through surveys.

How do you manage a large number of eaters in restaurant?

How can you manage a large customer base effectively?

Segment your customers.

Communicate with your customers.

Deliver value to your customers.

Streamline your processes.

Train and empower your team.

Learn from your customers.

Here's what else to consider.

How do you handle a large number of customers?

Understand Customer Needs & Set Expectations. A very important aspect of customer support is to know your customers in advance. ...

Use Knowledge Base to Tackle Frequently Asked Questions. ...

Use Canned Responses to Never Make Your Customers Wait. ...

Think About Proactive Engagement.

What is the food choice model?

The model includes the five major categories of influences upon food choice that emerged consistently during the course of interviewing participants: ideals, personal factors, resources, social framework and food context.

How does lifestyle influence food choices?

Lifestyle experiences are what confirm or alter perceptions that influence food choices. When a person regularly attends a sporting event and buys stadium food, they link the food with the game, which creates a long-term association.

What are the factors of quality in a restaurant?

Physical environment quality, such as ambient conditions and seating comfort, also plays a role in customer satisfaction. Interactional quality, which includes assurance, empathy, reliability, and responsiveness, is another important factor that influences customer satisfaction.

Why is food quality important in a restaurant?

In the restaurant industry, maintaining the quality of food is essential for attracting and retaining customers . Therefore, ensuring high food quality in menu offerings is crucial for enhancing customer satisfaction in various food service establishments.

What are the hidden factors of food quality?

Nutritive value is one of the hidden characteristics, which is now considered by the consumers as a quality attribute. Adulterants and toxicants are the other hidden characteristics. Toxic substances may be of microbial origin, veterinary drugs residues, pesticide residues or heavy metals.

How to increase restaurant sales by reaching new customers

Host a grand opening event to increase sales. ...

Establish and optimize a social media presence. ...

Focus on SEO to increase restaurant sales. ...

Optimize your Google My Business Listing. ...

Meet guests where they are. ...

Run digital ads to increase profits. ...

Run traditional ads.

How fast food attracts customers?

Firstly, the convenience and speed of service offered by fast food restaurants have attracted customers, as they provide food quickly and easily. Secondly, the expansion of the fast food industry has led to a wide variety of options for customers to choose from, allowing them to satisfy their hunger in different ways

What factors influence restaurant profitability?

The two big factors that affect the profitability of restaurants are labor and food costs. Food costs on their can be 10-20% higher than a bar's liquor cost. Couple that with labor costs of around 20-40%, and you can see how a restaurants costs substantially outweigh a bar's.

Here is a list of the factors general eater customers must consider when choosing a restaurant.

Reviews. To cater to all your needs is the aim every restaurant works towards, but not many succeed in doing that altogether. ...

Quality of Food. ...

The Proximity of the Restaurant. ...

Waiting Time. ...

Hygiene.

Who are the main customers of a restaurant?

The target customer of your restaurant is a specific segment of the larger dining market. Target markets are determined by a combined analysis of: Demographics: segments of the population as divided by shared characteristics, including age, sex, income, education, religion, race, and geographical location.

A hostess is the first person to meet a guest when they enter a restaurant, and they're in charge of the beginning part of the dining experience. Typically only sit-down, dine-in restaurants have hosts, as their main responsibilities are seating guests and managing reservations.

Which three factors are most important when choosing a restaurant location Why? When choosing a restaurant location, consider rent affordability, demographics that match your concept, and major market generators in the neighborhood. These factors will impact your restaurant's success.

How do people choose which restaurant they patronize?

What are the factors influencing customers' restaurant choices? People are influenced by word-of-mouth recommendations, online reviews, a brand's reputation, menu options, and pricing. Once you get them in the door, an emotional connection and the experience keeps them coming back

What are the 5 factors influencing consumer behavior?

Typically, there are five core factors that influence the decision to restaurant eaters which are:

Psychological Factors.

How the eater feels the restaurant environment, waiter service, food quality, meal choice and price.

Social Factors.

The restaurant can let the eater feel high or low class, social position

Cultural Factors.

The restaurant can present the eater whose education level

Economic Factors.

How many people are losing jobs or working in society.

Personal Factors.

The eater has restaurant distance feeling demand, e.g. Far or not far to go to the restaurant to eat, spending how long time to arrive the restaurant to eat.

CHAPTER TEN

Applying business development strategy to raise the educational robotic manufacturer sale number in recession period

What does business development strategy ?

An effecting business development strategy ought have these five steps: The first step is market analysis. Who are your clients , knowledge of your market? Second step is how to adopt for each penetration, your business needs to learn how to adopt for each group of clients, your first need to review your own capacbility. It is important that you are realistic and honest with yourselves over where clients truly sit, learn how to classify your clients into similar groups relative is the scale of the opportunity. Third step learns how to review your performance , market matrix to plot your results to help you determine your market penerstion. In addition, it will help you then discuss and consider various strategies for growth. By potting your clients you will get a sense of where your strengths and weaknesses are against the opportunity that total market offer.Fourth step learns how to consider alternative growth strategies on the market matrix. The final step , you need to consider these questions in order to decide whic is the most effective strategy for your business. For example, which model is the most (least effective? Why? which model work best for line managers, HR are finance, why? How might we most effectively progress from one model to the most reasonable questions?) Then, you will need to decide how to launch new services, new products, opening new markets, how accessing new geographic territories.

How to apply business development strategy to help educational robotic manufacturers to enter traditional education market ?

Many thinkers concern robots that are used in manufacturing workplaces, homes, roads, hospitals and care centre aspect, but they don't feel robotics may be possible to apply on social service aspect, e.g. educational service aspect . In fact, robotic may have both functions. Industrial robotics, e.g. manufacturing function as well as service robotics, e.g. professional robotcs, medical robotics, entertainment robotics, e.g. toy and education robotics and service robotics , e.g. personal and domestic robotics.

Educational robotic is on the birth stage in its industry life cycle. So, any educational robotic products will need time to persuade schools or any educational institutions to buy their products to assist teachers to teach students in classrooms. The question is how to apply business development strategy to help the educational robotic manufacturer to develop its educational robotic products to persuade educational clients to choose to buy ? I shall attempt to explain as below:

Due to educational robotic product is one new educational tool to assist any schools to buy to assist teachers to improve teaching service performance to let students to feel more learning satisfaction, so any educational robotic products must need time to introduce whether what it can bring schools benefits to let students and teachers to feel. When robotic can be popular to use on manufacturing, educational service industries aspect, e.g. warehouse , factory, shopping center, even restaurant's kitchen cooking robotics, office environment's accounting, law draft etc. clerical robotics may be invented to replace human 's general simple tasks. However, if future robots can be applied to educational aspect, e.g. classroom, school teaching students. Can educational robotic may assist or replace teachers to teach students in clasrooms? Will future teachers be replaced by teaching robotics . I shall attempt to explain whether it is possible that educational robotic can be developed to global educational organizations successfully as below:

Robotic technology has been invented to own " mind " ability, e.g. writing words, writing song, simple calculation tasks reading tasks . So, future robotics can be invented to own " mind " ability, when robotics' mind ability can be improved to own how to " communication" ability and " analytical" ability. Then can it be possible to apply robotics to do teaching tasks in classrooms, e.g. learning any books , the it applies the book's contents to analyze any "knowledge" in order to follow the logic mind to teach students in classroom. It is one major factor to influence any schools to explain why they need to buy any educational robotic in schools in any educational robotic product business development strategy. So, they need to find whether what their educational robotic strengths , any competitors won't own or their product weaknesses, they need to improve their educational robotic products in order to attract educational organizations to choose to buy.

Can future teaching robotics learn to do teacher individual same education tasks? It will be absolute competitive point to any educational robotic product manufactures. If it is true, can teaching robotics may be trained to exceed teacher individual teaching skill? It is another competitive point to any educational robotic product manfacturers. Is it ethic to apply robotic to teach students to replace teachers if teaching robotic can perform better teaching service to compare teachers? If the eduational robotic manufactuer can persude the school can accept eduational robotic ethic issue to assist or replace teachers to do teaching tasks, then it's sale chance will raise. So, ethic to educational robotic will be another factor to develop the educational robotic business. Can teachers be teaching robotic's teaching assistant role if teaching robotics can have teaching ability to teacher in the school? So, if the educational robotic manufacturer can persuade the school to feel that its products can be teacher's assistant to improve their performance to let students learn more easily. The educational robotics manufacturer may develop its product to sell in this educational market more easily, in business development strategy view.

All of these will be future any one educational robotic development challenges if they hope their products can sell more easily. They also need to know to let schools to know these disadvatages to their products to become advatanges in order to attract they to choose to buy their producte more easily. Such as what potential harmful consequences may come from the inventing of teaching robotics? What happends to important education moral, such as teacher or school privacy then robotic are starting to become an teaching tool to the school? Do such robotics hace any roght and responsibilities if the class has many students learning ability are influenced to poor or examination results are poor when the educational robotic has been bought to assist the school teachers to teach their students? Why does the school need to buy educational robotic to do teaching tasks? Any school organizations must need any one educational robotic product seller to answer any one of above questions, before they decide to buy their products. So, they must need to ensure teaching robotics will be used to help the school to teach students to learn more understanding to compare teachers only.

Future educational robotic are applied on development teaching maths market

In the future, business development to educational robotic market may be teaching maths. I shall explain as below:

It is possible that students can use mobile robotic to learn mathematics subject to compare teachers more easily. Why? For example, young age from 4 to 14 age, they may apply mobile robotics to learn add, multiple, divided, simple math equation more understanding than math teaches. Robotic kints and apps is currently available on the maket for teacher of 4 to 14 age students,due to mobile , kits app price is cheap. So, they can be popular to be accepted by any primary schools , even in secondary schools, robotics may be applied to teach computer science, statistical methods subjects of one robotic kit for teach team of 2 to 3 students, short theory lessons , and tutorials to link theory and practice, realistic but affordable tasks linked with curricular subjects, teachers at ease with the robotic etc. So, future primary and secondary , even university teachers may need to choose the more suitable robot kit for their students,and carefully design where and how to use it and with which role.In fact, children will be possible to raise interest to learn when they can contact for any kind of teaching robotic to learn maths in classrooms together. So, teaching robotics may help 4 to 14 children students to raise learning interest instead of learning about ability.

In the future, robotic role is school may be one tool to engage the students as teachers role may be transfer base knowledge when teachers teach maths, geography, statistics, computer science subjects to promary , secondary even university students. This is one good example , whether what subjects robotic may be applied when it is invented to own human mind and anlaytical skill and communication ability. Robotics can perform more better to be applied to teach these subjects. It can let students to understand easily, e.g. understanding how to create equations that describe numbers a relationship understanding solving equations as a process of reasoning and explain the equations and inequalities in one variable, helping students to find different solutions, then best solves the problem , given the criteria and the constraints, helping students have more understanding how science knowledge is based upon logical and conceptual connections between evidence and explanations, even robotc can ask questions that can be investigated within the scope of the classroom, outdoor environment, and museums and other public faciltities with available resources and when appropriate frame a hypothesis based on observation and scientific principles.

Even, robotics may help students to learn how construct, use and present oral and written arguments supported by evidence and scientific reasoning to support or refute an explanation or a model for a phenomenon, or robot can hep students to learn how obtain, evaluate and communicate information in 6-8 builds on k-5 and progresses to evaluating the merit and validity of ideas and methods, integiate qualitative scientific and technical information in written text with that contained in media and visual displays to clarify cliams and findings, helping students to anlyze data from texts to determine similarities and differences among several design solutions to identify the best characteristics of each that can be combined into a new solution to better meet the criteria for success, even helping students to learn how analyze data in 9-12 builds on k-8 and progresses to introducing more detailed statistical anslysis, the comparision of data sets for consistency and the use of models to generate and analyze data, analyze data using tools, technologies , and/or models e.g. computational, mathematical in order to make valid and variable scientific claims or determine and optinal design solution more easily than human teacher. So, there are human-made educaton machine advantage to students more than human teacher.

Educational robotic has been introduced as a powerful, in fact, flexible teaching / learning tool stimulating learns to control the behavior of tangible model using specific programming languages (graphical, or textual and involving them actively in authentic problem -solving activities. Howeverm in future educational robotic development, it may be divided two separate categories as below:

Robotics as learning object: This first category includes educational activities where robotics is being studied as a subject on its own. It includes educational activities aimed at configuring a learning environment that will actively involve learners in the solution of authentic problems, facing on robotics -related subjects, such as robot construction, robot programming and artificial intelligence as well as robotic as learning tool: In the frame of this second category, robotics is proposed as a tool for teaching and learning other school subjects at different school levels. Robotics as learning tool is usually, seen as an interdisciplinary, project -based learning activity drawing mostly on science, maths, informatics and technology and offering major new benefits to education in genera at all levels. However, I believe the role of teacher is crucial for the successful industry of technological and innovations in classrooms, when robotics are been particiapted to any education tasks in classrooms. Schools can focuse on the training of prospective and in-service teachers in the use of robotics technologies through courses.

In future electronic learning environment, robotics can be participated, such as recognised their active participation in all sessions of the course and their creative involvement even in the theoretical parts introducing principles and methodology for designing robotic-enhanced projects, very much liked the activity-orientation of the educational content, acknowledged the central role of the e-workspace during the face-to-face meetings and beyond ehem in enhancing sense of community, acknowledged the potential of educational robotics as a teaching tool but also as a subject, in different disiplines , such as technology, informatics and engineerinfg, highly appreciated the opportunity to create their projects.

How to develop robotic in technological subjects on teaching, learning and educational aspect? Learners can be encouaged hen robotics participate actively in the learning process. Through robotic learners build something on their own, preferably a tangible object, that they can both touch and find meaningful. In robotic learners are invited to work experiments or problem-solving with selective use of available resources, according to their own interest, search and learning strategies. Robotics can help them to seek solutions to real world problems, based on a technological framework meant to engage students' movitation. So, when students can have control of specific robotc in a rich learning environment, the construction of robots and programs to control them the emphasis might move on interesting learning actiities in the frame of specific learning areas , such as science and technology. Thus, the design of robotic construction activities is associated with the fulfillment of a project aimed at solving a problem. In such a learning environment, learning is driven by the problem to be solved. To engage students in activities requiring to design and manufacture real objects, i.e. robotic structures that make sense for themselves and should devise activities that will encourage students to support in order experiment. So, robotic participation any science experiments, they may encourage students to create problem solving and combining interdisiplinary concepts from different knowledge areas,: science, mathematics , technology and research educational tasks, the role of students will change, when preparing a work with a programmable robotics studies experiment with simple programmable sobotics devices , e.g. a car-robot, motors, sensor etc. Students are asked to synthesize their finds and reach conclusions and solutions to the problem uner investigation. SO, robotic is educaional participation to any scientfic technological or research experiments, they may help students to work with creativity , imagination and independence and finally organize the evaluation of the activity in collaboration ith studens. Also robotic participation to any technological or scientific research experiemtn, it also change teacher role . The teacher is such a constructist theoretical framework, like that teacher 's role that does not transfer ready knowledge to students, but rather acts as a organizer, coordinator and facilitator of learning for students. when educational robotics participate to any science or technological any research experiments, students may be organize the learning environment, raise the question , problem to be solved by students allow students to work with creativity, imagination and independence and finally organize the evaluation of the activity in collaboration with students. So, any educational robotic manufacturers must let their school clients to feel all these benefits which can bring to let students to raise learning abilty and learning interest to compare that are only taught by teachers, if they hope their educational robotics can be sold successfully in business development strategy view.

Why do some social challenges may influence customers number ?

In our societies , we shall have different challenges to our every day. However, in general , the challanges seem that they do not have relate to influence businessmen profit, but in fact, these social challenges have relationship to influence business profit and clients number. I shall indicate some social challenges to explain why these social challenges may influence any business profit indirectly as below:

In investment or raving individual preference decision aspect, for some people , it may be interesting or fun to think cbout the best investments or the right health care plan. But, for other people, these choices are unpleasant, they may be persuaded to buy anythings, e.g. car, computer. So, if car seller can have persuasive methods to influence many people feel the health care plan or investment plan is not prefereable choices, driving car enjoyable feeling or material enjoyment is the most preference choice. Then I believe that the car seller's car selling number may increase, because some people greatly enjoy thinking about their pension and the best investment or health care insurance preferable decision, their decision had been influenced to choose to buy the car seller's cars. When they feel driving car enjoyable feeling is more important than future benefit.

Hence, in behavioral economy view, they had felt the driving car benefit is much to compare pension investment or health care insurance future benefit. The question is how to car seller can persuade these investment ot pension plan or health care preference decision individual to change purchase car driving decision.

I suggest that the car seller may have discount or cash coupon or installment payment method to attract them to consider , instead of advertisement promotion method. because this preference investment or pension saving or health care plan decision individual customer group will be more difficult to persuade them to choose to buy car immediately at this moment. Hence, if the car seller can not implement cheap car discount strategy, it will be difficult to attract this prefeence long term future benefit consumer to make purchase ca r decision easily. Because they think pension or investment or health care plan ce help them to bring long term future benefit, also it means that purchase car may only bring short term present benefit. It is general social behavioral consumption model to influence their purchase choice. Hence, I assume that general social long term future benefit product or service, e.g. insurance, investment , pension may influence th scocial shor tterm present benefit product , e.g. car consumer. It is the main reason, it can explain why car sellers can not persuade this long term future benefit consumers to make decision to buy their cars easily, when they have no enough money to spend to buy car and make investment, saving , medical care insurance , pension plan in the same time. They must need to make either purchase car or insurance etc. decision in our nowadays societies.

So, in behavioral economic view, it explains why consumer individual purchase choice behavior has relationship to himself/herself spending budget. I assume that it has two kinds of behavioral economic consumers. One kind if long term future economic benefit in preference more than short term present economic benefit, such as purchase car and investment or health care plan insurace saving term present benefit consumer, he / she considers to earn driving enjoyment at this moment is not preference than purchase insurance or investment future benefit decision . So, our society, any business will encounter these two kinds of behavioral consumer. They persuade either long term futuer benefit consumers or short term present benefit consumer to change himself/herself products or services more easily. Otherwise, such as if car seller can not implement coupon or cash reward or discount or installment cash payment strategy to attracr the long term future benefit consumer. Then, it will lose this group car customers number absolutely. So, it explains why businessmen need to learn consumer behavioral consumption model in order to increase client number more easily.

" Social welfare" usually measured by people's prefences, and it also focuses for the conventional economists, on how to maximize social welfare. What then is the task of behavior law and economics? Such as, this cate seller case example, whether what social welfare the car seller can bring to society when the individual decides to buy its car to drive or when the individual chooses to buy health care insurance or pension plan or investment . When he/she chooses to buy health care insurance or make pension plan or buys any companies' shares. Then, these investment service companies will bring what benefits to our society? So, instead of consumer benefit, we also need to consider whether the kind of product or service will bring what long term social benefit . However, I think that when global many people own cars, then many cars are driven on the roads, it will bring serious air pollution to influence our health. Then, when many people are got lung diseases by air pollution. Then, many people will need to pay more medical expense. It will be long term negative medical cost increasing expense to future us, but it also bring possible income for insurance firms, when many people plan to buy medical care plans when they feel air pollution will influence them to need to pay future medical expense. So, it seems that the effect on many people own cars and their driving behaviors will bring serious air pollution, but it will also create the health care medical insurance need to be increased due to many people feel air polluton will bring lung disease and they need to pay long time medical expensein the future long time in possible. So, many people driving behavior may bring air pollution, but it also bring medical insurance need increases in our society in possible. It means that air pollution may create medical insurance market develops in possible, such as most smokers say they would prefer not to smoke, and many pay money to join a program or obtain a drug that will help them quit.If many smokers forgive to smoke, then the medical care insurance need for smokers number may be influenced to reduce.

In social benefit view, medical insurance for smokers insurance will be influenced to reduce, due to many smokers forgive to smoke. Although, many smokers may get health, when they do not smoke, they do not pay to buy any cigeratte often, they can save more money, but cigeratte sellers and medical insurance service providers , their income must be influenced to reduce. Hence, when our society government's advertisement concerns smokers often smoke cigeratte, it may bring poor drug health or many cars air pollution, these two messages may influence or dissuade many smokers forgive to smoke or many people do not buy cars. They choose to catch public transportation, or owning car people who do not often drive cares, then car gas or fuel suppliers income will be influenced to reduce, due to many car owning people do not often drive cars or many people do not choose to buy cars. Then, car sellers' income wil be influenced to reduced. Moreover, in long term social influence, when many people do not feel lung disease . Then, the medical care insurance need will also influenced to reduce.

It may bring insurance industry develops in difficulty for lung dissease medical care insurance. So, it explains why consumer behavior may also influence our social economic development in long term . They have cause and effect close relationship. When many consumers individual forgive or dislike to do the behavior in habit, e.g. driving car behavior or smoking behavior. Then, it will influence car seller market and cigeratte seller market to be poor in any countries , even global market.

Hence, in our society, when one individual feels that he.she has individual challenge, it may be economic or emotion or health problem, such as smoking influences health case, driving influences air pollution case. These both kinds of individual behavior may influence the individual may need to spend money for lung disease if he/she has continue smoking habit every day or he/she often drives car . Then, the individual will seek methods to solve these possible occurrence of problems before they do not occur. As it occurs in the natural environment, e.g. air pollution or lung disease is caused by cars or smoking. When individual begins feel these negative effect may case, if he/she continues to do smoking or dirving car behavior. He/she will begins to find methods to solve problem, problem solving is defined as the self-directed cognitive -behavioral process by which an individual , couple or group, such as smokers and drivers group in our society, they attempt to idcntify or disciver effective solutions for specific problem encountered in everyday living. More specifically, this cognitive -behavioral process (a) makes available a variety of potentially effective solutions for a particular problem and (b) increases the probability of selecting the most effective solution from among the various alternatives (D'Zurilla & Gold field 1971).

As this definition implies social problem solving is conceived as a conscious, rational, effortful, and purposeful activity. Depending on the problem solcing goals, this process may be aimed at changing the problematic situation for the better, reducing the emotional distress that it produces or both.

Hence, it implies that when any one feels he/she will have individual problem, e.g. health problem , economuc problem,emotion problem. He/she will avoid to continue to do the kind of behavior often every day ,e.g. smoking behavior or driving car behavior .When our society has many people make to forgive to do above themselves behaviors, such as smoking or driving habit. Then, it will influence cigeratte sale number and car sale numner to be reduced. So, when our society has any consumer groups, they forgive to do themselves behaviors in habit. Consequently, the kind of product seller or service provider may lose man customers. So, in our society , when one kind of product or service consumers , their habital behaviors are changed to reduce, then it may influence the kind of product sellers or service providers their income or clients number to be either decrease or increase. On conclusion, it explains that why social behavior has close relationship to influence business income or clients number in our societies.

Any organizations may experience organizational life cycle stages from birth stage to growth stage to maturity , then it may also experience decline and/or regrow stages. But this two stages, they are not all organizations must may attempt to experience. It depends on whether economic environment how changes, organizational itself SWOT strengths and weaknesses etc. unpredicted factors to influence that when the organization will experience decline life cycle stage. It means that if the organization has very poor performance, then the organization has possible to experience decline life cycle stage in short time or long time. Otherwise, if the organizationhas very good performance, it ought not experience decline life cycle stage in short time, when it can reach mature stage in its the topest level. Even, when the organization has poor performance, so it is experiencing decline stage, but if it may implement effective strategies to help itself organization to develop . Then, if its strategies are very effective , in consequence, the organization ought may experience regrowing stage to re-experience its mature life cycle stage again. So, it seems that if the organization can have very good performance. Client number can increase significant as well as profit can also growth rapidly. Then, the organization ought may experience long time in mature life cycle stage or it means that it will be difficult to reach decline life cycle stage. Unless, some sudden inpredicted economic environment, or strong competitors etc. influence its performance, then they will have chance to cause it experiences to decline life cycle stage from mature stage suddenly. Hence, all organizations must need to experience birht life cycle stage in beginning to this stage.

However, when the business founder starts to set up his/her business. He/she needs time to deal any difficulties,e.g. how to advertise his/her products to let customers have much knowledge, promote them to sell to market, how to implement strategies to solve organizational challenges. So, in birth stage, any organizations ought feel difficult to improve its whole performance or evaluate whether its future performance can improve to be better or can not improve or worse. Then, when the organization operates one period, it ought experience to growth stage, but it still depends on external factors to influence whether when it may experience growth stage, the factors may include: Whether strategies can be effective, economic environment is good or bad, customers purchase desire level is high or loe, cost expenditure is high or low etc. difficult factor.

So, before any organizatons may experience growth stage, there are many different complex factors to influence whether they can succeed to experience this stage easily. If the organization can not implement any effective strategies to solve its customers purchase emotion challenges, then its business is difficult to continue grow, also it means that the organization can not growor expand its business easily. Due to it can not continue to develop its business easily. It must not reach mature life cycle stage easily. Thus, any organizations can reach mature life cycle stage. It represents that its business has good strategies to solve any challenges in order to its products can attract customers to choose to buy or it can provide good service performance to satisfy clients needs to compare irs competitors in this market successfully.

In fact, it is not all organizations can attempt to experience the mature life cycle stage. This stage is any organization individual the topest stage. In this stage, the organization may have many clients increasing number significantly every year, its market can continue expand, profit can continue increases . All is the best to any organizations, if it can reaches this stage . All many organizations may only experience birth stage or growing stage . They reach this either birth or growth stage, then they have none good strategies to compete their clients number can not increase, but only decreases, profit reduces , even loss. They can not know how to change strategied to improve their performance or competitive effort to fight this competitors. Then, their businesses can not continue grow or expand. So, they have more chance to experience decline stage after either birth or growth stage only. They can not reach mature life cycle stage to attempt the topest level in whole business (organizational) life cycle stage or process. Thus, it brings these questions: Why do organizations need to learn organizational life cycle stages? What advantages to bring if they can attempt to learn how to reach growth or mature life cycle stages easily? I shall explain as below:

Why do organizations need to spend time to learn how may experience different business life cycle stages?

The business life cycle is the progression of a business in phases over time and is most commonly divided into five stages: Launch or birth, growth, maturity and decline or regrow. Each company begins its operations as a business and usually by launching new products or services. Because any organizations will encounter challenges in every stages . If they know what factos may help them to enter another new stage of business life cycle or what challenges may threaten them can not enter another new business life cycle stage easily. Because businessman need to learn and how adjust their business model to ensure profitability. That is why an awareness of what stage of the business life cycle , you are currently it can be helpful. Hence, how to maximize each stage of the business life cycle, the businessmen might still need to learn how to work in order to improve performance when the businessmen are experiencing any one life cycle stage. Moreover, each business life cycle stage comes still need to learn how to turn a profit and the first outlines of their governance and compliance and this is one big reason why most businesses fail at this stage.

So, I assume that business life cycle stage is similar to school examination, the student needs to spend time to learn in the birth learning stage, then he needs to test in the growth learning stage, next is examination in the mature learning stage, if the student fails, t is decline learning stage to the school. It may be due to the teachers can not teach students to learn easily. So, these are many students fail in tests or examinations. So, if the school teachers can improve teaching methods to let many students may earn high grades in tests or examinations. Then, the school may experience growth, even mature teaching life cycle stage in short time rapidly . Hence, teaching quality can improve or not , it will influence any school organizations ought feel to schools to learn how to improve teaching methods or strategies in order to let students can experience the maturity learning stage or it can also experience the maturity teaching stage. It means that it ought learn how to improve its teachers teaching service performance to satisfy students learning needs if it hopes to reach maturity learning and teaching life cycle stage in short time for itself school organization benefit.For example, the organization founder may ask himself/herself why he/she wants to start this business, learns how to manage exployees strategies? It is the learning needs in the third stage, such as maturity stage. Otherwise, in the first stage of the business entity birth life cycle is sometimes called the seed stage and a matter of iteraing, testing an learning , and trying again, knowing that the businessman is unlikely to have.

What advantages may bring to the organization if it can attempt to learn how to solve different challenges in different business life cycle stages ? What advantages to the organization, if it can know how to experience every business life cycle stage?

In fact, the business life cycle is the progression of a business in phases over time, and is consumer segments by advertising their comparative advantages and vale. For example, when the business is experiencing growth stage , in the growth phase, the business founder needs to spend time to learn how his company can experience rapid sales growth. This learning may assist his business to develop his business to enter next mature how stage easily , for example, he can learn how the rapid growth stage takes advantage from the proven sales model, e.g. online sale or traditional visiting shop sale model which is more suitable to his business, marketing model and operations model, e.g. how to advertise his product or promote his products can affect more audiences concern this will see the businessmen's jounrey from idea to start up, and if successful, how to keep to stay long time in the mature stage. Rememeber, when having a successful business model behind any businessmen is undoubtedly an advantage, it is not a disadvantage when the founder spends more time to learn hoe to run his business. In fact, he won't waste his time to learn how to improve his business in different business life cycle stages. So, a tactical plan will take any business strengths and reduces to avoid weakness cause to influence its development. So, knowing where you small product is in its product life cycle, it is important to continue to develop your business successfully. SO, any impacts of all life cycle stages, any businesses need to be considered comprehensively , for one new technological product firm example, its new technological product life cycle begins with the introduction or birth stage. The high technological product company must succeed at both developing new product and managing them in the face of changing tastes, competitors' technologies similar change. So, it is what it needs to learn in this stage for this new product technological firm preparing development to next growth stage.

On the conclusion, learning how to achieve in every business life cycle stage, it can bring these benefits to any organizations, such as : they can understand and redefine this role from a more, if the organization ony to learn sale frameworks what it could have picked up. It is not enough, because most organizations will only find that a majority of their total sale number which is to use solely supplier-specific data about the life cycle, but they neglect how to set targets to learn how to improve their sale to be better in the future time, it is one important factor explain why many organizations only reach the growth stage, but they can not experience to next mature stage more easily, due to they do not consider how to implement strategies in order to achieve their next targets. They feel often implment targets which will help them to know whether they need to how to do in order to improve their businesses to satisfy clients needs. As with any effort in your organization, communication plays a critical role, craft machine learning to predict and manage human for remote teams to work through the innovation lifecycle, serve them well. Any organizations need to learn how to satisfy any customer individual purchase jounrey (called purchase experience) which the customer has with the organization, because when the organization can learn how to satisfy any client individual real need in any life cycle stage. On consequence, its clients number with have possible to influence increase. Thus, any organizations can bot neglect to learn how to satisfy client individual real purchase experience need in any life cycle stages because improvement to salepeople sale performance, they need spend time to learn in every time sale experience . When the organization can build excellent sale teams, then they may help it to build famous loyalty and good client relationship in order to expand its business more easily. Hence, in any businesses' life cycle stages, they must need to spend time to learn how to improve product quality service performance to bring customers' satisfactory emotion in order to expand their business developmenr more easily. So, i recommend that all small organizations expand to large size, they must need time to learn and attempt to find the best methods to solve any difficulties when they are facing in any one business cycle stage, if they want to expand their businesses successfully.

The relationship between learning change management and rapid
reaching mature life cycle

It is one good question: Can the manager or CEO help whole organization to develop rapidly if he/she attempt to learn how to help his/her organization to implement different strategies to solve different challenges in different business life cycle stages? Does it easy to help the organization to grow up when a learning CEO or learning manager accepts to learn anything to compare a non learning manager in different business life cycle stages? Has it relationship between learning or non learning manager and rapid experiencing business life cycle stage and rapid developing business growth? I shall attempt to explain as below:

In fact, it is not essential to any managers or CEOs need to spend time to learn how any why what factors may influence their organizations to grow up to next business life cycle stage, but in comparison one learning how to change organizational life cycle stages manager and non-learning how to change organizational life cycle stages manger. Can learn attitude or strategy to help the manager to develop or expand his organization to next life cycle stage more easily or rapidly? I shall attempt to explain as below:

In fact, any organizations expect to change to next life cycle stage in success , can the manager(s) learn how to implement strategies to achieve to change management to their organizations' development in success? How the organizational management learns how to adapt organizational management change, it may be one important factor to influence whether the organization needs to spend how long time to reach growth life cycle stage from birth stage or reach mature life cycle stage from growth stage. So, it seems that how management spends time to learn how to change his/her organization. It will have relationship to the organization needs to spend long time to reach next life cycle stage successfully.

Hence, learning how to train employees in each life cycle stage, it is the important factor to influence any organizations succeed, the employee lifecycle is an ongoing process that starts and ends with competent employees in any managers' organizations. There are nine elements ofa successful change management process, if the organizational management expects whole organization can real reach to next life cycle stage in success. The nine elements of a successful change management process, any management needs to spend time to learn. They may include: readiness assessments, communication planning implementation, sponsor activities and sponsor roadmaps organizing, organizatons need to provide change management training for managers to learn how to achieve effectiveness as well as providing training development and delivery learning methods to them, resistance management learning and learning employee feedback and corrective action. Moreover, managements also need to spend time to learn change management steps in order solve any challenges in order to reach next life cycle stage easily.

The change management learning steps may include: Step 1: Urgency creation , step 2: Building every team serves to every department efficiently, learning how to create avision, how to communication of division, how to remove obstacles, going for quick wins, let the change mature, integrate the change. These elements are incorporated into change management phases process. For example, some elements of communication planning occur early in the lifecyle. At this stage, change management is not fully achieved effectively, so management needs to spend more time to learn how to achieve effective communication planning in order to achieve effective communication planning in order to keep whose organization employees can communicate to work efficiently. Also, it will help client service employees to know how to build good communication management method to deal or answer or satisfy their clients' sale service and improving service performance absolutely.

Because organizations are nor statis, they change , if one organization still stays long time in birth stage, it represents that the organization feels difficulties to continue develop . So, the management needs to find whether what challenges threaten its organization can not reach growth stage more easily. One failure changing management organization, it has these characteristics: failure to change, inexperienced management, not enough revenue, inadequate leadership. Hence, it has close relationship between employee life cycle and organizational life cycle . If the organizational management expects its organization can continue develop or reaches next life cycle stage in success, it needs to learn how to let employees to adapt when its organization is changing in order to keep efficience and improving service performance absolutely . So, I believe that it has relationship between learning change management and reaching to mature business cycle stage rapid and achieving long time staying in business cycle mature stage .

The question concerns that how management can learn to implement change management strategy in order to let his organization can reach mature cycle stage in short time as well as keep to stay in this mature life cycle stage in long time?

Firstly, we need to know what change management life cycle means ? For information technological industry example, it may be explained that the change management process is designed to help control of the life cycle of strategies, tactical and operational changes to IT services through standardized procedures. The goal of change managent is to control risk and minimize disruption to IT service and business operations. So, IT industry, the process change management maturity model presents five levels of organizational maturity in change management: The five level may include: from the lowest level 1 to the highest level 5, level 1: Absent or Ad hoc, level 2: Isolated projects , level 3: Multiple projects, level 4: Organizatinal standards and level 5: organizational competency. So, for IT , software manufacturing industry, if the management knows how to manage and change software manufacturing quality in order to satisfy manufacturing organization can follow software users' needs to change old function to new function and improve their qualities to achieve the highest level 5 organizational competency level.

Then, I believe that due to this organization's software management can learn how software user needs change and change its any kinds of software functions (software life cycle), when its all softwares can be often changed to more new functions to create many different kinds of new software functions to satisfy software users needs and fight its software compettors in this often changing needs market. Due to software product may experience often changing life cycle stages. So, for often one learning software manager example, I believe that he can help this software organization to reach growth life cycle stage, even mature life cycle stage more easily in short time as well as he can also help his software organization to stay in mature life cycle stage long time if this software organizational manager can keep learning attitude to continue to create any new kinds of different functions software to satisfy software clients‘ changing needs for long time . Then, I believe that this software organization may experience or reach growth life cycle stage, even mature life cycle stage as well as continue staying long time on mature life cycle stage or avoid to encounter decline life cycle stage occurrence chance, if this software organization's softeare management can learn how to change software organization operation and software manufacture and sale strategy in order to satisfy this software users' needs in this software users‘ need often changing market . So, it is one example to explain why it has close relationship between learning organizational management method and business life cycle stages. As this software organization case, the software management needs often to create and change any new kinds of software functions in order to satisfy software users' needs . So, the software managers need to spend time to learn software life cycle stage , it can help the software organization may reach products life cycle stage, even mature life cycle stage in short time,even the software product organization may also stay long time in mature life cycle stage , when it can reach this stage. Hence, learning how to change organizational management or strategy, which is one important factor to help any organization can reach growth or mature life cycle stage eadily in short time.

As Lewin describes that the change as a three stage process of unfreezing, change and freezing . In this phases of change model, Lewin emphasizes that change is that a series of individual processes, but rather one that flows from one process to the next . So, in general, services mature firms pace greater emphasis on more bureaucratic form, control systems might need to change throughout the life cycle to fit in with. He explains they have relationship between both organizational life cycle stage and management control.

Effective management control may help the organization to reach mature life cycle in short time rapidly. So, leadership managment and the way of thinking are required to balance control and through several stages of growth, maturity , decline or re-grow changes in the external environment influence. Hence, managers position in each of the stages of life cycle and providing practical solutions are, however world where environment changes have proven a rapid growth, the management of varios , they also need to implement how to change their organizational cultures, strategies in order to let their organizations to reach mature stage with a distinction-oriented rapidly. Hence, to successfully implement change initiatives, for each phase of life cycle. Any organizations need to produce resistance to change (the old model wins out over management boils down to improving the relationship) learning the relationship between leadership style and the organization life cycle were important. The change from one organizational life cycle phase to another, it depends on how the manager'c capacity to learn and change.

However, organizations at any stage of the life cycle are impacted by external environment, for example, threats in the start up stage differ from those in the maturity stage. So, managers must need often to learn when the right time is to be needed to change the goals, instead he also needs to learn types of changes in the maturity stage, comparisons with other, having strong personal and professional relationships in the organizaton's maturity stage. Hence, I believe that it has close relationship between learning change management and reaching maturity life cycle and staying long time in this stage.

How to achieve the experience of mature life cycle reaching stage rapidly for product and service ?

Any businesses expect they can have chance or possibility to attempt to experience this nature life cycle stage, but it is not guarantee any kinds of businesses must may experience this the topest stage, the question is that: Have any methods may help any kinds of businesses to reach this the topest level of business life cycle, when their businesses had been developing or expanding in a period, e.g. after five years? So, it has no absolute to guarantee any kinds of businesses must may experience this the topest stage in one fixed time. How businesses can adapt to birth and growth life cycle stages in order to reach this the topest mature stage in their business life cycle stages? I shall attempt to explain whether it is possible that achieving what strategies may help businesses bring high successful chance to reach the business life cycle mature stage as below:

Product life cycle with maturity stage, it foucs as an important strategic inflection point. A number of techniques can help their businesses to attempt to reach this stage more easily. In fact, the product life cycle contains four distinct stages: introduction, growth, maturity, and decline. Each stage is associated with changes in the product's marketing position . Any firms can use various marketing strategies in each stage to try to proplong the life cycle of their products.

How do the firm extend the maturity stage of a product? I shall recommend change price , place or promotion extension strategy , what does change price extension strategies mean? Change prices mean proces can be lowered to allow ew customers to buy it as well as change place means that products can be sold in different countries or territories to gain more sales, change promotion means different advertising or sales promotion techniques can proplong the life of the product, giving it a new image. So, any organizations can attempt to achieve this extension strategies in order to adapt in different birth, growth and maturity stages for ther product sale easily. This extension strategies' characteristics is at the product;s price, sold places and promotin methods can be changed in order to adapt clients needs when their products are selling in birth, growth and maturity three stages in order to achieve the most effective sale effort and clients growth increasing for long time.

In fact, any product is like human beings, products also have a limited life-cycle and they pass through several stages in their life cycle. A typical product moves through five stages, namely, introduction or birth, growth, maturity or saturation and decline stages. So, when the product needs the maturity life cycle stage, in this maturity stage, it has these characteristics: The maturity stage of the product life cycle shows that sales will eventually peak and then slow down. During this stage, sales growth has started to slow down, and the product has already reached widespread acceptance in the market, in relative terms, utimately, during this stage, sales will peak . Hence, any businesses ought need to consider what key strategies can be implement to achieve the best sale performance throughout the different product life cycle stages and how to make the most of each stage. For example, when the product is selling in the birth stage, e.g. one author's book , his book is selling to the publisher in the first year, there are not many readers knew this book existence, so this book is not popular, its price ought not change high to compare similar topic book, e.g. story book in this year, but after this year, if there are many readers know this book and readers number can grow up rapidly. This author's this topic story book does not change, either increases or decreases , but its sale number has been significant increasing after the first year . So, this author's this story book ought be raised book price to attempt to sell easily. It is one good example of extension strategy to this author's this story book in its life cycle stages. So, such as ths publisher book sale case, it may attempt to achieve extension strategies to every author's book sale, it can follow every author's book prices, publishing places and promotion methods to help every author to sell in the most competitive book sale price, sale place choice and promotin methods in order to earn their readers growth aim . So, any book , it is as product to book shop, it will experience introduction, growth, and maturity life cycle stages. Some books may attract many readers to consider or some books may not attract many readers to consider to read . So, it causes their reading life cycle stages staying time will be different. So, extension strategies can help any books to be sold easily.

In fact, instead of product has life cycle stage, any service also has life cycle stage. There are five stages in service lifecycle. Thay may include: Service strategy, service design, service transition, service operation and continual servce improvement five stages. The service strategy phase of the service lifecycle provides guidance on how to design , develop and implement service management. Because any service business needs to manage to any employee service performance in order to provide excellent service quality, e.g. property management service to building tenants or property owners , if the peoperty management furm can train employees to provide excellent property management service to let their managing building clients to feel satisfactory. Then, the property management firm ought may keep long time property management service to this building. So, service provider will also experience service performance different stages.

In different service performance life cycle stages, such as this property management service case, they ought implement dfferent strategies in order to let their employees to know how to achieve service performance improvement to let their servicing building clients (tenants or builgin owners) can feel their property management service can be continue improved to avoid to choose any property management service provider to replace it easily.

The purpose of the service strategy stage of the service life cycle is to define the perspective, position plans and pattern that a service provider needs to be able to execute to meet an organization business outomes. The objective of service strategy may include: An understandng of work strategy is thus either the concept of the product life cycle or the concept of the service life cycle is today at about to give a propsed new product or service , how and to what extent. This generally requires important changes in marketing strategies and methods, because any learning kinds of service or product lif cycle stage why and how to change to any organizational management, it may be an important tool for marketers, managers, and product and service providing designers alike, If specifies four individuals stages of a product's or service's life and offers guidance for developing strategies to make the best use of these stages and promote the overall success of the product or service in the marketplace.

Reasons managment needs to spend time to learn how to manage his/her product or service life cycle development stage? They may include: The product or service life cycle is determined by how long its marketable . Product or service life cycle also plays a critical role in marketing strategy . So, learning how to adapt your product or service to meet the coming trends , this is the stage what will occue in which differentiation when the kind of the product or service will have possible to reach the another new experience life cycle stage in order to adapt its business development more easily.

Hence, each stage is associated with changes in the product's or service's marketing postion . The organizational management can use various markting strategies in each stage to try to prolong the life cycle of your products or services . Any product or service reaches the marketplace, it enters the service or product life cycle . This product cycle typically has for stages: Introduction or birth, growth, maturity and decline (and possibly deaths stages for product as well as service strategy stages includes service strategy. service design, servic transition, service operation, and continual service stages four service stages. So, the organization management can spend time to learn how to develop its business product or service needs to change in order to adapt marketing change in its product or service different life cycle stages. It can bring these benefits, such as: true benefits of product or srvice life cycle management may include, reduced time to makret, reduced market entry costs, more efficient and profitable distribution challen, higher return on investment from promotional cappaigns in possible, extending the lifetime of your product or service by adapting your approach as it moves through the lifecycle , for example, any management needs to learn what can make its products or services move from growth to maturity. After the introduction and growth stages, a product or service passes into the maturity stage. IN the first two stages , companies try to establish a market and then grow sales of their product or service to achieve as large , a share of that market as possible. Hence, marketers must be sure that a product or service has moved from one stage to the next before changing its marketing strategy. At each stage, marketing strategy varies. Strategy for the different stages of the product or service life cycle strategies may include: such as more benefits may be provided to the customers, e.g. extending the warranty period, guarantee period etc. However, company's market strategy depends on which stages the product or service is in its life cycle, for example, when one software manufacture company expects to expand its software sale market to overseas from local in growth stage. If it expects that it can reaches maturity stage in short time rapidly. It needs to implement technology innovation strategy for competition advantage reasons in global software sale markets development. Thus, the software organizational manager needs to spend time to learn what its present organizational characteristics are what resources and skills it owns or lacks, that gives it to comparative advantages over different countries to the operating changes that result in the learning curve to prepare this software product sale organizational maturity life cycle stage development more successfully. So, it needs to look at the advantages of focusing on what kinds of software manufacture and sale services in this software development industry whole life cycle stages and find the best or the most suitable competitive straregy, e.g. a discountinuous change to the software product development marketplace, what the global software product development industrial stage is and the tertiary or sale services sector durig the maturity life cycle stage to this softare manufacturer and sale organization strategy to this software firm during this growth stage may include example of it how changed its software product sales channels to which countries will be its another expanding sale market choice.

On conclusion, any organization management ought spend time to learn whether which strategies are the most suitable or the best to implement as well as how to implement when it is experiencing in the prodiuct or life cycle stage in order to spend less time to reach the maturity life cycle stage and proplong its maturity life cycle stage more success.

Human Behavioral network job brings social economic benefits

What does human network job mean ? Why may human network job be popular? Why human network job behavior may influence economy ?

Nowadays internet is popular to use. We can apply internet to find data , search any new things, even earn money. Why does internet may become huma network job source. For example, e-publish may be one kind of new human network job. Any authors may apply internet channel to help them to sell electronic or paper books from e-publisher web store. They may apply facebook, you tub etc. any online channel to promote themselves new books to let new readers to know whether when they may buy themselves favourable new topic books to read from electronic publisher web store.

Thus, future electronic publisher industry may help any authors to build internet network platform to help them to sell and promote ot advertise their any one new electronic or paper book topic to let global any one reader to choose to buy their any new topic books from electronic publisher web store easily and conveniently. However, it implies that electronic network platform author may be one kind of future new human network job in our societies.

How electronic network platform author job may bring economy benefit in macro economy view? A person can have few friends, contacts and still be very influential if these few

friends and contacts are themselves highly influential, e.g. one author must not need to know any one reader in global society. When they like to choose any electronic books from electronic internet network platform. They may become the author's any one topic book buyer, when they feel the author's any one topic book is fun and attract they make decision to buth the strange author whose the topic book from electronic book publisher's platform web store conventiently in short time. Although, they are strangers, they do not know themselves , but the reader can understand what it way that made Google from writing platofrm to create new creative mind and typing network job method to replace traditional hand writing book method for global authors. It will be one kind of new human network writing job.

Hence, global any one reader can apply an innovative search engine , such as google.com to find whether whom author personal new topic books are value to read from internet. Then, the electroniuc publisher's web store may be new book store platform sale network to help the author to sell many electronic or paper books from electronic network platform in short time. So, internet may be future new network plaform to help global any one author to create network writing job absolutely. Furthermore, internet may be popular social media to help any one author to build goold relationship between his/her readers. It is one kind of new network, human network job. New authors do not need to buy many paper books to prepare to put in any one book shop warehouse. Their every book can print on demand to reduce out of book stock in any one book shop. They may choose to sell either electronic books or paper books both from any one book publisher web store. So, electronic network platform may be one kind of good writing channel to help human authors to create income and it can also help authors to bring new creative mind and new topic fun content books to let readers to know and buy to read from electronic publisher network platform.

Why does human behavior may be one kind of new human network job to bring global economic advantages. ALthough, it may be free income or without inocme, but the person does the network behavior, his/her behavior may be bring advantages to influence many other people's health. For this case, when a worker in a coffee shop in an airport gets a vaccination aganinst the flu, it does not only helps him or her stay healthy, but also helps the many travellers who might otherwise have been inflected if that workers caught the flu. So, the externality , the result implies the vaccination of even a part of a community conveys benefits to the whole community. For example, governments pay special attention to the vaccinations of school children, teachers, health mothers, and the elderly, categories of people particularly susceptible not only to catching, but also to transmitting a disease.

It is not accidential that governments are heavily involved with vaccination . When there are externalities, free market, fail to persuade individual incentives with society's

their the worker's decision of whether to get a vaccine ends up attracting whether other people get sick. The workers might not fully take all these other people's potential suffering into account when making her or his vaccination decision.

As Stanford University does many suggestions, understand this and tries to help them make the right decisions and so providers free flu vaccines for its staff and students.

Small pockets of unvaccinated individuals can allow a disease to gain a spread more widely well-being. For example, parent weighing the costs and benefits of a vaccine for their child is not always thinking of the consequences of that vaccination to other people. THese are markets in which subsidizing or regulating behavior can make everyone better off. Because the reason for requiring that a child be vaccinated before enrolling in school is not just to protect that child, because each child's vaccination affects others via potential contagions.

Robot job behavior brings economy influences

If one day robots can replace human to do simple, even complex jobs. They will bring what influences to our global societial economy.The popular economic refrain declares that the

global middle class is dying and robots will soon take our jobs, e.g. shopping center customer service jobs, library service jobs, cinema ticket sale jobs, restaurant kitchen cooker jobs,

even, bus drivers, taxi drivers etc. public transport driving jobs, accountant, doctors etc. professional jobs. Whether it is beautiful or petty matter if our future societies have many human jobs can be replaced to do from robots. Businessman must may reduce to employ employees and reduce to pay salary or wage, when robots can be replaced to do their employees tasks. But, societies must bring unemployement rate rises , due to societies will have many people loss jobs when their employers choose to buy robots to serve their clients or do any office tasks or customer service or cleaning etc. tasks.

In micro economy view, employers may save money in long term, but in macro economy view, it will cause unemployment ratio rises , even crime rate rises when there are many people lose

jobs in societies. These models of doom, though, fail to account for the hundreds of businesses riding the waves of change in their industries when robots may be invented to replace human to do many simple , even complex tasks in our future societies.

WE may image that one small factory needs to manufacture fishes canes to sell to supermarket, the small , cheaper stuff and higher margin parts of the fishes manufacture industry. Before, this factory needs to employe many human factory workers need to help every fresh customer makeing the perfect fishing gear, designed for performance, durability, and cost in order to achieve to manufacture every fish cane in whole fished processing manufacturing stages. Every worker needs to spend about 15 to twenty minutes to finish every fish cane , till to delivery to any supermarket to sell. If this fish canes manufacturing factory can apply manufacturing robots to help them to finish any one working tasks , every robot can only spend five minutes to finish whole fresh fish cane manufacturing process. Thus, every robot can

help this factory save 10 to 15 minutes time to finsh every fish cane manufacturing process. IN fact, time is money, because when every robot can help this factory to reduce 10 to 15 minutes time to compare human worker. Then, this factory can finish about 20 fish canes in one hour if it can use robot to help it to manufacture fish canes. Otherwise, if this factory still use human workers to help it to manufacture fish canes, then it can finsh about 3 to 4 fish canes in one hour. SO, the manufacturing efficiency ensures that robots must help this fish manufacturing factory to raise fish canes number more than human workers. So, in robotic behavioral economy view, manufacturing robots must help this fish canes manufacturing factory to raise fish canes manufacturing number and deliver increasing number to supermarkets to prepare to sell every day. Robots can help this fish canes manufacturing factory bring manufacturing time saving, rising manufacturing efficiency, improving performance and reducing wages expenditure long time advantages in micro economy view. However, manufacturing robots can also bring disadvanages to society, e.g. increasing unemployment ratio, increasing crime rate,

this factory workers will lose jobs and income, they need earn social welfare from government and increasing government finance pressure in short time, even long time in macro economic view.

Stanford University graduate program in economics, Scott lecturer explained that "in demand and supply economic theory for robots supply and demand case, robots supply number increasing may influence human workers demand number decrease. It sometimes calls " the efficient frontier".

No specific human beings were mentioned in any of economics classes. As robots supply and demand in market case, They (robots) may be purely theoretical " agents" who reached to the most reasonable sale prices in order to persuade any one businessman buyer to make manufacturing robot buying decision whether robots can help him / her to bring how much saving time , saving money, saving cost, improving performance, efficiency economic benefit before he/she plans to reduce workers number when he/she decides to apply robots to replace human workers in his/her factory or office or any service department, e.g. cinema ticket sale service, shopping center customer service, shopping center cleaning , supermarket customer service etc. service or sale tasks. When robots can replace human to do any one of these tasks in any organizations. So, robots may be human worker agents who reached to prices the way robots would react to a software command. There was nothing that explained why some people thrived and others did n't or why truly brilliant, hardworking people could fail when much lazier folks succeeded." Having been admitted to the Stanford University graduate program in economics, Scott lecturer hoped to get his answers there.

How robots influence our future social changing? Using the right technology can be a boon to your business in this economy. For internet example, it is easier than ever to find well-matched customers all around the world, to stay in contact with them, and to more quickly design the products they want. If you focus solely on being cutting -edge, though you risk letting the technology

take over what should be very robust relationships with your customers , employees, and colleagues. IN nowaddays society, technoligical advances and cutomation, personal relationships in business are more crucial than ever. I mean that robots can not replace human to serve clients to let them to feel more comfortable and passion more easily. For shoe shop case example, if the shoe shop apply one robot to serve its clients to replace human shoe salesperson to serve its shoe customers. Robots ensure that they can not persuade every shoe potential buyer to make shoe buying decision more easily when robots need to contact every shoe potential buyer. The reason is simple, because robots can not touch any one shoe buyer individual emotion very easier.

If the shoe buyer needs the robots to help him/her to choose any right shoe styles when he/she can not feel himself / herself can make the most right shoe style choice decision. The robots can not replace human shoe salesperson to make shoe style choice judgement more easily. They must need longer time to analyze whether which shoe style may be the most suitable to the shoe buyer. Otherwise, human shoe salesperson may attempt to make the most right shoe style choice decision to help any one shoe buyer to chooce the most right style shoe because he/she owns shoe style sale experience, shoe style knowledge, the most important reason is that they can feel every shoe customer individual emotion to touch whether he/she will feel comfortable or happy when they attempt to help every shoe customer to seek the most right shoe style in every shoe customer whole shoe searching processing. Othwerwise, serving robots are only one machine, they can not touch or feel every shoe customer individual emotion whether he/she feel comfortable or unhappy or happy when they need to contact them in whole shoe searching processing. Hence, I believe that some tasks robots can not repalce human staff to do very easily. Otherwise, robots may bring disadvanatges to let any one businessman to loss his/her customers, due to robots can not touch every customer emotion to compare human staff in service tasks more easily. Robots serving customer behaviors may cause money lose and customers number lose to the shop in micro economic view.

Intellectual human economic behaviors

What does intellectual human economic behaviors mean ? I believe that when we choose or decide to do intellectual behaviors, then our societies will be influenced to bring economic growth in consequence.I shall attempt to indicate pollution case to explain how and why eithet our intellectual or foolish behaviors may bring economic growth or recession in consequence as below:

On one hand, for air pollution social case aspect example, if we only consider to buy cars to drive for working aimr or holiday leisure aim. Then, our societies air will be polluted. Our health will be influenced to bad. Our car driving behaviors may cause global environment air pollution serously. In long tiem, global air pollution will bring our bodies health to be bad. Although, ourselves car driving behaviors may bring our driving travelling leisure enjoyment and comfortable feeling in short time, also we so not need to pay public transport fare often, but we need to compensate ourselves health economic intangible loss due to air pollution , when cars number increases, dirty air will cause ouselves health to become bad.

In the result, we will need to pay more medical expenditure when we are old age, due to ourselves bodies will become bad, due to we breathe global dirty air every day, due to ourselves cars pollute air in long time, e.g. 10 to 20 years, even 30 more without limited air pollution environment. So, driving cars behavior may be one kind of human foolish behavior and our foolish behavior may bring ourselves future long time medical expenditure absolutely.

One the other hand, water pollution social aspect, if we often keep much rubblish to pollute sea, oil exploration porcessing pollute ocean , ships gas pollute ocaen, then fishes will eat polluted food and drive dirty water, due to global ocean is polluted.

In fact, because human only to conside how to buy boats to carry on leisure enjoyment activities, or catch cruises to travel on the sea. Also, oil manufacturers only consider researching anywhere to find new oil exploration places to manufacture oil product, when their oil exploration processes pollute ocarn . Consequently, global fishes drink polluted warer or eat polluted food. They will have poison. SO, human will have high chance to eat poison polluted fishes, due to fishes are poison or are polluted.

So, human is doing foolish activities, we only hope to find oil exploration places to pollute ocean or we only spend money to buy ticket to catch ships to travel anywhere in global ocean. All of these human foolish behaviors will bring pollution to global ocean. On consequently, we will need to compensate to eat polluted or dirty or poision fishes, ourselves bodies health will be bad. In long time, we need have high chance to pay medical expenditure when we are old. So, pollution case may be one good example to explain how and why human foolish behavior may influence ourselves future need to compensate serious medical loss.

All of these human foolish behavior will bring pollution to global ocean. On consequently, we will need to compensate to eat polluted or dirty or poison fished , ourselves bodies health will be bad. In long time, we will have high chance to pay medical expenditure, when we are old. So, pollution case may be one good example to explain how and why human ourselves intellectual or foolish behaviors may influence future long time economic loss or economic growth or recession in micro and micro economic view.

On another water pollution aspect hand, if we often keep rubbish to sea, oil exploration processing pollutes ocean and ships‘ gas pollute ocean, then fishes will eat polluted food and drink dirty water, due to fishes will eat polluted food and drink dirty sea water because the global ocean is polluted seriously.

In fact, because human only consider how to buy boats to carry on any leisure water activities, or catches cruises to travel on the sea. Also, oil manufacturers only consider any where to find oil exploratin places to manufacture oil products from ocean, when their pol exploration processes can plooute ocean. Consequently, global fishes drink polluted water or eat direty food. They will have poison. So, human will have high chance to eat poison fishes.

Otherwise, such as pollutin case, it can infuence inflation or deflation. Consequently, the reason indicates supply and demand theory. If air pollution is serious, then we will consider health issue, global cars demand number may be influenced to reduce, when global cars number demand will reduce, global car prices and supply number will need to change to fall down in order to attract or persuade global car consumers choose to make car purchase decision.

Hence, global car manufacture number and car price will be influenced to reduce, due to global air pollution issue. Consequently, deflation will occur because when the country citizen usually does not spend much extra saving money to buy car expensive goods. Money value will be low. Otherwise, if global cair pollution is not serious, human considers to buy cars to enjoy driving leisure lives. So, global car demand is influenced to increase , also global car price will also influenced to increase.

Consequently, gobal human will choose to buy cars to drive. Due to we accept to spend extra saving to buy expensive car goods. Car sale price and supply may be influenced to rise up. Money value is influenced to reduce. Inflation may be influenced, due to global car consumers number increases, we would not have extra money to spend easily. Car expensive goods expenditure influences our spending habit to avoid to make car purchase decision more easily. So, human intellectual or foolish activities may bring inflation or deflation consequency in possible indirectly in macro economic view.

On conclusion, above pollution case explain that how and why human intellectual or foolish economic behaviors may bring inflation or deflation consequency as wll as economic growth or recession consequency as well as any goods demand and supply increasing or decreasing consequency. It implies that human behavior may have indirect relationship to influence any goods demand and supply number to either increase or decrease result as well as any goods price will be influenced to increase or decrease in micro and macro economic view.

The relationship between social change and human behavior

Why does economic changes may influence human individual behavioral change? I shall attempt to indicate shopping behavior and staying at home behavior to explain their case and effect relationsip as below:

Human behavior can be influenced by economic change or economic change can be influenced by human behavior? Why does recession may influence consumers reduce shopping desire? In social recession suitation, it is possible that many people lose jobs suddenly, due to businessmen lose many customers. They need to make decision to reduce employees number in order to continue to keep businesses. Consequently, many firms (organizations) their employees may lose jobs. When they have much time, due to lose jobs, they will feel to avoid to spend too much time and money to go to shopping often. Many losing jobs people, they will often stay at homes.

So, they will reduce time to go to shopping, then non essential products won't their preferable choice purchase products. Hence, recession will change many losing jobs people their shopping or consumption desires to avoid to buy non essential products often . Usually when economic boom, many people have jobs to do because consumers number must increase when many people have jobs to do. Then, many people can accept to spend money to buy non essential products often. Many people feel spend time to go to shopping can satisfy their purchase of any kinds of new products useful psychology or desire. So, recession is one good example to explain it can influence many people do not like often to leave homes to go to shopping easily. Many people like to stay at homes, becaue they feel worry about spending too much shopping time when they leave homes. Their staying home time is one good negative shopping behavior example. So, economic change may influence human individual behavior changes , they have direct cause and efect relationship in behavioral economic view.

May human behavior influence economic change? Is it possible that human behavior may bring the country social economic change in macro economic or micro behavioral economic view ? I shall indicate publishing industry example. Do you feel that if there are many students feel learning is very important when they read many books or many of students feel interesting to read or they have reading new books in habit, then it is possible that the country will have many students like to spend time to go to any book shops to choose the books, they feel that they can help they learn new knowledge. Then the country will increase students number, they often spend time to visit any one book shop every week. Their visiting book shops behavior which may become their habits. So, the country will increase students number, they often spend time to visit book shops. Also, it implies that visiting book shops behaviors may be their behavioral habits.

So, when the country has many students often spend time to visit book shops , their visiting book shops behaviors may help any one book shop to raise books sale chance. So, the country's student individual often visiting book shop behaviors, their habitual visiting book shops behaviors must may assist help any one book shop to increase books sale number absolutely.

Consequently, any one book shop , its books sale bumber must be influenced to increase to increase because the country will have many students like or feel need visit book shops habit in order to choose any suitable books to buy to read at home in order to raise themselves learning effort. When the country has many bok shops often have many students visit their book shops, then their books sale number may be influenced to increase. It explain why student individual visiting book shop behavior may help any one book shop sale number increases also.

How human productive behavior may influence economic development

May any country which citizen behavior assist themselves country development? It is one cause and effect economic question. I mean that if the country itself citicen can not concentrate mind or energy to choose to do one kind of industry in order to let themselves country can bring the most benefit, then whether the counry itself economy can bring the most serious economic benefit. I shall attempt to indicate these countries themselves indistry choice to explain whether these countries themselves citizen productive behavior may help themselves countries to achieve the largest economic benefits. I shall indicate as below:

New Zealand farmer individual wine productive behavior

For New Zealand country example, this country concerns itself effort is foucs on farming agricultural aspect. So, this country has many farmers concentrate on farming agricultural aspect. May New Zealanders choose to spend time to produce different kinds of wines, e.g. wine or red grape wine is for the people are eating meat, or they are eating dinner.

When these New Zealanders their behaviors choose to do farming or agriculture to grow and produce different kinds of taste of white or red grape wine drinking products job. Themselves grape agriculture behavior will influence these New Zealanders themselves, they can learn how to improve different kinds of grape wine drinking products in order to achieve every kinds of white or read grape wines taste improving aim during their white or red grape producing process.

Why can New Zealander every individual white or read grape wine producers improve their white or read grape wine taste more easily? In behavioral economic view, it can explain that why any one New Zealander white or read grape wine producer can be encouraged or excited or persuaded to concentrate nervous and energy and effort to learn how to improve their white or red grape wine products easily.

In fact, New Zealand is one agricultural food export country. It has good natural environment resource , e.g. land, seed to provide any one farmer to produce themselves any kinds of agricultrual food products, e.g. fruit, or wine food products. Because New Zealanders know themselves country has enough natural resource . So, in common, many New Zealanders choose to attempt to do farming agricultural jobs in order to export themselves any kinds of fruit or meat or wine products to overseas or sell to domestic in order to earn profit.

So, when these New Zealand farmers number has been increasing every year. This country farmers will feel themsleves competition between this New Zealand farmers themselves are serious due to they may feel New Zealanders choose to do agriculture businesses in order to export themselves different kinds of farming food to overseas or sell to local to earn profit.

Hence, when many New Zealand farmers feel that farmers number has been increasing every year. They will feel themselves competition is serious. They must need to spend much time and nervous and effort to research what method is the best how to produce the best taste of white or red grape wine products in order to let local or overseas wine buyers to choose to buy his/her producing white or read grpae products to drink.

Hence, in competition psychological view, may influence many New Zealand white or reaad wine producers had been beginning to change their learning behavior on researching what method is the best in order to produce the best quality of taste red or white wine products to sell in order to attract overseas or local white or read grape wine drinkers to choose to buy his/her wine products. Their behavior will focus on learning how to raising or improving white or read grape wine taste method more than only focus on producing a large number white or red grape wine products. They believe wine quality is more important to compare wine producing number. So, New Zealand wine producers themselves wine producers behaviors have been changing on concentrating on researching wine quality method aspect more then wine producing number aspect in behavioral economic view.

America high technological productive behavior

For America example, US is one high technological country, it owns many high technological knowledge talent inventors, e.g. computer science inventors. Hence, US must attract many diferent countries owning high technological computer inventors choose to go to US to develop their computer science profession career. Also, it seems that when many computer science inventors or professions choose to go to US to develop themselves computer science new career. In behavioral economic view, due to their leaving themselves countries choice, which may bring influence themselve country job behaviors need to be changed. They must need to adapt US new live. Because they will forgive their past computer science job. These computer science professionals need to spend time to adapt US new lives. They " past computer science job behaviors" will need to be changed to their new US any computer employer's new computer science job model.

Because their traditional computer science jobs needed to be forgot in their themselves countries. They will feel their old computer science job knowledge and behavior needed to change in order to let their US any one new of computer company employer feels satisfactory to accept their new working behavior in any one US computer organization.

So, on the other hand, many US computer company employer will feel that they must need time to accept any one new overseas computer science professions their working behaviors, their working attitude daily, because these foreign comouter science professional, their past computer working behaviors and working attitude must be different to US domestic computer science professions.

In behavioral economic view, these overseas computer science professions, their working behaviors and attitude must be needed to change in order to adapt any one US new computer company itself domestic or local computer science professional stafs themselves daily working behaviors and attitude because these overseas and local computer science professionals must need to team work together.

In behavioral economic view, it is only one way that foreign computer science professionals must need to change themselves past country traditiona daily working behaviors and attitude in order to cooperate with these US local computer science professionals in teams more easily.

Consequently, if these foreign compute science professionals can change their past working behaviors and attitude to let any one US local computer science professional feels to cooperate with them easily in short time. Then, the US computer company itself whole computer professional teams themselves efficiencies will be influenced to raised or improved by the changing past working attitude and working behaviors of these foreign computer science professionals. So, in behavioral economic view, only if US any one computer company hopes itself computer teams themselves efficiency can be raised or improved when it decides to employ foreign computer science professionals and US domestic computer science professionals. They need to work in teams together. They must need to let these foreign computer science professionals to know how to change their working behaviors and attitude to let their domestic computer science professionals feel easy to work together. Then, the US computer company itself whole team efficiency must be rasied or improved easily in short time.

China share market investing behavior

For China share market example, economic development depends on financial market. Because if many Chinese have interest to invest to carry on shares buying and selling activities in orde to learn how to earn shares interest and share profit when the China shareholder can make decision to sell himself/herself shares in the the high price, then he/she can earn money when he/she can sell the China company's shares in the high sale share price position.

If China has many Chinese like to spend time to carry on investing shares activities. Themselves shares buying and selling behaviors will influence China has many companies can increase fund from many Chinese shareholders in order to have enough money to expand or develop themselves businesses in China in long term.

Consequently, when China can have many Chinese like to attempt to carry on buying and selling shares investing behaviors in China share market. Themselves buying and selling shares behaviors can help many Chinese companies have effort to increase enough money or capital in order to continue to do their businesses in long term absolutely. So, it explains why when many Chinese become shareholders , they can assist China will have many companies continue to develop their businesses if many Chinese like to carry on shares buying and selling investing behaviors in long time in China financial investment market nowadays in behavioral economic view.

Why has any individual country have many people invest share behavior which can influence the country's macro consumption desire?

I shall apply shares market buying and selling investment behavior to explaiin why shares investment behavior which may impact the country's overal consumption desire as below:

In behavioral economic view, I assume that when the coutry has many people have interest to attempt to carry on shares buying and selling investment behavior, then their frequent shares buying and selling behaviors which may bring negactive consumption desire or shopping desire of these shares investors their consumer behavior.

The reason is simple, when the country has many share buyers number suddenly been increasing rapidly. Consequently, these large group share investors must need to spend much time to research any kinds of company shares variations, whether when their share prices will rise up of fall down in order to achieve buying the company's shares in the lowest price and selling the company's shares in the highest price level in order to earn profit.

Basic on this reason, they must need to spend much extra time to research share prices changing behavior every day, e.g. one working person will wait to leave his/her job, after he/she can spend time to gather data to research the day's share price changing behavior after dinner. So, the working person's right time may be his/her share price market research behavior. Before he/she may spend his/her night time to go to shopping after dinner, but nowadays, he/she will fogive to do his/her shopping behavior before dinner or after dinner at hight sometime. He/she will make decision to spend much night time to turn on computer to click on share market website to research his/her share purchase choice to investigate whether his/her share price whether it rises up or falls down at the moment in order to make his/her share buying or selling decision at ever night time.

I mean the when the country has many people are share investors, their shares investment behavioral spenging time which will influence many shops lose customers at might often because the country will have many people feel need to spend night time to turn on computer or watch television to investigate share price variation. So, the country will have many people / share investors choose to stay at home in order to carry on share price variation investigation behavior, they need to listen share market update news from radios or watch the share market update news from computer or TV at home every night. Consequenly, they must reduce times to leave themselves homes at night. So, their shopping behavior also will be reduced. Because these share investors feel need to spend time to investigate share price variation news at homes which can bring economic benefits (high opportunity benefits) when they choose to forgive to leave homes to go to shopping times (opportunity cost) every night.

On conclusion, it seems that when the country has many people are share investors, then their share price investigating behavior may bring negative shopping emotion at night. Consequently, the country's any one shop may lose many customers from this share investor consumer group in behavioral economic view. Hence, when the country's share investors number had been increasing rapidly, it will influence any shops lose many customers from this share investing customer group at night frequenly in short time, even long time in behavioral economic view, because their shopping desires or shopping emotion will be brought negative feeling when they make decisions to spend much time to listen radios or watch TV or computers share price update nes at night. Hence, share market will bring negative impact to influence consumer shopping desire or negative shopping emotion in behavioral economic view.

Can technology influence human shopping behavioral change?

Nowadays, technological development has reached mature stage, whether technological mature stage may bring positive or negative shopping emotion influence to global consumers. I shall aplly internet inventin or ecommerce shopping channel tool to explain whether internet technology can bring postive or negative influence to global consumer behavior in behavioral economic view.

Internet is a good technological tool, it brings e-commerce business chance. In fact, commonly, global has have many businessmen choose to use internet channel to carry on their products transactions between global online-buyers and their electronic websites. So, global many shoppers had begun to feel online shopping is more convenient to compare visiting shops shopping. Their shopping behaviors have been changed from internet technological tool. Global has many shoppers choose to buy any products from any overseas or local businessmen their web stores. They only need to spend time to find any businessmen their webstores to choose the most suitable products to pay visa to buy from their webstores. at homes. So, in general, global had have may shoppers had changed their shopping behaviors from visiting shops to visiting webstores at homes often.

So, it seems that internet technological tool had influenced global many shops disappear, but internet webstores will be replaced their actual shops on streets. Some of businessmen either they choose webstores to replace shops or choose websotes and shops both or still keep shops only. Hence, internet tool influences global businessmen have three kinds of products sale channels to let globa local and overseas consumers to choose how to buy their products.

However, in fact, many of global shoppers, youngers and olders had begun to accept to buy any products from webstores. They feel to spend time to leave homes to visit shops , their shopping behaviors will be wasted time to not essential part to their daily lives. Hence, since internet technological invention, it had changed many consumers their traditional visiting shops shopping habit to change to buying products from webstores channel.

However, on the one hand, internet creates webstores ecommerce shopping channel to let global many consumers do not need to leave homes to go to shopping. It brings negative visiting shops shopping emotion to global general consumers nowadays. But on the other hand, it also brings positive visiting internet webstores shopping emotion to global general consumer nowadays. So, it seems that global many consumers feel that they often do not need to spend much time to go out shopping. Many global consumers feel convenient and enjoy to choose any products to buy from different internet webstores, when the online buyer chooses the most suitable product, he she only needs to pay visa card to buy the product from the online seller's webstore conveniently at home.

Hence, online shopping can bring economic benefit to online buyers, e.g. avoiding walking time or spending transport fare to visit the shop to go to shopping, shortening or reducing shopping time to do another important matter.

On conclusion, global many consumers began feel online shopping can bring more economic benefits on shortening shopping time, avoiding transport fare spending aspect. So, online shopping will be popular shopping behavior for future long time. It may encourage global many shoppers can make rapid shopping decision in short time in order to carry on any products buying transaction to global any one online shopper in short time easily in behavioral economic view. So, global many businessmen had begun to build themselves one attraction webstore in order to persuade different countries consumers to choose to click themselves webstores from internet channel to buy any kinds of products in short time easily.

So, internet technology had changed consumers traditional shopping behaviors to build positive online shopping emotion as well as raise online sellers' any products sale chance easily in behavioral economic view.

Why and how human behavior may influence the country's economic growth or recession?

When one country has many people choose to do the same matter for one period, whether their behavior may influence the country's pvera; economic growth or recession . I shall attempt to indicate cases toexplain their relationship as below:

For flowing rubblish behavioral case example, do you feel that when the country has many people often flow rubblish on the streets, instead of their flowing rubblish behavior may bring streets dirty? But, their flowing rubblish behavior may explain that this country has people may have enough money to buy food to ear, or enough cloths to wear, enough bottles of water to drink, even they may have enough money to buy new television, radio, refrigeraters , washing machines, desktops or laptops electronic home products from old to new to use in order to satisfy their living needs. So, when they flow old electronic home products, their flowing old home electronic products behaviors may seem that they have enough money to buy other new home electronic products to replace old home electronic products to use at homes.

However, it seems thaat this country ought have many people have jobs to do. So, many of them, they can easy to make purchase decison to flow any old home electronic products and buy any new home electronic products to use . Because this country has many people have jobs to do. So, they can often not use old home electonic products to become rubblishs to flow on streets after they had bought any kinds of new home electronic homes.

In fact, it also implies that this country's economy grows rapidly. So, many businesses can glow up rapdly. When they expanded their businesses, they must need to increase employees number in order to let they help themselves to raise productivity or serve their clients absolutely. So, when the country has many businesses can grow up, it seems that its economy must be better or it is improved to compare past. Due to many different kinds of home electronic products had been often bought to use by this country people in this period. So, this country's any streets can be observed that expensive electronic home products were flowed on streets anywhere. then, this country will have many electronic home products sellers can sell their home electronic products very easily. When this country has many people can find any kinds of jobs to do easily. So, due to unemploymen rate had been decreasing.

In behavioral economic view, as this many electronic home products rubblish country case, we can observe this country may have many people have jobs to do. So, consumption number has been increased long time. So, cheap food, or expensive home electronic products may be rubblish on any streets. This country's people , their flowing rubblish behaviors may be explained that many of people have enough jobs to do, so they have ability to buy any good taste food to eat or buy any kinds of expensive electronic home products to use. So, this country's economy may be improved for this long period. So, in behavioral economic view, when this country can have many electronic home products rubblishs are flowed on anywherer in streets frequently. It seems that this country will have many people have jobs to do, so it causes they often change old home electronic products or replaced them easily, when they have enough income to spend to buy any kinds of new home electronic products to use at homes easily. Moreover, their flowing old electronic home products behaviors also indicate that this country has many people their salaries may be increased in possible from their emplyers. When this country can have many different kinds of home electornic products are sold. It means that this country's electronic home products needs or demand had been increasing, due to many people have jobs to do and income increases to excite their living of needs also improve. Consequently, this country may seem have better economic improvement. We can observe from this country's electronic home products rubblish increasing income in theis period.

On conclusion, this country ought experience economic growth at this period. So, " flowing expensive electronic home rubblish increasing number " may seem that this country's economic growth is rapidly in this period, due to many people have jobs to do as well as salaries increase in this period.

Technology how impacts human behavior changing?

Technology how influences human behavior to bring changing? For example, online share purchase and sale transaction from smart phone brings share investor can do share buying or selling transation in any where and any time conveniently, non manual driving auto vehicle, bring car owner feels comfortable and spends free time to do other matter, e.g. reading, listening mucis in himself or herself car freely. electrical energy vehicle can help car owner to reduce air polluton and it can brings the drivers do not feel drive long time in any journeys in order to avoid air pollution for environmental protection responsible car drivers in our societies. Thus, they will drive long time in any journeys when they can drive electronic energy cars to replace oil energy cars.

However, online technology can also bring consumers can choose to stay at homes to buy any things from seller individual online webstore conveniently. Such as online technology can bring shoppers do not need to spend much time to visit shops to buy any things. They can choose any kinds of products from any online sellers individual online webstores conveniently at homes. Online technology excite busy consumers can make purchase decision easily as well as it can help online sellers sell any kinds of products from internet easily.

In behavioral economic view, technology can change human behavior to be improved, it can let human feels comfortable, more free time ro use, rapid making any decisions, such as apply smart phones to make share purchase or sale transaction decision, online shopping decision, even travelling any where decision in short time, when the traveller finds the most cheap hotel accommodation room price and air ticket price frm any travel agent online tourism webstore, then the potential travel customer can follow the online hotel accommodation price and air ticket price data to make decision when to buy the air ticket from the airline travel agent or make decision when to prebook which hotel accommodation room to go to the country to travel from online travel agent tourism webstores. So, technology can encourage global any country travelers to make anywhere to trvel rapidly. If the traveler can find the country's general hotel rooms and airline tickets prices had been decreasing more sightly. The traveler may make travel decision to choose the country to travel in short time, then he/she can prebook the country;s any hotel room and airline ticket to pay by visa fraom the country's any hotel and airline travel agent webstores., before one week, even one month or more easily. Hence, online technology can also encourage traveler individual frequent travel times to be increased, due to global travelers can find any hotel rooms and airline tickets prices from internet conveniently at homes. They do not need to spend time to visit any airline travel agent to enquire travel choice country's hotel rooms prices and airline ticket prices. They can compare global travel of countries choices ' all hotels rooms and airline agents air tickets prices to make prebook airline seat and hotel room decision before one week, one month even six months early.

On conclusion, online technology can encourage global travelers can make travelling any where and when traveling time desicions easily. It can excite tourism industry develops in long time. Also, such as electricity cars invention can encourage environment protection car owners do car purchase decision easily, because they can choose to drive electronic energy cars to replace oil energy cars in order to avoid air pollution occurs easily. So, electronic cars can increase electronic car purchasrs number, due to many of environmental protection attitude of car owners can choose to drive electricity cars to bring air cleans, even non -manual driving cars can encourage lazy driving and free time driving car owners to choose to buy non-manual (artificial intelligent) cars to drive , because they can spend much free time to read, listen music or do any matters in themselves cars, they do not need to drive cars, robotic (AI) auto driving machine is such one non-manual driver to help them to drive themselves cars confidently. So, non-manual driving cars can attract lazy and enjoying free time driving car owners to choose to buy to replace traditional manual cars to drive easily. Moreover, online share transaction can help any share investors to make share buying and selling decision in short time easily. When they can apply smart phones technological tool to carry on share buying and selling activities easily. They can observe any share rising or falling price suitation from smart phones in any where any any time easily. So, smart phone technology can help global any shareholders to make share purchase and sale transaction easily. So, technology can encourage human makes decision in short time rapidly.

How and why employees behaviors may influence economy development?

In behavioral economy view,I believe the country's any organizational employees behavior may bring indirect relationship to influence the country's long term economic development. I shall indicate past manufacture industry social development period to explain their relationship. For many countries' past business activities had belonged to manufacturing industry, such as US, UK past before 1980 year, it focused on steel manufacturing and steel manufacturing related machine products. So, US, Uk developed countries manufacturing industries may be past main country's economic income sources. I assume US , UK past had one million number different kinds of industries. They ought had about seven houndred thousand number organizational businesses were belonged to manufactured industry. They may include:

Steel manufacturing and steel related machine manufacturing, e.g. vehicle manufacturing, home appliances, e.g. washing machine, television, radio, refrigerate cooler, heater, air condition etc. different kinds of different kinds of steel -related manufacturing machine, they were manufactured from US, UK steel machine manufacturers. So, US, Uk the other three hundred thousand number industry may be general service industry, e.g. hotel service, restaurent, cinema, public transport service, tourism lesiure , wine bar, supermarket etc. different kinds of non-manufacturing industries business organizations were operated in UK, US past before 1980 year.

So, in UK, US developed countries industry development history, they ought have high percentage of businesses belonged to steel related manufacturing machine and steel products. Also, in the past before 1980 year, US, Uk business employers , they employed many workers are manufacturing workers. They needed to spend long time to work in factories. They were skillful workers, and they are trained to manufacturing cars, washing machine, television, heater, etc. even steel itself different kinds of steel related products to prepare to deliver to their shops to sell to US, Uk local or overseas clients.

So, I believe that past UK, US ought employ many employees, they belonged to skillful manufacturing workers, manufacture increasing steel machine or steel related machine number of products rapidly daily. So, if UK, US had had many of these manufacturing factories owned high skillful workers, then their manufacturing steel-related machine or steel both kinds of products number must be influenced to raise rapidly. Consequently, their steel machine manufacturing products would been exported to overseas or would been sold to local both markets , they may be influenced to raise sale number. They (these manufacturing workers) needed to be trained to know how to manufactur these different kinds of machine products in the efficient teams and they ought to be trained to raise their efficiencies in order to shorten time to manufacturing many kinds of steel related manufacturing machine or steel itself products rapidly. So , if their efficiencies and manufacturing performance was improved, these US, UK any one manufacturing worker and their teams ought achieve raising productivities significantly.

Hence, when past UK, US manufacturing industry development period, if these two countries‘ any manufacturing factories could have many manufacturing workers could be trained to be skillful and proficient manufacturing workers. Then, in past every day to these factories workers, they ought help their steel or steel related manufacturing employers to raise any kinds of machine or steel products number in every team. So, when past in the manufacturing industry development, US, UK could have many factories’ manufacturing workers themselves steel or steel related machine products manufacturing skill could be trained to to improve to any kinds of these machine or steel manufacuring products quality as well as their products number could be influenced to raise by themselves skillful improvement significantly every day.

Then, what would be influenced to occur to past UK, US manufacturing industry period? In behavioral economic view, when these two manufacturing industry developed countries, such as UK, US , if they had many factories workers can be trained to improve their skill in order to achieve any kinds of steel or steel-related machine products quality could be improved as well as products manufacturing number could be also increased absolutely.

In consequence, past UK and US both countries ought increase themselves any kinds of steel and steel related machine products number to be supplied to themselves local shops to let local clients to choose any one kind of machine manufacturing products to buy easily as well as they could also export to supply overseas any countries to buy their different kinds of steel or steel related machine products to let overseas steel or steel related manufacturing machine product buyers, they can have many of these different kinds of these steel or steel-related different kinds of manufacturing machine from UK and UK these both countries easily to compare other countries.

On conclusion, I believe that past US, and UK macro manufacturing industry income GDP would increase significantly. So, they would have good economic growth performance because when many of these manufacturing workers themselves manufacturing effort could be improved. So, it explained when employees manufacturing abilities can influence economic growth indirectly.

Robots invention whether they can help organizations to raise efficiencies or inefficiencies?

In behavioral economic view, in any organizations, when the organization hopes its worker teams can raise efficiencies , the organization may choose to increase more workers number and/or it can provide training to improve these workets themselves skills in order to raise their efficiencies. For one warehouse example, when the warehouse increases many goods , they are needed to delivered these goods from the shelves to the delivering destination locations. If this warehouse supervisors feel these workers themselves goods delivery speeds are slow, which is possible due to this warehouse's workers number is not enough. So, this warehouse supervisor ought increase workers number in order to increase their goods delivery speed in order to deliver goods from the shelves to every indicated goods delivery destination in order to let any one lorry driver can transport the right kinds of goods and ensure the accurate goods number to transport to any one client home rapidly.

However, if this warehouse supervisor planed to buy several warehouse goods delivery robots to assist these warehouse workers to find the right kinds of goods from shelves and then deliver to the right destination location in the warehouse. So, these warehouse orkers can concentrate on counting the accurate goods number and ensuring the right kinds of goods in order to prepare to let lorry drivers to transport these goods to these goods of buyers themselvers homes rapidly. Consequently, in the first step, robots can concentrate on finding th right goods from shelves and delivers them to the right goods transportation of location destination. Then, in the second step, these warehouse workers can concentrate on counting the accurate goods number and ensuring the right kinds of goods in order to prepare to put them to the lorry. Consequently, when warehouse robots and warehouse workers can cooperate to work together, the most important, robots, can deal on finding the right kinds of goods and deal on delivering the accurate number of goods of job duty as well as these warehouse workers can only concentrte on counting the right kinds of goods number in order to avoid it has none any mistake of wrong kinds of goods and inaccurate goods of delivery number to be transported to the lorry and to deliver to any one buyer's home.

So, it seems that warehouse robots ought help any one warehouse worker to raise himself efficiency and avoid goods delivery of mistake occurrence easily as well as their help to warehouse workers that can let any one goods buyer feels their goods can be delivered to their homes rapidly. Moreover, warehouse robots can also help these warehouse workers to raise efficiencies because warehouse robots can help them to shorten goods delivery time between any one shelf and any one goods delivery destination of location in the warehuse because robots may help them to find the right kinds of goods from the right shelf in the short time. So, any one worker does not need to spend long time to seek anywhere is the right shelf location for the kind of goods when the kind of goods are needed to deliver to the buyer's home from lorry. Warehouse robots can help them to do this aspect of " finding the goods from the right shelf in short time job duty". So, any one warehouse worker only needed tospend less time to do the counting of any right kind of goods number and ensuring the right kind of goods job duty. Consequently, this warehouse 's any one worker, his any one kind of goods delivery time may be reduced, because robots' assistance and they may have more confidence to avoid mistake to deliver the wrong number of goods and/or the wrong kind of goods to any one goods buyer's home.

On conclusion, it seems that warehouse robots ought may help any one warehouse worker to raise efficiency for any one team in the warehouse as well as the warehouse any one supervisor does not need to spend much time to observe any one worker individual performance for " goods delivery job duty aspect" because their goods delivery job duty that had been replaced to do by these several warehouse robots. Robots can achieve the more accurate of right kinds of goods and the right number of goods delviery job performance to compare any one of human warehouse worker themselves right kinds of goods of delivery and right number of goods of delivery job performance. So, when robots can participate to cooperate with this warehouse's any one worker to do their goods of delivery job duty in this warehouse every day. Then, robots can raies any one of supervisor individual confidence in order to let they do not need to spend time to observe any one of worker individual whose goods of delivery job performane. They can concentrate on supervising any one worker whose goods transport to lorry in the final step in order to avoid to deliver wrong goods number and / or wrong kind of goods to any one goods buyer's home every day. Consequently, this warehouse's overall teams of their delviery of goods performance many be improved by robotss' participatin to goods of delivery task as well as this warehouse's oveall teams themselves efficiencies may be influenced to raise by robots' goods of delivery task participation.

Why social behavior may influence organizational strategy needs to be changed ?

Why any organizations need to know whether nowadays social behaivor how has been changing in order to implement the kind of the most right strategy to achieve the profit aim pursue in possible. I shall indicate nowadays ecommerce or online, customer shopping behavior to explain above question concerns they ought have close relationship between social behavior and organizational strategic choice or organizational behavioral changing need.

On nowadays ecommerce business, or online shopping model, this kind of shopping model in global many young and old age consumers like to apply internet tool to choose any country sellers website stores in order to stay at home to buy any kinds of products from themselves webstores in global societies.

In fact, online shopping model had been popular for long time above to twenty years. Most of global sellers will make decision to design themselves webstores in order to attract global many online buyers to choose to buy their products from themselves webstores. So, it seems that social consumers purchase behaviors had been changed to online shopping from internet invention.

Hence, social consumers purchase behavioral changes may influence any organizations' strategies need to be changed from visiting shops purchase strategy model to online purchase strategy model, if the seller still concentrate on concentrate on considerate how to design itelf , but neglects to considerate how to design itself webstore, e.g. how to design attract product photos to put on itself webstore, how to arrange sale price information location to be putted on webstore and visa card payment location on itself webstore in order to let any one online buyer can feel very easier to buy itself any kinds of products from itself webstore. Then, its potential online buyers will be influenced to increase number when they can find this online seller itself any kinds of products photes and every kinds of product sale price information and visa card payment channel locations easily from itself webstore.

So, it implies that nowadays any one seller ought need to design one webstore to let any one online overseas and domestic consumers can have chance to click itself webstore to choose any one kind of product to buy conveniently when he/she does not hope to leave him/her home to go to shop, because nowadays social shopping behaviors had been influenced to change when internet invention, them it gives another online purchase method to replace visiting shops purchase method to global any one buyer in nowadays societies.

So, if nowadays any one seller still concentrate on how to design itself shop display in order to put any kinds of product on shelf in order to let any one visiting shop customer to find the kind of product to buy, but it neglects to change to choose to pursue another new technological shopping method, such as webstore purchase method in order to implement effective strategy to design the most right webstore as well as in order to attract global overseas and local consumers to find itself webstore easily from website and find its any one kind of product phots and sale price and visa card payment button in order to choose to buy itself any kinds of products in the short time. Consequently I believe that the seller will lose many customers from overseas and local when its other same or similar product sellers choose to design themselves webstores in order to let global any one product buyer can buy themselves any one kind of product when they can pay visa card to buy their products from them webstores conveniently when they stay at home habitly. Then, the seller will lose many global potential customers in long time.

On conclusion, in behavioral economic view, any consumer behavioral social changing, which will influence any in order to avoid customers number loses significantly . In future time, organizations need to make rapid decision in order to implement the most reasonable and the most useful strategy in order to avoid global potential customers number reduces or lose them in long time. So, social behavioral changing environment ought influence any global organizations need to decide how to change themselves strategies in order to avoid customers loses significantly in future time.

CHAPTER ELEVEN

Explain behavioral economy theory

Behavioral economics combines elements of economics and psychology to understand how and why people behave the way they do in the real world. It differs from neoclassical economics, which assumes that most people have well-defined preferences and make well-informed, self-interested decisions based on those preferences. Behavioral economics is a field of study aimed at understanding why people make economically irrational decisions. Rational choice theory holds that consumers make choices that maximize their utility. In reality, people can be swayed or distracted from doing so. Behavioral economics is primarily concerned with the bounds of rationality of economic agents. Behavioral models typically integrate insights from psychology, neuroscience and microeconomic theory. The study of behavioral economics includes how market decisions are made and the mechanisms that drive public opinion.

When we can learn behavioral economy, can our future societies can be influenced to change to be better or improve our future lives to be better or comfortable or reduce social cost etc. advantages?

Behavioral economists work to understand what consumers do and why they make the choices they make. Such economists also **assist markets in helping consumers make those decisions**. Behavioral economists may work for the government to shape public policy to protect consumers. Behavioral economics plays a vital role in diagnosing what's driving current behaviors and increasing our effectiveness in designing interventions to shift those behaviors. While behavioral insights alone aren't sufficient to solve most of the complex social issues we face, ignoring them is a sure way to limit our effectiveness. For example,we spent a lot of energy, in many domains — technological, scientific, hard work, creativity, human ingenuity — to crack important social problems with technology solutions. That's been the discoveries of the last 2,000 years, that's mankind moving forward. When human learn behavioral economy, can our behavior can be influenced to spend lives expense, e.g. reducing driving time, or bath time in order to help global society to reduce social cost in behavioral economic view. Many times we (and our environments) are our own worst enemies. We know what we should do, but keep putting it off until tomorrow. Low and behold, tomorrow never comes.If you discover it's a problem of getting over these hurdles, it's a much different approach than if the intention isn't there. You might make the desired behavior the default choice so there's no hurdle. You might offer a small, immediate incentive to overcome the hurdle. You might get them to make a public commitment to take action. Or you may find ways to demonstrate that the desired behavior is the norm.If intention is there but action is lacking, look at their social network. Is there social pressure against the desired behavior? Is the dominant norm fighting your efforts? Is there competitive messaging pushing for a different behavior?

Behavioural economics is **a useful tool to help influence (or 'Nudge') the decisions people make**. It can potentially help them to do things which are better for themselves or for society as a whole. But it is just one of the tools available when planning and designing a social marketing program. The economy also affects things like **the cost of living, access to healthcare and education, and even things like crime rates**. When people have more money, they are generally able to afford better health care and education, and are less likely to turn to crime as a way to make ends meet. Behavioral economics **sheds light on most every day activities and why we consume goods and services the way we do, why we make certain choices about ourselves or others, and how we decide courses of action.**

ON conclusion, Social change occurs due to various factors such as **demographic, technological, cultural, political, economic and educational**. These factors often act in concert resulting in changes either in a serial manner or something in parallel too.

- What does behavioral economy mean?

(BE) Behavioral economics is primarily concerned with the bounds of rationality of economic agents. Behavioral models typically bring insights from psychology and micro economic theory. The study of behavioral economics includes how market decisions are made and the mechanisms that drive public choice. Moreover, behavioral economic plays a important role in our lives and in the economy because it can help businesses to explain why we consume the kind of goods and services , the way we do, why we make certain choices of action, the key contribution to behavioral economics, it uses psychological and experimentation to develop theories about human decision making, and has identified a range of biases as a result of the way people think and feel . (BE) is trying to change the way economics think about people's perception of value and expresses preferences.

- Have they relationship between consumer behaviors and economy ?

The success or failure of a nation's economy can greatly affect consumer behavior based on a variety of economic factors. If the economy is strong, consumers have more purchase power and money is spent , f the economy is poor, the reverse is true. Consumer behavior in economics means to explain of how individual customers, groups or organizations select, buy, use and dispose ideas, goods and services. A such, consumers play a role in the economic system of a capitalist economy. Without consumer demand, producers would lack one of the key motivations to produce to sell to consumers.
The motivates consumers behavioral economic perspective, it is the new field of behavioral economics has shown

them, in practice, people's decisions can be greatly influenced by seemingly irrelevant aspects of their personalities and by the environment in which their decisions are made. So, it seems that consumer buying behavior changes during economic crisis.

In organization how resources choices to use in behavioral economy view, though the number and variety of the different resources businesses require is limitless. Economists divide factors of production into three basic categories: Land, labour and capital. Land refers to all of the natural resources that business need to make and distribute goods and services, labours to make and distribute goods and services, labours refers how the organization chooses to employ the employee skill to make the kind of job, capital refers to how much the organization plans to spend in order to operate its business. Hence, behavioral economy can explains the economic model of employee, human behavior, working performance. It is a representation of people action. The concept is based on traditional economics, where human behavior is believed to spring from absolute rationality.

On behavioral economics in consumer lives and in the economy aspect, it explains it is a game theory, behavioral game theory. It is a game theory , behavioral game theory standard analytic game theory by taking into account how players (consumers) feel about the payoffs other players receive, limits in strategic thinking, as well as the effects of learning , the consumer individual past purchase experience, games (choices of purchases) are usually about cooperation or fairness.

For advertising how plays beneficial roles in a healthy economy example, advertising plays a strong role in the economy. It provides useful information to consumers that tells them about products and services choices as well as comparing features, benefits and prices, with more complete information, consumers and businesses often choose to purchase additional products and services . Hence, behavioral economics draws instead on psychology and economics to explore why people sometimes make irrational decisions, and why and how their behavior does not follow the predictions of economic models. Because humans are emotional and easily distracted being, they make decisions that are not in their self-interest. So, behavioral economics is the study of the effects that psychological factors have on the economic decisions making process of individuals. The importance of understanding behavioral economics for marketers is immeasurable as it shows for a better factors that can lead to irrational economic decision, e.g. overspend because of lack of availabiliey, such as buying expense gad because you are in the desert. Another irrational economic decision may be impluse buying or pressure.

● How to apply behavioral economic to explain why the employee does performance behavior?
A study on human behavior has revealed that 90% of the working population can be classified into four basic personality types: Optimistic, pessimistic, trusting. However, the latter of the four types. Envious is the most common, with 30% compared to 20% of each of the organization whole employee individual economic behavior,

economic behavior occurs in a climate of formal and informal organizational rules. These rules often act as incentives, e.g. appreciation, job promotion, increasing salary. These rules often act as incentives and influence the choices employees make , in general employees choose to work desk jobs that do not keep to fit, and how they have to make more time to stay healthy.

So, behavioral economic theory explain any organization will need have behavioral skills to dominate employee individual performance to raise. Behavioral skills are interpersonal, self-regulatory, and task-related behaviors that connect to successful performance in education and workplace settings. The behavioral skills are designed to help individuals succeed thorough effective interactions, stress management and persistent effort in any organizations. for task-oriented behavioral skills examples, they may include: active always buy with something, ambitious, strongly wants to succeed, cautious, being very careful, conscientious, taking time to do things right and creative, someone who can make up things easily or think of new things. The six important employee behaviors in organizations are employee productivity, absenteeism, turnover, organizational citizenship behavior, job satisfaction and workplace misbehavior. So, managers need have good behavioral management skills. They are all about learning appreciation and growth. Take the time to learn, try and grow strategies and leadership style.

● How to apply behavioral economic skill to help society to solve challenges ?

The three principles of social economics theory describes how the economy as a whole woks are (1) a country's standard of living depends on its ability to produce goods and services . (2) prices rise when the government prints too much money and (3) society faces a short-run tradeoff between inflation and unemployment. How to use behavioral economics for social impact. According to the American psychological association, social psychology is the study of how individuals affects and are affected by physical environment. Behavioral economics applies these concepts to the economic decisions that people make in addition to the ration thinking. It helps us understand how consumer participate in contest buy products and brand familiar choice in order to make the most rational purchase decision. Also, behavioral economists ask questions mostly about the way people make economic choices, judgments or the way particular financial purchase choice.

Hence, behavioral economic is the study of psychology as it relates to the economic decision making processes of individuals and organizations. In general, our societies ask two important questions: Are economists' assumptions of utility of profit maximization good approximations of real people's behavior? So individuals maximize subjective expected utility?

IN our societies, we need to satisfy and earn the greatest benefit, in economics, rational choice theory, states that when humans are presented with various options under the conditions of scarcity, they would choose the option that maximizes their individual satisfaction. Behavioral economics draws on psychology and economics to explain why people sometimes make irrational decisions and why and how their behavior does not follow the predictions of economic models, e.g. decisions such as how much to pay for a cup of coffee, whether to go to graduate school, whether to pursue a healthy lifestyle , how much to contribute toward retirement. For example, humans are emotional and easily distracted beings, they make decisions that are not in their self interest. For companies are increasingly incorpoarting behavioral economics to increase sales of their products case example, in 2007, the price of the 8 GB i phone was introduced for $600 and quickly reduced to $400, what if the intrinsic value of the phone was $400? If Apple introduced the i phone for $400, the initial reaction the price in the smart phone market might have been negative as the i phone might be thought to have too price. Buy by introducing the phone at a high-pricing and bringing it down to $400, consumers believed they were getting a pretty i phone deal for Apple. So, Apple i phone began to understand that its phone consumers are irrational, an effective way to behavioral economics in the Apple i phone's decision making policies that concern its internal and external stakeholders may prove to be worthwhile of done properly .

Behavioral economics is the study of the psychological, cognitive, emotional, cultural and social factors involved in the decisions of individuals or institutions, and how these decisions deviate from those implied by classical economic theory.

Behavioral economics is grounded in empirical observations of human behavior, which have demonstrated that people do not always make what neoclassical economists consider the "rational" or "optimal" decision, even if they have the information and the tools available to do so.

Behavioral economics combines elements of economics and psychology to understand how and why people behave the way they do in the real world. It differs from neoclassical economics, which assumes that most people have well-defined preferences and make well-informed, self-interested decisions based on those preferences.

Behavioral economics is often related with normative economics. It draws on psychology and economics to explore why people sometimes make irrational decisions, and why and how behavior diverges from the predictions of economic models. Behavioral economics is the study of psychology that analyzes the economic decisions people make. Moreover, behavioral economics explains that humans are not rational and are incapable of making good decisions. Because humans are emotional and easily distracted beings, they make decisions that are not in their self-interest.

CHAPTER TWELVE

Organizational behavior and consumer relationship

Consumer leisure need whether it has what relationship between economy?

Consumer leisure need whether is more and less whether it has what relationship between economy? Also whether the country's economy recession or growth, can it influence consumer leisure need to increase or decrease ? I shall attempt to apply behavioral economy theory to explain whether they have cause and effect relationship as below:

In our societies, there are so many different kinds of leisure activities, also any kinds of leisure consumers can follow the kind of leisure activity's price factor, enjoyable feeling factor, satisfactory feeling factor, leisure time need factor to influence the leisure consumer individual final choice to which kind of leisure activity among the different kinds of leisure needs. For example, travel leisure activity ought be the most experience, spending of leisure expense to compare general sport leisure, e.g. swimming , playing basketballs , table tennis, tennis, football, purchase tickets seeing movies, purchase tickets listening music, purchase electronic playing games to stay at homes to play.

In simple, it uses only considers leisure price aspect, we shall do the comparable and reasonable decision is that travelling activity ought be the kind of leisure activity, any leisure consumers ought spend the least leisure times to enjoy this kind of leisure activity, e.g. one year has only one time or two-to-five times for overseas for overseas travel. But, in fact, in global there are many travellers, they can make many times of travelling frequent decision, e.g. they can spend one week at least time to go to overseas to travel per month. Hence, it means that global some travellers like to buy air ticket to go to overseas to travel, they spend average one month and one time overseas travel.

In fact, tourism agents hope to attract travelers to choose travel leisure activity, they will attempt to decrease air ticket price in order to increase travelers number. However, some cheap travel package price can persuade global some travelers accept to pay cheap price to bu air ticket to spend several days to go to the country to travel enjoy their holidays.

So, it seems that cheap air ticket price strategy, it can attract some countries travelers to accept to spend some time for their overseas holiday their overseas travel leisure activity can explain why leisure price must be main element factor to influence leisure consumers to reduce spending amount to pay for the kind of leisure activity , such as travel leisure activity is one kind of good leisure activity example.
Otherwise, some kinds of leisure activities, ever their leisure prices are cheap, it must not influence them to like to spend much time to enjoy them, e.g. swimming, riding bicycles leisure activities, although those kinds of sport leisure activities prices must be very cheap to compare travel activities , it can must influence many young people like to buy bicycles to ride even they are proficient bicycle riders or they like to buy tickets to go public swimming pools to swim. The factors may include these both kinds of sports are tired sport leisure, any one must need more body energy to do these sports. Moreover, for student leisure consumers, although these both kinds sports prices, such as bicycles and swimming pool purchase tickets, they are cheap to students, but in fact, students must need to spend time to learn, if they often spend time to enjoy these both of sport activities, they will feel fear that they can not concentrate on spending learning time, if they spend on sport leisure time.

Hence, in behavioral economy view, it explains that leisure price whether it is high or low, it is not main factor to influence any leisure consumers to do leisure kind of choice, such as sport case to student leisure consumers, they will not choose to spend much time on sport leisure aspect, because the hard students must feel fear to influence their learning effort when they often spend time on sport leisure aspect. Otherwise, for a sport professional, e.g. proficient riding bicycle sport man, he may accept to spend expensive price to buy one expensive bicycle , e.g. when he feels the US$3,000 bicycle, it can help him to improve riding speed skills, he won't choose to buy the another US$1,000 bicycle, when he feels that it can not help him to improve riding speed skill, hence, it also explains that the leisure product high price , it must not influence leisure consumers number to reduce, it depends on whether the leisure product function to the leisure consumer, e.g. for riding bicycle sport men , they may accept to pay higher price to buy more expensive bicycles , because the hope that the bicycles can help them to compare their riding speed to more rapid. Otherwise, for student bicycle consumers, they won't compare different kinds of bicycles prices in order to decide whether which kind of bicycles are the most suitable to them to buy to ride.
Hence, behavioral economic theory can explain that price must not be the main factor to influence leisure consumers' leisure activities choices, their leisure need psychological and leisure product individual function factors was also influence their leisure activities choices.

● Can DNA reproductive technology bring only positive impact to influence our social behavior change?
Human's medical technology had been continue developed to improve to satisfy our medical need, such as cancer

patient medical different new drug research, it aims to help future cancer patients to avoid death. However, future human's new medical research will research on DNA biological medical improvement . So, future DNA biological medical technology may bring good or bad social impact, e.g. reproductive animal, such as pig, cow animals . So, when many pigs and cows can be reproduced. Then, pigs and cows number can increase. Consequently, pork, beefs meats food number can be also been increased by DNA biological medical reproductive cell technology improvement.

It is good aspect to bring enough meats supply to global , when future DNA biological medical technology can be developed to the reproductive many cows and pigs number stage in order to raise pork and beefs food number. However, DNA biological cell reproductive technology can also bring bad impact to our society, if one day human can apply DNA biological cell reproduutive technology to reproduce another ourselves, it means that reproductive human why is it bad new? if need DNA scientist decides to help one country ambitious leader to reproduce himself, then when the country ambitious leader dies, but his another reproductive himself person can contiue to bring war crisis to global, such as Japan's past leader, he was one ambitious leader to dominate global countries. If DNA reproductive technology is applied to help him to reproduce this Japan ambitious another himself . Then, the another new world war may be occurred easily. So, I also worry about future DNA reproductive technology may be applied to help the ambitous bad people to reproduce themselves to bring our societies safety and economic recession negative impact.
So, it brings this question: Can DNA reproductive technology bring only positive impact to influence our social behavior change? I shall attempt to explain as below:

How does DNA attract our behavior? In some situations, genes play a larger role in determining your behavior. How can genetic technologies impact society ? Although, genetic technology has a great potential to change the medical practice as we know it also has a potential to be misused , it also has a potential to be misused, and lead to further health disparities, discrimination and inequality in the human societies around the world.

However, I believe that those the ways that genetic engineering can help human society. Several works have been done on genetic engineering with major focus on its importance ranging from increasing plant and animal food production, diagnosing disease condition, medical treatment improvement, as well as production of vaccines and other useful drugs.

Can DNA reproductive technology bring only positive impact to influence our social behavior change? Human's medical technology had been continue developed to improve to satisfy our medical need, such as cancer patient medical different new drug research, it aims to help future cancer patients to avoid death. However, future human's new medical research will research on DNA biological medical improvement . So, future DNA biological medical technology may bring good or bad social impact, e.g. reproductive animal, such as pig, cow animals . So, when many pigs and cows can be reproduced. Then, pigs and cows number can increase. Consequently, pork, beefs meats food number can be also been increased by DNA biological medical reproductive cell technology improvement.

It is good aspect to bring enough meats supply to global , when future DNA biological medical technology can be developed to the reproductive many cows and pigs number stage in order to raise pork and beefs food number. However, DNA biological cell reproductive technology can also bring bad impact to our society, if one day human can apply DNA biological cell reproductive technology to reproduce another ourselves, it means that reproductive human why is it bad new? if DNA scientist decides to help one country ambitious leader to reproduce himself, then when the country ambitious leader dies, but his another reproductive himself person can continue to bring war crisis to global, such as Japan's past leader, he was one ambitious leader to dominate global countries. If DNA reproductive technology is applied to help him to reproduce this Japan ambitious another himself . Then, the another new world war may be occurred easily. So, I also worry about future DNA reproductive technology may be applied to help the bad people to reproduce themselves to bring our societies safety and economic recession negative impact.
So, it brings this question: Can DNA reproductive technology bring only positive impact to influence our social behavior change? I shall attempt to explain as below:

How does DNA attract our behavior? In some situations, genes play a larger role in determining your behavior. How can genetic technologies impact society ? Although, genetic technology has a great potential to change the medical practice as we know it also has a potential to be misused , it also has a potential to be misused, and lead to further health disparities, discrimination and inequality in the human societies around the world.

However, I believe that those the ways that genetic engineering can help human society. Several works have been done on genetic engineering with major focus on its importance ranging from increasing plant and animal food production, diagnosing disease condition, medical treatment improvement, as well as production of vaccines and other useful drugs.

- What is the focus of behavioral generics?

Behavioral genetics is the study of genetic and environmental influences on behaviors. By examining genetic influence, more information can be gleaned about how the environment operates to affect behavior. So, in behavioral economic view, gene DNA reproductive cell technology may seem to bring these benefits. Some benefits of genetic engineer in agriculture are increased crop yields, reduced need for food or drug production, reduced need for pesticides, enhanced nutrient composition and food quality , resistance to past and disease , greater food security, and medical benefits to the world's growing population . Also, the intangible , non economic measurement, possible benefit of genetic engineering may include more nutritious food, tastier food, disease -and-drought resistant plants that require fewer environment resources , such as water and fertilizers, less use of pesticides, increased supply of food with reduced cost and larger shelf life, faster growing plants and animals.

All of these benefits, they can not measured by economic calculation, but they can be felt by us. So, in our social behevioral economic view to genetic engineering, it may bring both positive and negative impact to our societies. On negative impact, these are many risks involves in genetic engineering, the release of genetically altered organisms in the environment can increase human suffering, disease animal welfare, and lead to ecological disasters are positive impact aspect, it can help to defeat diseases, getting rid of all illnesses in young and unborn children potential to live longer, produce new foods, organisms can be tailor-made , faster growth in animals and plants, pests and diseases resistance. But genetic engineering can also bring risks to our societies, e.g. new allergens in the food supply, antibiotic , production of new toxins, concentration of toxic metals, enhancement of the environment for toxic fungi, unknown harms, gene transfer to wild to weedy relations, change in herbicide use patterns.

By knocking out genes responsible for certain conditions, it is possible to create animal model organism of " human disease" as well as producing hotmenes, vaccies and other drugs. So, if DNA can bring human diseases, it means that it can also bring economic loss to our societies, because human disease may bring illness to any one to cause low productivity to any industry development, if the factory has many people human disease from reproductive animal cell accident risk. Then, the ill worker number increases, low productivity and inefficiencies will cause to the factory. If global has many factory workers got human disease from reproductive animal cell accident. Then, global factories products producing number must have been influenced to fallen down.

Consequently, global manufacturers will encountered serious loss, due to their products producing speed is slow and their different kinds of products supply number must decrease, if global will workers number increases, they are caused by reproductive animal cell disease. Hence, DNA genetic reproductive technology may also bring global economic loss crisis in possible.

Staff behavior how influences organization resource

In organizational behavioral economic view, whether they have cause and effect relationship between employees how to use resources behaviors and organizational resource excess use within organizations ?

In organizational behavioral economic view, whether they have cause and effect relationship between employees how to use resources behaviors and organizational resource excess use within organizations. For example, if the organization has many employees number, whether the organization will use its any internal tangible and intangible resources easily per day.

For construction organization example, one construction organization must need to buy different kinds of construction materials to prepare to let workers to help it to manufacture different kinds of properties or houses (products) in order to sell to property buyers. In its every building construction site, it will need more or less workers, they are needed to use different kinds of construction materials to build houses in different construction sites. I assume that construction site (A), it has 100 construction workers number, every day, construction site (A) 100 workers need to use different kinds of construction materials to help them to build 3 building floors wall at least floor number in the construction site (A).
I assume that these 100 construction workers , they include proficient workers and not proficient workers. For proficient construction workers group, they have 50 number, and not proficient construction workers group, they also have 50 number . Hence, the proficient construction workers only need to spend 3 hours maximum and use less number of constructoin materials, then they can finish to build 3 building floors wall per day.

I also assume that all construction material supply number is limited. It means that due to this construction firm needs to pre-booking to purchase this kind of the best quality of construction material from overseas before three months. So, it must not have enough time to pre-booking to purchase this kind of best quality of construction materials when they are used rapidly within one month, due to this one month is the final finishing time to this construction firm within one month. Hence, limited construction material supply number and limited finishing time to build this new 40 floors house within this final one month .

So , not proficient construction workers number , limit number of construction material and per day 8 hours which is its limited resources in behavioral economy view. Moreover, total 50 proficient and not proficient 50 construction workers (human resource employees number) will cause this construction firm , it will possible need to build this new 40 floors house are more than one month, if these 50 proficient construction workers , they have more than 30 at least number, they are absent to cause their overall construction workers' efficiency to be fallen down, due to the other 50 not proficient construction numbers must need their teaching how to cooperate ad how use less materials to build this new 40 floor house rapidly in order to raise overall construction team efficiency and avoid to delay more than one month time to build this 40 floors new house successfully within this final one month time.

Hence, it explains that when one organization has more employees, it does not represent that this organization must need to use more resource to achieve its any mission, such as this construction firm case, although it has 50 not proficient construction workers, they need to use more construction materials to build this new 40 floors house in this construction site (A). But, in fact, it has other 50 proficient construction workers, they know how to reduce construction materials to build every building floor wall for this new 40 floors building house. So, they can teach the not proficient building workers to know hoe to avoid to use extra excess construction material to finish to construct every building floor wall. SO, although, it has 50 not proficient construction workers number, but they can be taught to learn how to reduce to use these limited the best quality of construction materials to build this 40 floors new house. It implies that if the construction workers number can increase, e.g. increases more 50 not proficient construction workers, this the best quality of construction material resource number must not need to increase demand, because this construction site (A) has 50 proficient construction workers , they can teach these 50 not proficient construction workers how to avoid to use extra excess this kind of high quality construction material to build this new 40 floor house efficiently and effectively within this one month.

Hence, if this construction firm won't have more than 30 proficient workers number is absent in this final one month, it will have enough proficient construction workers to teach these 50 not proficient construction workers to know how to use this high quality of construction materials to build this 40 floors new house building in order to avoid waste or construction material need shortage challenge occurs in this final one month time.

Consequently , it ought finish to build this 40 floors new house building within this month. Hence, it explains why its this kind of high quality of construction material resource need must not increase, because if its all proficient construction workers is absent and their absent number is less than 30, then they have enough proficient construction workers number , they can teach this 50 not proficient construction workers how to avoid to use extra excess construction materials resource number in order to have enough construction material resource supply to satisfy this new 40 floors building house to finish construction within one month finishing date need.

On conclusion, in organizational behavioral economic view, it explains that resource use need must not be influenced to increase when the organization's employees number increase. It depends on whether the organization has how many talent and proficient workers number in order to assist them and teach the not proficient employees how to use resource to manufacture any kinds of products in order to avoid to spend extra excess of resource need. Hence, organizational behavioral economic view, it can explain that any organization's increase to employees number, it does not mean that its resource number is also needed to increase. Moreover, in organizational behavioral economic view, it also explains that if the organization can have many proficient workers to help it to do any complex tasks, they will help it to bring avoiding waste or excess extra resource to use advantage, because they ought know whether how they work, they can help the organization to improve performance or raise efficiency e.g. car manufacture, computer manufacture, television manufacture etc. home electronic products or car leisure products. Due to that manufacture processes are complex, if the organization can have more proficient high skillful workers to help it to manufacture their products. They ought help it to use lesser manufacturing time and less manufacturing resource to finish any above these products to compare not proficient or low skillful manufacture workers. So, in long time, the organization must may earn economic low cost benefits from proficient worker individual high manufacturing skillful knowledge behavior or performance. So, organizational behavioral economic theory explains why even the organization plans to increase employees number, it's resources number won't be influenced to increase rapidly because when the organization's proficient high skillful workers number is more 2 times at least than not proficient low skillful workers number. They ought have enough effort to train and teach and cooperate with the not proficient low skillful manufacture workers to improve their manufacture skills in order to raise manufacturing efficiency and reduce extra excess resources waste and avoid to bring long term resource waste economic loss.

So, any manufacturing organizations must need to increase proficient workers number to assist the not proficient low skillful workers to learn how to improve their skills and know how to reduce to use excess resources to keep to manufacture the highest number of products aim frequently. Consequently, the organization will bring long term low resource use manufacturing economic benefit.

CHAPTER THIRTEEN

How organization improvement may bring economic benefits

Can organizational economies, e.g. transaction cost economics, agency theory, organizational theory , e.g. models of formal organizational independent of the strategies, improve organizational behavior in order to bring economic benefit, e.g. development potentially valuable resources and capabilities, it can raise internal organizational strengths and avoid weaknesses in SWOT strategy in order to improve performance and bring organizational internal economic benefit in organizational behavioral economic view.

For manufacturing industry example, if the car manufacturers can attempt to discover the most efficient steel, or different kinds of car components material, but they can help it to manufacture many high quality cars. Then, their manufacture cost reduce , but its any model of car quality does not caused to poor. Then, this car firm can apply the most efficient and the most high component materials to help it to manufacture high quality cars. Although, it must need to spend time to research how to invest the most efficient and high quality car manufacture components, but if it can apply the most efficient and the high quality components to help it to manufacture any new model of cars. Then, new components research spending time can bring long term low manufacturing cost and high quality of cars to achieve long time economic benefits.

So, on behavioral economic view, organization's spending time on different kind of cheap and high quality car manufacture manufacture components research and research expenditure spending on new kinds of different car manufacture components, it can help it to sell the high quality of different model of cars to satisfy car buyer comfortable needs. Moreover, it can earn high profit, when it 's any car manufacture component cost reduces. So, SWOT internal strengths (high quality and low cost) to this car manufacturer. It may help it to bring long term raising profit economic benefit, when its any new model of car prices do not need raise, but their compared material manufacture cost reduce, due to new kinds of car manufacture component materials can be invented in success.

Hence, high quality and low cost of car manufacture component invention researching on spending time and research experiment expenditure is value to this car manufacture company, because if high quality and low cost car manufacture component experience succeeds, it can help it to improve any new model of cars quality , but the most important factor is that its any new model of cars prices do not need increase. So, car buyer individual purchase desire won't be influenced to choose any brand of car seller to replace it more easily.

For one drug development process, case example ,I assume that this drug manufacture firm can attempt to spend 10 years time, but it can help it has possible to help it to invent one kind of new pharmaceutical drugs to kill cancer cells for global cancer patients. So, its spending time research on new drugs to kill any kinds of cancers and experimentation expenditure is value, because it can help it to bring economic benefit when global will have many cancer patients believe its new discovery of cancer drugs , it may help them to kill cancer cells to get health or reduce death chance ratio raises after 10 years.

Consequently, in soon future, it's global cancer patients number may increase when they choose to buy its future new cancer drugs product. It may bring high profit economic benefit. So, on organizational behavioral economic view, when the organization spends long time and experimentation expenditure to research new resources, if these new resources can be invented in success and it ensures help it to increase clients number to order to bring future economic benefit. The organization is value to spend time and expenditure to carry on new resources research.

- Can organization apply behavioral economic demand to evaluate work performance for whole different departments?

Behavioral economies investigation may include evaluating demand for a commodity (such as drug experimentation and car manufacturing component material etc.) is given changes in price, using hypothetical purchase tasks, which are a reliable and efficient assessment method. Can behavior management examine work performance evaluation? The work performance evaluation target includes that employee individual and different department will performance evaluation in organization.

I believe high quality or low quality training , which can be evaluated whether the employee individual work performance or the department overall employees work performance can be improved after training. So, if the department employee individual or all employers work performance can be improved, e.g. work efficiency raises, client satisfactory feeling raises, product sale number . Then, the training is a high quality training to help the organization to earn future high economic benefit. Otherwise , if the organization can not earn above any one good result. Then, the training in a low quality training.So, any organization can attempt to observe any department

overall performance and employee individual performance in order to evaluate whether it can provide high or low quality of training to let employees to learn.
So, employee individual behavior can bring performance evidence to let the organization to evaluate whether its training is useful or not useful to achieve its training aim, e.g. when the car manufacturer provides money, time, effort training arrangement to teach all workers to learn how to manufacture car skill. After training provision, many of them, they do not need to work over time more than one hour to manufacture daily of least 10 cars per employee.Before, any one worker must need to spend more than one hour over time to manufacture daily 10 more cars.

So, when this car manufacture skillful improvement train is provided more than one hour more than one hour , none of them, they need work over time in order to manufacture more than at least 10 cars number per day. It seems that training improvement arrangement can be used to evaluate whether employee individual efficiency can be raised in organizational behavioral economic view.

Hence, any organization's internal training provision knowledge resource, it can be evaluated employees' behavioral performance can be improved, about being available to work, about role performance . It assumes that employees are likely to come to work and remain in the organization if they obtain satisfaction from their jobs, and that they are likely to put use effort and work more effectively if they are to be reward more for their effort and performance can be confirmed to improved by management after they are taught by training. So, when the employee hopes to raise salary, he must hard to learn any new knowledge from the organizational training. Then, training can help the " expectation good reward employees" can improve performance in organizational behavioral economic view.

It is one important successful factor to help the organization to innovate and bring economic benefit, when the organization can implement any new useful training to improve any new useful training to improve employee skills. It means that training is one long term economic organizational strategy, it depends on whether the training is useful or is useful in order to help any old employees to raise or improve their skills to achieve raising efficiency and satisfactory client service , sale product number, product manufacture increasing number aims.

- How organizational ethic influence employee behavior ?

Organizational ethic behavior concerns with explaining employee individual behavior in organization, e.g. ethical decision making, ethical conduct for example, when one marketing department manager does not attempt to carrying on any data research about new market research to sell the new model i phone to any country. He only depends on his personal judgment, he believes that this new invention of US i phone products, they ought to be sell to Korean new i phone market, because he feels Korean must prefer to choose to buy US brand of new i phone products to compare other countries i phone product. However, this i phone marketing development manager lacks enough data research for different Korean i phone buyer age target, purchase experience, purchase desire to conclude Korean i phone buyers must like to buy any brand of US i phone products in preference.

His non ethical new i phone invention decision making to choice Korean i pohone buyers market will bring time waste rick to satisfy Korean i phone buyers' needs to replace other new model i pone users market, e.g. Hong Kong, China, i pone market. So, his ethical decision making to Korean i phone buyers , i phone invention market may bring less economic benefit to this US i phone manufacture firm. So, this new model i pohone marketing development immoral judgment of this i phone marketing development manager individual decision making to Korean new model i pone invention to Korean i pone users, it can bring high economic loss to this US i phone firm.Otherwise, if this marketing department manager can spend time to carry on data gathering to make more accurate new model i phone invention decision making to choose which one country, then his ethical decision making may help his this US ip hone firm to reduce new i phone invention loss risk. So, it explains that why ethic organizational behavior may influence the firm can earn more or less economic benefit. SO, ethic or moral behavior can influence the organization can earn how much economic benefit in long term significantly in organizational behavioral economic view.

● Can improve energy efficiency by organization building occupant's energy consumption relative behavior to bring economic benefit?

Reducing energy consumption in building , it must improve efficiency by building, but whether they have close cause and effect relationship between occupant's energy consumption behavior and improvement energy efficiency to the building? IN fact, high efficiency equipment is being developed, it can help any building to save energy and economic effectiveness, if building energy is subject to uncertainties, such as whether variations, human operations, human behavior changes and government policies. So, building technology equipment improvement may be one main factor to help buildings to save energy . But why occupant behavior may help building to save energy by their daily energy consumption behavior.

The occupant energy behavioral user inputs factor may include: Weather influences, internal heat gain, efficiency, simply normal occupant behaviors, e.g. a high efficiency chiller can save very limited energy in cold climates due to minimal cooling load, and a good designed natural ventilation building won't work if the occupants do not open windows when outdoor air favors cooling. So, it seems that if one living building hopes to reduce energy consumption, instead of building equipment technological change , e.g. air condition facilities, building occupants , artificial intelligent light, life, their daily energy consumption behaviors, they can influence the living building's energy consumption level in occupant energy consumption behavior and building energy saving economic benefit view.

In fact, when the occupant considers hot water, air condition, energy gas electricity expenditure, he won't use excess electricity, gas resources, because he needs to pay more energy expenditure , when gas and electricity energy consumption expenditure is applied to any business organization offices, warehouses , shops working facilities environment, such as offices, warehouses , shops can often use less electricity, gas energy far their employees daily work . In long time, the organization must may reduce much electricity, gas energy expenditure for whole organizations business activities. In organizational behavior economic view, organizational energy consumption reduces it can help it to bring less expenditure spending economic benefit.

Can Amazon e-commerce activities bring economic benefit to global societies

Amazon e-commerce is one online product sale e-commerce organization. Any one country e-buyer can use his/her home computer to click to Amazon web stores, when he/she saw the product phone and price, then he/she feels the product's price is reasonable and he/she believes that he/she can make the best choice to buy the product. Then, he/she can pay visa to buy the product from Amazon web store.

Amazon can bring the most convenient online sale channel to global any one e-buyer. The e-buyer can buy the overseas product from its e-web stores . He does not need to catch air plane to fly to the e-sellers' shop. he can pay visa to pay the product from Amazon e-web stores any time immediately. All Amazon e-web stores . He can open 24 hours, so all web stores have no close time. So , it can bring busy working people, they do not need to spend long time to visit any shops to make purchase decision. For busy working people example, time has important value to them, they do not want to waste time to make any purchase choice.

So, Amazon gives " economic purchase time benefit " to global any one full time working people. In their psychology, Amazon can help them to save much time to go to online shopping purchase chance at homes. They can stay at homes to shopping. Even, when they give their their address to Amazon to know, Amazon will deliver their products to their homes within several days rapidly. Also , they do not need to pay money to buy its products immediately. They can only pay visa to buy the product from Amazon web stores. So, they can save " consumption money" to use for another need in short time. So, one individual e-air ticket buyer, Amazon can bring economic benefit to him, he does not need to buy air ticket to fly to another country to buy the product. Amazon web stores are given more different kinds of similar brand products to let him to choose in order to pay the most reasonable price, working people do not need to spend much visiting shop time to choose any products in order to make the final purchase decision at home rapidly, any one has visa card , he/she can buy the product from Amazon web stores at homes.

Instead of individual e-buyer e commerce time benefit, spending little time product choice, reducing catching air plane to visit another country seller shop to pay air ticket expense and travel time spending activities to every e-buyer . Amazon also brings global economic benefits to any one country. When the e-buyer lives in one country to buy the product, it is saved in the overseas country's warehouse. Then, the product must need to deliver to his home by air plane. So, all of Amazon products can bring global goods air transport delivering service to any one overseas buyer, when the product is saved in the overseas seller's warehouse. Any one Amazon product overseas transport delivery service activity, it can help air goods transport service need increases as well as their goods air transport service income will also increase. Amazon can bring global air goods transport service need increases. It can assist global GDP air goods transport industry grows, and economic benefit for the country's air plan goods delivery service industry development in long term. Hence, on behavioral economic view, Amazon online sale channel ,it can help global economic benefit to air plane goods delivery service industry as well as individual different country e-buyer individual time saving and short term money saving economic benefit by visa payment method.

Moreover, Amazon also creates more high technology employment chance to any one country because Amazon owns many offices and warehouses in different countries, due to it is one high technological e-commerce online sale organization, It must need many high skillful website designers to help it to design different countries web stores in order to satisfy any one e-buyer online purchase need. So, it creates high technology job chance to any one country web store designers . It can help them to raise competitive effort when any one graduate pursues website designer career. IN Amazon provides good employment chance for any one country computer e commerce designers in order to let them to earn high salary. Also, Amazon public e-commerce organization provides good chance for any one country author to earn royalty income when he/she publishes any electronic or paper books to sell from Amazon publish. It gives good writing skillful authors have more writing chance to help them to sell electronic books and /or paper books from its different countries web book stores to different countries' readers in short time. It can help them to increase book sale chance to let different countries book buyers can know whether new book topic to the author, he/she will publish soon. So, it brings author's new writing mind training chance when he/she needs to compare book sale rank from Amazon web stores.

Hence, Amazon can bring social employment benefit and author individual skillful training advantage and royalty income benefit to any on country author in nowadays online published industry. So, Amazon online business activities can increase global social employment chance, encourages global authors attempt to train writing skill, helps e-buyers to save visiting shops shopping time and air ticket expenditure for global overseas buyers.

● How and why Amazon e-commerce organization influence global consumer behavioral changes to bring e commerce benefits to sellers?

In behavioral economic view, Amazon changes consumers behavior as well as product sellers sale method, such as global consumer sellers began to accept online purchase method to replace frequent visiting shop purchase method and global sellers began to accept to apply Amazon web stores to help them to sell products from its online sale channel to replace opening shops locate to the country sale channel.
The advantages to global sellers may include they do not need to pay rent or buy the shops, they can use Amazon web stores to show their different kinds of products photos and prices to let any one online buyer to know . The

advantage to global buyers, they do not need to spend time to visit any countries shops to choose products in order to make purchase decision. They only need to spend some time to visit amazon any one country's web store to see any brands of product photos and know their prices to different kinds of products to compare design and price and functions among of them in the online visiting short time when they stay at home to turn on themselves home computers . So, future home consumption behavior may replace visiting shop consumption behavior. Amazon 's online purchase method will encourage global many sellers have began to believe traditional visiting shop purchase model can not be accepted to global any one consumer more easily, when any one owns computer and internet service at home in common. Then, global shops number will reduce, due to different kinds of product websites purchase model needs number increases to global product sellers, they will close their shops and open themselves web stores or choose Amazon web store to help them to sell their products conveniently. Consequently, global online purchase and sale transactions number will be influenced to increase by e-commerce organization development.

Global consumer behavior how influence
global economic growth or recession
Have they close relationship between consumer behavioral change and economic change?

- How does consumer behavioral change impact economic change?
- How does consumer behavior bring positive or negative influence to economic growth or economic recession to the country?

I shall attempt to apply behavioral economic theory to explain their cause and effect relationship why and hoe global economy growth or recession may be impacted by global consumer behavior change reasons as below:

I shall indicate travel leisure and goods air plane transport industries example, since air planes are invented, it is a kind rapid air transport tool, it can help human to do both kinds of transport service, one is goods transport and another is human transport . So, any individual or business goods can be delivered to another country offices or homes by air planes transport tools rapidly. SO, air planes can create more overseas purchase and sale business activities chance between different countries nowadays. Moreover, internet invention, it also increase more e-commerce online purchase and sale business activities to global any one online buyer, he/she only needs to apply computer tool to click to the online seller web store, when he /she likes the product, he/she can pay visa to buy the product from the online seller web store at home conveniently.

Hence, e-commerce encourages global consumers to choose to buy any products from internet channel, it also brings global goods are needed to transport by air planes between different countries, e.g. one US online buyer makes purchase decision from online channel, then he chooses the product from Korean one online seller web store. After he pays visa to the Korean online seller web store , then the Korea seller will follow his US address to send the product to the US buyer's home after several days rapidly.

Hence, it explains that if future global consumers like to buy any products from any one country's online sell web store. Then, the product must need to be delivered to the online buyer's home. When the seller's product is not located to the online buyer's country warehouse. It needs to be delivered by air plane. When, global there are man consumers, their traditional visiting shops purchase habits are influenced to change online visiting web stores habits. Then, when their purchase habits are influenced to change by rapid, convenient, visa card payment online purchase method at home, time online purchase technological new payment channel method.

In future new online purchase trend development, it may influence future global traditional visiting shops consumption model to change visiting webstores consumption model. Consequently, consumers will choose to pay visa online purchase at home in preference. Also, it encourages visa card purchase , consequently, online purchase may influence these industries development, airlines goods transport service needs increase, it can increase new visa cards number to the frequent online channel e-buyer number. So, online consumption encourages global households save long time money in banks, because we can pay money by visa card payment after we buy any products from online. Global bank may have more money to save longer time from global households, long time money save , because we do not need to withdraw money to buy any expensive products, immediately, e.g. computer , television, furniture etc. When global households begin to accept online purchase method is better to compare visiting shop purchase method. So, future global airline goods transport and bank saving businesses these two industries may have positive impact by future global online buyers raising number.

Hence, when global consumers behaviors began to change online purchase , their online purchase activities may influence global banks can have long time saving money and airlines goods transport need increase rapidly. However, online purchase activities will bring negative consumers emotion impact to some businesses, e.g. property rent business, because when the country has high population of consumers, they choose online purchases, they won't often visit shops to choose any kind of products frequently, they only like to stay at home and turn on themselves home computers to find whether global whom sellers, they have web stores to let global consumers to buy their products from online channel. Due to the country will not have many consumers like to spend time to visit any shops in the country. It means that the country will have many shops are needed to be close, because there are less number people visit the businessmen shops every day. It will cause property rent service providers can not increase rent income, even decrease rent income, when there are many businessmen close their shops and change online web stores to replace actual shops. Hence, it seems that online buyers number increases, it may also brings positive impact to influence shop rent service income decreases to the property rent developers.

On global macro economic changing environment, online buyers number increases, it can encourage any kinds of

products, they can sell more more easily. So, global product sale number may be influenced to increase rapidly, when global online purchase and sale transactions number increase, GDP on any kinds of product income may be influenced to increase . So, online buyers number increases, it must may bring positive impact to influence global trading GDP high growth, but global shops rent income property developers may be influenced to reduce, due to there are many shops may be caused to close in possible.
How travelers' leisure need change, it may influence travel leisure service industry development? I shall attempt to explain how COVID 19 disease influences global travelers leisure need change and airplane and travel service providers, e.g. hotels, travel agents, their leisure service needs change. Nowadays, COVID 19 disease has caused global many travelers feel fear to catch airplanes, because air planes all windows are needed to close, he/she has COVID disease, then he/she can bring any one passenger to get this kind of disease by air plane close window air environment. So, when global many travellers feel afraid to catch air planes, this kind of COVID 9 air contact disease, it can cause global travellers number has began to reduce, many of travellers began to reduce travel times per year, even 0 time travel per year. Consequently, it will bring negative impact to global travel industry development.

Firstly, COVID 19 disease influences global traveler individual travel desire decreases, every traveler began to avoid to catch air planes to travel. So, any country;s airlines air planes flying times began to reduce, because it is no full seats booking to any airlines. It means that airline must decrease income, also they need to pay parking airplanes rent to any countries airports. So, fixed rent expenditure will need to pay, and many airlines began to dismiss the excess extra number of airline front service staffs, e.g. airport front service staffs, air plane check in /out staffs, even pilots number began also decreased.
So, airline unemployment ratio increases , it causes pilots, airlines service staffs need to change jobs even some countries pilots , choose to do simple goods delivery jobs in supermarkets or securities. Also, COVID 19 disease influences hotels, travel agents income began to reduce, because there are none many travellers need to live hotels, and they do not need travel agents to help them to arrange any travel journeys. So , COVID 19 disease influences many different countries travelers began choose any leisure activities to replace travel, because they feel afraid to get COVID 19 disease when they need to sit in closed window air plane environment.

This kind of disease can influence any one traveler individual leisure choice began to change, such as they began to forgive travel sure activities, they will spend holiday to do other leisure activities in themselves countries , e.g. climbing mountain, swimming, running, playing table tennis, tennis etc. different outdoor sports. all of these leisure sports have same features, global any one leisure need, he does not catch air plane to fo to another country to carry on playing these any one sport and he/she does not need to pay more price to enjoy these sports. Otherwise m travel leisure activity, it must need any one leisure need to spend much expenditure to enjoy this kind of leisure activity . So, it explains why many travellers began to choose to do any kinds of sports to replace spending money to enjoy travel leisure in their holidays,

On conclusion,this COVID 19 disease had influenced global travel leisure businesses and travel related leisure service industries income and travellers number began to reduce and any countries GDP on travel industry will have negative economic recession occurrence in this COVID 19 disease global environment. Hence, it implies that consumers (travellers) behavior leisure activities need, it may influence global business activities increase or decrease , global economic growth or recession, they have close cause and effect relationship between consumer behavioral change and industries GDP changes in behavioral economic view.

CHAPTER FOURTEEN

Vehicle owner individual driving times and income level relationship

Can behavioral psychologist apply vehicle owner individual driving times to measure or evaluate whether he/she has high income level or whether his/her income increases or decreases?

Can drivers' driving time reflect his/her general income level ? In general, whether private car owners , their driving times can be influenced by income changing level? It depends on different factors, e.g. the car driver does not want often spend 10 minutes to wait bus from home to working places or from working places to home two ways frequently.

I assume that, in general, private car owners do not want often drive themselves cars to go to anywhere, e.g. working people usually only like to drive themselves cars , when they need to work, even holiday leisure activity, they need to drive cars to arrive the leisure activity destination. So, it seems that any car owners , their cars purchase aims, they are either for working needs or leisure aims mainly. So, I bring this question: Suggesting that any countries car owners, their cars purchase usually for leisure and working both intention. Can the car owner's per month driving times, it can reflect his/her income level whether it increases or decreases? It means that the car owner will increase driving car times, when his salary has increased or the car owner will decrease driving car times, when his salary has decreased? Can driving car times represent the car owner his/her general increasing or decreasing salary? Have they relationship between increasing or decreasing to car owner's driving times and his/her salary increasing or decreasing level?

Behavioral economists can attempt to apply behavioral economic view to research general car owners their driving behaviors. In general, when can fuel price increases, it may influence car owners to reduce driving times because when they drive themselves cars frequently, their cars must need to use much fuel. Consequently, they will need to pay higher price to buy another long driving time useful fuel. So, when any one car owner knows that car fuel prices are general increasing. They will be influenced to reduce to drive themselves cars to avoid more expenditure spending on car fuel aspect.

So, I assume car fuel price increases, it can influence general car users reduce themselves driving car times per day. They won't drive themselves to go to far destination, unless the destination is not too far. It means that general car owners like to drive cars to go to short distance destination only, if general car fuel price has increased significantly in local car fuel market. Hence, it seems that car fuel price whether rises up or falls down, it can influence many car owners avoid often drive themselves cars to go to long distance destination, in order to avoid frequent high fuel price expense. Also , it means that any car fuel seller ought not often rise fuel price in order to avoid many car owners reduce driving times behaviors. Consequently, car fuel and car purchase number will be influenced to reduce when the country has many car owners reduce driving times to go to long distance destination. It is driving car and using car fuel behavioral market principle, it means that when the car fuel price general increases, it influences general car owners reduce driving car want more times, because they do not want often buy new car fuel rising price level to avoid not essential economic loss on rising price of car fuel expenditure.

Hence, if this supposion to " general rising car fuel price level, " it will influence general car owners avoid to drive themselves cars to go to long distance destinations. It is reasonable and their driving car times will be influenced to reduce in society. Then, it explains that behavioral economists can attempt to gather general social car owner individual driving car times increases or decreases between last month and this month to evaluate whether it is direct car fuel price as well as whether it rises or falls down. This factor can judge whether what factor can cause general car owner individual driving times increases or decreases in society. Also, it implies that we can depend on general car owner individual driving behavioral times to judge whether the car owner's salary level had been increased or had been decreasing in the past. It is possible that general social car owner individual driving time behavior is significantly increasing or decreasing, it may reflect whether the car owner has present salary , it has been increasing or has been decreasing. Because if the car owner whose salary has been decreasing significantly, the significant decreasing salary, it may influence the car owner reduces to spend long time to drive car to arrive another long distance far away destination frequently.

The reason is that he avoids to increase economic loss to use more car fuel for non essential driving use, when he feels that his income is significantly decreased.

Hence, any behavioral economists may attempt to gather household individual general expenditure data in order to conclude what factors influence the household changes his/her family behavioral consumption or consumption attitude. It means that any household individual consumption attitude changes, it may be influenced by any product price changing factor, such as car fuel price case or the household overall rising or falling income level factor in household behavioral economic view.

CHAPTER FIFTEEN

How transport brings economic development

What factors may influence public transport passenger psychology

What factors may influence public transport passenger psychology ? How these factors may influence any kinds of public transport passenger choice? Specifically there are following characteristics to influence any kinds of pubic passengers transport tools choice , they may include these factors : speed of means of transport, length of stay of means of transport in the stops and stations, waste of time and value of time savings, fare, comfortable feeling etc.

A passenger's only job is to ride along. In the fourteenth century, a passenger was simply a "passer-by," from the Old French passenger, "passing, fleeting, or traveling." The first instance of the modern use was recorded in the early 1500s.Public transport tools are very import to help working people, students, retire people daily transport need. It reduces congestion in towns and cities. using public transport is cheaper than owning and operating a car. no more sitting in traffic jams in rush hour thanks to bus lanes and other bus priority measures. However, any kinds of public Transportation need to consider how to avoid negative emotion to passenger, e.g. Air pollution may cause to reduce environment protection passengers number to bus, taxi etc. Public transport tools, especially road transport, or noise can influence bus passengers number reduce. It has a significant negative impact on the environment, including pollution, greenhouse gas emissions, noise pollution, congestion, and traffic accidents.

Any kinds of public transport need to considerate these need to let every passenger feels comfortable. Here are some ways to be a considerate passenger: Keep your belongings organized and out of the aisle. Respect others' personal space and try to keep noise levels down. Use headphones if listening to music or watching a movie.

However, any kinds of public transport may help social economic development. It enables the movement of people and goods, supporting social progress and a vibrant economy . Transportation is an important component of urban infrastructure and contributes to the overall system of life, government, and social systems .

In order to meet demands for traveling of passengers and the requirements to the quality of the service, the construction level of terminals is to be higher. Passengers' activities in terminal are becoming complicated, so there is no doubt that the operation and management of terminal faces much higher request. In order to fully understand the psychological characteristics of the passengers and improve the transportation service and make people-oriented management measures based on the passengers' demands.

The factors affecting passengers' traveling psychological activities

Passengers are the users of subway, train or other means of transport. Passengers are the crowds that combined with the people in passenger transport system as the social individuals. These individuals get together because of common purposes, forming a temporary group. All the psychological activities passengers did in trip, as well as all the behavior results that are produced under the control of psychological activities are influenced by the factors inside and outside the transportation system environment, the main factors are:

The environment factors: people live in certain circumstances; the environment can be divided into the natural environment and social environment and the economic environment created by people. Transportation, especially road transport, has a significant negative impact on the environment, including pollution, greenhouse gas emissions, noise pollution, congestion, and traffic accidents.

Personal factors: in the personal growth process, everyone forms relatively stable psychological characteristics through environment edification, the education accepted, the social status and identity formed in personal development, which affect one person's psychological activities and results of behaviors.

Group factors: the passengers on travelling will inevitably interact with other passengers and have mutual influences and restraints between each other.

Transportation tools and services factors: the comfort, economy, safety, efficiency of transportation tools and the quality of the services provided by transportation departments will affect passengers' selection of traffic tools, which is also the direct reason for Due to passengers' traveling psychological activities affected by the comprehensive functions of all aspects

above, who inspect every factor and its mutual relations so that the inner mechanism of the psychological activities can influence any one passenger emotion when they need to sit in any kinds of public transport tools in long time. So, I believe that psychological factor is the main influence to any one of public transport tool passenger choice.

In general, passengers may include these kinds :Transit (e.g., bus, rail, tram, taxi, ferry, plane) workers (e.g., drivers, ticket inspectors, conductors, attendants) play a critical role in providing safe travel to and from work, school, and leisure activities for community members. However, like workers in hospitality, retail, and other service industries, transit workers may face hostility from their customers or, in this case, their passengers.

The subject of psychology can be applied to this project as we are analysing social behaviour and psychological anthropology as our main themes. Therefore, the inclusion of this subject is valid because we apply these theories to passengers in public transportation and analyse their behaviour.

This project is concerned with seeking general patterns in people's behaviour when being in the public transportation system, and thus it is essential to look into social psychology. The connection between social psychology and the observations the group has conducted will be elaborated further on in the project, yet it is of great importance to make a short introduction of what social psychology entails before applying the theoretical aspects to this specific project.

Understand train transport psychology : The underground provides advertisements on both sides on the train, which gives the passengers information, or little entertainment for the duration of their journey. Since the passengers have pre-purchased a ticket, and must prove purchase at the gates prior to entering the underground, there is no ticket controller needed. However, in any event, security cameras are placed throughout each station in order to secure the safety of the passengers using the underground.

To reach the platform, passengers use the escalators or the stairs to reach the lower level in order to get to the area of departure. Upon entering the train, the seats are divided length wise, and include an aisle in between. The seats are also 10 divided into 'sections' and these are able to seat four to six passengers. Since the train is above ground, the use of cell phones and other electronics is available.

Bus transport psychology: In Copenhagen, the busses are designed much the same as automobiles, and they are two seats wide. However, when passengers move further away from the front of the bus, they will enter the back of the bus, which is the same as the front of the bus, with the exception of the back seats, which are five seats wide. There are two exits in the bus, and one entrance. The entrance is located next to the driver, who is not confined in a partition, where passengers can either pay with coins, show a clip card or monthly pass, directly to the driver. There is also seating available for handicapped passengers and strollers and is located at the front, near the centre exit door.

Most people engage in more than one group on a daily basis, this might not be something that the individual is aware of, rather it might be an implicit part of moving around in everyday life. For instance when being at work you are engaged in a group consisting of colleagues, bosses and other employees. This group might be composed of both in-group as well as out-group, depending on the internal relationships. Another example on participating in a group could be after work meeting up with a friend, then you have moved from one group to another. Thus it is most likely that the number of different groups you engage in is more than you might be aware of. It is important to be aware of the fact that engaging in one or more groups presumably leads you to take on a certain role. This role might differ from group to group and can even be two different roles within the same group. Being part of a group and taking on a role might influence the individual in either increasing or decreasing ones' self-esteem. Ones' self-esteem is of high importance when determining what kind of person you are and will become in 24 your further life, since your self-esteem influences the way you think and feel both about yourself but surely also about the people who are part of your life. Having a high self-esteem might affect your participation in the groups that you have an affiliation with (Bertelsen, 2008). One vital aspect of social psychology that cannot be ignored is the fact that people become aware of themselves and their behaviour. In becoming aware of ones' behaviour most people have a tendency to evaluate their choices and find the positive in what they choose to do, and in addition find the negative aspects of what they did not choose to do (Bertelsen, 2008).

The transportation such as Mass Rapid (MRT), Bus Rapid Transit/Transjakarta, Light Rail Transit (LRT), Commuter Line (KRL/Electric Train) and the Airport Train (Railink) are developed to create an integrated transportation system. The main purpose of an integrated system is to provide public transport users with a "wide spectrum" of destination choices and also with a convenient, accessible, comfortable, safe, speedy, and affordable transport system (Luk and Olszewski, 2003;Ulengin et al., 2007) and when is supported by related regulation, it will encourage the use of public transportation (Chowdhury and Ceder, 2013a).

These factors depend completely on the individual and their beliefs and personal preferences, and some are related to the controllability experienced by the user. According to the Theory of Planned Behaviour (TPB), users manifest a stronger intention to take routes involving transfers when they have greater control over the situation (Chowdhury & Ceder, 2013a). Health status is also important in determining both actual and perceived walking distance and time.

One suggestion provided by Chowdhury and Ceder (2013) used the theory of planned behavior (TPB). The TPB approach explained that an individual tends to plan their behavior, and this is done consciously or unconsciously

According to this theory, human behavior is guided by three factors, which are beliefs about the consequences of things related to the behavior (resulting in a specific attitude towards the behavior), beliefs about the expectation of significant others (resulting in the perception of social pressure), and beliefs about things that facilitate or inhibit behavior (resulting in the perception of difficulty of displaying the behavior); these three factors (attitude towards behavior, subjective norm, and perceived control) forms the base for behavioral intentions that will be done when there are no actual obstacles to do the behavior (Ajzen, 2002). Chowdhury and Ceder (2013) discovered the presence of a psychological model on individuals who have the intention to use public transport. This condition is often found on people who need to transfer from one station/terminal to another before reaching their destination.

Public transport plays a crucial role in the movement of people. With the growing demand for public transport, the safety of public transport becomes a pertinent issue. Although collisions caused by drivers have been extensively investigated, passengers' safety behaviour is largely ignored. This study examines the determinants of passengers' safety behaviour on public transport.

Public transport plays a crucial role in the movement of people because of the affordable rates and low private car ownership in many countries (Pettersson and Hrelja, 2020; Rao et al., 2019). Taxis, trains and buses, which are three main modes of public transport, play a key role in providing transport services to the public (Ma et al., 2010), and a vast majority of residents travel by public transport daily. With the increasing global population and, hence, the growing demand for public transport, the safety of public transport becomes a pertinent issue given the catastrophic consequences often associated with public transport collisions. In fact, road traffic injuries are the leading cause of death for young people (from five to 29 years old) globally

I identify and test the factors affecting the passengers' safety behaviour of public transport by synthesising theoretical insights from different psychological theories. To illustrate, the theory of planned behaviour (TPB) is one of the most influential psychological models which explains road safety behaviours by considering individuals' attitudinal, normative and control beliefs (Ajzen, 1991; Kaplan et al., 2018; Ledesma et al., 2018). Furthermore, as public transport is often considered the most reliable mode for daily commute, we argue that passengers' safety awareness and perceived threat of unsafety behaviour are particularly relevant to our study.

The instruments include three subsections: demographic, physical, and psychological behaviors that commuters might experience. An indicator was also used to obtain the passengers' opinions about the impacts of delay on the level of the perceived quality of the transport. The ordered mixed logit model was employed for the analysis. The mixed model was considered to provide more flexibility and to prevent biased point estimates. That is especially important as it is expected that the point estimates of some commuters' feelings might vary across population based on factors such as the commuters' objectives of travel, or level of urgency to reach the destination. The results highlighted, for instance, the feelings of being tired or nervous to be random in predicting the perceived quality of the transport. The results also indicated that the interactions between age, gender, and level of education, and also neck pain, and an increased heartbeat should be considered, instead of their sole main effects. Also, evaluating the heterogeneity in taste revealed that the change in a random parameter of feeling nervous is dependent on the parameter of commuters' gender.

Public transportation systems play a vital role in reducing traffic congestion, gasoline consumption, carbon emission, and consequently creating cleaner air (Mees, 2000). Thus, extensive efforts have been made by public transport planners to enhance the satisfaction of public transport. The higher satisfaction could be achieved, for instance, by an improvement in the quality of a certain service, which could lead to greater use of public transport. One of the aspects of public transport, which received much attention, is the delay. Delay is part of waiting time and can be defined as the difference between the actual arrival of public transportation and the expectation of a commuter.

Traveling in a more sustainable way draws attention to the relationship between people and their environment. For instance, sustainable transport choices such as moving on foot or by bicycle could allow a slower and more intense place experience. On a different level, the promotion of public transport use should suggest a specific attention on the appearance of waiting areas, such as bus stops or train/bus stations, whose design features could affect the travel experience of transport users, especially in terms of perceived safety (Loukaitou-Sideris, 1999; Kooi, 2015). In this regard, Abenoza et al. (2018b) have pointed out how particular sites, such as bus shelters and the surrounding environment of bus stops, may influence the perceived safety and crime perceptions of the travelers, which in turn affect the travel mode choice. It was also noted and supposed that the strong relationship between security and overall travel satisfaction (Abenoza et al., 2018a) can influence the intention to use public transport. Therefore, this research has focused on identifying which features of public transport waiting areas trigger people's security perceptions. A literature review by Tucker (2003) reported that lighting, shelters, benches, the surrounding environment and their maintenance, and cleanliness are among the most important features to be considered when designing safe environments related to travel behavior. A recent study pointed out the strong effect of security and economic arguments as significant predictors of positive attitude toward sustainable transport (Manca and Fornara, 2019).

Above bus and underground train public transport psychology factors may influence passengers number increase or decrease in possible.

Understanding individual passenger behaviour is essential for the design MTR transportation, because who can choose to catch bus, taxi, tram, train ferry etc. different kinds of public transportation tools. Individual traveler who decides to catch which kinds of public transportation tools, it depends on whether the public transportation tool can provide real time travel information, liking link travel time schedule. So, MTR underground train needs to understand where it has terminal to give convenience to the local living areas of time travelers to choose to catch MTR easily. Although, MTR ticket fare is one factor to influence any passengers choice. But, those other factors can also influence them to choice. e.g. MTR any terminal location of convenience, short time travelling, none crowding in busy (peak) time, MTR platform waiting arrival time, none sudden MTR engineering machines broken accident events occurrence frequently etc. different factors, any one of these factors which can influence passengers who choose to catch MTR or other kinds of transportation tools.

Why route choice can influence passenger behavioural choice

Usually, the busy time passengers will regard the route choice as a coordination problem to influence them to choose to catch which kinds of transportation tools. The route choice is as an opportunity costs to influence any busy time passengers to decide to choose to catch which kind of transportation tool which is the best right choice in the right time among of them. In the short time, for example, it seems any busy time passengers will choose to catch bus to substitute MTR underground train transportation tool, due to who feels the bus can arrive any destinations to compare other kinds of transportation tools in the most short time. However even if the MTR can either charge cheaper ticket fare to sell full day or charge discount ticket fare to sell in the busy (peak) time to compare to bus fare. It is possible that the busy time passengers will still choose to catch bus, if between the bus terminal and the another bus terminal that distance is the shorter time route to spend time to arrive destination to compare between the MTR terminal to the another MTR terminal arrival time . Also, although the busy time passengers will feel to enounter traffic jam to influence sitting or waiting bus time to be longer time in possible and who also feel MTR can avoid traffic jam problem. However, usually any busy (peak) time passengers will feel the chance of traffic jam occurrence will be less. So, the short bus route choice is more potential factor to influence the busy (peak) time passengers still to choose bus to catch.

However, if anyone wants to investigate results of day-to-day route choice which can be transferred to more realistic environment. It is necessary to explore individual behaviour in an interactive experimental set up to ensure busy (peak) time passenger transportation behavioural choice. For example, a passenger has a choice between a main road (M) and a side road (S) for travelling from (A) to (B). (M) is faster if (M) and (S) are chose by the same number of passengers. So, this method can be researched whether MTR terminal station is located at the main road (M) or the side road (S) where is more suitable to accept to passengers generally.

Why trip time reliability and
crowding factors can influence

MTR passenger choice.
Other problem is MTR busy (peak) time's crowding in public transportation occurrence of MTR underground train transportation tool is becoming a growth to concern as MTR demand growth at a busy (peak) time. To capture the MTR passengers benefits with reduced crowding from improved MTR public transport service and image. It is necessary a identify the relevant dimensions of crowding that are meaningful measures of what crowding means to MTR passengers. Two main influences on MTR model choice that are growing in relevance are trip time reliability and crowding. It represents a benefit-cost framework. In fact, MTR passengers can be willing to pay more expensive ticket fare, it MTR can avoid crowding and short and the accurate arrival trip time between terminals is reliable to occur. How to measure of MTR crowding, e.g. weighting the gap between the busy time, the standard (i.e. objective) and the perceived (i.e. subjective) metrics. We are not in a position to definitely map the two dimensions, which is a crucial requirement for translating objective improvements into equivalent subjective gains that then can be applied, willingness to pay estimates MTR ticket fares to obtain the additional MTR passenger benefits of MTR public transportation investment to any terminal stations. Because MTR crowding has a negative impact on passengers in terms of psychological on emotional distress. MTR passengers are willing to stand for up to 20 minutes of the service is fast and reliable. However crowding outweighed these benefits from a MTR passenger's perpective, experienced crowding leads a increased dissatisfaction. e.g. stress and less privacy during who needs to stand up in MTR. Due to there are no enough places to supply to them to stand up in MTR. If the MTR trip time was longer time between the passenger's terminals, who will feel more dissatisfaction and it will cause who feels whether who ought need to choose to catch other transportation tools to substitute MTR next time. e.g. bus, train, tram, ferry, taxi etc. So, from an operator's perspective, the MTR service frequency or MTR size is significantly influenced by the level of ridership, which sends a signal to respond if the monitored crowding level exceeds the benchmark standard in the busy time. e.g. in the morning time or at the night time, the students or employment people who need to go to schools or offices (working places). The locations of different places between MTR terminals and crowding are regarded as a key service attribute for MTR pubic transportation along with other factors, such as travelling time and reliability, e.g. service quality, none engineering machines are broken to cause MTR stops suddenly.

Given the increasing importance of crowding on both the disutility to existing MTR public transportation users and the influence to it. MTR passenger can choose to use either the MTR public public transportation or other public transportation. It is timely to review the MTR current measures of crowding defined by transportation authorities. MTR operators ought evaluate whether they apporpriately reflect MTR each traveler experiences and perceptions of crowding in busy (peak) time. I suggest that MTR needs to buy other underground trains to supply to the busy (peak) time passengers to let them have enough seats to sit down, so who do not need to stand up in any MTR underground trains when they catch MTR underground trains in busy time. It aims to let who are willingness to pay the estimation of reasonable ticket fares to compare the other kinds of transportation tools in the busy (peak) time.

What is the crowding difference between train and MTR underground train?
In fact, crowding won't be happened to brother these transportation tools easily in the busy time and non busy time both. e.g. bus, taxi, train, tram, ferry. Because passengers can not choose to stand up in these transportation tools easily, due to these transportation tools have no enough areas (spaces) to let them to stand up easily . So, the crowding will be avoided to occur in these tranportation tools usually. Otherwise, MTR will have many passengers who can choose to stand up because MTR design of length is very long and it has enough areas (places) to let passengers to choose to stand up, even there have none any seats are provided to let them to sit down. So, MTR passengers will feel more dissatisfaction and crowding easily, especial in any peak (busy) time every day.

Comparing to bus, much more diverse crowding measures are defined in the passenger rail industry. For passenger, different specifications for measuring crowding are found across countries and even within a country. For example, rail crowding measures in the UK, the passengers in excess of capacity is crowding measure that applies to all London and South east operators weekday train services at a London terminus during the morning peak from 0700 to 09: 59 , and those departing during the afternoon peak from 16:00 to 18:59 (office of rail regulation 2011 year). The overall PIXC figure is considered the planned standard class capacity of each train service as well as the actual number of standard class passengers on the service at the critical point. i.e. the location on a trains of standard class passengers that surpass the planned capacity as the difference between the number of actual passengers and the capacity of the train divided by the number of passenger is within the capacity . So, it seems train and MTR underground public transportaton tools had been encountering the crowding problems in peak time, the difference in train passengers need to wait next train or more train arrival is who doesn't plan to enter the train, when who discovers the current train has no seats to provide to them to sit down in whose trip. Otherwise, MTR passengers can choose either to stand up within the large areas (places) if who discovered there are no any seats to provide to them to sit down or who can wait the next MTR arrival in order to who can sit down. It seems MTR transportation tool crowding environment includes in waiting platform and inside of the MTR underground train. Otherwise, train transportation tool crowding environment only includes the waiting platform and the passengers will not have crowding feeling inside of the train, due to none of passengers choose to stand up inside any trains because any train inside has no enough places to let them to stand up.

How MTR can attract many passengers.
On the commuter departure time choice of any reference point researching hand, the departure time decisions of communters are of fundamental importance of peak period MTR traffic congestion. However, whether on the demand side, MTR underground train congestion relief measures, such as MTR ticket fare to every terminal station needs to be charged cheaper fare or discount fare in the peak (busy) time every day. To aim to attract many passengers to choose to catch MTR Underground train public transportation tools, substitute to choose other public transportation tools in the peak time.

Over the past decades, there have been very active research efforts in the departure time problem, both in econometric modeling and dynamic user equilibrium fields. Although, these works provide valuable insights into dynamic commuter decision making, they do not identify the commuters' response to gains and losses related to whole actual arrival time to reference points who may have relative. The appliability of the reference point hypothesis of prospect theory to the commuter's departure time decision making to obtain a better understanding of how departure time choice in MTR platform during their waiting underground train arrival time. However, every MTR underground train actual arrival time and deviation variables related to reference points (gains and losses) are the key factors in the departure time choice model. How the MTR underground train of every communter's daily departure time decision can be modelled when the reference point hypothesis of prospect theory. The MTR underground train's schedule delay is defined as the difference between the preferred arrival time (PAT) and the actual arrival time (AT) for a given MTR communter. In a daily MTR commute, a commuter in the indifference band actual arrival time is an essential feature of MTR schedule study. Two reference points are the earliest acceptable arrival time and the work starting time for a given MTR platform waiting passengers. In psychological view point, prospect theory proposes that the displeasure of a loss is perceived or greater than the pleasure of a gain of the same attitude and therefore, the value function is stronger for losses than gains.

To conclude, it seems that if MTR waiting passengers need not spend long time to wait underground train arrival in platform and it can provide seats to let them to sit down in the busy (peak) crowding time. It will make them to feel pleasure, even the MTR ticket fare is not fair and reasonable to charge higher fare to compare other kinds of public transportation tools fares. So the peak waiting time factor can influence the passengers to choose other kind of transportation tools to catch easily. Moreover, MTR's two reference points are the earliest role. Similarly a loss is observed when the MTR platform waiting commuter experiences or actual arrival time which is beyond that the MTR schedule time. Due to that a MTR waiting commuter is as an early side arrival of whose actual arrival time is earlier than whose preferred arrival time.

Reference

Bailey, L., Mokhtarian, P.L. Little, A. (2008). The broader Connection Between Public Transportation, Energy Conservation And Greenhouse Gas Reduction, Report Prepared As Part Of TCRP Project J-11/Tasks Transit Cooperative Research Program, Transportation Research Board Submitted To American Public Transportation Association in http://www.apta.com/research/into/online/land_use.cfmi, accessed 17 April 2008.

The UK Standing Advisory Committee On Trunk Road Assessment (SACTRA) (1999). Transport And The Economy (Report To UK DETR). Retrieved From: http://webarchive.nationalarchives.gov.uk/20050301192906 ; http://dft.gov.uk/stellent/groups/dft-econappr/documents/pdf/dft_econappr_pdf_022512.pdf

Wikipedia Contributors (2008). Arterial Roads In Wikipedia, The Free Encyclopeda, http://en.wikipedia.org/w/index.php?title=Arterial_road&oldid=212832640(accessed May30,2008).

- Reasons we need to improve public bus transport tool service quality

The ways that we need to improve public transport, e.g. bus transport service, we try our best to ask these questions: During periods of stress on the bus, like weather conditions or maintenance failure that slows the bus service system? How to improve mass transit on bus service frequency, when looking at ways to improve public bus service transport , riders want frequency? Interestingly, speed is not as much of an issue, if they are waiting downtown in the rain, or on some suburban backstreet, riders want to know that a bus will arrive soon, preferably in less than 15 minutes. Therefore, the wait becomes part of the transportation cycle. Even, if the bus is lightning fast, in the mind of the rider, the trip begins right when they arrive at the bus station, and start waiting for the bus to pick them up.

`

`What does efficient bus ticketing system mean? It is big part of how to improve bus transportation efficiency is improving transit ticketing system, because ticketing systems have to be quick and practical to allow for prompt loading and unloading of passengers. So, inefficient ticketing systems also slow down bus frequency, as drivers need to wait for everyone to tap before they can drive away to the next stop.

How to let passengers feel comfortable? Riders want comfortable buses that can seat as many people as possible. Face-to-face seating is not appealing and being knee-to-knee in a confined space creates awkward moments between strangers. However, comfort also extends beyond the buses' seating arrangements. A smooth riding, quiet bus plays a significant role in reducing the overall stress of a public transit experience. Among the consistent feedback from riders of fuel cell electric buses is a surprised delight about how quiet the buses are when in motion.

On reduce greenhouse gases environment prote3ctoin aspect, exhaust spewing buses are on ongoing concern. One of the significant factors that commuters consider when deciding to take public transit is the environment impact of their alternative transport method. And although a diesel bus packed with 40 people may be less environmentally damaging than 40 separate diesel cars, it will still have negative impacts on both local air quality and the overall climate situation , when given the choice, we've found nearly all riders prefer " zero-emission buses" to conventional diesel buses nowadays.

IN fact, we are always thinking of ways to improve public transportation by dev4eloping new clean fuel technologies. Fuel cell electric buses resolve some of the above issues for both transit bus operators, bus performance is continually being proven and improved over millions of miles of operation in environments ranging from mountain villages to desert communities to busy cities. Hence, the first step to creating better public transit networks is becoming aware of the available options. Many communities are taking measures to improve public transport by implementing innovative sustainable transport solutions that have profound impacts on the live ability of their communities.

So, I shall recommend these ways to improve public transport methods to bus service as below:

Firstly, making interchanging easy for public transport has most efficient public transport service improvement aim at linking areas that are outside a city to the city center., doing this is beneficial in two ways. It helps people who should not at the city center , but needed to pass through because the outlying areas are not connected together to keep off and hence reduce congestion at the center. Also, connecting the outlying areas provide a backup for the public transport system in case of a problem which often happen.

Secondly, minimize the number of stops/ stations, stops and stations improve the efficiency of public transport , but there should be a balance between enabling accessibility with more steps or stations and reducing the costs of operation by increasing transit need of ensure trips are covered in time. Therefore, core should be taken to ensure that stops and stations are located on streets to balance accessibility by commuters on one hand and reduces operating cost on the other hand.

Thirdly, lessen traffic congestion by deploying a number measures. Reducing traffic congestion at city streets could be done, implementing a number of strategies, such as providing lanes dedicated specially for the use of public transport, deploying strict regulations , such as queue bypasses or queue jumps. Another means of reducing traffic congestion is by providing feeds and data from public transport systems, freely to commuters to educate and help them avoid areas of traffic congestion and finally, giving priority to public and trams operating efficiency, increasing the travel time of these engineering mechanism whereby a traffic signal turns green at the light of a public transport at an intersection. All of above these improvements may be future public transport bus passengers service improvement need, if any bus companies hope to increase their bus passengers number absolutely.

● What rail passengers really want rail innovation improvement

Public transport systems, such as rail provides benefits including less traffic congestion, less pollution, safe travels, lower expenditures , less effort and better predictability in comparison to road transport. In fact, bus and train riders experience the most negative emotions in comparison with other transport modes, such as private cars , walking and cycling. Hence, technology has the potential to bring about the changes, needed to increase efficiency of rail transport, e.g. cost-effective ways to improve the quality of public transport and increase ridership may involve comfort and convenience improvement, or technology has the potential to provide more up-to-date information and customized service to train passengers and therefore improve the rail journey experience . On the overall, passenger journey , e.g. the importance of automated traveller information systems, and electronic fare payment collection systems can bring rail passengers look for this information in different interfaces from localized displays installed on platforms to smartphone applications.

Moreover, technology can also improve fare collection and management which of made manually can be prone to error, and time consuming , unified cards, smartphones can make it easier for rail passengers to obtain ticket, with the potential to increase the user satisfaction with the rail system. Because rail passengers demand not only pre-trip information for planning their travels, but also information during journeys, such as punctuality, connections and platform allocation. One extensive review indicates that accurate communication, for example, giving effective way finding information, can optimize passengers' experience with public transport.

Also, technology can facilitate the process of finding free seats on trains, which is a current demand from rail passengers and the cause of stress during the boarding process. IN fact, many rail passengers have specific preferences regarding seats and would appreciate having control of where to sit. So, navigation and way finding information can be delivered directly to passengers to inform where they could stand aiming to board less busy carriages, for example, choosing to travel on a less crowded train, or spreading themselves out on the platform before boarding in respond to crowding information, e.g. smartphones are frequently used by passengers of public transport and can make waiting times seem shorter. Furthermore specific system features designed for train passengers have the potential to improve the journey experience of the travelling public.

What ferry passengers service improvement need

- How can ferry service be improved affordable, reliable, convenient, flexible and clean will get drivers out of their cars ad onto environmentally responsible to passenger ferries?

Ferry transportation provides an environmentally friendly commuting alternative to the congested roadways in many of countries , so ferry transport service needs to meet long term air quality goals, it is critical to move beyond traditional technologies to zero-and near zero emissions technology. Clearly putting a transit system in operation that demonstrates emission control technology and the development of zero-emissions, ferries will help achieve air quality goals to our societies, for example., new shipping rout4es are needed to increase in order to satisfy ferry passengers different rapid ferry journey short distance need, when they need to choose one kind of public transport service either bus or rail or ferry transport service among of them.

None ferry accident occurrence, ferry service needs to let passengers to feel it is the safest sea pubic transit, expanded recreational service is also needs, particularly on weekends when bridge , corridor traffic congestion is becoming an increasing problem. Ferry service needs have uniquely provided flexible, vital transportation supports in response to a natural or man-made disaster that shuts down bridges and roads, fuel –cell technology is needed , that will lead to zero-emissions ferries, e.g. on-board emissions monitoring is far less polluting than previously through, e.g. 149 passenger boats are designed to travel 25 knots or less , and 300-350 passenger vessels designed for speeds up to 30-35 knots.

This emissions standard will perform specifications and the cost of this technology is accounted for in the ferry company vessel capital budget ,e.g. vessel design capabilities to accommodate existing and new docking configurations . This maximizes fast ferry passenger loading, including bicycles, carriages and wheelchairs. Hence, future global ferry service needs have these positive influence to our societies: Need for flexibility, desire to help the environment, need for time saving, which includes the importance of reliability, sensitivity to personal travel experience, such as a need for personal space or quiet feeling ferry seat any time, insensitivity to transport cost, e.g. the ferry ticket price is cheaper than rail or bus fares sensitivity to stress.

However, ferry service is different unlike rail, bus because expanded ferry service can be launched quickly at low initial cost and with great flexibility. Unlike buses, ferries are not hindered by traffic congestion on roads and highways or in tunnels. So, ferry service can be safely expanded to bring new service to new places and add more service to existing routes more easily than bus and rail public transport both, e.g. expanded ferry transport service can operate safety and provide with a robust, flexible and effective emergency response capability if the region is hit with a natural or man-made event that disables roads, other transit, bridges , before any.

Hence, ferry companies need to decide to improve their ferry transport service, they need to answer these questions: Is the new shipping route a good transportation investment? Does the new shipping route have fatal environmental negative impact? Does it offer a transit option that can be initiated in a timely and cost-effective manner? Can it provide ferry transport service that is reliable, safe and fully accessible after the ferry recovery would be unreasonably high charge to ferry selection is decided to implement to increase?

Also, ferry safety is needed to consider because it can influence any ferry passenger choice, when the ferry is moving on the sea, when the passenger is sitting on the boat. The ferry safety issue may include: Ensuring that access to all ferry operational areas, including, machinery spaces, pilothouse and gear lockers, remain locked at all times and accessible only to authorized crew, posting night watch security guards at terminals, conducting diligent onboard inspection for unattended passenger bags, briefcases and packages after each run, before the next boat load is allowed to board, creating coded signals and response to report suspicious activity, requiring positive identification before allowing any contractors, vendors or others access to ferries, providing additional security training to crew, developing a security plan to account for potential threats, outlining preventive measures and detailing an action plan in the event of a threat or actual emergency.

How future our transport need change? What factors influence our future transport need change? In general, these factors may influence our transportation need change. They may include fuel cost, the labor market for commercial drivers, demand for frieight , customer loyalty , vehicle capacity, government regulation, geographical events, the public transport tool reputation to passegners as a merchant. However, the factors that influence the development of transport system in an area? They may include as below:

Environment at the local scale existing hydrographical and geomorphological characteristics are string, factors in transport development, particularly in terms of the technical challenges (bridge, gradients,) they present to construct, other factors may include historical, technological, political and economic factors. All of these factors may influence our future transport system how develops. For raiway development influential factors, they may include: Geograohical factors, e.g. the North Indian plain with its level land, high density of population and rich agriculture presents the most favourable conditions for the development of railways in India. However, the presence of large number of rivers makes it necessary to construct bridges which involve heavy expenditure to

Indian Government publich transport expenditure.

How transport has changed from past to present?

There has been a remarkable development in modern transportation. The stream engine and then the stream trains have emerged and spread at this time and in abundance until the discovery of natural gas and oil was an evolution of transportation. Thus, the sedams and vehicles began to run in oil, until present battery changes energy vehicle need, even future non-manual driving artificial intelligent driving vehicle need. These new transport technology may influence our future public transportation from gas energy to battery changed energy, even non-manual driving vehicles need to our daily transport need.

So, our future purpose of public transport need is the unique purpose to oversome space, which is shaped by a variety of human and physical constraints, such as distance, time. These both is our future main public transport need main purpose factors, short distance and reducing journey time, they influence that why we need to choose to catch any kinds of public transportation tool to replace purchase private cars to drive transport tool choice. So, future any kinds of public transport tools, they need to consider above both main factors , how to attract passengers to choose to catch themselves public transport tools choice in this competitive public transport tools market.

On the other hand, the economic importance of transportation development can be defined as improving the welfare of a society, through appropriate social, political and economic conditions , such as US Government spent too much money to assist MTR (MAss transport railway firm) to develop underground thrain transport. Its aim to let many passegner can reduce journey time and reduce distance between destinations, it also hopes US citizen passengers can pay cheap transport fare to buy ticket to catch underground transport train for many families their transport expenditure in social transport welfare view.

However, US Government neds to solve those challenges, before it implements to develop rapid underground railway , e.g. lack of knowledge of geographical fwatures, lack of manpower necessary to operate the rapid underground railway construction work, lack of construction materials within the US itself. For Brazil rail network transportation development example, the factors influence the use of rail network for transportion is highly restricted in Brazil. Thus, the development of roadways and waterways is the main modes of transportation that caould be used in Brazil given its topography and drainage benefit to society . So, brazil can develop rail network for transportation development in success.

So, transportation system is important in the development of any nation, because transportation plays important role in rapid economic growth of a nation. Thrapsortation increases the quality and variety of consumer goods, thereby stimulating the demand and development of trade and economy of the nation. Moreover, transport provides various employment opportunities and boosts up the economy of the country.

Also, any transport tools need to improve themselves transport service in order to attract passengers to choose their public transport service more easily. They may attempt to sign up for an autonomous vehicle pilot program, free phone enquiey concerns whether the passegner can catch which bus bumber to go to the destination, hou much bus fare, how long journey time, when the bus will arrive teh bus stops or leave the bus stop etc. bus service questions, before any one passenger prepares to choose to catch bus (free bus go phone call enquiry), free download a public transport tool transit app. even water taxi tranport tool innovation can replace ferry public transport tool, it can let passengers have more fun an enjoyable catching feeling. So, water taxi tranport tool is one kind of future new transport tool change to replace ferry , it can influence ferry passengers to choose water taxi public transport tool to replace ferry. Although, its fare may be more expsnse to compare ferry, but it can reduce jounrey time and distance between both water stations, when ferry can not arrive the other destinations, but water taxi can arrive any one water station destination. It can bring convenient to future any one ferry passengers. So, water taxi may be developed to some countries, e.g. New Zealand , Auckland city, US , Washington and New York cities they had developed water taxi public transport tools to let ferry passengers have one kind new water public transport choice.

However, instead of new transport innovation improvement to water transport service public transport with input from the public on bus transport service aspect, bus frequency improvement, it means when booking at ways to improve, bus frequency from long times to less times, efficient bus ticketing system, a big part of how to improve tranportation efficiency is improving transit ticketing system.

In fact, my future transport system may still include these five types, modes of transport are: railway, roadways, airways, waterways and piplelines. Also, among different includes of transport, railways are the different modes of transport, railways are the cheapest. Trains cover the distance in less time and comparatively, the fare is also less to other modes of transporation. Therefore, railways is the cheapest mode of transportation to compare ferry, water taxi , sea transport, bus, taxi, road system.

On conclusion, transport price is not the main factor to attract passegners to choose to catch. The importance to have a good public transport system in place. It may be one main factor to help the kind of public transport tool to attract passengers to choose to catch, because a good transport links can widen people's job search area and help them find employment. It can also reduce commuting times and reduce the cost of living, and high skilled workers are more likely to travel across longer distances to work, especially if they are following good job opportunities. So, future any one kind of public transportation tool service provider ought consider how to satisfy working people working time need to shorten journey time to any working places or student learning time need to shorten jounrey times to any schools as well as let they feel comfortable to sit on comfortable chairs or provide free internet service to themselves mobiles , laptops, when they are sitting down or standing up in the kind of public transport . It is the important factor to influence any kind of public transport service in success.

Future Non-Manual driving vehicle How
Influences Public Transport Tool Passenger Need

Nowadays, artifical intelligent (non-manual) driving vehicles are invented, it may be accepted to any countries families to feel comfortable to drive on roads, because any people choose to buy any kinds cars, when any people choose to buy kinds of non-manual (artificial intelligent) vehicles, they do not need to use their hands to drive cars, because artificial intelligent (robotic auto control wheels, it means that robots can help human (drivers) to control wheel to drive to avoid any cars crash occurrence on the roads more easily.

If one day, non-manual driving robotic control whoole vehicles are invented in successful, whether it will persuade many different conuntries families choose to buy non-manual (robotic auto control wheel) vehicles, then it will cause bus, tram, train, underground train, road transport need will be influenced to reduce or even if non-manula boats are invented, whether it will cause ferry sea transport needs will b influenced to reduce. Hence, future non-manual driving vehicles or bats invention whether they will influence public transport tool of road and sea transport passengers number reduces. It is one interesting question. I shall attempt to discuss as below:

In fact, non-manual vehicles are very attraction, to excite any person chooses to buy to drive, because people do not need often touch wheels and touch foots button to control cars to move often forever, when robotic can be invented to help human to control car wheel and foot button, any person only needs to sit on his/her car, then the car can move rapidly, because any drivers is lazy, he/she hopes machine can help her/him to drive car on the road safely. So, he/she can read book or listen music or eatch mobile movie to enjoy his/her entertainment when he/she is sitting on his/her car.He/she will feel more comfortable and enjoyable when robotic can help him/her to drive car. So, robotic (non -manual driving vehicle) can encourage people to choose to buy cars because any drivers won't need to drive cars, robotic can help drivers them to drive on the road easily, when global any one family can own one robotic auto control (non-manual driving) car at least, it may influence these owning non-manula diriving vehicle owners do not feel need to pay any fares to buy road public transport tools of bus ticket, train ticket, underground train ticket , tram ticket to go to anywhere. So, it seems that robotic (non-manual driving) vehicles may influence future any road transport passengers number reduces , because traditional catching any kinds of road public transport tool passengers will be influenced to choose to sit themselves auto (non-manual) driving cars to go to offices to work, parents do not need to follow their sone/daughters to sit on themselves non-manual auto driving cars to go to schools, because their sons/daughters can sit on themselves non-manual driving cars to go to schools more easily. In holidays, they can sit on themselves non-manual driving cars to go to cinemas, music halls, breachs, theaters, shopping centers, gardens different entertainment places to enjoy their any leisure safely because robotic can help them to drive their cars on roads safely.

So, it means that robotic auto control driving cars can influence global every family to feel that they do not need to catch any kinds of public transport tools, e.g. bus, train, tram, taxi underground train to go to anywhere because robotic auto driving cars can help any one, he/she does not know how to drive car to go to anywhere safely. So, future any one won't need to learn driving car skill, when he/she likes to buy one auto driving car. So, in passenger public transport need view, non-manual driving cars will influence them to feel any kinds of road public transport tools can help them to go to anywhere conveniently, because themselves non-manual driving vehicles can help them to drive cars to go to anywhere conveniently. They only need to tell robotic that where they want to go, when they sit on their non-manual driving cars, then robotic knows whether where destination, they want to go, their cars will auto move on the road immediately. It is one exciting and enjoyable ourney when the driver does not need to drive his/her car on the road. So, it seems that robotic (non-manual driving) vehicles invention may bring negative influence to any kinds of public transport tools service needs to passengers , when passengers had owned one non-manual driving car at least.

Why and how non-manual driving car owners need raise public transport quality on travel time and fare aspects

- How non human driving behavior can be influence by non-manual driving cars

In fact, impact of automated vehicless on travel mode preference, it can bring both trip purposes and distances aim raising need to any kinds of public transport service passegners. Because of technology penetration in the transportation system, the automated vehicle is set to be a future mode of transport, it may bring negative impact to future any kinds of public transport passengers needs, in special on the potential impact of these non-manual driving automated vehicles on travel behaior negative impact to public transport passenger behavior. Automated vehicles will influence future public transportation passengers feel it can bring more short time travel distances and short trip purposes more benefit than any kinds of public transport choices, e.g. bus, taxi, ferry, train, tram, underground tram etc. road and sea public transport tools, e.g. ferry, water taxi. It means that when future any passenger feels above these any one kind of public transport tool needs to spend longer travel time on journey distance and trip to compare future automated vehicles, then they will choose to sit on automated vehicles in preference, due to automated vehicles can help global any one person needs to go to anywhere rapidly.

So, automated vehicles may replace general traditional public transport tools in possible, when they are popular accepted in societies. On the other, instead of shortening journey travel distance time, (travel time) aspect, public transport fare, travel cost will be another influential factor to influence future public transport tool passengers to choose automated vehicles to replace to catch any kinds of public transport tools.

In fact, conventional cars and public transport s are perceivd as being the least attractive alternative in relation to in-vehicle travel time on short and long distance communting trips. So , future automated vehicle drivers (non -human driving) behaviors will be likely changed to prefer this mode for long distance leisure trips rather than short distance commuting trips by automated vehicles.

In fact, advanced technologies have revolutionized many aspects of human life, include the automated vehicle transport system. Also, transport system is one of the essential development aspect to particular , such as non-manual driving automation , vehicle aims to make trips safer, faster , more efficient, automated vehicles passengers and drivers can feel enjoyable to do themselves leisure behavior , e.g. read books, listen, music, listen mobile, watch laptop movies when any one does not need to consider whether their cars are safe to be driven , even any one needs to drive the automated car, because robotic can help them to control how to automatic drive this car on the road safely.

Robotic will bring confidence to let them feel that themselves cars are moving safely on the roads . In recent years, the concept of automated driving has been introduced as on outstanding platform for the next generation of driving systems that is expected to improve safety, traffic flows efficiency, reducing traffic jams occurrence chance, avoiding traffic accidents occurrence chance, e.g. avoid to crash any one person when he/she is walking across road or crach any car is moving on the road easily, capacity, accessibility , and reducing congestion through the application of some technologies , such as vehicle to vehicle and vehicle to infrastructure communication.

So, future automated vechicles can have good driving facility systems to be installed in their cars, in order to raise safety, rapid driving speed level to let any one to feel , when they are sitting in their automated cars, e.g. using cameras, sensors, global positioning system adaptive cruise control, light detection and ranging, and advanced driver assistance system, automated vehicles can steer the vehicle and drive it automatically when passengers delegate control to a computer. Absolutely, ny replacing the driver role with an automated driving system , future one automated vehicle is able to totally free up passengers under automation levels.

So, unless future any kinds of public transport tools may apply automated robotic automated driven system replace the bus driver, taxi driver, train driver, tram driver, underground train driver to raise automated driving system service improvement level to let any one passengers to feel. Otherwise, when automated vehicles are popular to be accepted to buy in any one country in global. Then, global public tansport tool passegners number may be influenced to reduce when global any one family owns at least one automated vehicle at themselves homes .

In other words, automated vehicles can bring thes benefits to let global any one household family feels, future automated vehicles users , they can mostly behave like passengers inside the vehicle, which implies that they will be able to multitask and productive by allocating the travel time to do other activities, e.g. reading, eating, working, drinking, watching movies, listening musics, even sleeping. So, automated vechicles will motivate humans to change non-humanly driven behaviors from conventional humanly driven behavior. This non-humanly driven behavior may be one main factor to influence or encourage future any one kind of public transport passenger won't choose to pay fare to buy ticket to catch any one kind of public transport tool again, because non-manual driven behavior may hel many lazy people do not need to consdierate how to learn to drive cars skills to prepare pass any road test in order to earn the driving licnece to permit to drive cars forever. When automated vehiclesa re popular to be accepted to replace manual-driven cars in societies.

Hence, automated vehicles could potentially change the traditional human driven vehicle market to cause their manual driven cars sale buyers number reduces, when the automated vehicle buyers number increases, also they can chance globa public transport passengers behaviors to reduce to pay fares to catch any kinds of public transport tools when automated vechicles users may sit on themselves automated vehicles to go to anywhere in short time rapidly and safely in any countries.

On conclusion, future global public transport service competition is serious, because instead of global passengers had began to compare whether which kinds of public transport fares are cheaper, more safe, shortening journey time between leaving place and destination, more comfortable feeling, e.g. clean and comfortable chairs , mre free internet service facilities in order to make any one kind of catching public transport tool choice in preference. On the other hand, future automated vehicles number will increase when traditional manual driven car users begin to believe that automated vehicles can bring more safe , more comfortable, more fee- time using, more leisure satisfactory feeling, more than traditional manual driving cars. Then, when global any one household family had made choice to buy at least one automated vehice to replace themselves car(s) at home. When, they are habit to sit in themselves automated vehicles to go to anywhere, however, short or long trip . Consequently, global any one household family won't feel any kinds of public transport tools may bring personal economic saving cost, comfortable, enjoyable, free-time using benefit to compare themselves automated vehicles . It will cause global public transport tools passengers number will reduce , when many different kinds of home automatic vehicles are purchased to replace manual driving cars by global household automated vehicle users. So, in passegner transport tool choice psychological view, automatic vehicles will be possible to replace future public transport service tools. So, any public transport service providers can not neglect how to desing and improve their facilities , charge reasonable transport fare, provide more comfortable, and enjoyable sitting feeling , even applying automatic driving system to replace human drivers in order to attract passegners ' catching need choice more easily.

In airline transport industry strategy, I shall attempt to indicate some useful strategies to help airlines to keep travellers number in order to avoid to reduce. I shall indiate as below:

● Airline Oil Price Variable Factor strategy

Positive social change influence to vehicle fuel consumers

What suitation is positive social change to vehicle fuel consumers. We are entering globalizational competitive society, such as airline fuel case, if the country, e.g. US is increasing vehicle consumers in this year, then US vehicle fuel demand will increase. So, the US vehicle fuel price will be caused to increase. Due to much vehicle fuel demand increases in US this year, so foreign fuel import and US fuel manufacturers will increase to supply to US for vehicle market in this year, due to many US vehicle consumers need to buy fuel to drive their vehicles in US. However, due to fuel natural resource will have limited number to be supplied to manufacture airline fuel, due to much fuel is used to manufacture vehicle fuel in US this year. So, it will cause airline fuel manufacturing and supply shortage challenge. Due to this year, US decreases airline fuel supply, but the US airlines demands fuel number is still increasing.

Consequently, vehicle fuel increasing demand factor will cause airline fuel price to be rised in US this year. For example, air tickets can be bought from internet, so travellers won't need to go to travel agent to buy conventienty. It is due to the global travel industry is increasingly competition. Thus, global travel industry competition will bring negative social change to influences fuel price rising because it will increase traveller numbers and airline flight times to fly. When, traveller's travelling desire demand numbers will be grown up fastly, then their online electronic-ticket buying or consumption behaviors will be rise. Thus, it will also cause online e-ticket price is decreased to attract many travellers to choose to buy e-ticket from online channel more than paper-ticket visiting travel agent channel. Thus, it is negative social change influences to cause fuel price rising due to plane flight flying times will increase and airline company will increase demand to buy many fuel to prepare to fly often. When fuel demand will rise, then the fuel sellers will rise fuel price in possible. Thus, airline industry global competition will being negative social change to influence fuel price raising up and air ticket price falling down to attract many traveller numbers to choose to buy among different travel agents.

Negative social change influence

What suitation is positive social change. I shall indicate economic growth example. When one country has better economic development in the year. Then, employers will have more effort to do businesses. Then, they will create many jobs to provide to the country citizen to do. When, these unemployed people have jobs to do, they will have extra income to save. They can spend extra to prepare to spend to enjoy their entertainment every year, such as travelling. Thus, the positive social change will influence traveller number increasing, then the plane fliging flying times will also increase, it will cause planes need to use much fuel to fly. The result, it will also increase fuel demand, but the fuel natural resource number will decrease , so fuel supply will also decrease. Finally, it will also cause fuel price to be risen.

Also, I shall indicate the financial risk of airline industry evidence from Cathay Pacific airways and China airlines against key determinants of which include interest rate, exchange rate and fuel price risk for the period of January 1996 year to December 2011 year. During this period, these key external factors which were the most serious influence to cause these two airlines choose to change their strategic behaviors.

Due to any these financial risks is difficult to predict and it was also changing often, these factors will also affect any airlines stock returns which arise from changing economic conditions, e.g. fuel price movements and fluctuations in exchange rates. These external unpredicted changing factors will attribute to the air tickets cyclical demand, capital investment, fixed costs of labor and landing rights to this global airline industry.

However, the relationship between fuel price and stock prices varies across economies. The effects of oil price changes in sub-sector indices, such as wood, paper and printing, insurance and electricity. In the past, on global stock exchange market was positively significant in 2011 year. Otherwise, with respect to the U.S.A. aviation industry, some economists suggested that global airlines stock returns were negatively to percentage change in fuel prices related to any airline firm value, e.g. Qantas and Air New Zealand were negatively share price growth to fuel price risk in the short term in the 2011 year.

Thus, it brings this question. Whether positive or negative social change will be one important factor to impact fuel price rising. I feel positive social or negative social change will be one important factor to impact fuel price rising. The reason is such as below:

Nowadays, airline transportation demands are increasing, due to many travelers need to catch planes to travel as well as many cargoes need to be carried to planes to transport to different countries to sell. It seems aviation transportation industry is important to influence the health of the global economy growth nowadays. However, ignorance of internal or external market dynamics, catching travelers business can be detrimental to airline profitability more than carrying cargoes business. Because the demands of travelling different countries' travelers' consumption are still more than the demands of businessmen carrying cargoes in any countries every year. Thus, the travel industry will increase demand to human travelling business more than cargo transportation business. However, the cargo flying transporation demand will rise, due to many global fast speed post businesses are growing. Base on both global cargo flying transportation demand and travellers' flying travelling demand are increasing. Thus, the fuel demand will increase, but the fuel supply will be shortage. So, it will cause fuel price rising consequently.
How can positive or negative social change influence any airlines' air ticket prices to be risen or fallen? In fact, the increase in petroleum price can have chance to affect airlines in a negative manner because increased oil prices have resulted in the reduction of services operations, the number of airline schedules flights, even airline bankruptcies.

Thus, it seems that plan travellers and air flying cargo transportation both demand have been increasing. This social increasing demand change factor, it will be the most influential cause the bad effects to cause airline industry share price reducing or reducing air ticket price or decreasing traveler numbers more than the other factors influence, such as inflation, terrorism, oil shortage, bank interest rate etc. unpredictable external suitation factors.

To support this hypotheses, this are my research questions, such as : Does a combination of terrorism and price of petroleum significantly influence airline profit changing mostly? The alternative hypothesis was base on a significant relationship exists between terrorism, price of petroleum and airline profitability more than other factors, such as inflation, bank interest rate or air ticket price changing of these factors influence. I shall indicate that the first assumption was that terrorism has a negative effect on airline profitability and another assumption was that only external factors as oil prices or terrorism affect airline profitability.

Terrorisms attack influence

Whether terrorisms attack will influence fuel price rises up or falls down. I feel terrorisms attack to any country, which will cause plan fuel price falls down. Because travellers will feel dangerous and worry about their life safety when they catch the plan to enter the country if the country has serious terrorisms attack risk to cause plan crash accidently.

However the effects of oil price and terrorism on airline profitability was limited to a regional perspective, e.g. the terrorism attack of plane crash event to USA on 11 Sept. After the terrorism attack happened on USA 11 Sept.

incident of terrorism attack was restricted to events of skyjacking, attacks on oil production, refinery and distribution. Thus, USA on 11 Sept. terrorism attack will cause oil price falls down , due to it will influence travellers fear death , so who will reduce times to travel to USA after 11 Sept. date terrorism attack occurrence at the year. The oil sellers will reduce oil sale price to attract many airline companies to buy more supply, due to airlines will decrease demand to buy fuel to provide planes to fly when the traveller numbers has decreasing and flying times will be decrease also. Thus, the fuel price will be decreased consequently after the terrorism attacks to any country.

Other types of terrorist activities, such as attacks on financial targets or senior government officials could have an adverse effect on the petroleum and airline industry. I think the disruption of the production or distribution of petroleum because of incidents of terrorism was costly in terms of loss of business and the inflationary effect on fuel dependent products or services.

In fact, some airlines have adopted more fuel saving technology, so whose fuel consumption would not use more than other non fuel saving technology airlines. So, the owned fuel saving technology airlines which will buy less fuel to use. It means that they won't need fear fuel rising to increase their expenditure because they only need to buy less fuel to use and their fuel demand won't fall , even fuel price has risen.

However, it seems fuel price increasing will not be the only factor to influence the airline industry's traveler numbers decreasing, due it is possible that the airlines need to rise air ticket price to riase their profit, sue to their fuel cost has risen. However, due to some airlines which have fuel saving technology, so which can avoid to use more fuel to provide planes to use and which fuel costs will be reduced, then which can provide cheaper air ticket fare prices to compare the non fuel saving technology airlines. The result will cause some non owned fuel save technological airlines will lose travelling customers in this global airline travelling market, also the non fuel saving technology airlines need to renew their fuel technology if which want to keep their competitive abilities to avoid to close down their businesses.

Can airline fuel self-organization avoid fuel price rising cost ?

I feel one airline fuel self-organization can avoid fuel price rising to influence cost rising because it doesn't often buy any fuel from fuel suppliers. However, there are some airlines which are the characteristic of airline fuel self organization and they are present in that both of oil fuel production and providing flights service in airline industry. So, these airline fuel self organizations can control the oil fuel price by themselves. However, one airline fuel self organization is also evident in efforts by businesses acts of terrorism against economic targets by adopting proactive steps, such as airline and airport security. So, it seems airline fuel self organization can reduce the risk to avoid oil price raising and terrorism attacks to raise cost in airline industry risk management sector.

Beside, these airline fuel self organizations which have high technology of fuel efficient aircrafts, the use of one aircraft model, the adoption of direct routes versus customer loyalty programs and other operational cost reductions are strategies for increased profitability. It seems these airline fuel self organizations can solve oil price, terrorism etc. external factor influences to raise cost.

Instead of high technology of fuel efficient aircrafts and airline fuel self organization methods can solve terrorism attacks and oil price rising risks. However, I believe that there are other risks are caused to these airline fuel self organizations to raise their airline cost possibly. The risks include such as user factor, such as culture, tradition, education ; economic factor, such as costs, human resources and macro economic factor, such as political stability, economic development, educational policy, health policy, environmental policy. However, these risks occurrences are resulting in the relationship of cause and effect events. These events are not directly observable. Such as, the complexity of relationship between terrorism and airline profitability. Hence, if global airline industry can predict when those risks occur to do protective strategic behavior. It is possible that which can understand when these risk events will occur and to adopt their protective strategic behaviors to influence their outcomes to be positive to avoid any external risk threats on the long term. However, I think hierarchy, airlines fuel self organization efficiency methods which are as possible predictors of user preferences to avoid risk threat events to cause whose airline businesses cost rising to cause failure occurrences in airline industry.

Can tourism industry influence airline profitability ?

In my study, I suppose terrorism and the price of petroleum both factors which had properties of distinct and interrelated close relationship to raise airline cost. Moreover, these variables (terrorism and the price of petroleum) displayed differentiation, self replication, efficiency and hierarchy which can cause risk events to airline industry. However, I also think the other internal and external threat factors of airline industry, such as inflation, bank interest rate, business model, service quality, airline fuel or plane engine technology, air ticket pricing, brand loyalty, airline strategic management, government policy and fuel hedging of these factors which can also raise the risks to threaten any airlines existence in airline industry.

There are two basic business models in tourism industry. They are network (full service) and low cost (discount) carriers. The network carrier model employs diversification strategy by increased domestic destinations, serving international routes, providing diverse seating arrangements (business, economy and first class), maintaining a complex system of offering high quality service. Otherwise, low cost (discount) airlines focus on lower air fares. To keep operating costs down, discount airlines offer shorter routes and provide point-to-point destinations rather than through sophisticated flights are primarily in domestic destinations. So, discount airlines operate a common model aircraft fleet, offer a single seating arrangement and cheaper flight services offered to compare network airlines. However, these two basic business models have their unique competitive abilities to provide any airlines existence in tourism industry nowadays.

In fact, natural resource of oil is decreasing in our earth. But as the same time, human demand is increasing and oil supply is decreasing, so it also causes the oil fuel price is increasing to supply to airline industry. It influences not only to airline industry, it also impacts of higher oil fuel price to tourism, such as expansion of airports are made based on expected demand increase.

Tourism has been proven to many adverse events, including terrorism, flight disruptions. Beside, the bad natural climate change influences, such as the volcanic ash cloud event occurred in April 2010 year. So, airline industry need to concern climate change because it will cause high fuel prices indirectly. For example, the event occurred the extreme increase in operating costs for airlines in 2008 year, due to unprecedented prices for aviation fuel also meant, that despite the introduction of fuel charges, so this event causes the global tourism industry recorded losses seriously. Even if alternative fuels become commercially available for airlines which are still likely to be more expensive than present aviation fuel.

Higher airfares in the future are likely to lead to reduction in travel and cause tourists to shift from more distant to closer destination. When some of the economic responses to higher oil prices are obvious assessing the overall economic impacts on tourism is difficult. However, long term changes in global oil price rises will be similar to global changes in other commodity prices, exchange rates and income. It is therefore important to consider the impact of high oil prices on tourism from a general equilibrium perspective rather than relying only on bottom partial equilibrium approaches.

However, I believe tourism and airline industries have close relationship, such as tourism and airline industries are likely to suffer in an environment of high oil prices. Given that tourism destinations receive tourists from a range of origins, it would be useful to understand of some countries are increasing oil prices than others. Such as the net oil importing countries are selling higher oil prices than oil exporting countries generally. For example, New Zealand is an oil import country to provide planes for international visitor arrivals, so its oil fuel price is usually higher to charge to NZ airlines because any NZ airlines need to pay to foreign countries to buy any oil more expensive price. So, NZ airlines usually charge higher airfares to its visitors to compare the other exporting oil countries' airlines. It will impact NZ has negative influence to domestic tourism industry as well as planes need will also be decreased , due to NZ charge high fuel price to cause air ticket price to be raised.

In economic theory, on income effects indicate negative impacts on tourism demand, the exact effects of higher oil fuel prices for specific destinations are far from clear. However, airline industry's different market segments show different sensitivities to air ticket fares changes.

On the first hand, if the visitors are long destinations generally wealthier than average and therefore potentially less affected, as energy costs would be a smaller proportion of their income compared will be those from less wealthy groups. Thus, the more wealthier travelers who won't decrease travelling desire, even the fuel price raises to case the air ticket price to be increased.

On the second hand, oil prices don't translate into higher transport costs especially not on air routes that are highly competitive and that are maintained for strategic reasons. So, non air transportation industry won't influence customer number to be decreased easily.

On the third hand, many other factors shape tourists' decision making, including emotion drivers or those related to images, fashions and perceptions. Increasing environmental protection awareness of tourists could also be an important factor to influence tourism consumption, instead of oil fuel price raising causes air ticket fares raising factor to reduce traveler numbers. However, oil price raising reason causes also due to high use of cars, vans and domestic air transport in some countries, e.g. Hong Kong, China countries, there are many people like to buy cars to drive. So, the private driver numbers are increasing demand to cause these countries' oil fuel prices raise in the short time suddenly. It implies airlines need to consider their country car number whether is increasing or decreasing. If their country car number is increasing, it is possible to cause fuel price to be risen up because car demand is increasing to need to use more fuel and it has less supply of fuel in the year. Otherwise, if their country car number is decreasing, it is possible to cause fuel price to be fallen down because car demand is decreasing to need to use less fuel and it has more supply of fuel in the year.

Is fuel price rising only factor to cause airline risk in short term ?

In long run, fuel raising price will not cause risk to airline, due to implications of changes to supply and demand side conditions of oil fuel energy may differ qualitatively. For example, due to investment responses of producers, consumers and governments in alternative energy sources and more energy efficient plants, vehicles are supplied in order to achieve oil fuel price can't be risen seriously.

However, I believe oil fuel rising charge will be an important factor to influence global airline ticket fares to be increased in the short term to cause risk because oil fuel rising charge will be influenced to raise any airlines pressure from other unpredicted factor risk influences.

Firstly, on the bank interest changing factor, e.g. bank interest rate rising which only attract more bank saving. But it can not influence the bank savers who choose to reduce relax time to go to other countries travelling. Otherwise, when the bank savers can save more money to earn higher interest in banks, who will prefer to choose to use their saving to consume travelling. Due to who can earn higher interest rate after a period of saving time. So, I believe who behavioral travelling consumption will be raised when the banks will raise interest rate, then the bank savers won't choose to save more money in banks. So it is possible that who will withdraw more money to consume to go to travelling from banks. It seems bank interest rate changing won't influence bank savers' behavioral travelling consumption to be reduced.

Secondly, on the exchange rate changing factor, although any country's exchange changing will cause other

countries' money value to be fallen down or risen up. However, it won't influence any travelers' behavioral consumption to be reduced seriously. Although, it is possible that the traveler won't spend too much to go to shopping when who travel to the another country and arrive the country. But, it is not possible to influence the traveler decides to reduce consumption to buy any air ticket to go to travelling in short time.
Thirdly, any country inflation also can not reduce travelers' travelling consumption easily because inflation can influence consumers who choose to buy cheaper foods and clothing and reduce entertainments in their every day life. But, one country's inflation can not influence it's citizen do not spend much travelling expenditure because travelers only spend one time or two times of travelling every year usually. So, the travelling expenditure rate of any households is not too much to compare daily essential expenditure.
So, it seems that bank interest rate and exchange rate changing and inflation won't influence any travelers' travelling consumption of decisions to be reduced easily in short time. Otherwise, if the oil fuel price raises too much, then global airlines' cost will be raised in long term. So, the airlines only choose to increase their air fare prices to aim to avoid loss possibly in long term. It seems that oil fuel raising price and bank interest rate and exchange rate changing and inflation factors will have direct influence airline income in long term.

- Methods to solve rising air fare prices to decrease travellers'demand

Biofuels energy increases supply
I suggest these methods how to avoid the oil raising price factor to cause airline air fare prices to be risen to lead the risk of traveler numbers to be reduced as below:

The first method: Whether aviation fuel markets will have what benefits from biofuels supply to planes. I shall refer the scope includes trends in jet fuel price, airline response to fuel price, increases and volatility and environmental goals for aviation. The aviation fuel supply industry includes production, distribution and consumption of aviation fuel and it outlines players in the aviation fuel supply chain. For example, at each airport, fuel supply chain organization and fuel sourcing could differ with regard to the role of oil companies, airlines, airport owners and operators and airport service companies. However, major jet fuel purchasers are airlines, general aviation operators, corporate aviation and the military, with most of the jet fuel in global different countries demanders being used for domestic commercial and civilian flights carrying passengers, cargos or both.

Commercial aviation fuel efficiency has improved dramatically over time, largely due to aircraft and engine upgrades and operational and air traffic control improvements. So, it seems that fuel supply factor can influence airline fare prices majorly. However, jet fuel prices generally correlate with prices of crude oil and other refined petroleum products, such as diesel. So, increasing prices and the persistent price volatility of jet fuel markets import airline industry finances in any countries.

However, airlines use various strategies to manage aviation fuel price certainty, including financial hedges, increased vertical integration and adjustments in aircraft utilization and size to avoid the jet fuel raising price risk.

Investments in alternative aviation fuel could be a mechanism to diversity expose to the price of petroleum. It seems the use of alternative aviation fuel would serve to diversify the fuel mix to reduce the risk of jet fuel monopoly raising price threat. If a diversified fuel mix were to avoid either fuel raising price in short term or to avoid fuel raising price in long term. Potential benefits include reduced actual fuel costs from only choice of jet fuel supply increased price certainty and lessened fuel costs. This diversify could allow airlines to become more consistently profitable and to make other investments in their businesses.
So, biofuels have potential to meet aviation industry needs, possibly including managing risks of upward fuel price trends and fuel price volatility and avoid risks with greenhouse gas emissions. So, the aviation fuels market could use biofuels to reduce greenhouse gas emission and mitigate long-term upward price trends, fuel price volatility or both.

What are the challenges of high priced oil for aviation? In fact, nowadays not the resources of oil as such, but much more the insecurity of supply, due to geopolitical instability in combination with a tight oil market makes a scenario with much higher oil prices than the world is currently experiencing not unlikely.
Aviation is completely dependent upon oil as its fuel source. Since no practical energy substitute is readily available for commercial aviation, a scarcity of petroleum relative to demand will present a major aviation policy. In addition, efficiency gains, due to operational measures and new aircraft medium term. In particular, it has been demonstrated that the annual reduction rate in fuel consumption traffic unit is not a constant, but is itself also falling, in contrast to past estimates.

So, a high-priced oil scenario will have severe consequences for demand, airline revenues, the competitive position of airports and eventually airline networks, strategies and fleet development. In particular, transfer demand, short-haul and leisure traffic can be expected to be heavily affected by high oil prices, due to their relative high price sensitivity. Also, different countries‘ governments or/and airlines are valuable to research another new and potential biofuel energy to substitute oil energy to supply our planes to reduce the threat of oil monopoly supply to influence the cause of air fare raising prices. Because the elasticity is very high to travelers, when the travelers feel air fares are rising high or even low level to influence travelers who will choose not to buy the air tickets to go to travel easily.

Whether will the fuel (oil based inputs) risk be high to compare other costs, e.g. engineering maintenance, employees salaries, general cleaning, security office expenses etc. expenditures to airlines? If the probability-weighted upside effect on firm value when a risk is resolved favorably is greater the risk than the probability-weighted downside effect if the risk is resolved badly, then expected value work not be enhanced by hedging. So, the risk will be resolved badly to any commercial airlines.

Airlines are an interesting case because the direct effect of source of risk resides squarely within the no offset in revenue functions (unlike for oil producers, for example), so value effects from costs feed directly into equity value. Most directly, the risk source is fuel costs to commercial airlines. Jet fuel is of course, a mix product of crude oil, so airlines indirectly face oil price risk. There are reasons to expect that airlines' fuel costs might to convex in oil price (i.e. absent any hedging). For example, oil prices, being generally pro-cyclical in recent times, tend to be highest when airline demand is strong.

In conclusion, airlines are therefore apt to use more high priced fuel than low-priced fuel over time. Airlines can raise air fare benefit is limited by the elasticity of demand. Also, cost functions could be influenced from fuel cost corresponds to upturns in economic activity overall (due to demand pressures on oil related prices), so it causes that airline's capacity delivers their services given their level of fixed capital. The essence of airlines basis risk in the case of jet fuel is essentially the time profile of the refining margin between crude and jet fuel, or the time profile of the price differential between other refined distillates and jet fuel. Thus, it is far from clear that risk management with oil is sure to add value to any airlines. It seems the impact of airline energy and any countries' domestic or foreign airline passenger travel numbers which have direct close relationship.

Reducing terrorism occurrence

Can reduce terrorism occurence to reduce airline failure risk? It needs to judge to determine if a combination of terrorism and the price of petroleum significantly predicted airline profitability and which variable whether the further period was the most significant between the terrorism occurrence and the price of petroleum influence.

I suggest that different countries' governments or airlines need to collect samples of financial records from which country's any airline commercial passengers and cargo airlines on costs of fuel and any airline profitability. Also, gathering the terrorism data were comparison of terrorist attacks on petroleum in oil-producing nations, and incidents of high jacking aboard any country's aircraft.

When any countries' airlines or governments can judge whether the impact of airline energy and terrorism risk level is high or middle or low level. Then, which can use this sample data to measure how to do positive social change to decide either ought rise or reduce employment in commercial aviation industry, or ought need to invest other higher commercial activity in tourist and other travel related service businesses and when is the most right time to adopt of green technologies by the civil aviation manufacturing industry after the terrorism attacks occurrence to any country. It seems that any countries' governments or airlines which ought concern that the event of when the terrorism attacks will occur and gather past sample data to predict when the next time terrorism attacks event will be occurred and the risk will be high or middle or low level to influence global airline industry development.

Will airline industry's ticket price elasticity be influenced by demand and supply factor
In fact, the airline industry is largely dependent on the supply of the oil industry. Otherwise, the oil industry is inelastic. However, the increase or decrease of the price of airfare is directly related to the increase or decrease of the oil's price to fuel the aircrafts because there has no any new energy which can be substituted to oil fuel to airline industry.

So, it seems oil fuel producers are monopolies to control its sale price to be raised easily. Another factor that can affect airline industry to be directly targeted by a tragedy brought about by terrorism. The past four years, from 2001 year to 2005 year, there had been at least $40 billion worth of losses in the airline industry because of the September 11 date terrorism attacks in 2000 year. There had been an expected and significant decrease in the demand for the airline industry services because of the attacks that involved planes hijacking and crashing into key locations like the World Trade Center and the Pentagon in USA. Although, terrorism attacks can bring risk to influence fuel price rising in airline industry. However, this risk occurrence to airline industry is only that after the terrorism attacks occurred. It is possible that terrorism attacks won't occur again in the future.

Otherwise, our concerning ought be the greenhouse emissions and how it affects global warming. The air quality would be better once this new regulations are adopted. However, it would affect large airlines. So, it would increase the price of airfares because of economic fees that airline companies have to cover. Air pollution can give a negative impact on the domestic or oversea owned airline companies for long term. If airlines' planes can use clean fuel to fly, e.g. biofuel, then it will bring benefits to global airlines for long term.

On the positive side, the environment would be healthier as the earth's temperature would rise, and greenhouse effect would be dramatically reduced. This positive effect can come at a cost that is greater than most people perceive. On the psychology view point on travelers, who will be more preferable to catch planes to go to different countries to travel, due to the chance of air pollution and global environmental warm issues will be reduced to low risk to influence our health if planes can use biofuel to be energy to fly in the future one day.

It seems that spending expenditure to research other non polluted biofuel new energy is one solvable method to global airline industry in the future. To solve, any airlines or countries' governments or oil producers ought choose to spend more time to research new biofuel. Otherwise, the predicting when terrorism attacks event will be occurred, it is more difficult to predict the time more than researching to produce new biofuel energy method in the future. So, I recommend that researching the new biofuel energy or other kinds of energy to substitute the oil energy is the urgent behavioral economy which the airlines or oil producers or different countries' governments which need to concern nowadays.

● Boeing 747 manufacturing fuel cost strategy

For Boeing 747 air plane manufacture example, how it can help airline to avoid travellers number reduces. Boeing 747 air plane manufacture company how achieve air plane manufacturing strategy to reponse airline traveller number market changing. What is fuel conservation strategy to Boeing 747 air plane manufacturing firm? The cost index, (CI) feature of the flight manufacturing computer (FMC) can help airlines significantly reduce operating cost. However, many operators do not take full advantages of this powerful tool. What does CI ratio mean? The CI is the ratio of the time-related cost of an air plane opertation and the cost of fuel. The value of the CI reflects the relative effects of the fuel cost on overall trip cost as compares to time-related direct operating costs.

The equation form, CI= time cost-$/hour / fuel cosst -cents/lb

The numerator of the Ci is often called time refrated direct operating cost (minue the cost of fuel). Items, such as flight crew wages can have an hourly cost associated with them, or they may be a fixed cost and have n variation with flying time engines, anxiliary power units, and air planes can be leased by the hour or owned, and maintenance costs can be accounted for an air planes by the hour, by the calendar or by cycles . As a result, each of these items may have a direct hourly cost or a fixed cost over a calendar period with limited or no correlation to flying time.

What does this air plane fuel, cost strategy advantages to airline companies? In the case of high direct time costs, the airline may direct to time costs, the airline may choose to use a larger CI to minimize time and thus cost . In this case, where most costs are fixed, the CI is potentially very low because the airline is primarily trying to minimize fuel cost. Pilots can easily understand minimizing fuel consumption, but it is more difficult to understand minimizing cost when something other than fuel dominates. So, the cost of the CI ratio. Although, this seems straight toward, issues such among the operating locations, fuel tankering, and fuel hedging can make this calculation complicated. So , this fuel consumption cost, air plan manufacturing strategy can help any airlines to reduce air fuel useful cost and waste fuel.

However, CI can be an extremely useful way to manage operating costs. Because CI is a function of both fuel and non-fuel costs. It is important to use it appropriately to gain the greatest benefit. Appropriate use varies with each airline, and perhaps for each flight.

How low fuel situations can bring less fuel consumed benefit in the more environmentally friendly flight? Fuel conservation strategy can help airlines significantly reduce operating costs. However, many operators do not take full advantage of this powerful tool. Cruise flight is the phase of flight that falls the largest percentages of trip time and trip fuel are consumed typically in this phase of flight, which also impact trip time and fuel significantly can

often be avoided through appropriate cruise planning. This fuel conservation strategy includes these characteristics. These objectives which depend on the perspective of the pilot , dispatcher, performance engineer, or operations planner can be groups into five categories , such as:
1. Maximize the distance traveled for a given amount of fuel (i.e. maximum range).
2. Minimize the fuel used for given distance covered (i.e. minimum trip fuel).
3. Minimize total trip time (i.e. minimum time).
4. minimize total operating cost for the trip (i.e. minimum cost, or economy speed).
5. Maintain the flight schedule . The first two objectives are essentially the same because in both cases the airplane will be flown to achieve optimum feel mileage.

In addition to one of the overall strategic objectives for cruise flight, pilots are often forced to deal with shortage term constraints that may require them to temporarily abandon their cruise strategy one or more times during a flight. These situations may include:

Flying a fixed speed that is compatible with other traffic on a specified route segment. Flying aseed calculated to achieve a required time of arrival at a fix. Flying a speed calculated to achieve minimum fuel flow when holding (i.e. maximum endurance). And when directed to maintain a specified speed by a air traffic control. Hence, when the air plane faced with a low fuel situation at destination, many pilits will opt to fly LRC speed, thinking that it will give them , the most miles from their remaining fuel. Also, if fuel prices increase relative to other costs, a corresponding reduction in CI will maintain the most economics operation of the air plane. If however an airline experience rising hourly costs, an increase in CI will retain the most economical operation . For this reason, flight crews typically reserve a recommend CI value from their flight operations department, and it is generally not advisable to deviate from this value unless specific short term constraints demand it.

How it can help air planes to execute for maximum fuel savings efficiently? For example, but times have clearly changed. Jet fuel prices have increased over times from 1990 to 2008 year. At this time, fuel is about 40% oa a tycpical airline's total operating cost. As a results airlines are reviewing all phases of flight to determine how fuel burn savings can be gained in each phase and in totel.
Boeing 777-200 extended range and 747-400 and (long-range, e.g. short range e.g. 717, medium range, e.g. 737-800 with winglate commercail air planes can impact fuel usage. However, flap setting must be appropriate for the situation to ensure air plane safely. Higher flap setting configurations use more fuel than low flags configurations.

The difference is small, but at today's prices the savings can be substantial especially for air planes that fly a light number of cycles each day. Hence, top fuel conservsation strategies for flight crews include: Take only the fuel you need, minimize the use of the nuxiliary power unit, taxi use efficiencly as possible, take off and climb efficiently ,

fly the air plane with minimum drag, choose routing carefully, strive to mantain optimum attitude, fly the proper cruise speed, descend at the appropriate point, configure in a timely manner.
Fuel conservation is a significant concern of every airline . An airline can choose an approach procedure and flap setting policy that was the least amount of fuel, but it should also consider the trade off involves with using this type of procedure.

Hence, Boeing flight crew can earn benefit, when they fly or air planes, such as to conserve fuel and reduce noise and emissions or to accommodate speed requests by air traffic control. All of these are fuel consumption reducing strategy to airlines.

● How airlines and airports implement successful netwpork strategies
What is airline network strategy ? Network management includes route planning, scheduling optimization, airline business planning and data analysis . How implement airline network strategy, airlines need to evaluate strengths and weaknesses of the current network strategy, identification of additional potential, recommendations for adjustments, network integration, due to merger or cooperation. Fleet and capacity evaluation , analysis of estimated passenger volume over time combined with option aircraft size and frequencies for current and potential future rotes / markets; competition response, modeling of results as an impact of competitor's action and reaction; establishing best practice network managment for new carriers include: route selection, network planning, scheduling, airline business planning includes forecasting of revenues and costs. Finally, any airlines need to establish network planning, such as network optimization and development, traffic and revenue forecasting, market -and -competitor analysis, scenarios for profit-optimized networks include: hub-strategies, evaluation of aliances, cooperation includes: route joint ventures in industry environment.

● Performance measurement system strategy
Any airlines may apply performance measurement methods to design the indicates of performance. Different models and frameworks are excellence models. Any airlines hope to achieve useful performance meaurement strategy. They need to answer these kep questions: Who are the key stakeholders and what they want and need? What strategy airlines have to put into place to satisfy the key stakeholders' want and need? What critical process do airlines need if they want to implement this strategy? What capability do they need to operate and improve this process? What does cost leadership strategy mean? Competitive price is decided for customer . Indoneasia, Malaysia , India and China countries are implementing, it can provide cheaper workforces and the cost of production will be covered.

In aviation service industry, cost strategy , it much relevant to be applied cost carrier, such as Vigin Blus, Ryanair Airways are implementing . However, some airlines combined the low cost carrier and full service ,which is known as low fare limited services.

Innovative marketing strategy is not only how to carry many more passengers, but also how to enable significant reduction in the costs of distribition and marketing. Such a strategy is used as a competitive strategy of low cost tariffs . For example, low cost focus strategy serve tourists or groups with certain destinations, e.g. the flights are carried out by certain airlines.

There are also tourist groups who travel to certain tourist destinations. Passengers only are transported be the tourist destinations, thus departure schedule won't be a basic need, lower price of ticket and flexible departure schedule as well as comfortable cabin are still the standard.
Another improvement of performance method, it is market orientation, it is believed to give psychological and social benefits to the employees , in the forms of greater pride and sense of belonging, as well as greater commitment to the organization.

Another strategy improves to service performance, it is distribution management strategy . Everyone can be brought benefits. It may achieve these benefits: Raising passenger numbers, as some airlines and airports are running at near full capacity. The effects of disruption are only becoming compounded. Social media can help airlines and airports to tackle dissuption management and avoid damaging their reputation with consumers.

So, when discuption is solved. It can help airports reduce discuption cost and damaging their reputation with consumers . Innovation may include: airlines attempt to develop standard procedure for common disruption situations, responding to regulations, such as the delay rule and compensation for cancellations with faster, more proactive decisions, collaborating with air traffic control facilities, airports, themselves views of resources, identify available options.

● What factors influence cost-related management quality ?
Thus, the reduction of costs lies at the core of the low cost airline model, which aims to offer lower fares, elimating some comfort and services that were traditionally quaranteed, e.g. employed to refer to low-cost flight. The use of an airline booking system, the suppression of free-in-flight catering, the use of secondary airports connected through a point-to-point network, and the use of homogeneous fleets are only a part of the innovative choices made by low-cost airlines. However, these are main important factors to influence route structure, type and characteristics of the aircraft cost of labor and management quality . For example, if the airline's pilot, airline passenger service people, cleaners , all salaries can be reduced to employ. Then, the airport or airline's labor cost will be reduced and it can influence it's air ticket price to be also decreased.

When the airline's air tickets price reduces, it will bring competitive low air ticket sale price to win other airline competitors more easily. How air ticket sale attractive prices ? The airline's air plane type and characteristics,, whether they ae comfortable to let passengers catch in their whole trip time. Whether their air planes are new or old model ? Whether their air planes' facilities can satisfy passengers entertainment need, e.g. chair can be bed to let passengers to sleep, television or movie is attractive to watch, music is soft sound etc. psychological entertainment facilities can let the airline passengers feel satisfactory or not.

Final view is management quality, such as whether the airline or airport CEO's management ability performance is either excellent or good or general or poor . They can influence whole airline or airport front -line service staffs' service performance to let passengers or airport visitors feel their services can satisfy their needs when they choose to catch the airline air planes to fly to the country to travel or work, but the country's airport staffs' service performances and airport facilities will influence their revisiting to the country's airport or rebuying the airline's air tickets again.

The final strategy is flying route strategy. I believe that whether the flying route is attractive or not, it can influence passengers to choose the airline preference. Which factors determine choice of flights on the Dhaka-London route? How could the airline be able to cope with the competitive advantages of its major rivals in this flying route? How is the competitive environment for airlines operating in this route? How could the airline sustain its competitive advantage and what can it do to gain more market share in this route?

A successful and attractive flying route design needs to amend and adjust its flying route design strategies and capabilities as the airline firm goes through its flying route design life cycle, when changes in passenger's flying route choice preferences. Hence, any airline needs to know whether what its SWOT (strengths, weaknesses, opportunities, threats) before it decides to implement which flying route(s). Because manay flying routes choicew will be influenced by its current SWOT environment situation. For organization of new flying route to the UK airport from UK , e.g. London ciry airport, the HK airline needs to know whether what its strengths , e.g. customer loyalty, its strengths can provide the most rapid .

The most cheapest, the more comfortable flying feeling from HK airport flys to UK London airport or from UK , London city airport flys to HK airport, its UK , London city flying route can provide competitive fare al promotion, extra baggage allowance, airline brand image , whether is famous to UK travellers, providing online seats reservation for any UK , London flights services, airline organization size and airline brand , whether it can get travelling passegners, loyalty or confidence either to fly to UK , London city from UK city airport, or flying to HK city from UK, London city airport, providing regular UK , London flying route schedule, network presence how much UK flying route cost cutting, Uk air planes' aircrafts facilities whether are enough to satisfy HK or UK to catching the airline's air planes flying entertainment needs. Does it one new route development opportunity of direct flughts from HK airport to UK , London city airport. HK air port has enough terminals number to let facilities to provide passengers stay in HK airport when UK , London city travellers arrive HK airport? Does HK airport lacks technologica facilities to satisfy new UK , London city airport flying route development , e.g. providing enough spaces to let air fleets stay in HK airport, aircraft manintenance whether is enough? Does HK airport encounter shortages of experienced front line counter service staffs to serve UK , London city travellers in airport? When the seasonal time is holiday travelling time for UK visitors, is UK new flying route rising fuel cost? Does new entrants to develop another UK , London city flying route from HK? Has new UK , London city from HK flying route , these weaknesses , such as lacking enough resource to develop another another new flying route or no direct flight or long hour flight after the HK airline developed the new UK , London city flying route to the HK airline from HK airport. Has new Uk, London city flying route development enountered these threats: strong competiton, high interest and UK foreign currency exchange rates, raising fuel cost, economic recession decline in the UK airline industry, environmental pollution etc. issues influence UK travellers choose to travel to HK desires. So, SWOT analysis must be needed to consider in order to develop any new flying route in order to avoid servious high cost expenditure loss to any airlines.

So, above these tangible , e.g. fuel cost control , route choice, network cooperation choice and intangible, e.g. service performance factors can influence whether the airline's network cooperation strategy, route choice strategy or low cost strategy can succeed or fail. So, airlines or airports can not neglect these factors to be revised in order to achieve any strategies in success more easily.

Economic Environment Influences Airport
service performance

Airline employee positive emotion method

Emotional labor factor

Airline service industry, front line travelling passengers service workers' emotional challenge concerns cabin crew and airline ground service employee whose service quality or performance how to serve travelling passengers in order to reach service level or satisfy their service performance needs to be accepted. So, how to influence airline service labour individual emotional matter which will be one major factor to let travelling passengers how they feel satisfactory to the airline service.

The question concerns how to let airline service cabin crews and air ground service employees build long term good emotion to serve their airline travelling passengers. Because
bad emotional airline service labors will damage the whole airline employers' loyalty as well as reducing travelling passengers number in possible.

Will a lot stresses at work cause bad emotion to airline ground service employees? The hospitality industry comprises of travel and tourism and the major segments include lodgings and cuisines (hotels, restaurants), transport(airlines, rentals, cruise and railway companies), travel and tour operators. All of these related travelling industries‘ employees , they are emotional labor, whose service performance or service attitude will influence future potential travelling passengers' airline choices to the airline operating servicer again. Any airline service employees in these service sector industries, have to interact with their travelling clients, be its customers on a regular emotion reflecting basis. So, they must be patient to listen any travelling passengers‘ enquires in order to help them to solve any problems considerably.

Emotional labor is managing one's feelings to generate a publicly accepted facial and bodily display of emotion. Emotional labor is an expression of emotion for a wage. Jobs involve face to face or voice to voice interactions with clients (travelling passengers), jobs demanding the employee to produce and alter an emotional state in other person, and jobs allowing the employer to implement certain amount of control over the emotional activities of the employees, produce or create emotional labor among the employees.

Thus, long time bad emotional airline front labors number increasing, it will influence the airline whole service member performance to be its airline passengers. However, many airline organizations have their owning set of norms or policies that determine these feeling rules. These are specially seen in customer service industries. IN long term, these strict policies will let airline front service staffs feel stress or pressure, because they won't feel to be punished in possible, e.g. without salary continue increasing, dismissal (lose jobs), changing to another position to do more simple or boring job duties, if they are discovered that their working service performances are not satisfied to their airline employers in any time.

So, strict airline organizational policies will be one strict or pressure emotional regulation to any airline front service staffs. This emotional regulation refers to a person's capability to accept and understand his or her experience of emotions to get involved in healthy strategies in managing emotions which are uncomfortable whenever required, when they need to contact their airline passengers every day. In fact, it has possible that they will accept unreasonable complaint from their airline passengers, even they perform very good or they have help their airline passengers to solve any enquiries when they feel any needs, they stay in airports any time. So, it has close relationship among airline front service staffs' emotions and the airline's policy as well as their service attitude. Thus, good airline policy will build good airline service staffs‘ emotions and good service attitude or service behaviour to serve their airline passengers every day in possible.

Any airline organizations can not neglect to consider how to build (keep) good airline front labor emotion issue. Because they are any airlines' representatives, if they can build good
images to let the airline the airline passengers to feel. Then, it will influence many airline passengers to choose to buy the airline tickets to replace other airlines because they like its front airline front staffs‘ services. SO, any airline organizations need to consider front service staffs' health status and definite psychological or mental diseases more than physical diseases, because many airline front service staffs only need to serve their airline passengers and they

do not need to move any heavy things in airports in general. They need to spend more time to contract their passengers more than any things. When their passengers give their passports or/and any related travelling documents, e.g. air tickets to them to check in to find whether they can allow to enter airport restrict areas, and if they give their luggage to them, they also need to help them to measure its size and weight heavy to decide whether they need to pay extra fee and their luggage are permitted either to keep to them together to enter the air planes to fly or separate air planes to fly to destination. So, they need to make accurate judgement need to avoid any error occurrence. They do not allow to do any wrong judgement or error in order to be complain by their airline passengers often. Hence, any airline organizations need have good method to help their airline front service staffs to avoid to do any wrong judgements in order to influence any flights delay or customers' complaints , due to their personal wrong judgement to their passengers cause in possible.

Thus, any airline organizations require to enquire themselves these questions: Is there any influence of emotional labor (surface acting and deep acting) on the general mental health or psychological disease of airline employees? Is these any difference in the experience of emotional labor across demographics (age/gender/mental status/work experience of airline employees influence their service performance? Because above any one factors , such as every airline front service staff individual age, airline service experience, marital status of these factors will influence their emotions to be good or bad to serve their airline passengers every day. Hence , any airline organizations need to investigate every airline front service employee individual background in order to arrange the most suitable policy to train their front line or ground airline service staffs' skill in order to let them to feel less stress or pressure

or they can feel happy to enjoy to serve their airline passengers.

On conclusion, reducing airline front or ground service staffs' psychological stress or mental pressure issue which will be the most effective or the best solution to assist them to raise confidence to serve their airline passengers in airports in long time. I believe that it is the most rapid psychological solution method to assist any one airline front or ground service staff to raise service level in short time.

Airports service environment factor

The environment of airports service environment for the airline services, which will also influence travelling passengers' travelling destinations and travelling frequent times choices. The airport price factor includes income growth, aviation technology and local economic / geographical features of the country's domestic or overseas airports both. IN fact, airports, airports are indeed two sides businesses, it has commercial relationship between both airlines and passengers. So, airports' pricing will influence passengers' travelling demands to the airlines in the country. Any countries' airport(s) need(s) to respond how to help themselves country airlines how to increase passengers number and airlines choices in order to achieve attracting traffic on frequent air planes flying aim. Because the country's travelling passengers number increases , it will influence the country's airport(s) ' income increases indirectly, instead of the countries' any airlines themselves incomes.

Hence, any country's airport(s) will be one good platform to let travelling passengers to stay in the country's airport(s). It means that id the country's airport(s) can build good service image and reasonable products sale price and comfortable shopping environment to attract any countries' passengers feel comfortable and worth to stay in themselves countries' airport(s), when they need to transfer air planes to stay in the country's airport, e.g. one hour to five hours short time, even overnight long time staying. However, if they feel the country's airport(s) are(is) more comfortable and clean to stay, less noise, as well as they have enough chairs to let them to sit or sleep and large area to let them to work in the airport ground floor.

Moreover, the country's airport(s) can have enough restaurants , bookshops, any electronic or other kinds product shop[s, even cinema etc. shopping or entertainment services to satisfy
the passengers whose eating needs, entertainment needs, shopping needs in the airport. Then, I believe that the country's airport(s) can help itself airlines to attract many passengers
to choose to increase travelling times to the country frequently. For example, when the country's airport passengers feel that the airport restaurant food concessionaires will probably provide enjoy positive external gains from having more flights at the airports, additional or better eating facilities are unlikely to provide external benefits to the airlines by stimulating many more passengers with local origins or destinations to use the airport. I believe these airport restaurants can influence the choices of transit passengers whether which country will be their transfer air plane's short journey staying airport destination to fly to their final destinations. Although, transit passengers usually stay to the transfer air plane airport in short time, but they hope that these any one transit staying airport can have any restaurants to provide good taste food to them to eat when they feel hungry, if the transfer air plane country's airport can provide enough restaurants and they can have different food taste choice and reasonable price. Then, the airport's restaurants may attract many short time transit passengers to choose to eat their food, even many passengers will like to choose the country's airline to buy tickets to stay short time to wait to transfer another air plane to fly to their final destination to replace another country's airport to stay short time.

Hence, it seems that any countries' airports' entertainment, eating and shopping service environment will influence any countries transit passengers whether they ought either choose to stay short time this country's airport in prefer or another country's airport to stay short time in prefer in order to decide to buy the country's airline air ticket for transfer airplane to another destination. Hence, any airports service environment will influence any countries passengers how to make transit airport destination short time staying choice.

However, I also suggest that an airport will place a lower revenue -over cost burden on that side of the travelling market that benefits the other the most. Assuming one passenger
can earn benefit enjoyed by airlines from an extra- passenger using the airport, the airlines will be willing to pay up to this amount to increase passenger enjoyed benefit feeling.

The airport can extract rent from the airlines up to above their allocated costs for providing the airport short time staying platform (transfer air plane short time staying airport) for eating, entertainment, shopping need service of increasing their destination arriving passengers or transfer another air plane passengers number base.

This involves transferring the external benefits derived by airlines from additional passengers using the transfer airport to the another destination airport.

On the another view, from a airport location choice perspective, locating or expanding an airport near a city center can reduce or at least contain passenger access costs . But, because land is like to be more expensive, the airside costs to airlines are serious higher and if the various other external costs of aviation are included. Hence, countryside or the airport is built far away from city center in the country. This location is one reasonable location choice, because it can reduce noise to influence people who are living when air planes are often flying or landing on the airport and the rent cost to the airport's any business renters will be influenced to reduce. Then, their food , product or entertainment service prices charge to the airport consumers will also be reduced. Thus, any airports ought nor neglect their building location choices in any countries because they will influence airport business renters sale prices.

Lean maintenance repair and manual error factor

Any airlines must need air plans to catch passengers to fly to travel. So, any air plans will need often to fly. Every flight will need long time to fly, e.g. short trip needs to fly less than five hours, even long trip needs to fly more than five hours, even ten hours. If many passengers choose the country to travel, the air plan needs to fly frequently to catch every flight passengers to go to the travelling destination frequently. So, any airlines air plans often need to check whether they have any engine machines has broken, need to be repaired in possible in order to let passengers feel the airline air plans are safe. If the airline's any air plans have occurred any accidents when they are flying, even the accidents cause any one passengers hurt, even death. Then, these flying accidents will let passengers feel life risk to choose this airline's any air plans to catch to fly. IN special, long time trip(s) flight(s). So, lean maintenance and engine check is needed to consider for any one airplane to any airline in order to improve efficiencies and minimize costs, maintenance, repair, and overhaul services in the aviation industry sector, even avoiding any flying accident occurrence or reducing serious flying accidents occurrence chance to bring any one passenger hurt, even death when they are catching any one of the airline air plans to travel. Thus, any one of airline safety is one important successful factor to any airlines.

Instead of passenger safety aspect, the flying logistics safety factor is also important. The central tenet of the lean to a flying process can mainfest in a variety of ways , as over stalled and underused inventory and misallocated labour, time transportation and logistics. From a customer's perspective, value-added activities are necessary and customers are willing to pay for activities(Bamber, 2000, Glass, 2016). For example, improvements caused by lean introduction in aviation industry in order to avoid misallocated labour time, increasing number of old broken tools, and obsolute jigs and fixtures. Aviation MRO services have been reported by the MIT Lean Aerospace Initiative (2005) to result in:

(1) Set up time: 17 to 85 percent improvement.
(2) Lead time: 16 to 50 percent improvement.
(3) Labour hours: 10 to 71 percent improvement.
(4) Cost: 11 to 50 percent improvement.
(5) Productivity: 27 to 100 percent improvement.
(6) Cycle time: 20 to 97 percent improvement.
(7) Airline airplane manufacturing factory floor space: 25 to 81 percent improvement.
(8) Travel distance (people and products): 42 to 95 percent improvement.
(9) Airplanes engine inventory or work in progress: 31 to 98 percent improvement.
(10) Scape, rework , deflects or inspection: 20 to 80 percent improvement.

Hence, any airlines' airplanes need to be achieve any one of above improvement at least percent level in order to keep airplane's accident occurrence chance to the least level.

Moreover, airplanes' pilot employees their flying experiences or flight numbers factor is also important to influence airplane safe flying issue. Because if the pilot has less flying expereince or he is not proficient pilot, or his flight number is less. This pilot's individual flying factor will also influence the airplan's safety when he is driving the airplane.

So, any airlines need to consider how to train any one of pilot to be one proficient pilot, because id less experienced pilot , he/she is not proficient to drive any one airplane to fly. Then, the flying accident occurrence chance will also raise. It is one critical successful factor to influence passengers' confidence to choose the airline's airplanes to catch, instead of maintenance repair and checking engines factor.

On conclusion, raising travelling passengers' safe confidences factor will be one critical successful factor to influence any airlines' services level, because flying safety issue must be one important matter to be considered to any passengers when they decide to choose the airline's airplane to catch to fly to any destinations. If one airline can not guarantee any flying accidents won't occur, to cause any passengers hurt or death. Then, any passengers won't have confidence to feel its others services level can satisfy their basic flying enjoyment needs. Due to passengers' life cost must be no worth calculation more than other service cost. When they choose to catch the airlines' any one airplane to fly to the another destination form the country's airport. Hence, the influence of human factor in airport maintenance factor will influence any airlines' services feeling level to their passengers because human factor is one of the safety barrier which is used in order to prevent accidents or incidents of aircraft.

Therefore, the question is to which extent the error caused by human factor is included into the share of errors that are made during aircraft maintenance, such as flying accidents, incidents, injuries, death, damages related to aircraft operation and maintenance. More airlines' detailed analyses have led to the knowledge that it is necessary to study the interrelation of repair people, machines, airline factory maintenance and manufacturing working environment, and the air planes production processes. Human is the key factor production process and in the process of operation of technical means since gives new value to the object of any one airplane manufacturing process.

As a factor, the human is not perfect and introduces unintentional error in the system. It is important to develop a system of ever identification and to work constantly on error prevention. The works and activities on aircraft maintenance can produce hidden and active errors on the aircraft. Hidden errors are a type of errors that are seemingly invisible during aircraft flying. Active errors are errors that occur immediately and result in immediate aircraft damage or injury , even death to any travelling passengers.

Hence, non human or without human factors will be less number to compare human factors to cause any flying incidents or accidents occurrence easily, e.g. damaging engine, old engine (no renew engine), fire, crash etc. different kinds of causes. However, the main causes of human errors to cause any flying accidents may include: lack of communication between the pilot(s) and airport airplane landing staffs, complacency (assessment of work according to previous working experience), lacking of flying knowledge to the pilot, distraction, lack of team work, fatigue, lack of materials and technological support), pressure on the work performer, lack of assertiveness (lack of self-confidence or technical approach to work),stress (working under pressure), lack of awareness etc. different human factors. Any one of above human factors will influence any flying accidents cause.

Moreover, instead of human factor, the flying working environment which refers to the space and place for work as well as the conditions of work factor will also influence human error occurrence increasing chance, e.g. time pressure, equipment and tools enough number supplies, night shift, all of any one work environment factor will also influence human error occurrence increasing chance in any flight flying. However, the factors that lead to cause of maintenance error may be caused from wrong information system supplies of equipment , aircraft manufacturer, wrong working equipment and tools, wrong design of aircraft equipment and parts, incorrect working task arrangement, lacking technical education to the aircraft maintenance workers, employee’s bad personality, poor aircraft factory manufacturing working environment, poor airline company organization structure, working management and control and poor communication etc. different manual or non manual factors.

Hence, all of above any one non manual factors will also raise manual error factor to cause any flying accidents occurrence chances. However, if any airlines hope to satisfy their passengers‘ flying service level. They must consider non manual and manual both factors for aircraft lean maintenance repair service aspect.

Influence of airside and off airport to airport geographical choice factor

What does airport airside means ? It includes a system of three components: runways, taxiways and agron-gate areas, on which aircraft and aircraft support vehicles operate. It brings this questions: Why can airport airside operation influence passengers feeling to the country's airport and airline services? How does it influence airport ground service staffs' service performance?

In fact, this airside airport physical area choice has direct relationship between aircraft and apron gate areas of the terminal processing of passenger and cargo. They are major factors to influence operations on runway component. It means that airport ground service staffs' service efficiency, used for the passengers and air fright catching any airplanes processing.

Hence, in a geographical sense, landside and airside capacity on how designing and building og geographical area can bring indirect influence to passengers. They need to enter or indirect influence the airport , in special, many flights are staying on the airport runway as well as many passengers need to leave from the airplanes or enter to the airplanes in the same time on the airport boundary. Hence, if the airport has good airside design , then many passengers will feel convenient to leave or enter the airport from the airside areas.

Airports are perhaps truly intermodel terminals in the transportatoin system. They provide an intersafe among air highway, rail and even water way travel. They are an important part of the medium and long distance intercity transportation system in our future transportation tools. Hence, it has enough reasons to support airside geographical airside and off airport factors can influence an airport and its airline flying service providers on its capacity as well as how it's capacity can influence passengers' satisfactory level when they arrive the country's airport. Hence, airport's congestion growth problem that is needed to consider to any airports because when one airport 's congestion is growing.

It will influence passengers service satisfactory level to be fallen down in possible, e.g. capacity is increased by the addition of a new access road, such as additions provide a major increase.Thus, the stair step growth, it will cause congestion growth because if the airport had used many areas for stair step growth and passengers will have less space to let them to walk on the ground and their airport congestion feeling will also increase when passengers are staying to leave the airport or waiting for check in or check out or waiting to transfer another airplane in the country's airport.The major airside factors to influence travelling passengers whose airport service feeling may include as below:

Availability of enough land for expansion for runways, availability of aids to navigation and air traffic control techniques that could result in reduction of separation between aircraft , noise, aircraft mix, load factor, exclusive use and use of gates , enough airside and outside facilities, availability of airspace, whether aircraft large size is enough capacity and where is location of gates, staffing, equipment freight, environmental protection regulation, and community attitudes toward airside operation.

Thus, whether the airport has enough facilities to satisfy passengers staying in its airport service need, it will have indirect influence further passengers increasing or decreasing number problem. For example, if the airport terminal functions are spread over a large geographic area, access and facilities have to be expanded to accommodate the spread-out configuration of the terminal or if terminal facilities are grouped together, the access facilities can be congregated into a smaller geographical area.

The capacity of the landside is a function of the terminal design , which has a major influence on the relative to between airside and landside capacity. Also, these off airport factors can also influence landside capacity, they may include: off airport parking, off airport terminals, urban development pattern, multiple jurisdiction, financial resources etc. issues. The sub factors of the off-airport access functions , they can influence passengers‘ services feeling to the airport. They may include: user and vehicle characteristics, e.g. occupants per vehicle, separate and preferential guide way subsystems, roadway traffic management, access link to major transportation , transportation connections. All of these airside and off-airport facilities will influence passengers’ servicing feeling when they arrive any countries‘ airports. Hence, any countries’ airports ought not neglect any one of these minor airside facilities of inside airports to outside airports both.

The another geographical choice airport building issue, it is also one critical factor for how the development of airport cities. It will influence passengers‘ service feeling to any country airport. The questions may include: Why may any country need to develop an airport city? Can it bring economic benefit and attract many passengers to choose to travel the country? Can the airport city reform to raise airport service performance or service level? Airports have become new dynamic centers of economic activity, incorporating several commercial and entertainment services inside passenger terminals, when developing a hotels and accommodations , office complexes, conference and exhibition centers or leisure facilities choices for leisure passengers and business passengers both.

Airport-centered development may occur at different spatial scales (from the micro scale of the passenger terminal to the regional or metropolitan scale), thus assuming different shapes and mainfestations. Different concepts to address these developments can be found in the " airport city", airport corridor, and aerotopolis (Guller, M. & Guller, M, 2003).

I shall explain how airport city concept can help to raise passenger service performance feeling in airports and airlines as below:

In general, airport passengers hope airports ought provide these different kinds service and achievement the lowest satisfactory service quality or performance level to let them to feel, such as air transport needs have complex airport -neighborhood interactions (in what concerns an eventual development towards the concept of airport city) requires the identification of thes takeholders involved and an awareness of the relationships between them. Any airport’s main task needs to provide traveling, air transport, shipping, entertainment services to the dual market of airlines and travelers. As such, its primary interaction consists of the supply and demand relationship with the users stakeholder group (passengers and airlines), which results in broad terms in the airports aeronautical revenues. Furthermore, non-aeronautical (commercial) revenues also result from the interactions between airport and users, namely from agents such as cargo and passengers oriented organizations who pay rents or concession feeling to the airport authority, depending on the commercial arrangements binding these agents.

Thus, one successful airport city, it ought provide good neighborhood transport service to travelling passengers, e.g. bus, taxi, ferry etc. public transportation service. It aims to avail any airport passengers can catch any one of these public transportation tools to arrive airport or leave the airport easily. It also needs to provide hotel, conference service for business visitors as well as retail shops, cinemas for shopping visitors or entertainment visitors when they are staying in the country's airport(s). Also, it ought provide facilities to any cargo -oriented organizations to deliver any cargo in short time rapidly. So, one airport's any neighborhood facilities have relationship to influence any passengers and airport organizations' service performance feeling between different user agents including: service provision (e.g. between passengers and businesses), business transactions, supply and demand (e.g. between public transport providers and passengers and passengers or visitors) and employer-employee relationships (businesses and workforce , such as airport airline ground service workers). Because if they feel that they can work in one comfortable airport working environment, they will feel happy and enjoyable to serve their passengers more everyday. It means that any airports' facilities will have indirect relationship to influence airport ground service workers' psychology to feel either enjoyable or hate to work in the airport environment often.

On conclusion, airports ought need to consider themselves airside and off airport facilities whether they have enough supplies and innovate their facilities to be better , even perfect in order to satisfy any airport visitors, travelers, user organizations and airport ground service employees to enjoy to work and use their services if they hope their service level or performance is satisfied to their service needs for long term.

Influencing air connectivity to service quality factor

Can air connectivity growth decreases travel costs for attracting travelling passengers, consumers and businesses and facilities global productive growth? This seems to be particularly an issue when airport capacity is scare or when new airports are added to an existing airport system. What is air connectivity ?
Why does air connectivity raise passengers services? How to measure air connective service?

When direct and indirect connectivity relate to the airport connectivity available to local travelling passengers, any airports ought need to raise extra
airline services to raise service quality , e.g. cheaper air ticket price, in-flight service extra service provision, e.g. comfortable and clean and quiet air port waiting environment
service provision and feeling. However, passengers will generally prefer direct, non-stop connections over indirect air connectivity service.

Air connectivity service can assist airlines to raise competitive effort an offer and they provide access to the many destinations with too little demand for a direct flight, such as minimum connecting time differs in quality , due to in-flight time differences, the inconvenience and risk of missing a connection and transfer time for direct or indirect flights. Hence, any airlines can reduce passengers indirect or direct flight in-flight time to wait airplanes arrive to catch when they arrive any airports. This air in flight waiting time shorten service will attract many passengers to choose the airline to catch airplanes if its inflight waiting time to airport passengers is lesser than other airlines‘ in-flight waiting time in any airports. It can raise airline service quality, due to the airline has many passengers feel in-flight waiting time is shorten than other airlines often.

In fact, airport connectivity is one good concept method to raise passengers’ satisfactory service level. One of the important factors for the connectivity of airports may include: The size and economic strength of the local catchment area how drives outbound demand, size and economic activities as well as tourism attractiveness are an important cariable factor in explaining inbound demand (including the propensity to flying demand), landside accessibility drives the size of the catchment area that airlines can serve from a particular airport within a certain landside travel time, apart from the socio-economic variables factor, also cultural , political and the historical ties play a role in explaining demand the origin-destination level factor. All of the research on the factors that explain air level, demand at the origin-destination or airport level is widespread, including gravity modelling (e.g. a bed at al., 2001) and regressions on aggregate
airport demand (Dobruszkes, 2011). All of any one factors may be airport connectivity service to influence passengers‘ service feeling level in airports and airlines both service quality.

ON airport visit costs aspect, airlines also need to consider airport visit costs in their route development strategy. Visit costs may also influence passenger choice behavior when
airlines pass on higher/lower charges to the passenger through air fares. Although, airport visit costs generally represent a limited share of an airline’s total operational costs, this share can be more significant for short haul flights as well as fair airlines. All of any one these airport charges and passenger fees variable may influence passengers airlines choice. They may include:

Fees variable, landing charge, parking charge for their vehicles or aircraft, passenger luggage charge, security charge, boarding bridge charge, noise charge, emission charge, airport development service increasing charge, check -in charge, terminal charge, cargo charge. So, if any one of these charges influence the airline ticket price rises, it will influence passengers’ air ticket purchase choice to the airline in possible.

On airport service levels aspect, for keeping and attracting passengers, airlines and airports need to compete with services that improve the passengers experience. Such service
factors concern for immigration and luggage, but also relate to the terminals, waiting transfer another air plane time, shopping facilities, toilets, atmosphere and space cleaniness, friendliness of staff and availability of delicated lounges. Together they determine the image of an airport and its perceived value by passengers and airlines.

On airline routes development aspect, it can also influence passengers choices to the airline, e.g. Australia airline had developed long route to England destination. Any Australia
passengers can fly to England route directly. They do not need to transfer another air plane to go to England. Although, flying time is above 12 hours long time, but it can bring available to
passengers. They do not need to spend time to wait another air plane to transfer to go England in Australia any airports. THus, airline route development strategy airline planners require detailed, accurate information to make

new route decisions, but airlines usually do not have the resources to fully evaluate every new route market. So, they need a sound well articulated business case, can convince airlines to introduce new air services, as well as airport / destinations can influence the airline planning process.

For example, Interviewer indicates that new routes are a huge investment and risk to an airline in airline economic view point, if the airline had not gathered any data to evaluate
whether the new route is worth to develop and predict passengers' new route choice behavior. It assumed 75% lead factor will influence any new route development in success. It indicates these different aircraft type and seats per flight, annual passenger requirements data for these aircrafts: Boeing 747 aircraft needs to satisfy 400 at least seats per flight and annual passenger requirement need 219, 000, aircraft airbus A340 aircraft needs 280 at least seats per flight and annual passenger requirements need 153,300 , Boesing 767 to 300 aircraft needs 220 at least seats per flight and annual passenger requirements need 120, 450 . Boeing 737 to 700 aircraft needs 76,650 and regional Jet aircraft needs 100 at least seats per flight and annual passenger requirements need 54,750.

Hence, any airlines need have route priorities strategy before they decide which new flight route(s) will be developed , in order to achieve airlines add service in order of expected profitability, different airlines have pursued different strategies, destinations can move up the priority board with: solid research and analysis (always) and incentives (sometimes).However, any airline questions for new routes may include as below:

What is the current, actual market for a potential route?
How much can my airline stimulate the flight flying market?
How will the competition react?
How much market share will achieve?
How will be the connectivity contribution?
Will the new route be a financial success?

Hence, any airlines need to reduce uncertainty and risk, before they decide to develop any new route market.

The air service development process may include as below:

Step one: market assessment, required a quantify the time size of the existing air travel market

step two: strategy, deficiency analysis and detailed route analysis

step three: business case analysis, packaging and presenting the information to airlines

step fourth: evaluate and negotiate airline incentives

It is the final steps an appropriate incentive, in certain circumstances, helps airlines commit to new air service to satisfy any new route passengers' more satisfactory flying needs.

Similarly, the strategy steps follow: benchmark air services, identify deficiencies, identify new route opportunities, identify potential air service providers, assess viability of potential air services and prioritize route opportunities and target carriers.

Any airlines may find any information concerns new route business cases to decide their countries flying new routes choice , such as: catchment area profile: demographics, economy, tourist etc. information, airport profile :

traffic and facilities information market profile; market sizes , top city pairs, traffic leakage etc. information, suggested service : frequency , schedule, airport routing information, route analysis: market share, load factor, stimulation potential, self-diversion etc. information, any airlines‘ past flying routes strategic considerations etc. information in order to predict and evaluate whether how many further passenger number is flying that they accept to choose the new flying routes travelling needs.

Hence, how to design to impact either the supply or demand for any new flight routes that is only important because of the country has less number of passengers accept to choose the new flying route to fly. Then, the new flying route does not needed to be design to supply to the country's travelling passengers because their acceptance to this new flying route ends are very less. However, the demand level is low new flying route needs to satisfy these three qualifying services criteria, such as: Are new routes only? Increase on existing routes? Does it work service rent incentives? Will the new flying route be satisfied to air service to the airline passengers and airport waiting passengers, e.g. strategically important? Marginally (unprofitable) self-sustaining in the short term? New flying routes only? Increase an existing routes? Service rent incentives?

How can airports afford aggressive airline incentive / fee discounts and still fund route development marketing in a difficult economy? I recommend that the solution method may include new flying route design and developing and maximizing non-aeronautical revenue streams both, such as retail and duty free, food and beverage, parking , loyalty and premium programs and land development to airport building. Marketing funding strategy may be an ineffective incentive for travelling destinations. However, it may not differentiate a market, as route marketing incentives are used by over 80% of communities in the U.S. marketing incentives can be: Unilateral airport pays 100% or cooperative airlines matches some portion, funding amounts are often tied on the capacity of inbound seats to be available on the new flight (flying) route. By calculating the economic impact of new visitors (spend at the destination), a destination can calculate the return on investment in cooperative new flight (flying) route market.

On conclusion, air connectivity is one important factor to influence any country's travelling passengers to the airline's service quality or service level in order to achieve new flying (flight) route design , reducing inflight transfer another airplane waiting time in airport, or marketing development in success. So, any airlines can not neglect this air connectivity will influence their passengers' service quality. Hence, air connectivity factor is also very important to influence any travelling passengers‘ service satisfactory level.

How to measure and rise airline service quality

How are airline performing ? Nowadays, the rise of the low cost airlines' competition is serious, due to airlines hope to rise themselves attractions to influence passengers to choose to use their travelling services. So, different airlines have spend long time to build their unique person-to-person passenger services, which passengers use of different airlines, e.g. digital electronic air tickets purchase method. Any airlines hope to make each journey personalized to the individual will gain market share and improve its service quality to be more unique in order to reach the efforts of airlines to build high levels of customer service appears to have been generally noticed by passengers, when they choose to buy the airline's digital electronic ticket or paper air ticket to use its flying service.

Hence, improvement their digital e-ticket purchase experience and communications factor, for example, if any passengers can enter the airline's air ticket purchase website to buy electronic ticket to pre-book seats in the short time rapidly as well as there are enough seats number to supply to them to pre-book. So, they do not need to worry about without any seats to supply to them to catch the airline's flight to fly to anywhere in any time available conveniently. So, it seems that there is plenty of space for airlines to grow and improve their digital experience and communication method to let any passengers to feel, if the airline hopes to let its passengers to feel that it has unique service to compare others airlines.

The aviation industry plays a major role in the aspect of work and leisure to passengers around the global. So, nowadays passengers' demands to any airlines' service quality had been raised. Hence, any airline service industry messengers are under pressure to prove their services are customers oriented service improvement of performance that guarantees competitive advantages to the global travelling marketplace. So, it also implies that any airlines' services performance will be influenced to cause many passengers feel more poor and let passengers dissatisfy the airline's service performance. The, the airline will possible lose many passengers, due to passengers have many airlines choices, they can find any airlines to replace which any one airline to buy air ticket from internet at home immediately.

However, airlines' comfortable seats arrangement service provision feeling factor is still important in preferable to compare other factors, because passengers must need to sit any seats in any air planes. So, whether the air plane can provide new comfortable seats to let passengers to feel this factor is still the most important factor to influence any passengers to choose to the airline's air plane to catch. For example, service comfortability is how passengers observed the quality of service offered them by the airline's cleanliness, quiet zone, shops, restaurants and business pavilion in functioning like staffs, information desk, and in flight announcement are included as tangible features by the passengers (Geraldine et a.,2013). All of these factors are needed often to measure whether their service performances are satisfactory to themselves passengers service needs.

Moreover, the other factors may include service affordability , it can be regarded as given passenger the opportunity to select from inclusive air ticket prices made available to the different group of passengers by the airlines, as a gesture of goodwill , to establish and reinforce customer loyalty and repeat purchases essential for the airline continuity as well as service reliability. it is the probability that airline will carry out its expected function satisfactory as stated in the flight schedule. Hence, there is a strong link between different airlines' service quality variables, airline image and repeat patronage from the passengers.

Service quality is a measure of how well the service level delivered matches passengers expectations to measure service quality based on input from focus groups. It consists of five factors (tangibles, reliability, responsiveness, assurance and empathy). All of these factors will be identifies that how the airline service quality can be satisfactory to its passengers ' psychological and emotion enjoyable service needs.

Any one of these any five service factors will be important to influence the airline's passengers service feeling level to the airline. It means that the passenger will have more chance to choose the airline's service again (repeating purchase its air ticket). Hence, any airlines can not neglect any one of service feeling to its passengers. It needs often to enquire questionnaires to evaluate whether its these five aspects of service quality , if it discovered any of these five aspects of service level is poor, e.g. 5 scale is the best service performance level, then it can attempt to find its error whether which aspects, it needs to very need to reach the 5 scale , the best service performance level when many passengers feel, e.g. enquiring 100 passengers who give 5 scale to reliability service aspect, before reliability service aspect has less than 50% passengers from 100 passengers who feel the airlines concerns this reliable service level aspect questions to be the best. It is one kind of measurement service quality method to any airlines.

Other service performance evaluation factor is satisfaction in the job to every airline front service or ground service staffs to the airline. Job satisfaction describes how content an employee is with his or her job. It is how the employee responses to a job. It can be considered as a part of life satisfaction to one organization, when the employee is working in the organization. Hence, if one airline front service as ground service staff who can feel more job satisfaction to compare his/her prior airline employer. Then, he/she won't be easy to change his/her present airline employer.

However, some factors can influence job satisfaction are pay and benefit, fair performance appraisal, career and promotional opportunities, proper reward and recognition, work-family life balance, the job itself, proper working conditions, leadership chance, autonomy in work.

Job satisfaction can also involve complex number of variables, circumstances, opinions and behavioral tendencies and a variety of work related outcomes, such as commitment, involvement, motivation, satisfaction, attendance. Hence, any airlines also need to concern how let their employees feel job satisfaction issue in order to avoid their leaving turnover number increases, due to job satisfaction and dissatisfaction depend on the expectations what the job supplies for an employee not the nature of the job.

Finally, instead of concerning employees job satisfaction issue, any airlines also need to concern passengers satisfaction issue because it will have any passengers will choose the airline, if it can bring more service satisfaction to let them to feel , then they will become repeat passengers to the airline.

What kinds of factors passengers were looking for and what were the reasons of choosing a specific airline? When one airline often is complained from its passengers. It will have more mistakes to let them to feel or dissatisfy its service. Hence the airlines needs to find which are its mistakes and improve in order to satisfy its passengers' expectations, e.g. finding what are the mistakes to the airlines' serious concern regarding passenger complaints and complaint satisfaction in order to make the airline more likely to meet its passengers' expectation in case of a problem. Hence, any airlines need to concern how to improve its employees' satisfactory service as well as its passengers' satisfactory service both issues as well as how to measure their service quality whether is enough to achieve general service acceptable performance to its passengers.

Artificial Intelligent In Road Transportation Strategy

- How artificial intelligent vehicle may interact intelligent transportation tools

Can artificial intelligence (AI) and machine learning (ML) be used in the search for new " consumption" behavioral type variables that affect consumer individual or transportation service organization individual different transportation tools choices, such as road or sea or sky transportation tools? Can artificial intelligent vehicle may interact intelligent transportation tools market development?

Consumers usually have bargaining and on risk choice when they are already shopping, such as who need to accept to use any (AI) new technological products to replace human traditional behaviors, such as intelligent non-manual driving transportation market, e.g. cars are needed to be driven by human drivers on road, but it has bargaining and on risky choice, when non-manual (AI) vehicle buyers who need to depend on non-manual artificial intelligent (ML) system assists them to drive their cars on the roads.

So, any non-manual driving auto car buyers must need to believe (AI) non-manual driving vehicles (ML) systems can make accurate driving judgement to reduce or avoid any traffic accident occurrences more than human drivers' driving judgement when the (ML) systems are driving their cars on the roads. Then the intelligent vehicle manufacturers will have possible to sell their non-manual driving vehicles success.

This is the first reason or idea influences consumer individual choice to buy any kinds of (AI) non-manual driving vehicles, when consumers believe (ML) systems are more safe and make more accurate judgement to compare human or computer systems, when they are sitting in one non-manual auto driving vehicle on the road.

The another second reason or idea is that some common limits on driving consumer prediction might be understood as the kinds of errors made by poor implementation of machine learning.

Supposing driving consumers believe (AI) machine learning ability is worse to compare to human learning ability. It will also influence driving consumers do not accept to use any (AI) non-manual auto driving vehicles to replace every driver is essential on driving by himself/herself on the road. The third idea or reason is that it is important to influence driving customers believe how (AI) non-manual auto driving technology is used in them can both overcome and exploit human driving skill and safe limits and raise more auto driving safe judgement to compare human driving safe judgement.

However, how to predict any kinds of (AI) non-manual driving vehicles future consumption effort, due to different kinds of (AI) non-manual driving transportation vehicles which have different unique functions and designs to be used by different kinds of road transportation or driving demand of consumers. For example, lorry drivers need non-manual intelligent system can help them to drive fast, but safe to assist them to transport cargo to arrive destinations from their factories or offices. Otherwise, private car driver expects whose (AI) non-manual driving

vehicle can auto drive to send to whom to arrive destination in safe way and non-too fast and non-too slow speed in order to avoid accident occurrences.
So, a different road intelligent consumer demand is to define whose individual driving behavior and driving habit and driving attitude and driving judgement and driving speed demand to decide how to design whose intelligent vehicle to satisfy those driving demand more generally, as simply being open-minded about what variables are likely to influence every consumer economic choice, when who decide either to buy any kinds of (AI) products or not to buy any kinds of (AI) products to replace the different demand of consumers their different (AI) useful demand.

Hence, for these three (AI) products group of stakeholders, such as home (AI) consumer group, firm (AI) consumer group and government (AI) consumer group . These consumer groups may consider whether different kinds of (AI) products can give what is special beneficial interest to them to use. These variables can be measurable properties of choices to influence them to choose to buy any (AI) kinds of (AI) products to use, e.g. psychophysiological, biological, social influences, consumer's wealth, moods and personality, (AI) product price etc. variable factors which will influence them to decide to attempt to buy any kinds of (AI) products to use.
If behavioral economics is as open-mindedness about what variables might predict. Then , (AI) machine learning system is a way to do behavioral economics because it can make use of a wide set of variables and select- which ones predict.

In behavioral economic view point, when general consumer overall demand to the product is much than the other similar (AI) non auto driving vehicle products, such as any kinds of (AI) non-manual auto driving vehicles and any kinds of manual driving vehicles case, then any kinds of (AI) non-manual auto driving vehicles will be more attractive to cause many manual driving vehicle buyers choose to buy (AI) non-manual auto driving vehicles. Hence, it seems if any kinds of (AI) non-manual auto driving vehicle products can make more attractive variable efforts to influence overall driving consumers to feel that they have more needs to drive non-manual auto vehicles to compare more than driving manual driving vehicle.
What is the main variable effort to intelligent vehicles to attract driving consumers to choose to accept to drive them ? However, I believe that (AI) machine learning system is a main factor to raise overall driving consumers‘ acceptances to drive it to replace manual driving vehicle. If it can persuade or prove (AI) machine learning system ability and judgement effort is more accurate than human or computer learning effort or judgement effort, then it is possible that any kinds of (AI) non-manual driving vehicle products will be accepted to drive on the road in popular.

Machine learning system is able to find prediction value in details of how the bargaining occurs. This discovery is the beginning of the next step for driving consumer individual driving behaviors or driving habits. It raises questions that include: What variables predict to influence driving consumers to change whose driving habits or driving attitudes? How can driving consumer individual emotion, face-to-face talking with whose friends when they are sitting in the non-manual driving vehicle to influence whom driving habit or driving attitude to be changed ? Do driving consumers consciously understand why those habit driving attitudes variables are important when they are sitting in one intelligent vehicle? Can (AI) driving machine learning methods capture the effects of motivated cognition to influence driving consumers decide to buy any kinds of (AI) non-manual auto vehicle products more attractively. So, it seems (AI) driving machine learning method is a main variable factor to influence driving consumers to feel who have more confidence to drive them more than any other kinds of similar manual driving vehicles on the road.

Consequently, (AI) driving machine learning system will be one important psychological method to influence driving consumers to choose to buy (AI) auto driving vehicle products to replace manual driving vehicles. The reason is because human and driving machine learning system both which will have limited variable factors to influence general different countries (AI) driving consumers' need desire to be raised.

- Why can (AI) driving machine learning system main factor influence driving consumer individual desires ?

Driving consumer expectations are hard to measure or predict driving attitudes and driving behaviors in (AI) non-manual driving vehicles market. Artificial intelligence is another kind of computer science development to apply intelligent vehicle market. Why do driving consumers feel need to buy any kinds of (AI) auto driving vehicles to drive to replace manual driving vehicles on the roads? What are (AI) auto driving features different to manual driving features?
(AI) is the recreation of cognitive functions in computers; it enables machines to perform tasks like humans and perhaps even better than human. In the real world, scientists develop the technological singularity, in which a superintelligence emerges with unfold human consequences.
Professionals in many industries are intensely interested in the specifics of what (AI) can do today, and how can it helps. They are considering the impact of applied (AI), in which computers are used to address a particular problem, extracting and utilizing patterns found in large volumes of data. Of all (AI)'s subfields, machine learning is attracting the most attention. I shall explain why (AI) machine learning system is the main factor to lead consumers feel need to buy any (AI) products to use. Such as below:

For smartphone, fraud detection to medical diagnosis etc. applied (AI) technological products examples. (AI) machine learning systems can help any one of these products to do any exceed general computer learning systems which (AI) learning systems can do any skills to supply (AI) users to use to compare computer learning systems can not do any skills to supply compute users to use. It seems that (AI) machine learning system is the unique

feature to attract consumer consideration in technological product market.
An term for different types of learning, and can be accomplished using different techniques. This has led to a perception that all marketing teams should have (AI) to bring a unified personalized customer experience, when consumers choose to buy any (AI) products to feel what are the different or unique characteristics to compare general computer products. Such as (AI) product has this unique machine learning characteristics, we can predict (AI) and machine learning is connected to influence consumers to feel needs.

Furthermore, over the same time period, and in contrast to predictions for roles in many industries. (AI) won't take the place of marketers and merchandisers themselves although it is already a new value to analytical and strategic marketing skills to persuade consumers to buy any (AI) products. It means different kinds of (AI) products will have different machine learning effort and unique characteristics to attract consumers to choose to buy them to use. Such as, when intelligent vehicles need have unique road driving or sea transportation or flying machine learning system when they are applied on these three kinds of transportation tool aspects. They need have good response safety driving and immediate response learning systems to avoid any boats or air planes or vehicles to crash to them to reduce accident occurrences immediately on any one of either road or sky or sea journey environment.

What is the reason why (AI) driving machine learning system can influence good at making sense to driving consumer desire? Only humans (drivers) , preferably experienced, well informed humans can understand their driving customer needs and decide how to design or reengineer any (AI) intelligent vehicle product functions. (AI) intelligent vehicle can give these professionals the means to do this better to compare manual driving immediate response control function when any vehicles are driving or they will stop immediately to close / near to them in order to reduce crash occurrence on the road, and then maximize relevance through real-time customization of the non-manual auto vehicle driving user experience.

For example, as ever, senior decision makers need to be informed, decisive and results-oriented or risk losing out. Harvard Business Review indicated : Over the next decade, (AI) won't replace managers, but managers who use (AI) will replace those who don't. Such as intelligent vehicle won't replace drivers, but drivers who use intelligent vehicles will replace those who can not control how to drive their vehicles in the most safe way. So, (AI) driving machine learning system will have possible to do any drivers' (human's) driving judgement, driving analytical mind and driving effort to be more accurate than manual driving skills. Such as how to control to drive the intelligent vehicle in the most safe way. It is general manual driving skill can not achieve to drive in the safe way.

For another (AI) digital commerce example, (AI) and machine learning are the most exciting developments in marketing and merchandising to be applied to digital commerce, such as making better decisions through trend and cluster analysis, deploying product and content in mutually reinforcing combinations, increasing customer engagement and satisfaction in real time.

Hence, the key attraction in digital commerce circles is that machine learning is designed to be self-optimizing. Optimizing for revenue example will surface are increasingly profitably selection of products (within the brand parameters selected).

When to apply (AI) capabilities and what value (AI) is delivering for customer and company like. Unlike any technology before it, (AI) is analytical and predictive capabilities offers the prospect for each and every individual. It can maximize real time and engagement. Effective tailored (AI) technology, such as digital experience cloud technology is available now. And once integrated, (AI) starts learning and delivering incremental value from day one. So (AI) could transform the digital experience to any business organizations.

Hence, (AI) driving machine learning system can be applied to road driving skill aspect. When intelligent vehicles are invented to own the most safe driving judgement skill and they can know when either they may auto drive fast speed, when they are feeling to know when there are not many vehicles are moving close/near to them or when they need auto drive slow speed, when they are feeling to know when there are many vehicles are moving close/near to them. Then driving consumers will have more confidence to choose to buy any kinds of intelligent vehicles to replace manual driving vehicles to drive on the roads.

- Non-manual driving transportation tool market development

If Non-manual driving vehicle manufacturers expect their (AI) automatic vehicles can attract drivers to buy. I feel them to need to consider how (AI) driving machine learning system can achieve these requirements in order to satisfy manual driving vehicle drivers' requirement to change their traditional driving habit to choose non-manual driving needs. It means (AI) driving machine learning systems can help them to drive vehicles to replace manual driving vehicles on the road. This is the main factor to influence car buyers choose to buy intelligence driving vehicles replace to manual driving vehicles. I believe (AI) non-manual driving vehicle machine learning systems, need to be designed as below:

(1) Improving driving safety by preventing accidents from happening.
Every year, drivers are facing a large number of casualties, due to traffic accidents. The amount of killed and injured road traffic related accidents is increasing every year. The real cost of an accident can go well beyond the limits of immediate material destruction, and is impossible to evaluate.
Hence, researchers and car manufacturers are looking for solutions in order to reduce the amount of accidents. They already developed a considerable set of technologies in order to decrease the amount of casualties. Most of them (like airbags, seat-belts, anti-lock systems, shock absorbing car bodies) are efficient in decreasing the impact of an accident, and in protecting the passengers of the cars. The technologies already saved a lot of lives, but they are rarely able to avoid accidents because they do not anticipate them. Moreover, if they are protecting in many

cases, the passengers of the car, they do not prevent most traffic participants, like pedestrians on bicyclists from getting injured. it causes (AI) non-manual automatic car manufacturers need to consider how to design machine learning safety system is to prevent accident from happening instead of just reducing their impact.
This can only be possible using intelligent systems that can observe the driving environment, reason and decide if there is a danger, determine how to avoid it and act if necessary

(2) Reducing energy consumption by optimizing the driving.
Nowadays, global air pollution is serious. (AI) non-manual driving car manufacturers need to concern how to design (AI) machine learning system can reduce degree of air pollution to be the most minimum level to compare to traditional manual driving vehicles.

The reduction of energy consumption if certainly one of the main challenges. Transportation is one of the major factors in fossil energy consumption, and it is also responsible for a large amount of CO2 pollution. It is difficult to ask individuals to voluntarily limit the use of their vehicle of they do not have a strong incentive to do so. Specially in regions where vehicles are needed to drive to go to work every day. It stands to reason that if it is difficult to decrease the amount of vehicles, part of the solution is to make them more energy efficient.

Hence, non-manual driving car manufacturers need to design how to improve engines, which are more optimized and need less fuel to operate, and hybrid and electric cars have been developed and are continuously being improved. But we can go beyond these solutions that do not take into account the environment in which a vehicle is driving. A growing number of scientific contributions presented intelligent systems used in order to improve energy efficiency and reduce fuel consumption, based on the optimization of the way (AI) non-manual driving (AI) vehicles are performing. Such as recharge batteries and electric engine will be predicted the popular fuel in order to limit fuel consumption to future (AI) non-manual driving vehicles. They can reduce air pollution, consume less fuel for (AI) non-manual driving vehicles.

(3) Improving comfort by anticipating (AI) non- manual driving vehicle drivers.
Finally, another application for intelligent vehicle is the improvement of driving comfort. Car industry is very competitive market. Many potentials (AI) intelligent vehicle customers need to enjoy to sit more comfortable intelligent vehicles, who will be attracted by (AI) comfortable systems improving when driving, so part of the research in intelligent systems from cars focuses on how to improve the driving experience, i.e. make it easier and more enjoyable, more comfortable to compare to traditional manual driving vehicles.

As an example, lane keeping assistant systems are technologies that actively keep the vehicle in the lane in highways of the driven drifts out of it. Automatic speed regulation keeps the car at a certain speed without requiring to touch the gas pedal. This can be really interesting for, e.g. (AI) non-manual driving truck drivers that spend a lot of time on highways. But these technologies have a limitation in the case of automatic speed regulation, this technology can not copy of a vehicle ahead drives slower than the desired speed, or if another vehicle cuts into the lane.

This case requires the driver to have a constant focus on the road. In order to achieve more comfort, it is better of the system can adapt to changes in its dynamic environment: let the (AI) intelligent vehicle adapt to the speed of the man-manual vehicle, or autonomously change lane when requires. Again, this requires knowledge about the environment, detection capabilities, reasoning and action planning. Intelligent systems can be used in order to create more attractive and more comfortable and more safe, less energy consumption and less fuel expenditure by intelligent vehicles.

HOW DESIGNING UNDERGROUND MASS TRANSIT RAILWAY TO BRING PASSENGERS

- Designing transportation system advantages

Many commercial users depend on road transport facilities, with movement of products and services from place to place on the roads, aspect of global and urban economic survival. Hence, developments of various transportation modes have become important to physical and economic developments. For example, urban locations with such relative advantages are found where different transport routes with high degree of connectivity, within the intra and inter urban road networks. On similarly, commercial activities like banking, retail/wholesale businesses and professional services can take advantage of nearness to concentration of activities attracted consumers service providers. This partly caused increase in demand for commercial space and its effects on commercial property values along commercial roads can be rose. However, some countries' roads need to provide pedestrian movements more than the businesses activities, e.g. shorten the time of lorries parking on the road to let pedestrian movements on the narrow road. If the country government did not consider the roads need to let more pedestrian movements or shorten the time of lorries parking on the road. It will cause traffic jam or traffic density of the individual roads. Hence, governments need to concern the locations of commercial property buildings and the relationship between the explanatory variables of the design road networks.

What are construction of roads design networks benefits? In fact, construction of roads increased substantially with the opening up of residential environments that also is getting much benefits from increasing demand for spaces in commercial properties. Many private companies, retail stores, commercial banks aggregate in the main roads of cities, which get advantage of opportunities afforded by locations near central of cities to attract many pedestrians concerning their businesses existence. This led to high concentration of vehicular and pedestrian movements. Specially along the access main roads in the central of cities. The main roads exhibits linkages to form networks of minor routes along which commercial properties locate. If commercial users are displaced residential users, causing sites to be at the highest and best uses with increases in the values of commercial properties. However, it seems road network development is affected by the compact nature of various routes that sometimes causes volume of traffic jam. Thus, demand for transport can't be treated solely as a derived demand road. Improved main and minor roads access an city or rural areas is a necessary (but not sufficient). Precondition for increased productivity, the UK Standing Advisory committee On Trunk Road Assessment (SACTRA, 1999) noted "various ways in which transport can affect economic growth, for example benefits include through reorganization and rationalization of production, distribution and land use: reducing labor costs by expanding catchment areas etc."

What is land use and road transport design system relationship? Land use refers to the whole range of human activity and of the built environment, and to some aspects of the natural environment. This is a way relationship between land use and road transport. Governments need to design how to use land and how to design road transportation systems. e.g. where are built the main roads and/or where are built the minor roads are the most suitable locations in the cities or rural areas ? If the main roads is located in the not suitable locations at the centers of the cities or rural, it will case the increasing traffic volumes and levels of congestion, including air pollution, noise, ground water pollution from run-off , loss of soil functions and loss of bio-diversity to natural environment. By influencing the spatial structure of locations in the urban environment, so land use planning can help to mitigate any negative effects resulting from land use changes.

Modelling and land use transportation interactions has become an important aspect of road design transport planning. On the one side, for example, design roads in urban centers, it can increase land use and it can also reduce employees or students catching buses or driving cars' time spending to go to workplaces or schools users. Hence, the land use and roads designing transportation can give benefits to residents and employment people to reduce time to wait buses or taxies etc. public transportations to go to workplaces or schools or shopping centers etc. anywhere. It seems to assist bus companies or taxi drivers to earn more income, On the other side, designing urban transport systems is also important . Increased densities mean more destinations become within convenient walking and cycling distances and consequently the use of these modes tends to be higher. Also in dese cities public transport systems are able to offer higher levels of service and operate more economically, when the provision of sufficient road space to meet potential demand becomes impractical. It aims to reduce the danger of driving or walking in urban areas. The transport modes (that is walking, cycling, public transport) and the extent of car dependence is less, due to driving users dependency is less on rural roads. Hence, building main roads can concentrate on designing convenience to pedestrian walking to close to their houses on the streets. However, poor transport design and land use can cause to spend too expenditure not only transport costs on governments and transport users both and also the costs of providing other services. These include the usual utilities and also education and health services as well as negative externalities , such as greenhouse gas emissions. Most such studies concluded that there are significant financial and economics cost advantage of inner city redevelopment compared with fringe development.

However, such policies won't necessarily be successfully, in particular because of the two ways road problem, they may result in additional private investments and employment opportunities flowing into the region, buy may equally result in population and employment opportunities flowing out of the target region because of the improved access to other centers. Hence governments need to analyze how to arrange the land use to assist the property developers to choose where are the suitable locations to build offices or factories or shopping centers or houses at capital or urban cities to adapt to whose the growth of living population. For example, to judge where the land use whether where main roads or junior roads are built where are the suitable locations to satisfy the lorry drivers to park their lorries are the safe locations ; to design the minor roads to let the pedestrians to feel no danger to walk on the streets when the cars are driven to near to the streets on the minor roads. Thus, the factor of choosing where the land use to design the main or minor roads areas, sizes and lengths and of the minor or major roads can influence the drivers and pedestrians feel safe or dangerous when who are driving whose cars on the roads or who are walking on the streets to arrive the offices, schools, cinemas, church, houses etc. destination.

Designing road transportation networks how to assist economic growth ? I feel it is not all transport investments will be equally effective in enhancing economic growth. Designing road transport investment is a necessary, but on its own not sufficient requirement to earn significant economic growth at either a national or regional level. There are conditions under three categories: economic conditions, investment conditions and political conditions. In fact, although in some circumstances, transport investment may be a necessary condition for enhancing economic growth, it is rarely on its own a sufficient condition. Other factors including the broader policy environment, need to be present if the investment is going to be successful in addressing regional economic objectives. My some suggestions the following key aspects as being most relevant including:

a. Scale economies for example, where these dominate, lower transportation costs through improved accessibility may encourage increased concentration of firms in core regions, until the point that diseconomies set in.

b. Size of the local market.

c. Local land and labor conditions.

d. The nature and scale of transport improvements.

e. The nature of backward and forward linkages
in the country 's local economy.

In any countries, road transportation improvements don't guarantee increased economic development. To increase economic development, an improvement needs to assist any lorry drivers to drive in short trips to reduce transportation costs and shorten time driving on the road or to make transportation more reliable, e.g. reducing the numbers of traffic jams on any roads. A proper economic climate must also exist as well as other support services. With these factors to influence transportation improvements can become catalysts for economic expansion. However, road transportation improvement that intends to induce job creation, when employers need many lorry drivers to help them to transport products and to move products on the roads often. So, the employers need to employ many transportation workers and lorry drivers to help who to transport their products to send to clients, due to the transportation time is shorten and work efficiency is rasied, so the transportation times are also increasing every day when the road transportation roles are improved. On the other side, improving transportation can raise productivity when many customers need to buy many products and the lorry drivers may drive whose lorries to transport many products between factory and office or between factory to the client's home or between the shop and the client's on the road in the short time fast.

I recommend one model links in an overall road transportation network includes these four modes.
I. Maximizing use of the existing road highway system.
II. Extending or improving the multi-lane divides system local roads and connectors.
III. Continually improving the entire road highway network in response to business activities demand.
The improvement of modern road transportation successful factors include:
● How to improve the highway network

modernization includes obsolete interchanges and other segments of the road, transport network of new designs to improve the life and service of pedestrian walking streets, rebuilding certain in main or minor roads. To the extent that labor markets operate more efficiently and more jobs are created to raise economic expansion if our governments can improve road transportation system to design to satisfy business users demand when lorry drivers need to move or transport whose products on the streets, but who will not influence pedestrian are walking on the streets. Hence, excellent transportation design network can subsequent plan efforts, it can also rise economic efficiency, community and social effects, it can also encourage transportation users to attempt to drive lorries to transport products a lot of times in one day fast and who can also avoid traffic jams occurrence on the road easily. On the one side, economic development is a concept referring to the material aspects of community welfare. There are numerous factors need of development: growth in income and wealth, equitable distribution of income, decreased infant mortality rates, increased literacy rates. On the other side, economic growth means which is sustainable increase in community income and /or wealth. (wealth is the net of resources that generate income). It seems the link between transportation facilities and economic growth has close relationship. Good transportation facilities support economic growth by lowing the transportation costs of users of the transportation network, such as roads. Direct users benefits are reductions in travel, times and fuel consumption, increased reliability and increased safety in the movement of people and products, users' transportation costs are reduced, resources are used for other purpose.

The relationship between transport and economic development occur in two directions, in the sense that (i) land use and economic development are major drivers' of demand for transport (in terms of quantity , type, location and mode); and (ii) transportation investments and other initiatives (such as regulations, pricing) can influence levels, patterns and locations of economic development. The principal role of road transportation is to provide access between spatially separated locations for the business and household sectors, for both commodity (lands transportation) and person movements. For the business sector, this involves connections businesses and their input sources between business factories and other business shops and between business and their markets. For the households sector, it provides people with access to workplaces and education facilities, shops and social recreation, community and medical facilities etc. on the roads. I feel different countries' road transportation system can be self funded in the sense that the majority of the costs of transportation system investment operation and maintenance are either paid directly by users (for example, through car operating costs) are funded initially by governments and recovered from transport users (for example, through petrol duties and road user charges). Governments' road transportation system and their use also give rise to some external costs(externalities). These include global environmental impacts (greenhouse gas emissions) and local environmental and health impacts (for example, noise partial pollution and road accident costs). The direct effects of transportation investments are to reduce road transportation time and costs through reducing travel time, decreasing the operating costs of transportation and enhancing access to destinations within the road network. A good road transportation network also needs to reduce any economic disbenefits, for example where projects reduce congestion or the risk of injury. These incremental benefits of transportation investments may be measured through commercial cost benefit analysis. Other indirect consequences of road transportation network should also be considered when evaluating effects on productivity and the spatial pattern of economic development. Good road transportation design network benefits can include lower costs and enhanced accessibility, due to better transportation links and services expand markets for individual transportation using business and improved access to input.

The economic contribution of road transportation policy can be assessed from various perspectives. These include:

- Effects on aggregate economic welfare (e.g. the sum of consumer and which is the times of cost benefit analysis, as linking to transportation productivity effect.
- Micro economic, for example, enterprise or household level productivity effects.
- Macro economics, for example, contributions to GDP investment or employment and the spatial patterns of economic activity.

One key characteristics of road transportation is split between infrastructure and operations. Infrastructure refers to the right of way on which vehicles operate, which may include ancillary facilities to ensure efficient and effective operations (for example, traffic signals, railway stations). In developed countries, are in most transportation is operated by the private cars, road trucks, the majority of bus and coach services. In long term , overall purpose, to ensure transportation system helps to develop that maximizes the economic and social benefits and minimizes harm. Hence, governments need to concern who are their main target users to use every road. Such as the road is used to near to park and leisure, or local and national economic conditions, keep clean natural environment etc.

facilities to provide different benefits to different target users to enjoy to use. It seems that good transportation networks designing can influence economic activities, shopping convenience or business convenience etc. activities to cause whether the country's economic behavior to achieve close relationship successfully. Possible relationship between road networks, location attribute, demand and supply and accessibility and commercial property values of these factors which will influence different countries' concerning to choose where to build main roads and sub minor roads in different cities and rural locations. However, I shall suppose hypotheses how governments to find the most suitable places to build main roads and sub minor roads to whose cities and rural. There is no significant relationship between commercial property values and individual contributions of explanatory variables to variability in commercial property values in whose countries.

In conclusion, I suggest methods how to design suitable transportation networks to governments to build, such as it is essential to establish a technique that may be useful for determining relative accessibility of locations in the network of main roads and sub minor roads. Even, when relative advantages are determined, there is need to develop models that will be useful for predicting commercial properly values. The model may become tool for professional estate surveyors and values to change their practice of using intuition to determine relative access of locations in a road network. Similarly, there is the need to predict the supply of, demand for, and fair market values of commercial properties by developers. Hence if the cities or rural locations can attract many businesses to build commercial properties, governments can build the main roads in the locations. Otherwise, if the cities or rural locations can not attract many businesses to build commercial properties, governments can build the sub minor roads in these locations. Hence, the main roads must have high transportation valuation to let big lorries to drive and park in these main roads easily and conveniently. It seems capital cities may not influence to build the main road factors. Natural environment, commercial properties values, the lands areas size and shape and pedestrian walking numbers on the streets and lorries available numbers on the areas will be other factors to influence where to build main roads in any cities or rural in the country.

In road concept, the route network consists of primary and secondary roads, known as main roads and minor roads respectively. Main roads are usually moderate or high capacity roads that are below highway level of service, carrying large volumes of traffic between areas in urban centers and designed for traffic between neighbors. They have intersections with collector and local streets and commercial areas, such as shopping centers, petrol stations and other businesses are located along such roads. In additions, main roads link up to expressways and freeways with inter-changes in cities or rural. Road network constitutes an important element in urban development , due to urban areas have many farms, gardens, forests , so roads and building needed to provide accessibility required by different land uses and the proper functioning of such urban areas depends an efficient transport network existence. In computing des, the network indicator are used to partition road network into different parts in reasonable way. The results in number of connection to describe density differences in road networks. The parameter records how many roads connect to each road in a network. For two roads with the same length, the ones in the dense area will connect to more roads than that in a sparse area and the connection differences will indicate the density differences to some extent, so road density can also be calculated as the total length of all known roads divided by the total land area in a road divided by the total land area in a road network. Hence, governments need to consider road length to decide how to build main or minor roads to design its transportation systems for businesses activities , such as driving lorries and parking lorries and products are been moving on the streets from roads easily and conveniently. As Wikipedia Contributors (2008) indicate that ''transport networks are spatial structures designed to channel flows from the points of demand to points of supply and to link the points together in a transportation system. They are useful for transport network analysis to determine the flow of people, products, services and vehicles.'' Hence, governments need to research whether where the shopping centers, cinemas, houses, hospitals, schools, offices, factories etc. are located, then, which need to follow these location datas to predict the cars, lorries, taxies, buses etc. of the demand numbers of transportation users to design the lengths, width and distances and the construction of main and minor roads locations and their supply numbers in different capital cities or country roads. It aims to reduce traffic jams and shorten time and air pollution as well as increasing the available spaces to let the lorry drivers to move their logistc on the road easily and reducing the accidents occurrence when the pedestrians are walking on the streets. If the vehicles can be moved on the roads easily. It will also increase time efficiency and productivity to any businessmen. Hence, how to design of the main roads and/or minor roads in any capital or country cities. It will influence any country's economic growth long time in the future.

- Underground train transportation needs to know passenger behaviour reasons

Understanding individual passenger behaviour is essential for the design MTR transportation, because who can choose to catch bus, taxi, tram, train ferry etc. different kinds of public transportation tools. Individual traveler who decides to catch which kinds of public transportation tools, it depends on whether the public transportation tool can provide real time travel information, liking link travel time schedule. So, MTR underground train needs to understand where it has terminal to give convenience to the local living areas of time travelers to choose to catch MTR easily. Although, MTR ticket fare is one factor to influence any passengers choice. But, those other factors can also influence them to choice. e.g. MTR any terminal location of convenience, short time travelling, none crowding in busy (peak) time, MTR platform waiting arrival time, none sudden MTR engineering machines broken accident events occurrence frequently etc. different factors, any one of these factors which can influence passengers who choose to catch MTR or other kinds of transportation tools.

Why route choice can influence passenger behavioural choice ? Usually, the busy time passengers will regard the route choice as a coordination problem to influence them to choose to catch which kinds of transportation tools. The route choice is as an opportunity costs to influence any busy time passengers to decide to choose to catch which kind of transportation tool which is the best right choice in the right time among of them. In the short time, for example, it seems any busy time passengers will choose to catch bus to substitute MTR underground train transportation tool, due to who feels the bus can arrive any destinations to compare other kinds of transportation tools in the most short time. However even if the MTR can either charge cheaper ticket fare to sell full day or charge discount ticket fare to sell in the busy (peak) time to compare to bus fare. It is possible that the busy time passengers will still choose to catch bus, if between the bus terminal and the another bus terminal that distance is the shorter time route to spend time to arrive destination to compare between the MTR terminal to the another MTR terminal arrival time . Also, although the busy time passengers will feel to enounter traffic jam to influence sitting or waiting bus time to be longer time in possible and who also feel MTR can avoid traffic jam problem. However, usually any busy (peak) time passengers will feel the chance of traffic jam occurrence will be less. So, the short bus route choice is more potential factor to influence the busy (peak) time passengers still to choose bus to catch.

However, if anyone wants to investigate results of day-to-day route choice which can be transferred to more realistic environment. It is necessary to explore individual behaviour in an interactive experimental set up to ensure busy (peak) time passenger transportation behavioural choice. For example, a passenger has a choice between a main road (M) and a side road (S) for travelling from (A) to (B). (M) is faster if (M) and (S) are chose by the same number of passengers. So, this method can be researched whether MTR terminal station is located at the main road (M) or the side road (S) where is more suitable to accept to passengers generally.

Why trip time reliability and crowding factors can influence MTR passenger choice? Other problem is MTR busy (peak) time's crowding in public transportation occurrence of MTR underground train transportation tool is becoming a growth to concern as MTR demand growth at a busy (peak) time. To capture the MTR passengers benefits with reduced crowding from improved MTR public transport service and image. It is necessary a identify the relevant dimensions of crowding that are meaningful measures of what crowding means to MTR passengers. Two main influences on MTR model choice that are growing in relevance are trip time reliability and crowding. It represents a benefit-cost framework. In fact, MTR passengers can be willing to pay more expensive ticket fare, it MTR can avoid crowding and short and the accurate arrival trip time between terminals is reliable to occur. How to measure of MTR crowding, e.g. weighting the gap between the busy time, the standard (i.e. objective) and the perceived (i.e. subjective) metrics. We are not in a position to definitely map the two dimensions, which is a crucial requirement for translating objective improvements into equivalent subjective gains that then can be applied, willingness to pay estimates MTR ticket fares to obtain the additional MTR passenger benefits of MTR public transportation investment to any terminal stations. Because MTR crowding has a negative impact on passengers in terms of psychological on emotional distress.

MTR passengers are willing to stand for up to 20 minutes of the service is fast and reliable. However crowding outweighed these benefits from a MTR passenger's perpective, experienced crowding leads a increased dissatisfaction. e.g. stress and less privacy during who needs to stand up in MTR. Due to there are no enough places to supply to them to stand up in MTR. If the MTR trip time was longer time between the passenger's terminals, who

will feel more dissatisfaction and it will cause who feels whether who ought need to choose to catch other transportation tools to substitute MTR next time. e.g. bus, train, tram, ferry, taxi etc. So, from an operator's perspective, the MTR service frequency or MTR size is significantly influenced by the level of ridership, which sends a signal to respond if the monitored crowding level exceeds the benchmark standard in the busy time. e.g. in the morning time or at the night time, the students or employment people who need to go to schools or offices (working places). The locations of different places between MTR terminals and crowding are regarded as a key service attribute for MTR pubic transportation along with other factors, such as travelling time and reliability, e.g. service quality, none engineering machines are broken to cause MTR stops suddenly.
Given the increasing importance of crowding on both the disutility to existing MTR public transportation users and the influence to it. MTR passenger can choose to use either the MTR public public transportation or other public transportation. It is timely to review the MTR current measures of crowding defined by transportation authorities. MTR operators ought evaluate whether they apporpriately reflect MTR each traveler experiences and perceptions of crowding in busy (peak) time. I suggest that MTR needs to buy other underground trains to supply to the busy (peak) time passengers to let them have enough seats to sit down, so who do not need to stand up in any MTR underground trains when they catch MTR underground trains in busy time. It aims to let who are willingness to pay the estimation of reasonable ticket fares to compare the other kinds of transportation tools in the busy (peak) time.

What is the crowding difference between train and MTR underground train? In fact, crowding won't be happened to brother these transportation tools easily in the busy time and non busy time both. e.g. bus, taxi, train, tram, ferry. Because passengers can not choose to stand up in these transportation tools easily, due to these transportation tools have no enough areas (spaces) to let them to stand up easily . So, the crowding will be avoided to occur in these tranportation tools usually. Otherwise, MTR will have many passengers who can choose to stand up because MTR design of length is very long and it has enough areas (places) to let passengers to choose to stand up, even there have none any seats are provided to let them to sit down. So, MTR passengers will feel more dissatisfaction and crowding easily, especial in any peak (busy) time every day.

Comparing to bus, much more diverse crowding measures are defined in the passenger rail industry. For passenger, different specifications for measuring crowding are found across countries and even within a country. For example, rail crowding measures in the UK, the passengers in excess of capacity is crowding measure that applies to all London and South east operators weekday train services at a London terminus during the morning peak from 0700 to 09: 59 , and those departing during the afternoon peak from 16:00 to 18:59 (office of rail regulation 2011 year). The overall PIXC figure is considered the planned standard class capacity of each train service as well as the actual number of standard class passengers on the service at the critical point. i.e. the location on a trains of standard class passengers that surpass the planned capacity as the difference between the number of actual passengers and the capacity of the train divided by the number of passenger is within the capacity . So, it seems train and MTR underground public transportaton tools had been encountering the crowding problems in peak time, the difference in train passengers need to wait next train or more train arrival is who doesn't plan to enter the train, when who discovers the current train has no seats to provide to them to sit down in whose trip. Otherwise, MTR passengers can choose either to stand up within the large areas (places) if who discovered there are no any seats to provide to them to sit down or who can wait the next MTR arrival in order to who can sit down. It seems MTR transportation tool crowding environment includes in waiting platform and inside of the MTR underground train. Otherwise, train transportation tool crowding environment only includes the waiting platform and the passengers will not have crowding feeling inside of the train, due to none of passengers choose to stand up inside any trains because any train inside has no enough places to let them to stand up.

How MTR can attract many passengers. On the commuter departure time choice of any reference point researching hand, the departure time decisions of communters are of fundamental importance of peak period MTR traffic congestion. However, whether on the demand side, MTR underground train congestion relief measures, such as MTR ticket fare to every terminal station needs to be charged cheaper fare or discount fare in the peak (busy) time every day. To aim to attract many passengers to choose to catch MTR Underground train public transportation tools, substitute to choose other public transportation tools in the peak time.

Over the past decades, there have been very active research efforts in the departure time problem, both in econometric modeling and dynamic user equilibrium fields. Although, these works provide valuable insights into dynamic commuter decision making, they do not identify the commuters' response to gains and losses related to whole actual arrival time to reference points who may have relative. The appliability of the reference point hypothesis of prospect theory to the commuter's departure time decision making to obtain a better understanding of how departure time choice in MTR platform during their waiting underground train arrival time. However, every MTR underground train actual arrival time and deviation variables related to reference points (gains and losses) are the key factors in the departure time choice model. How the MTR underground train of every communter's daily departure time decision can be modelled when the reference point hypothesis of prospect theory. The MTR underground train's schedule delay is defined as the difference between the preferred arrival time (PAT) and the actual arrival time (AT) for a given MTR communter. In a daily MTR commute, a commuter in the indifference band actual arrival time is an essential feature of MTR schedule study. Two reference points are the earliest acceptable arrival time and the work starting time for a given MTR platform waiting passengers. In psychological view point, prospect theory proposes that the displeasure of a loss is perceived or greater than the pleasure of a gain of the same attitude and therefore, the value function is stronger for losses than gains.

To conclude, it seems that if MTR waiting passengers need not spend long time to wait underground train arrival in platform and it can provide seats to let them to sit down in the busy (peak) crowding time. It will make them to feel pleasure, even the MTR ticket fare is not fair and reasonable to charge higher fare to compare other kinds of public transportation tools fares. So the peak waiting time factor can influence the passengers to choose other kind of transportation tools to catch easily. Moreover, MTR's two reference points are the earliest role. Similarly a loss is observed when the MTR platform waiting commuter experiences or actual arrival time which is beyond that the MTR schedule time. Due to that a MTR waiting commuter is as an early side arrival of whose actual arrival time is carlicr than whosc prcfcrrcd arrival time.

● How to let passengers feel impact of undergrouund train transport to their working time efficiency

Any countries must need road, sea and air transport to assist businessmen to transport products in local or overseas. If the country's road , sea or air transport system service quality is poor. It will influence any products transport time, speed, inefficient transport to anywhere.

How to raise the country's transport system in order to improve efficiencies to let any businessmen can deliver their products to anywhere easily,e.g. warehouses, client homes, supermarkets destination in the most short time to avoid delay occurrence to let clients feel unsatisfactory or complaint their perform their delivery services poorly. I shall discuss the factors how to improve any countrues' transport systems to achieve the most efficient way as below:

Any countries' transport systems will create economic value, e.g. demonstrate value for money, economic worth, viable commercial worth, financial affordable worth, achieveable worth. Any countries' transport systems can bring welfare value by economics. It has direct relationship to take the form of measured economic activity, i.e. GDP. The form of measured economic activity can impact on any countries' economic economic geography, locally , regionally and nationally's local GDP impacts. The welfare impacts may include: leisure time savings, e.g. the local people drive cars or catch any public transportation tools to go to any geogrpahical location's shopping centers, big gardens, swimming pools, cinemas etc. places to carry on any kinds of leisure activities.

Environmental impacts may include avoiding noise, air pollution on road transportation aspect , when the main road is only on on focus on the main city,
but the city lacks other roads to let any drivers can choose them to drive, instead of the main road in the city. Then, when many cars are driven on the busy transport
time, e.g. morning working time or night busy time between 6:00 and 9:00 AM, between 6:00 and 9:00 PM. When either many working people need to catch public transport or drive themselves cars to go to offices to work or they need to catch pubic transport tools or drive themselves cars to home. Then, the only one main road problem will need them to stay themselves cars on roads, due to traffic jam or traffic accidence occurrence problem causes when many cars are driven on the road in the busy transport time. It will influence they can not go to offices or homes easily daily, even in the busy transport time, their cars' gas need to be used much to cause air pollution and traffic noise is easily caused easily in the busy transport time on the road. When the city has only one main road for drivers in the busy transport time. So, poor road transport system can bring poor impact on economic welfare benefits arising from proved labour supply from commuting, time savings, including exchequer benefits. Consequently, the county's GDP will be fallen down, due to labour market effects which do not add to welfare

value.

Whether can poor transport system impact indirectly on GDP or not on local, regional , or national economic geography impacts? Does transport lead to greater economic activity i.e. higher GDP? DO they lead to change in economic activity location? Does transport impact the existence of business location and new economic activity opportunities? The measurement on every country's transport how impacts on economic change, facilitating geographic division of labour and specialization. It can be analyzed on these general aspects:

Costs and speed of travel time (Economic value of travel time savings) . Travel time savings to users from improved transport is a key of economic value, but it has only less influence,journey time reliability is more important to business frieght as well as business travellers, network connectivity enhancements as well as business travellers, network connectivity enhancement can help people and goods travel more quickly (i.e. linked to jounrey time and journey time reliability, as well as opening new destinations and new journeys, comfort and quality service provision is relevant to public transport, e.g. detering jounreys at particular times or by certain modes (e.g. overcrowding), impact on productivity at work for commuters, safety and security , due to loss of output from workers, transport accidents occur easily. All of these issues will impact any countries' standard of living to local people (geography) , even GDP income.

Why does the direct and indirect effects of transportation have a positive impact on the economic growth and development of a country? Does it influence acccess to goods, services and employment opportunities in any regions? Underdeveloped countries must need to consider how transport system influences their economic growth. For example, the costs of transportation and production are reduced through timely delivery and enhancing the economies of scale in the production process, when the road is often traffic joam, gas cost, time waste , air pollution cost, noise has many roads, but if one lorry drivers needs drive more than one day to day to deliver goods to another city's warehouse every day. It will bring psychological pressure in terrible, when they need long time to drive on the road. They can not sleep easily because road accident will occur easily when they need to spend long time to drive lorries on the road.

So, how to solve the long driving time on road transport problem will be one issue concerns human life welfare benefit aspect, instead of economic benefit aspect. The transport system welfare worth needs to include human life worth. It is a valuable insight into the causality (ot lack of causality) between transport and economic growth and will serve to compare to any countries' national level and local geographical location level both.

In special, underdeveloped countries' public transport time whether it is long or short factor, it will influence workers their going to offices to work time. If they often need spend long time to catch buses, due to traffic jam,then it will influence their efficiences to be reduced, productive number is influenced to reduce also, because traffic jam causes they often go to offices too lately.It can influence workers' bad emotion to work every day. So, traffic jam will bring negative relationship between low efficiency and bad emotion to the workers, because they need to spend long time to wait, public transportation tools and traffic jam also influence their working emotion. Consequently, service and working performance will be influenced to poor, because long time traffic jam problem causes their bad emotion to work. It is one critical factor in the path of more widely spread economic growth and urbanization for traffic jam problem to underdeveloped countries.

However, transport system can also influence developed countries' economy. How does it influence on environmental impacts aspect from mature stage. Its business activities must raise, dramastic expansion during this period, such as underdeveloped country, US, UK. In order to acheive long term sustainable development , new demands are being placed on transport sector, such as underground mass transit rail transport , ferry, local air frieght transport, train , e.g. Japan, Fance, US high speed prior rail. Because their developed countries , business and entertainment activities needs increase, it influences high time efficient and rapid speed public transportation tools needs are also needed in societies. These new technological public transport tools invention will impact on climate, noise, human health, land use and damage to ozene layer, acidification aspects, instead of economic beneficial aspect.

For long -term sustainable development to be achieved, the various activities within developed and underdeveloped societies must be adapted to what can be tolerated by humans and by the natural environment. Transport is an activity which affects humans and the natural environment for both the development of society as a whole as well as for the mobility for the individual. For Swedish underdeveloped country example, air pollution in Swedish urban areas has beed reduced, but in many places concentrations of certain substances deiving from transport activities are still at unacceptable levels and much more has to be done. Carbon dioxide emissions and noise are examples of environmental problems demanding further efforts. Measures to limit the exploitation of valuable natural and cultural environments to protect biological diviersity are also needed. So, if Swedish still hopes to develop its tourism industry to attract many travellers to choose to travel itself country. It needs to solve environmental problems from different modes of transport are of different dimensions, such as improving its air transport to avoid cause different problems and rail transport differs in turn from road transport.
The transport problem to Swedish may include poor technological communication information to its public and purchasers of transportation and communication services as to the environmental effects of different solutions is significant in creating the demand for environmentally sound public transport service concepts. It is therefore important that such lacking high technological communication and information system is presented in as completem accurate and clear way as a method for non-monetary comparison of the environmental public transport service system aspect.

In real, it's public tranport service system is needed to be improved and upgraded in order to let travellers feel Swedish's any rail, underground train, ferry, bus , taxi etc. different public transport travelling service can provide excellent performance to serve their travelling passengers, when they need to catch any kinds of public transport tools to go to travel. They can feel convenient and comfortable to attract them to visit Swedish to travel again. Then, its tourism industry GDP income will be raised, if Swedish government can innovate any new kinds of purchase ticket equipment to install in and public transport stations to let travelling passengers feel that they do not need to spend long time to queue to buy tickets to catch ferry, train, underground mass transit rail on stations conveniently. Because long time purchase ticket queue waiting will cause travellers feel its public service performance dissatisfaction and they will complain , even they won't choose to catch the kind of public transport, even the travellers won't choose to travel Swedish again, if they feel Swedish is one developed country, but it neglects to take care about travellers' catching public transport travelling service needs.

It is one poor or bad feeing to let travellers choose to Swedish again. Hence, Swedish needs to improve its public transport service performance in order to achieve to raise their comfortable and satisfactory catching public transport tools needs to let travellers to feel. They may include efficient land use for transportation tools, comprising issues concerning natural and cultural environment, natural resources, biological diversity and aesthetics, noise reducing, public transportation energy consumption and time consumption reducing, raising public transport service facilities performance functions and other issues concerning the model. For example, Swedish government can facilitate the public transport price conparison and journey time spending comparison information gathering enquiring machines public transportation selection method of public transportation services to let every travellers can evaluate different modes of public transport when they are staying in ferry, bus, train, underground mass transit rail, taxi stations.

A travelling family can seek its sustainable transport selection system for passenger transport tool. When they touch the enquiry machine, they can compare busm ferry, train, underground train, taxi price and journey spending time from their transportation stations to another destinations. Then, travelling passengers can compare these public transport tools ticket prices, journey spending time immediately when they touch the public transport enquiring machines in stations any time. Then, they can make the most righ choice to decide whether they ought catch which kind of public transport tool to arrive the another journey destination. It is one every attractive high technological enquiry method to help any travelling passegners to choose which kind of public transport tool, it can be the most cheap transport tool at the moment in any public transport stations. So , for developed countries innovative its public transport service performance will need future passengers' journey needs daily. Hence, they can not neglect how to improve public transport service needs to satisfy passengers to feel satisfaction, if Sweden government hopes its tourism industry can raise GDP income in long time.

- How underground train MTR can let passengers to feel catching time reducing

It has close relationship between globalization and global tranport development. How globalisation impacts on the environment via changes taking place in the transport sectors. In fact, it is not clear how the relative price changes that result from openness will affect the environental composition of economic activity. For example, some countries will produce more environmentally intensive goods, others will produce fewer. On the other hand, liberalisation will raise incomes, perhaps increasing the willingness to pay for environmental improvement. These potential income effects increased outweigh the negative scale effects with increased economic activities. When combined with the positive effects with technology transfer, the net effect on local pollutants could be positive . Hence, we need to find methods to solve the problem of raising transport economic activities and serious environmental pollution creating as the same time occurrence.

Globalisation helps to facilitate greater division of labor, and to exploit its comparative advantage more completely. In longer term, globalization also stimilates technology an dlabour transfers, and allows the dynamism that accompanies economic activities to stimulate the development of new transport technologies and short time transport processes that lead to global welfare improvement.

On shipping transport industry aspect, shipping will increase ocean pollution, when international shipping activities are increasing. Trade and shipping encourages energy use in shipping is coupled with the movement of waterborne commerce. The estimates depending on the transport goods number of at-sea or in port days much increase globally every day. The energy demand of international shipping fuel sale number and domestically assigned fuel sales number also increases for global fuel usage. Estimates of ocean going ships now consume about 2% to 3% and perhaps even as much as 4% of world fossil fuels.Hence, when global shipping energy fuel usage number increases, because global shipping trading activities number increases. It will bring the environmental pollution to ocean level increases.

On air transport industry aspect, their travellers‘ catching air plans travelling needs and businesses' goods transport air delivery service needs are increasing from the requirements for high quality , fast and reliable international transport. Moreover, the networks that airline companies operate have changed often to hub-and spoke networks, many new often low -cost companies have entered the air freight market, any long time air journey is needed, e.g. Australia airline expands its one new air journey flies to UK, it needs two days flying time. It means that every flight to UK from Australia , it needs to use more fuel to fly. Then , air pollution will increase also.

On road transport industry aspect, global road transport cost and transit times, traffic jam occurrence chances also increase because when the road building number is increasing globally. So, it will cause traffic jam and long journey time spending , even fuel usage spending number is also increased. Then, accident occurrence chance is raised. Hence, global business or entertainment transport activities number increasing , it will bring much negative impact on environmental pollution, traffic jams number increases, long journey spending time increases, fuel usage number increases. Although , frequent transport activities may bring GDP income.

On transport service industy aspect, but is also brings negative influence to standard of living. It means that when transport fuel demand increases, transport activities number increases, GDP income on relative any transport activities needs industy , e.g. logistic demand needs, when lorry drivers need to drive lorries to deliver goods from one warehouse to another warehouse or supermarket or office etc. different business places on the road driving activities increase. But, it also bring air pollution , traffic noise and traffic jam etc. transport problems to road and natural environment and raises worse standard of living , bad emotion to working people or learning emotion to students , due to frequent traffic jam causes , low efficiency and productivity to workers, even student individual learning time can be reduced if they need to spend long time to wait bus, ferry, rail, underground train to go to schools , due to frequent long time traffic jam occurs on the roads to influence they can not go to schools on time often when they are catching buses to go to schools absolutely in busy transport time.

Thus, although any countries need to consider how to design their transport system, e.g. how to e.g. how to choose the right locations to build roads to let many cars can be driven available easily when the morning and evening (office and school transport busy time, e.g. 6:00 to 9:00 AM morning, 6:00 to 9:00 PM in the evening transport time usually because these two transport periods are usually , there are many students and working people need to catch any public transportation or drive cars tools to go back homes. So, enough roads number and long and not narrow road area must be needed to design in order to let enough cars be driven on the roads in the transport busy times to the countries have many big cities or have high population , such as UK, US, China, India, Hong Kong. They have many people , but drivers and cars numbers both are increasing. So, efficient road design and road number are also needed to increase in order to let drivers can transport goods to deliver, students and working people can catch any public transport tools to arrive any destinations on reads in the short time rapidly in order to avoid to spend long time transportation time and late to arrive any destinations in possible occurrence. So, any sudden traffic jam is not hoped to be caused by easy traffic accidents occurrence any time.

Hence, global efficient road transport system is needed, when global transport activities are increased, because any road logistic transport activities are increasing, they will also influence the students and working people when they also need to catch any public transport tools or drive themselves cars to go to working places or schools on the roads at the same busy transport time between 6:00 to 9:00 AM morning busy transport time and between 6:00 to 9:00 PM evening busy transport time. Because these both times will be have many students, working people , they need either go to offices or schools or go to homes. Hence, if the country had many lorry drivers need to drive their lorries to deliver goods on the roads in the transport busy morning or evening time in the same driving time on the roads. It will increase the risk to cause frequent traffic jam or traffic accident occurrence easily in possible in the country. So, any countries' governments can not neglect how to design roads and choose anywhere are the roads suitable locations to be built as well as anywhere land useful number to build road location choices in order to solve geographical traffic jams occurrence chance.

Hence, globalization of transport activities may bring geographical GDP growth, but it also bring traffic jams and traffic accidents occurrences, hearing impairment due to traffic noise, air pollution, traffic crashed, bad working emotions to workers and bad learning emotions to students, due to spending long transport time when traffic jam or traffic accidence occurs more easily.

However, transportation is an important tool if a country's progress. Rapid economic growth and increasing level of urbanization enhances a person's living standard have, it leads to a greater travel demands. Hence, governments ought not neglect have to design its roads , measure every road's length or width whether it has how many cars need to drive in morning or evening transport busy time for students, working people and delivery goods drivers of public transportation tools or private transportation tools easy driving needs in order to avoid frequent traffic jams or traffic accidents occurrences in possible.

Moreover, any governments also need to solve these issues, if they hope to develop their transport system successfully. These issues include : What mode of transportation to cost-effective in meeting a region's transportation needs to the country? How should a state department of transportation prioritize its highway delivers to maximize economic growth? What is the trade-off between additional growth in urban area and the cost of expanding transportation systems to accommodate greater growth? What effect does the expansion of transportation systems have on the need to invest in other types of transport modes? For example , the transport expansion may include the construction of additional highway segments, rail lines, runways, or additional sea, air, rail or bus terminal capacity using traditional technology; highway may include the additional of lanes to an interstate highway system; the conversion of an existing two-lane road to a four lane limited access highway, replacement or widening of bridges, and the extension of an existing road. Airport examples, include runway lengthening, apron expansion, and additional terminal gates.

On the other hand, enhancement to new transport technologies may bring efficiency of the existing highway system, examples may include intelligent highway systems, congestion pricing, intermodal freight facilities, geographic positioning systems, and instrument landing systems to mention of a few major transport innovations. So, transport policy makers need to understand the effects of these new transport mode innovations on economic development or GDP growth on transport activities growth transportation services and a more efficient use of limited land supplying scarce resources , air quality ,and noise pollution, traffic jams, long spending transport time to students, working people, entertaining people, even deliver goods lorry drivers their every day essential driving activities or catching public transportation tools needs problems. For example, the concept of intelligent highway systems needs increase trend. In simply , vehicles are being linked to each other and to traffic control devices to improve the efficiency of the total highway system. Similar types of innovations in intelligent traffic management are increasing needs for air, sea, and rail systems. The question is that whether intelligent highway systems can attribute of highways on economic development, raising on productivity of reducing highway congestion or improving pavement condition.

In fact, many developed countries' transportation system is mature. The nation has gone beyond the frontier of building, the interstate highway system and connecting most cities (markets). Tweaking the system with additional lanes and the new intelligent highway systems are useful in China, US, UK, because they have many cities. SO, road efficient traffic congestion control is needed when many students, working people, delivery goods transport people need to drive cars or catch cars on every city's roads in the transport busy time between 6:00 to 9:00 AM morning transport busy time as well as between 6:00 to 9:00 PM evening transport busy time.

However, transportation investment must be needed, if the country hoped to have good economic productivity, efficient transport service can bring good effects on the flows goods and people on roads every day when they use the country's transport system. So, any countries need to collect data, they can not be lack of enough transport information in any time that links anywhere locations of any drivers to the locations of the transport system that provide them with services in any time, e.g. every day morning and evening transport busy time, radio can report the real transport time of any roads traffic jam or traffic accident message to let drivers to listen to know whether anywhere roads are occurring traffic accidents or traffic jams or when the road traffic accident or traffic jam is solved to let the drivers can know whether when the roads can be opened to drive again. So, real time road transport message information is needed to report by radio, in order to let any drivers to know whether they ought choose to drive themselves cars on the road when they need to choose anywhere road to drive to the destination if they can know when the road has traffic accident or traffic jam occurs. They won't drive their cars on the road in the moment immediately.

On conclusion, globalization can being frequent transport economic activities. So, road , air, sea, transport service users' transport service needs are also increased. Every country ought not neglect how to innovate their transport service in order to satisfy their transport needs to achieve economic growth, efficient and short transport time spending, productivities increase, reducing air pollution, traffic noise , raisins standard of living on transport influence aspect to satisfy working people, students, entertaining people, delivery goods transport users' efficient road transport time behavioral spending aspect.

Artificial intelligent public transport how influences passenger psychology

How technology influence passenger psychology

Nowadays, robotic invention can be applied to factory manufacture, hotel, restaurant, shopping center, customer service, accounting, law document draft etc. general office tasks aspect, evem hospital surgen patient medical operation health service aspects. If future robotic non -manual driving vehicles can be invented to reach the safe auto driving mature skill stage. Any one driver begins to believe robotic, driving safe level is bette than he/she drives himself/herself car. I assume that if future robotic public transport tool drivers can replace human public transport tool drivers to drive bus, taxi, train, tram, ferry, underground train, tram , even air plane ets. different kinds of public transport tools. How non maual driving public transport tools influence our social change either to improve better ot worse? How non manual driving public transport tools influence passenger psychology, e.g. increasing any kinds of public transport tools passengers safe feeling to choose to catch any kinds of public transport tools to go to anywhere or feeling more dangerous when the passenger himself/herself chooses to sit the non manual driving public transport tool.

In past, traditional public transport tools are driven by human drivers, if one day non manual driving skills are invented to reach the most safe level, when the car owner or passenger is sitting on the non manual driving vehicle or public transport tool, the artificial intelligent driver can help the driver to control the car wheel to avoid to crash any other cars or pedestrians to o to any far places on the roads easily. The public bus does not human driver to drive the bus, artificial intelligent driver won't feel tried, when it drives the bus long time, it does not need to leave the bus to go to toilet, to go to restaurant to eat, to go to rest room for rest, because it is one (AI) machine. So, the (AI) driver won't have negative emotion to feel angry when the bus passenger complaints its service is poor when he feels dissatisfactory to the (AI) driver bus service performance.

However, human bus driver may be complainted for unpolite or rude bus service attitude. It is common human bus driver will encounter any unreasonable passenger complain in general . Hence, when non manual driving technology can be invented to reach the most safe driving skill level, whether (AI) machine driver is the most suitable to replace any public transport tool drivers, such as bus, taxi, train, underground train, ferry, tram, even air plane to drive for future passengers service need.
In fact, any public transport tool drivers may cause traffic transport accidents, due to their careless driving to crash any other vehicles or pedestrians (walling people). Consequently, any passengers may have chance to be killed by public transport tool crashing accident. So, it seems that global public transport tools are dangerous to any passengers, when they are sitting on the bus, taxi, train, tram, underground train road public transport tools, or ferry sea public transport tools, because any human public transport tool drivers will feel tried to drive any one kind of public transport tool long time, for example when the bus driver has no enough nervous to drive the bus, he wants to sleep, due to he often needs to follow night time bus timetable to drive bus long time at night. When he often want to sleep and he is driving the bus, traffic accidents will be caused easily. So, any passenger individual life is dominated by the sleeping bus driver. His bus dirving behavior is not safe to any one bus passenger when the bus passegner chooses to catch this feeling sleeping bus driver's bus to catch.

Otherwise, (AI) non manual driver must not feel tried or need sleep often. It is one automative driving mature, it can drive any kinds of public transport tools all day, because (AI) machine drivers do not need sleep, (AI) none human auto-driving driver can bring this important unique benefit to any kinds of public transport tools to compare human drivers. Instead of (AI) automatic driving tools' non need sleeping advantage, (AI) non-manual control auto-driving tools must not own sad, disappointing feeling , tried feeling, anygry emotion feeling when it needs to contact angry passengers every day. So, I mean that any traffic accident occurrence will reduce, when (AI) drivers often feel happy to drive any kinds of public transport tools. Otherwise, any human public transport drivers will be influenced to feel angry when they are complaint by angry passenger in any driving time easily. So, public transport traffic accident will be caused to occur easily. Althoug, it is not guarantee that it is obsolute none any public transport accident occurrence, due to crash to other vehicles, during the non manual driving (AI) driver drives the bus, tram, train, taxi, on the road, nut when (AI) non manual driving skill can be improved to the most safe driving level. I believe that non manual driving public transport tools ought be bring more safe to compare human public transport tools drivers to any one passenger individual life safety.

How non manual driving automated vehicle influences future mode of public transport service change? A survey distributed in the Netherlands in which respondents had to choose between conventional cars, public transportation for different travel distances and trip purposes. having collected information from 663 respondents, conducted a study on classic trip attributes (such as travel time, car owner self driving time and non manual driving public transport tool driving time as well as travel costs, car owner car fuel purchase expenditure and general non manual driving public transport tool fare comparison), attitudinal factors and socio-economic variables to understand future non manual auto driving public transport tools choices. The repor indicates that automated driving transport service which they defined as an automatically controlles door-to-door transport service provided by a vehicle with similar features to a conventional car, albeit driveless. Results suggest that travellers' mode preferences vary significantly for different travel distances and purposes. They found that conventional cars and public transportation are perceived as being the least attraction altererrnatives in relation to vehicle travel time and short -and -long distance commuting trips respectively, preference for passegner choice is between the non-manual driving auto car and non manual driving auto public transport tool.

They indicated that future passengers will consider how non-manual driving public transport tools whether they can bring trips are safer, faster and more efficient to let them to feel as well as traveling time and time cost is also another factor to influence them to choose to catch non-manual driving public transport tool, when they feel safe to arrive the destination rapidly. Then, future many passengers will be persuaded to choose to catch non-manual auto driving public transport tools in preference. So, if future all public transport service providers can let passengers to feel fares are reasonable price, when their non-manual driving public service transport tools, bus, taxi, tram, train, underground train etc. they can let them to feel safe to arrive destinations rapidly, they won't need worry about passengers number will reduce when human drivers are replaced by AI robotic drivers.

In fact, when one needs to drive to arrive destination in long driving time. The car owner will feel tried, bored and he/she can not spend driving time to do his/her interesting activites in his/her car, e.g. reading, listening music, watching TV, playing electronic games from smartphone, phone talking etc. personal behaviors. So, it means that future long time trip passengers may be persuaded to catch non-manual auto driving public transport tools if they believe that this kind of new non manual auto driving pubic transport tools can provide more safe, efficient, rapid, comfortable feeling to them, when they are sitting on them.
All of these may be the main factors to influence them to choose to catch non -manual auto driving public transport

tools. In general, these other factors may influence future passengers to choose to catch non manual auto driving public transport tools, they may include: whether automated vehicle would drive on populated streets better than conventional cars, whether an automated car would be comfortable entrusting the safety of a close family member, whether automated vehicle might produce fewer pollutant emissions. Because , when future non-manual auto driving vehicles are popular, many car owners will choose to buy automated vehicles to drive. So, future non manual auto driving public transport tool service providers , their competitors may be automated vehicles. If automated vehicles can let car owners to feel car prices are reasonable, they can provide safe, rapid speed, comfortable feeling to any one car owner, then he/she can sell his/her traditional car to change new automated car easily, when global many car owners begin to accept automated cars.

On conclusion, future passengers may be persuaded to choose to buy fares to catch any kinds of non manual auto driving public transportation tools. It depends on these factors, such as reasonable fares, safe feeling, efficient and rapid arriving to destinations short time journey, comfortable and clean seats facility, free personal behavior, e.g. quite reading , listening music, watching TV , free internet provision transport environment, when future any one passenger is sitting in the auto driving public transport vehicle. So, (AI) technology will have possible to influence our future social public transportation development may bring more significant new travelling experiences and it can let global passengers to feel indeed. Moreover, it will be future global public transportation service providers, they need to consider that they ought need to change their public transport tools services in order to satisfy future passengers transport needs more easily. I conclude that future global public transport service will be influenced to change non manual auto driving public transport services by future global passegner public transport service needs within 10 years. So, nowadays, any kinds of public transport service providers ought need to spend time to research how to design themselves traditional public transport service moods to change to non manual auto driving moods in order to satisfy future global passenger individual new public transport services needs successfully.

Can non-manual driving cars dominate traditional car market

Nowadays, non-manual driving car invention may influence traditional car market development. In car development history, human had been habitly driving gas energy cars, but since battery energy cars invention, it can influence environmental protection car buyers feel gas energy cars may pollute global air. So, many different countries car buyers begin to choose to buy battery energy cars to replace traditional gas energy cars to drive. For example, US, Uk, China , they haver many big cities, their different cities living car buyers had begun to choose to buy battery energy cars to replace their old gas energy cars to drive to different destinations from their living cities every day.

So, it seems that nettergy energy cars had been beginning to replace some old gas energy cars in some countries cities, e.g. China Shanghai large cities, US, New York, Washington large cities, UK London large city. However, it brings these questions: Can non-manual driving cars may dominate future traditonal gas energy cars market? Because, cattergy energy cars bring environmental protection advantages to reduce air pollution.

So, battery energy cars may influence nowadays many gas energy car buyers to choose to buy battery energy cars to replace gas energy cars to replace gas energy cars to drive to avoid air pollution problem serious occurrence in our future societies.

In car market demand and supply view, I assume that if future many gas energy car owners accept to battery energy cars can reduce air polution continue influences our health when we often breathe dirty air due to gas energy cars' emission.

Hence, I estimate the demand number of battery energy cars pollution will be influenced to increase by air pollution. If future global air pollution will continue seriously influence global human health, it will influence global many car owners make choice either not buy any cars to drive, they will choose to catch public transport tools, e.g. bus, tram ,ferry, taxi, underground train etc. to go to anywhere or they will choose to buy battery energy cars to avoid gas continue pollute air to influence our health. So, it seems that battery energy cars will replace traditional gas energy cars to cause gas energy cars demand number decreases and battery energy cars demand number increases.

The other questions concern: Can battery energy cars influence future non-manual driving cars demand number reduces? Can non-manual driving cars replace battery energy cars and gas energy cars to dominate global car market?

In fact, non-manual driving cars may let many lazy car drivers or car buyers do not need to drive their cars, robots may help them to drive cars when they are sitting in themselves cars. So , they may read books, lsten music or sleep when their non-manual driving cars are still running on the roads. Although, non-manual driving cars can let many lazy car drivers feel comfortable and free when they are sitting in themselves cars. But non-manul driving cars can let they feel not safe, when robots help they to drive cars.

It means that their lifes are dominated by robots. However, traffic accidents may occur in any time, if robots help them to drive their cars in whole road journey time. So, they will feel more dangerous to compare they drive themselves cars on road busy time. Moreover, non-manual driving cars also need gas energy. So, non-manual driving cars still cause air pollution when many non-manual driving cars are being driving on the roads.

Hence, non-manual driving cars can also let environmental protection drivers feel that they can cause air pollution when they are driven on the roads by robots. Otherwise, battery energy cars must not pollute air , because they are using battery charge energy to replace gas or oil energy. Moreover battery energy cars won't let many car drivers feel safe to drive themselves cars on the road, due to they can still drive themselves cars and they won't need robots to help them to drive cars on the roads.

On conclusion, it seems that battery energy cars can attract many car buyers to choose to buy more than the kinds of both non-manual driving cars and gas energy cars. In supply and demand view, if future non-manual driving car manufacturers hope to raise sale price and demand purchase number. Unless, they can reduce their future any kinds of non-manual driving manufacture number to less than battery energy cars sale number to let future non-manual driving buyers feel that they can not buy any kinds of non-manual driving cars easily if they make purchase decision to buy them leter. Then, any kinds of non-manual driving cars prices may be influenced to raise to sell more easier when car buyers feel their supply number will begin to reduce to sell in global non-manual driving car market. However, future battery energy cars will be non-manual driving cars main competitive choice target to global car buyers. So, non-manual driving cars will be difficult to dominate the primary car choice tool to car buyers in future global car market.

CHAPTER SIXTEEN

Organizations learn behavioral economy bring what benefits

- What does behavioral economy mean?
-

(BE) Behavioral economics is primarily concerned with the bounds of rationality of economic agents. Behavioral models typically bring insights from psychology and microeconomic theory. The study of behavioral economics includes how market decisions are made and the mechanisms that drive public choice. Moreover, behavioral economic plays a important role in our lives and in the economy because it can help businesses to explain why we consume the kind of goods and services , the way we do, why we make certain choices of action, the key contibution to behavioral economics, it uses psychological and experimentation to develop theories about human decision making, and has identified a range of biases as a result of the way people think and feel . (BE) is trying to change the way economics think about people's perception of value and expresses preferences.

-

● Have they relationship between consumer behaviors and economy ?
The success or failure of a nation's economy can greatly affect consumer behavior based on a variety of economic factors. If the economy is strong, consumers have more purchase power and money is spent , f the economy is poor, the reverse is true. Consumer behavior in economics means to explain of how individual cstomers, groups or organizations select, buy, use and dispose ideas, goods and services. A such, consumers play a vitual role in the economic system of a capitalist economy. Without consumer demand, producers would lack one of the key motivations to produce to sell to consumers.
The motivates consumers behavioral economic perspective, it is the new field of behavioral economics has shown

them, in practice, people's decisions can be greatly influenced by seemingly irrelevant aspects of their personalities and by the environment in which their decisions are made. So, it seems that consumer buying behavior changes during economic crisis.

•

In organization how resources choices to use in behavioral economy view, though the number and variety of the different resources businesses require is limitless. Economists divide factors of production into three basic categories: Land, labour and capital. Land refers to all of the natural resources that businessed need to make and distribut goods and services, labours to make and distribute goods and services, labours refers how the organization chooses to employ the employee skill to make the kind of job, capital refers to how much the organization plans to spend in order to operate its business. Hence, behavioral economy can explains the economic model of employee, human behavior, working performance. It is a representation of people action. The concept is based on traditional economics, where human behavior is believed to spring from absolute rationality.

•

On behavioral economics in consumer lives and in the economy aspect, it explains it is a game theory, behavioral game theory. It is a game theory , behavioral game theory extened standard analytical game theory by taking into account how players (consumers) feel about the payoffs other players receive, limits in strategic thinking, as well as the effects of learning , the consumer individual past purchase experience, games (choices of purchases) are usually about cooperation or fairness.

•

For advertising how plays beneficial roles in a healthy economy example, advertising plays a strong role in the economy. It provides useful informatin to consumers that tells them about products and services choices as well as comparing features, benefits and prices, with more complete information, consumers and businesses often choose to purchase additional products and services . Hence, behavioral eonomics draws instead on psychology and economics to explore why people sometimes make irrational decisions, and why and how their behavior does not follow the predictionsof economic models. Because humans are emotional and easily distracted being, they make decisions that are not in their self-interest. So, behavioral economics is the study of the effects that psychological factors have on the economic decisions making process of individuals. The importance of understanding behavioral economics for marketers is immeasurable as it shows for a better factors that can lead to irrational economic decision, e.g. overspend because of lack of availabiliey, such as buying expense gad because you are in the desert.

Another irrational economic decision may be impluse buying or pressure.

-

- How to apply behavioral economic to explain why the employee does peformance behavior?

A study on human behavior has revealed that 90% of the working population can be classified into four basic personality types: Optimistic, pessimistic, trusting. However, the latter of the four types. Envious is the most common, with 30% compared to 20% of each of the organization whole employee individual economic behavior, economic behavior occurs in a climate of formal and informal organizational rukes. These rules often act as incentives, e.g. appreciation, job promotion, increasing salary. These rules often act as incentives and influence the choices employees make , in general employees chooce to work desk jobs that do not keep to fit, and how they have to make more time to stay healthy.

-

So, behavioral economic theory explain any organization will need have behavioral skills to dominate employee individual performance to raise. Behavioral skills are interpersonal, self-regulatory, and task-related behaviors that connect to successful performance in education and workplace settings. The behavioral skills are designed to help individuals succeed thorough effecttive interactions, stress management and persistent effort in any organizations. for task-oriented behavioral skills examples, they may include: active always buy with something, ambitious, strongly wants to succeed, cautious, being very careful, conscientious, taking time to do things right and creative, someone who can make up things easily or think of new things. The six important employee behaviors in organizations are employee productivity, absenteeism, turnover, organizational citizenship behavior, job satisfaction and workplace misbehavior. So, managers need have good behavioral management skills. They are all about learnings appreciation and growth. Take the time to learn, try and grow oen strategies and leadership style.

-

- How to apply behavioral eocnomic skill to help society to solve challenges ?

The three principles of social economics theory describes how the economy as a whole woks are (1) a country's standard of living depends on its ability to produce goods and services . (2) prices rise when the government prints too much money and (3) society faces a short-run tradeoff between inflation and unemployment. How to use behavioral economics for social impact. According to the American psychological association, social psychology is the study of how individuals affects and are affected by physical environment. Behavioral economics applies these concepts to the economic decisions that people make in addition to the ration thinking. It helps us understand how consumer participate in contest buy products and brand familiar choice in order to make the most rational purchase decison. Also, behavioral economists ask questions mostly about the way people make economic choices, judgements or the way particular financial purchase choice.

•

Hence, behavioral economic is the study of psychology as it relates to the economic decision making processes of individuals and organizations. In general, our societies ask two important questions: Are economists' assumptions of utility of profit maximization good approximations of real people's behavior? So individuals maximize subjective expected utility?

•

IN our societies, we need to satisfy and earn the greatest benefit, in economics, rational choice theory, states that when humans are presented with various options under the conditions of scarcity, they would choose the option that maximizes their individual satisfaction. Behavioral economics draws on psychology and economics to explain why people sometimes make irrational decisions and why and how their behavior does not follow the predictions of economic models, e.g. decisions such as how much to pay for a cup of coffee, whether to go to graduate school, whether to pursue a healthy lifestyle , how much to contribute toward retirement. For example, humans are emotional and easily distracted beings, they make decisions that are not in their self interest. For companies are increasingly incorpoarting behavioral economics to incrase sales of their products case example, in 2007, the price of the 8 GB iphone was introduced for $600 and quickly reduced to $400, what if the intrinsic value of the phone was $400? If Apple introduced the iphone for $400, the initial reaction the price in the smartphone market might have been negative as the iphone might be thought to have too pricely. Buy by introdicing the phone at a hgh-pricing and bringing it down to $400, consumers believed they were getting a pretty iphone deal for Apple. So, Apple iphone began to understand tht its phone consumers are irrational, an effective way to behavioral economics in the Apple iphone's decision making policies that concern its internal and external stakeholders may prove to be worthwhile of done properly .

•

- Behavioral economics is the study of the psychological, cognitive, emotional, cultural and social factors involved in the decisions of individuals or institutions, and how these decisions deviate from those implied by classical economic theory.
-

- Behavioral economics is grounded in empirical observations of human behavior, which have demonstrated that people do not always make what neoclassical economists consider the “rational” or “optimal” decision, even if they have the information and the tools available to do so.

• •

Behavioral economics combines elements of economics and psychology to understand how and why people behave the way they do in the real world. It differs from neoclassical economics, which assumes that most people have well-defined preferences and make well-informed, self-interested decisions based on those preferences.

•

• •

Behavioral economics is often related with normative economics. It draws on psychology and economics to explore why people sometimes make irrational decisions, and why and how behavior diverges from the predictions of economic models. Behavioral economics is the study of psychology that analyzes the economic decisions people make. Moreover, behavioral economics explains that humans are not rational and are incapable of making good decisions. Because humans are emotional and easily distracted beings, they make decisions that are not in their self-interest.

•

● Consumer leisure need whether is more and less whether it has what relationship between economy?

Consumer leisure need whether is more and less whether it has what relationship between economy? Also whether the country’s economy recession or growth, can it influence consumer leisure need to increase or decrease ? I shall attempt to apply behavioral economy theory to explain whether they have cause and effect relationship as below:

In our societies, there are so many different kinds of leisure activities, also any kinds of leisure consumers can follow the kind of leisure activity’s price factor, enjoyable feeling factor, satisfactory feeling factor, lesiure time need factor to influence the leisure consumer individual final choice to which kind of leisure activity among the different kinds of leisure needs. For example, travel leisure activity ought be the most experience, spending of leisure expense to compare general sport lesiure, e.g. swimming , playing basketballs , table tennis, tennis, football, purchae tickets seeing movies, purchase tickets listening music, purchase electronic playing games to stay at homes to play.

In simiarity, it uses only considers leisure price aspect, we shall do the comparable and reasonable decision is that travelling activity ought be the kind of leisure activity, any leisure consumers ought spend the least leisure times to enjoy this kind of leisure activity, e.g. one year has only one time or two-to-five times for overseas for overseas travel. But, in fact, in global there are many travellers, they can make many times of travelling frequent decision, e.g. they can spend one week at least time to go to overseas to travel per month. Hence, it means that global some travellers like to buy air ticket to go to overseas to travel, they spend average one month and one time overseas travel.

In fact, tourism agents hope to attract travellers to choose travelling leisure activity, they will attempt to decrease air ticket price in order to increase travellers number. However, some cheap travelling package price can persuade global some travellers accept to pay cheap price to bu air ticket to spend several days to go to the country to travel enjoy their holidays.

So, it seems that cheap air tcket price strategy, it can attract some countries travellers to accept to spend some time for their overseas holiday their overseas travelling leisure activity can explain why leisure price must be main element factor to influence leisure consumers to reduce spending amount to pay for the kind of leisure activity , such as travelling lesiure activity is one kind of good lesiure activity example.
Otherwise, some kinds of leisure activities, ever their lesiure prices are cheap, it must not influence them to like to spend much time to enjoy them, e.g. swimming, riding bicycles leisure activities, although those kinds of sport leisure activities prices must be very cheap to compare travelling activities , it can must influence many young people like to buy bicycles to ridem even they are proficient bicycle riders or they like to buy tickets to go public swimming pools to swin. The factors may include these both kinds of sports are tired sport leisures, any one must need more body energy to do these sports. Moreover, for student leisure consumers, although these both kinds sports prices, such as bicycles and swimming pool purchase tickets, they are cheap to students, but in fact, students must need to spend time to learn, if they often spend time to enjoy these both of sport activities, they will feel fear that they can not concentrate on spending learning time, if they spend on sport leisure time.

Hence, in behavioral economy view, it explains that lesiure price whether it is high or low, it is not main factor to influence any leisure consumers to do leisure kind of choice, such as sport case to student leisure consumers, they will not choose to spend much time on sport lesiure aspect, because the hard students must feel fear to influence their learning effort when they often spend time on sport leisure aspect. Otherwise, for a sport professonal, e.g. proficient riding bicycle sportman, he may accept to spend expensive price to buy one expensive bicycle , e.g. when he feels the US$3,000 bicycle, it can help him to improve riding speed skills, he won't choose to buy the another US$1,000 bicycle, when he feels that it can not help him to improve riding speed skill, hence, it also explains that the leisure produt high price , it must not influence lesisure consumers number to reduce, it depends on whether the leisure product function to the leisure consumer, e.g. for riding bicycle sport men , they may accept to pay higher price to buy more expensive bicycles , because the hope that the bicyces can help them to comprove their riding speed to more rapid. Otherwise, for student bicycle consumers, they won't compare different kinds of bicycles prices in order to decide whether which kind of bicycles are the most suitable to them to buy to ride. Hence, behavioral economic theory can explain that price must not be the main factor to influence lesiure consumers' lesiure activities choices, their lesiure need psychological and leisure product individual function factors was also influence their lesiure activities choices.

● Can DNA reproductive technology bring only positive impact to influence our social behavior change? Human's medical technology had been continue developed to improve to satisfy our medical need, such as cancer patient medical different new drug research, it aims to help future cancer patients to avoid death. However, future human's new medical research will research on DNA biological medical improvement . So, future DNA biological medical technology may bring good or bad social impact, e.g. reproductive animal, such as pig, cow animals . So, when many pigs and cows can be reproduced. Then, pigs and cows number can increase. Consequently, porks beefs meats food number can be also been increased by DNA biological medical reproductive cell technology improvement.

It is good aspect to bring enough meats supply to global , when future DNA biological medical technology can be developed to the reprodctive many cows and pigs number stage in order to raise porks and beefs food number. However, DNA biological cell reproductive technology can also bring bad impact to our society, if one day human can apply DNA biological cell reprodutive technology to reproduce another ourselves, it means that reproductive human why is it bad new? if ne DNA scientist decides to help one country ambitious leader to reproduce himself, then when the country ambitious leader dies, but his another reproductive himself person can aontiue to bring war crisis to global, such as Japan's past leader, he was one ambitious leader to dominate global countries. If DNA reproductive technology is applied to help him to reproduce this Japan ambitious another himself . Then, the another new world war may be occurred easily. So, I also worry about future DNA reproductive technology may be applied to help the ambitous bad people to reproduce themselves to bring our societies safety and economic recession negative impact.
So, it brings this question: Can DNA reproductive technology bring only positive impact to influence our social behavior change? I shall attempt to explain as below:

How does DNA attract our behavior? In some situations, genes play a larger role in determining your behavior. How can genetic technologies impact society ? Although, genetic technology has a great potential to change the medical practice as we know it also has a potential to be misused , it also has a potential to be misused, and lead to further health disparities, discrimination and inequality in the human societies around the world.

However, I believe that those the ways that genetic engineering can help human society. Several works have been done on genetic engineering with major focus on its importance ranging from increasing plant and animal food productio, diagnosing disease condition, medical treatment improvement, as well as production of vaccines and other useful drugs.

● What is the focus of behavioral generics?
Behavioral genetics is the study of genetic and environmental influences on behaviors. By examining genetic influence, more information can be gleaned about how the environment operates to affect behavior. So, in behavioral economic view, gene DNA reproductive cell technology may seem to bring these benefits. Some benefits of genetic engineerinf in agricultures are increased crop yoelds, reduced need for food or drug production, reduced need for pesticides, enhanced nutrient composition and food quality , resistance to past and disease , greater food security, and medical benefits to the world's growing population . Also, the intangible , non economic measurement, possible benefit of genetic engineering may include more nutritious food, tastier food, disease -and-drought resistant plants that require fewer environment resources , such as water and fertilizers, less use of pesticides, increased supply of food with reduced cost and larger shelf life, faster growing plants and animals.

All of these benefits, they can not measured by economic calculation, but they can be felt by us. So, in our social behavioral economic view to genetic engineering, it may bring both positive and negative impact to our societies. On negative impact, these are many risks involves in genetic engineering, the release of genetically altered organisms in the environment can increase human suffering, disease animal welfare, and lead to ecological disasters are positive impact aspect, it can help to defeat diseases, getting rid of all illnesses in young and unborn children potential to live longer, produce new foods, organisms can be tailor-made , faster growth in animals and plants, pests and diseases resistance. But genetic engineering can also bring risks to our societies, e.g. new allergens in the food supply, antibiotic reistance, production of new toxins, concentration of toxic metals, enhancement of the environment for toxic fungi, unknown harms, gene transfer to wild ot weedy relations, change in herbicide use patterns.

By knocking out genes repsonsible for certain conditions, it is possible to create animal model organism of " human disease" as well as producing hotmenes, vaccies and other drugs. So, if DNA can bring human diseases, it means that it can also bring economic loss to our societies, because human disease may bring illness to any one to cause low productivity to any industry development, if the factory has many people human disease from reproductive animal cell accident risk. Then, the ill worker number increases, low productivities and inefficiencies will cause to the factory. If global has many factory workers got human disease from reproductive animal cell accidently. Then, global factries products producing number must have been influenced to fallen down.

Consequently, global manufacturers will encountered serious loss, due to their products producing speed is slow and their different kinds of products supply number must decrease, if global will workers number increases, they are caused by reproductive animal cell disease. Hence, DNA genetic reproductive technology may also bring global economic loss crisis in possible.

● In organizational behavioral economic view, whether they have cause and effect relationship between employees how to use resources behaviors and organizational resource excess use within organizations ?

In organizational behavioral economic view, whether they have cause and effect relationship between employees how to use resources behaviors and organizational resource excess use within organizations. For example, if the organization has many employees number, whether the organization will use its any internal tangible and intangible resources easily per day.

For construction organization example, one construction organization must need to buy different kinds of construction materials to prepare to let workers to help it to manufacture different kinds of properties or houses (products) in order to sell to property buyers. In its every building construction site, it will need more or less workers, they are needed to use different kinds of construction materials to build housess in different construction sites. I assume that construction site (A), it has 100 construction workers number, every day, construction site (A) 100 workers need to use different kinds of construction materials to help them to build 3 building floors wall at least floor number in the construction site (A).

I assume that these 100 construction workers , they include proficient workers and not proficient workers. For proficient construction workers group, they have 50 number, and not proficient construction workers group, they also have 50 number . Hence, the proficient construction workers only need to spend 3 hours maximum and use less number of constructoin materials, then they can finish to build 3 building floors wall per day.

I also assume that all constructoin material supply number is limited. It means that due to this construction firm needs to pre-booking to purchase this kind of the best quality of constructoin material from overseas before three worths. So, it must not have enough time to pre-booking to purchase this kind of best quality of constructoin materials when they are used rapaidly within one month, due to this one month is the final finishing time to this construction firm within one month. Hence, limited construction material supply number and limited finishing time to build this new 40 floors house within this final one month .

So , not proficient construction workers number , limit number of construction material and per day 8 hours which is its limited resources in behavioral eocnomy view. Moreover, total 50 proficient and not proficient 50 construction workers (human resource employees number) will cause this constructoin firm , it will possible need to build this new 40 floors house are more than one month, if these 50 proficient construction workers , they have more than 30 at least number, they are absent to cause their overall construction workers‘ efficiency to be fallen down, due to the other 50 not proficient constuction numbers must need their teaching how to cooperate ad how use less materials to build this new 40 floor hourse rapidly in order to raise overall constructon team efficiency and avoid to delay more than one month time to build this 40 floors new house successfully within this final one month time.

Hence, it explains that when one organization has more employees, it does not represent that this organization must need to use more resource to achieve its any mission, such as this construction firm case, although it has 50 not proficient construction workers, they need to use more construction materials to build this new 40 floors house in this construction site (A). But, in fact, it has other 50 proficient construction workers, they know how to reduce construction materials to build every building floor wall for this new 40 floors building house. So, they can teach the not proficient building workers to know hoe to avoid to use extra excess constructon material to finish to construct every building fllor wall. SO, although, it has 50 not proficient construction workers number, but they can be taught to learn how to reduce to use these limited the best quality of construction materials to build this 40 floors new house. It implies that if the construction workers number can increase, e.g. increases more 50 not proficient construction workers, this the best quality of construction material resource number must not need to increase demand, because this construction site (A) has 50 proficient construction workers , they can teach these 50 not proficient construction workers how to avoid to use extra excess this kind of high quality construction material to build this new 40 floor house efficiently and effectively within this one month.

Hence, if this construction firm won't have more than 30 proficient workers number is absent in this final one month, it will have enough proficient construction workers to teach these 50 not proficient construction workers to know how to use this high quality of construction materials to build this 40 floors new house building in order to avoid waste or construction material need shortage challenge occurs in this final one month time.

Consequently , it ought finish to build this 40 floors new house building within this month. Hence, it explains why its this kind of high quality of construction material resource need must not increase, because if its all proficient construction workers is absent and their absent number is less than 30, then they have enough proficient construction workers number , they can teach this 50 not proficient construction workers how to avoid to use extra excess construction materials resource number in order to have enough construction material resource supply to satisfy this new 40 floors building house to finish construction within one month finishing date need.

On conclusion, in organizational behavioral economic view, it explains that resource use need must not be influenced to increase when the organization's employees number increase. It depends on whether the organization has how many talent and proficient workers number in order to assist them and teach the not proficient employees how to use resource to manufacture any kinds of products in order to avoid to spend extra excess of resource need. Hence, organizational behavioral economic view, it can explain that any organization's increase to employees number, it does not mean that its resource number is also needed to increase. Moreover, in organizational behavioral economic view, it also explains that if the organization can have many proficient workers to help it to do any complex tasks, they will help it to bring avoiding waste or excess extra resource to use advantage, because they ought know whether how they work, they can help the organization to improve performance or raise efficiency e.g. car manufacture, computer manufacture, television manufcture etc. home electronic products or car leisure products. Due to that manufacturre processes are complex, if the organization can have more proficient high skillful workers to help it to manufacture their products. They ought help it to use lesser manufacturing time and less manufacturing resource to finish any above these products to compare not proficient or low skillful manufacture workers. So, in long time, the organization must may earn economic low cost benefits from proficient worker individual high manufacturing skillful knowledge behavior or performance. So, organizational behavioral economic theory explains why even the organization plans to increase employees number, it's resources number won't be influenced to increase rapidly because when the organization's proficient high skillful workers number is more 2 times at least than not proficient low skillful workers number. They ought have enough effort to train and teach and cooperate with the not proficient low skillful manufacture workers to improve their manufacture skills in order to raise manufacturing efficiency and reduce extra excess resources waste and avoid to bring long term resource waste economic loss.

So, any manufacturing organizations must need to increase proficient workers number to assist the not proficient low skillful workers to learn how to improve their skills and know how to reduce to use excess resources to keep to manufacture the highest number of products aim frequently. Consequently, the organization will bring long term low resource use manufacturing economic benefit.

What factors influence student makes subject choice decision

Behavioral economic on law and economy subject choice how to student individual subject learning choice behavior in universities economy and law subjects choice example, whether students will make subject either law or economt subject choice, it depends on future lawyer and economist salary whether which occupation can earn long term more salary comparision in order to decide wither law or economy degree learn.

Some university students make these two subjects either one learning choice, they will decide whether school fee is how much more than future salary earns, or personal interest psychological factor influences. So, if the student feels more interest to learn law degree , then he won't choose economy degree between these two degrees. Behavioral economy theory can be applied to explain this student individual economy and law degrees choice behavior because his subject choice decision is depended on personal psychological interest factor more than school fee or future salary possible earn economic salary reward factor influences. But, I assume that if the university can give scholorship for economic and law degree student when the student feels the law degree scholarship higher than economic degree. Then, he will decide to choose law degree to study more than economy degree. He chooses to study law degree because he hopes to earn higher scholarship.

IN behavioral economy principle , it can be applied to explain this student degree choice behavior. However, applying behavioral economy view, it assumes these principles to analyze whether how the student chooses to study the degree. The principles or factors may influence his degree choice may include: Cost and benevits, e.g. the student fee and future salary for the degree, when the student has interest to study law and economic degree. So, he needs to do degree choice. Then, he may compare whether how much law and economy degree school fee, it may be possible future earn salary, scholarship possible reward. All of these factors concern the price for law and economy degree (external cost) and future possible income (salary) for economist and lawyer occupation. It is behavioral law and economic factor to influence how the student chooses either law or economic degree to study in the university.

For example, when the (A) university on student enrolls to the (A) university before, he needs to choose wither law or economy degree to study. I assume that he only feels interest to study these two degrees. Then, he will compare school fees, if law degree school fee is per year US$5,000, 4 years is US$20,000 and economy degree school fee is per year US$3,000, 4 years is US$12,000. Although, it seems that economy 4 year school fee is more less US$8,000 to compare law degree 4 year, but this student also compare possible future salary for lawyer and economist occupation. He believes that future lawyer salary may pay more 4 times to compare economists salary after 5 years working experience. Although, if this student chooses economy degree to study, he may have chance to earn scholarship if his examination can be good, but it is one time short time economic researd and this scholarship reward is not sure that he must earn, if he can not get at least 5 (A) grade any one economic subject papers in this university economy degree structure. Otherwise, if he chooses to study law and get 5 (A) grade any one law subject papers in the university law degree structure, he can not get scholarship for this law degree. hence , he makes final choice to study law degree, although he can not get scholarship and school fee is more than economy degree. But he believes that he can earn higher salary when he can be one lawyer and he works after 5 years, his salary may be paid more than one economist salary.

In behavioral economic view, it can be applied to explain this university student his degree choice behavior, then he has interest to study law and economy degree. He must need to make one degree choice to graduate, then he may make degree choice decision by external economic cost (degree price) and future reward (possible income) behavioral economic factor . Then, he can judge whether which degree is more suitable to choose to study in this university.

- How organization improvement may bring economic benefits

Can organizational economies, e.g. transaction cost economics, agency theory, organizational theory , e.g. models of formal organizational independent of the strategies, improve organizational behavior in order to bring economic benefit, e.g. development potentially valuable resources and capabilities, it can raise internal organizatonal strengths and avoid weaknesses in SWOT strategy in order to imporve performance and bring organizational internal economic benefit in organizational behavioral economic view.

For manufacturing industry example, if the car manufacturers can attempt to discover the most efficient steel, or different kinds of car components material, but they can help it to manufacture many high quality cars. Then, their manufactury cost reduce , but its any model of car quality does not caused to poor. Then, this car firm can apply the most efficient and the most high component materials to help it to manufacture high quality cars. Although, it must need to spend time to research how to invest the most efficient and high quality car manufacture components, but if it can apply the most efficient and the high quality components to help it to manufacture any new model of cars. Then, new components research spending time can bring long term low manufacturing cost and high quality of cars to achieve long time economic benefits.

So, on behavioral economic view, organization's spending time on different kind of cheap and high quality car manufacture manufacture components research and research expenditure spending on new kinds of different car manufacture components, it can help it to sell the high quality of different model of cars to satisfy car buyer comfortable needs. Moreover, it can earn high profit, when it 's any car manufacture component cost reduces. So, SWOT internal strengths (high quality and low cost) to this car manufacturer. It may help it to bring long term raising profit economic benefit, when its any new model of car prices do not need raise, but their compared material manufacture cost reduce, due to new kinds of car manufacture component materials can be invented in success.

Hence, high quality and low cost of car manufacture component invention researching on spending time and research experiment expenditure is value to this car manufacture company, because if high quality and low cost car manufacture component experience succeeds, it can help it to improve any new model of cars quality , but the most important factor is that its any new model of cars prices do not need increase. So, car buyer individual purchase desire won't be influenced to choose any brand of car seller to replace it more easily.

For one drug development process, case example ,I assume that this drug manufacture firm can attempt to spend 10 years time, but it can help it has possible to help it to invent one kind of new pharmaceutical drugs to kill cancer cells for global cancer patients. So, its spending time research on new drugs to kill any kinds of cancers cellers and experimentation expenditure is value, because it can help it to bring economic benefit when global will have many cancer patients believe its new discovery of cancer drugs , it may help them to kill cancer cells to get health or reduce death chance ratio raises after 10 years.

Consequently, in soon future, it's global cancer patients number may increase when they choose to buy its future new cancer drugs paroduct. It may bring high profit economic benefit. So, on organizational behavioral economic view, when the organization spends long time and experimentation expenditure to research new resources, if these new resources can be invented in success and it ensures help it to increase clients number to order to bring future economic benefit. The organization is value to spend time and expenditure to carry on new resources research.

- Can organization apply behavioral economic demand to evaluate work performance for whole different departments?

Behavioral economies investigation may include evaluating demand for a commodity (such as drug experimentation and car manufacturing component material etc.) is given changes in price, using hypothetical purchase tasks, which are a reliable and efficient assessment method. Can behavior management examine work performance evaluation? The work performance evaluation target includes that employee individual and different department will performance evaluation in organization.

I believe high quality or low quality training , which can be evaluated whether the employee individual work performance or the department overall employees work performance can be improved after training. So, if the department employee individual or all employers work performance can be improved, e.g. work efficiency raises, client satisfactory feeling raises, product sale number . Then, the training is a high quality training to help the organization to earn future high economic benefit. Otherwise , if the organization can not earn above any one good result. Then, the training ia a low quality training.So, any organization can attempt to observe any department overall performance and employee individual performance in order to evaluate whether it can provide high or low quality of training to let employees to learn.
So, employee individual behavior can bring performance evidence to let the organization to evaluate whether its training is useful or not useful to achieve its training aim, e.g. when the car manufacturer provides money, time, effort training arrangement to teach all workers to learn how to manufacture car skill. After training provision, many of them, they do not need to work over time more than one hour to manufacture daily of least 10 cars per employee.Before, any one worker must need to spend more than one hour over time to manufacture daily 10 more cars.

So, when this car manufacture skillful improvement train is provided more than one hour more than one hour , none of them, they need work over time in order to manufacture more than at least 10 cars number per day. It seems that training improvement arrangement can be used to evaluate whether employee individual efficiency can be raised in organizational behavioral economic view.

Hence, any organization's internal training provision knowledge resource, it can be evaluated employees' behavioral performance can be improved, about being available to work, about role performance . It assumes that employees are likely to come to work and remain in the organization if they obtain satisfaction from their jobs, and that they are likely to put use effort and work more effectively if they are to be reward more for their effort and performance can be comfirmed to improved by management after they are taught by training. So, when the employee hopes to raise salary, he must hard to learn any new knowledge from the organizational training. Then, training can help the " expectation good reward employees" can improve performance in organizational behavioral economic view.

It is one important successful factor to help the organization to innovate and bring economic benefit, when the organization can implement any new useful training to improve any new useful training to imprve empllyee skills. It means that training is one long term economic organizational strategy, it depends on whether the training is useful or is ot useful in order to help any old employees to raise or improve their skills to achieve raising efficiency and satisfactory client service , sale product number, product manufacture increasing number aims.

- How organizational ethic influence employee behavior ?

Organizational ethic behavior concerns with explaining employee individual behavior in organization, e.g. ethical decision making, ethical conduct for example, when one marketing department manager does not attempt to carrying on any data research about new market research to sell the new model iphone to any country. He only depends on his personal judgement, he believes that this new invention of US iphone producs, they ought to be sell to Korean new iphone market, because he feels Korean must prefer to choose to buy US drand of new iphone products to compare other countries iphone product. However, this iphone marketing development manager lacks enough data research for different Korean iphone buyer age target, purchase experience, purchase desire to conclude Korean iphone buyers must like to buy any brand of US iphone products in preference.

His non ethical new iphone invention decision making to choice Korean ipohone buyers market will bring time waste rick to satisfy Korean iphone buyers‘ needs to replace other new model ipone users market, e.g. Hong KOng, China, ipone market. So, his ethical decision making to Korean iphone buyers ne iphone invention market may bring less economic benefit to this US iphone manufacture firm. So, this new model ipohone marketing development immoral judgement of this iphone marketing development manager individual decision making to Korean new model ipone invention to Korean ipone users, it can bring high economic loss to this US iphone firm.Otherwise, if this marketing department manager can spend time to carry on data gathering to make more accurate new model iphone invention decision making to choose which one country, then his ethical decision making may help his this US iphone firm to reduce new iphone invention loss risk. So, it explains that why ethic organizational behavior may influence the firm can earn more or less economic benefit. SO, ethic or moral behavior can influence the organization can earn how much economic benefit in long term significantly in organizational behavioral economic view.

● Can improve energy efficiency by organization building occupant's energy consumption relative behavior to bring economic benefit?

Reducing energy consumption in building , it must improve efficiency by building, but whether they have close cause and effect relationship between occupant's energy consumption behavior and improvement energy efficiency to the building? IN fact, high efficiency equipment is being developed, it can help any building to save energy and economic effectiveness, if building energy is subject to uncertainties, such as whether variations, human operations, human behavior changes and government policies. So, building technology equipment improvement may be one main factor to help buildings to save energy . But why occupant behavior may help building to save energy by their daily energy consumption behavior.

The occupant energy behavioral user inputs factor may include: Weather influences, internal heat gain, efficiencies, simplied/ normal occupant behaviors, e.g. a high efficiency chiller can save very limited energy in cold climates due to minimal cooling load, and a good designed natural ventilation building won't work if the occupants do not open windows when outdoor air favors cooling. So, it seems that if one living building hopes to reduce energy consumption, instead of building equipment technological change , e.g. air condition facilities, building occupants , artificial intelligent light, life, their daily energy consumption behaviors, they can influence the living building's energy consumption level in occupant energy consumption behavior and building energy saving economic benefit view.

In fact, when the occupant considers hot water, air condition, energy gas electricity expenditure, he won't use excess electricity, gas resources, because he needs to pay more energy expenditure , when gas and electricity energy consumption expenditure is applied to any business organization offices, warehouses , shops working facilities environment, such as offices, warehouses , shops can often use less electricity, gas energy far ther employees daily work . In long time, the organization must may reduce much electricity, gas energy expenditure for whole organizations business activities. In organizational behavior economic view, organizational energy consumption reduces it can help it to bring less expenditure spending economic benefit.

● Can Amazon e-commerce organization business activities bring economic benefit to global societies?

Amazon e-commerce is one online product sale e-commerce organization. Any one country e-buyer can use his/her home computer to click to Amazon webstores, when he/she saw the product phone and price, then he/she feels the product's price is reasonable and he/she believes that he/she can make the best choice to buy the product.

Then, he/she can pay visa to buy the product from Amazon webstore.
Amazon can bring the most convenient online sale channel to global any one e-buyer. The e-buyer can buy the oveseas product from its e-webstores . He does not need to catch air plane to fly to the e-sellers' shop. he can pay visa to pay the product from Amazon e-webstores any time immediately. All Amazon e-webstores . He can open 24 hours, so all webstores have no close time. So , it can bring busy working people, they do not need to spend long time to visit any shops to make purchase decision. For busy working people example, time has important value to them, they do not want to waste time to make any purchase choice.

So, Amazon gives " economic purchase time benefit " to global any one full time working people. In their psychology, Amazon can help them to save much time to go to online shopping purchase chance at homes. They can stay at homes to shopping. Even, when they give their their address to Amazon to know, Amazon will deliver their products to their homes within several days rapidly. Also , they do not need to pay money to buy its products immediately. They can only pay visa to buy the product from Amazon webstores. So, they can save " consumption money" to use for another need in short time. So, one individual e-air ticket buyer, Amazon can bring economic benefit to him, he does not need to buy air ticket to fly to another country to buy the product. Amazon webstores are given more different kinds of similar brand products to let him to choose in order to pay the most reasonable price, working people do not need to spend much visiting shop time to choose any products in order to make the final purchase decision at home rapidly, any one has visa card , he/she can buy the product from Amazon webstores at homes.

Instead of individual e-buyer ecommerce time benefit, spending little time product choice, reducing catching air plane to visit another country seller shop to pay air ticket expense and travelling time spending activities to every e-buyer . Amazon also brings global economic benefits to any one country. When the e-buyer lives in one country to buy the product, it is saved in the overseas country's warehouse. Then, the product must need to deliver to his home by air plane. So, all of Amazon products can bring global goods air transport delivering service to any one overseas buyer, when the product is saved in the overseas seller's warehouse. Any one Amazon product overseas transpor delivery service activity, it can help air goods transport service need increases as well as their goods air transport service income will also increase. Amazon can bring global air goods transport service need increases. It can assist global GDP air goods transport industry grows, and economic benefit for the country's air plan goods delivery service industry development in long term. Hence, on behavioral economic view, Amazon online sale channel ,it can help global economic benefit to air plane goods delviery service industy as well as individual differeent country e-buyer individual time saving and short term money saving economic benefit by visa payment method.

Moreover, Amazon alsoo creates more high technology employment chance to any one country because Amazon owns many offices and warehouses in different countries, due to it is one high technological e-commerce online sale organization, It must need many high skillful website designers to help it to design different countries webstores in order to satisfy any one e-buyer online purchase need. So, it creates high technology job chance to any one country webstore designers . It can help them to raise competitive effort when any one graduate pursues website designer career. IN Amazon provides good employent chance for any one country computer ecommerce designers in order to let them to earn high salary. Also, Amazon public e-commerce organization provides good chance for any one country author to earn royalty income when he/she publishes any electronic or paper books to sell from Amazon publish. It gives good writing skillful authors have more writing chance to help them to sell electronic books and /or paper books from its different countries webbook stores to different countries' readers in short time. It can help them to increase book sale chance to let different countries book buyers can know whether new book topic to the author, he/she will publish soon. So, it brings author's new writing mind training chance when he/she needs to compare book sale rank from Amazon webstores.

Hence, Amazon can bring social employment benefit and author individual skillful training advantage and royalty income benefit to any on country author in nowadays online published industty. So, Amazon online business activities can increase global social employment chance, encourages global authors attempt to train writing skill, helps e-buyers to save visiting shops shopping time and air ticket expenditure for global overseas buyers.

● How and why Amazon e-commerce organization influence global consumee behavioral changes to bring ecommerce benefits to sellers?

In behavioral economic view, Amazon changes consumers behavior as well as product sellers sale method, such as global consumer sellers began to accept online purchase method to replace frequent visiting shop purchase method and global sellers began to accept to apply Amazon webstores to help them to sell products from its online sale channel to replace opening shops locate to the country sale channel.
The advantages to global sellers may include they do not need to pay rent or buy the shops, they can use Amazon webstores to show their different kinds of products photos and prices to let any one online buyer to know . The advantage to global buyers, they do not need to spend time to visit any countries shops to choose products in order to make purchase decision. They only need to spend some time to visit amazon any one country's webstore to see any brands of product photos and know their prices to different kinds of products to compare design and price and functions among of them in the online visiting short time when they stay at home to trun on themselves home computers . So, future home consumption behavior may replace visiting shop consumption behavior. Amazon 's online purchase method will encourage global many sellers have began to believe traditional visiting shop purchase model can not be accepted to global any one consumer more easily, when any one owns computer and internet service at home in common. Then, global shops number will reduce, due to different kinds of product websites purchase model needs number increases to global product sellers, they will close their shops and open themselves

webstores or choose Amazon webstore to help them to sell their products conveniently. Consequently, global online purchase and sale transactions number will be influenced to increase by e-commerce organization development.

- Have they close relationship between consumer behavioral change and economic change?
- How does consumer behavioral change impact economic change?
- How does consumer behavior bring positive or negative influence to economic growth or economic recession to the country?

I shall attempt to apply behavioral economic theory to explain their cause and effect relationship why and hoe global economy growth or recession may be impacted by global consumer behavior change reasons ae below:

I shall indicate travellingleisure and goods air plane transport industries example, since air planes are invented, it is a kind rapid air transport tool, it can help human to do both kinds of transport asrvice, one is goods transport and another is human transport . So, any individual or business goods can be delivered to another country offices or homes by air planes transport tools rapidly. SO, air planes can create more overseas purchase and sale business activities chance between different countries nowadays. Moreover, internet invention, it also increase more e-coomerce online purchase and sale business acitivities to global any one online buyer, he/she only needs to apply computer tool to click to the online seller webstore, when he /she likes the product, he/she can pay visa to buy the product from the onlin seller webstore at home conveniently.

Hence, e-commerce encourages global consumers to choose to buy any products from internet channel, it also brings global goods are needed to transport by air planes between different countries, e.g. one US online buyer makes purchase decision from onlin channel, then he chooses the product from Korean one online seller webstore. After he pays visa to the Korean online seller webstore , then the Korea seller will follow his US address to send the product to the US buyer's home after several days rapidly.

Hence, it explains that if future global consumers like to buy any products from any one country's onine sell webstore. Then, the product must need to be delivered to the online buyer's home. When the seller's product is not located to the online buyer's country warehouse. It needs to be delivered by air plane. When, global there are man consumers, their traditional visiting shops purchase habits are influenced to change online visiting webstores habits. Then, when their purchase habits are influenced to change by rapid, convenient, visa card payment online purchase method at home, time online purchase technological new payment channel method.

In future new online purchase trend development, it may influence future global traditional visiting shops consumption model to change visiting webstores consumption model. Consequently, consumers will choose to pay visa online purchase at home in preference. Also, it encourages visa card purchase , consequently, online purchase may influence these industries development, airlines goods transport service needs increase, it can increase new visa cards number to the frequent online channel e-buyer number. So, online consumption encourages global households save long time money in banks, because we can pay money by visa card payment after we buy any products from online. Global bank may have more money to save longer time from global households, long time money save , because we do not need to withdraw money to buy any expensive products, immediately, e.g. computer , television, furniture etc. When global households begin to accept online purchase method is better to compare visiting shop purchase method. So, future global airline goods transport and bank saving businesses these two industries may have positive impact by future global online buyers raising number.

Hence, when global consumers behaviors began to change online purchase , their online purchase activities may influence global banks can have long time saving money and airlines goods transport need increase rapidly. However, online purcahse activies will bring negative consumers emotion impact to some businesses, e.g. property rent business, because when the country has high population of consumers, they choose online purchases, they won't often vitis shops to choose any kind of products frequently, they only like to stay at home and turn on themselves home computers to find whether global whom sellers, they have webstores to let global consumers to buy their products from online channel. Due to the cuntry willl not have many consumers like to spend time to visit any shops in the country. It means that the country will have many shops are needed to be close, because there are less number peple visit the businessmen shops every day. It will cause property rent service providers can not increase rent income, even decrease rent income, when there are many businessmen close their shops and change onine webstores to replace actual shops. Hence, it seems that online buyers number increases, it may also brings positive impact to influence shop rent service income decreases to the property rent developers.

On global macro economic changing environment, online buyers number increases, it can encourage any kinds of products, they can sell more more easily. So, global product sale number may be influenced to increase rapidly, when global online purchase and sale transactions number increase, GDP on any kinds of product income may be influenced to increase . So, online buyers number increases, it must may bring positive impact to influence global trading GDP high growth, but global shops rent income property developers may be influenced to reduce, due to there are many shops may be caused to close in possible.
How travellers' leisure need change, it may influence travelling leisure service industry development? I shall attempt to explain how COVID 19 disease influences global travellers lesiure need change and airpine and travelling service providers, e.g. hotels, travelling agents, their leisure service needs change. Nowadys, COVID 19 disease has caused global many travellers feel fear to catch airplanes, because air planes all windows are needed to close, he/she has COVID disease, then he/she can bring any one passegner to get this kind of disease by air plane close window air environment. So, when globa many travellers feel afreaid to catch air planes, this kind of COVID 9 air contact disease, it can cause global travellers number has began to reduce, many of travelles began to reduce travelling times

per year, even 0 time travel per year. Consequently, it will bring negative impact to global travelling industry development.

Firstly, COVID 19 disease influences global traveller individual travelling desire decreases, every traveller began to avoid to catch air planes to travel. So, any country;s airlines air planes flying times began to reduce, because it is no full seats booking to any airlinees. It means that airlinee must decrease income, alsoo they need to pay parking airplanes rent to any countries airports. So, fixed rent expenditure will need to pay, and many airlines began to dismiss the excess extra number of airline front service staffs, e.g. airport front service staffs, air plane check in /out staffs, even pilots number began also decreased.
So, airline unemployment ratio increases , it causes pilots, airlines service staffs need to change jobsm even some coutnries pilots , choose to do simple goods delivery jobs in supermarkets or securities. Also, COVID 19 disease influences hotels, travelling agents income began to reduce, because there are none many travellers need to live hotels, and they do not need travelling agents to help them to arrange any travelling journeys. So , COVID 19 disease influences many different countries travellers began choose any leisure activities to replace travel, because they feel afraid to get COVID 19 disease when they need to sit in closed window air plane environment.

This kind of disease can influence any one travller individual leisure choice began to change, such as they began to forgive travel siure activities, they will spend holiday to do other leisure activities in themselves countries , e.g. climbing mountain, swimming, running, playing table tennis, tennis etc. different outdoor sports. all of these leisure sports have same features, global any one leisure needer, he does not catch air plane to fo to another country to carry on playing these any one sport and he/she does not need to pay more price to enjoy these sports. Otherwise m travelling leisure activity, it must need any one leisure needer to spend much expenditure to enjoy this kind of leisure activity . So, it explains why many travellers beagan to choose to do any kinds of sports to replace spending money to enjoy travel leisure in their holidays,

On conclusion,this COVID 19 disease had influenced global travel leisure businesses and travel related leisure service industries income and travellers number began to reduce and any countries GDP on travelling industry will have negative economic recession occurrence in this COVID 19 disease global envionment. Hence, it implies thaat consumers (travellers) behavior leisure activities need, it may influence global business activities increase or decrease , global economic growth or recession, they have close cause and effect relationship between consumer behavioral change and industries GDP changes in behavioral economic view.

- Can economic environment influence individual learning performance ?

Why does student enrollment rise when the economy recession? When a strugging economy certainly forces extra pressure on young students seeking funds for loans and tuition cost, the enrollment rates for colleges continuous to rise. In fact, some experts theoritize that a poor economy environment actually helps a stimulate student enrollment. Whether it is the economy , new academic programs or better recruiting, community colleges are seeing an enrollment boom, when enrollment has been growing steadily , it may increase year institutions. To help prospective student interests when providing all current students with diverse support.

What the motivation had factors that are encouraging students to enroll, e.g. whether it is that the country 's young people feel the country begins have poor economy, so many of them choose to enroll schools to learn new knowledge, because scoial poor economy environment, it won't have many employers like to pay more salaries to employ new employees, consequencey, unemployment rate will rise, it causes students feel difficult to find jobs to do in general, even graduate students. So, it seems that economy recession may encourage students further study, because job supply is decreasing. so, it causes many young people choose to spend time to further study in order to wait economy recovery later. Then, they can prepare to seek any new jobs more easily when there are many employers like to increase employees number.

So, it explains that they have case and effect relationship between student enrollment number and the country's economy growth or recession or recovery, For example, when the country economy growth, in society, it will have many employers like to spend more salaries to employ new employees, because there are many people like to consume, when most of them have jobs to do and earn higher income. so, it seems that in society consumer individual increasing consumption attitude/desire that can help businesses grow, when businesses have more customers, they have effort to pay money to buy any things to use.

Businessmen ought need to increase employees number to help them to develop themselve businesses more successfully. So, it is economy growth period, moreover, many young people feel economy growth can create more employment chance in society. So, it encourages many students choose to forget to continue to pursue high level academic education, e.g. when the student had graduated undergraduate degree, due to he feels social economic environment is improved. So, employers are seeking new employees to help them to develop businesses. So, employment chance increases and salaries level will also rise. So, it encourages many undergraduate students do not want to pursue master degree. Because they believe that they can find jobs to do more easily in this time. So, it seems that the society's present economy suitation is either goos or worse, it can impact students to choose continue pursue higher learning stage or not. So, it explains that student individual learning desire and the social economy have close influential relationship.

● Why does economy scenarios can influence student learning behavior?
Why does economy scenarios can influence motivation and learning behavior on student achievement? Quality in higher education is not only determined by lecturers, it also depends on student individual learning desire, because if economy scenarios can influence the student learning desire to pursue continue learning or seek jobs in society.

Then, quality in higher education won't be main factor to influence student individual learning in success or failure. If the student does not plan to continue to learn, even the school has good quality in higher education , it won't attract the student to choose to enrol to the school to continue learn easily. It is due to whether economy scenarios how influences the student decides to pursue or forget further study.

In fact, any countries must encounter or experience economic recession or economic growth or economic recovery period different social economic environment changes. It will bring negative or positive emotion impact to the country's every student learning attitude, in order to decide whether continue pursue learning is better or forget pursue learning is better. So, school fee whether is high or less, it is not main factor to influence student individual continue learn.

In macro economic view, the social's economic growth, or economic recession or economic recovery , any one of these economic scenarios change, it will bring positive or negative emotion impact to encourage the student either chooses to further learning pursue or forgive further learning pursue, in student further learning social behavioral economic view.

ON conlusion, on behavioral economic analytical theory, it explains our social macro economic environment new changes to be better or worse, it may bring indirect impact to influence the country's student individual learning desire or learning behavior either on pursue continue learning or forget continue learning in global societies. So, it also implies that whether the school's fee whether it is more or less, it is not main factor to influence student individual continue pursue to learn or not. If the student feels that movement, himself/herself country's social economic scenario is worse, or it is experiencing recession. The student will be influenced to choose continue to go to school to pursue further learning. So, worse economic environment or recession macro economic environment feeling, it may persuade any country's students trend to choose to pursue further study intention more than seeking jobs to work intention, because they feel social jobs provisin chances are influenced to reduce, and no many jobs to supply to them to choose, salaries will be reduced etc . these factors , they can caes the country will have many students make school enrollment choice more than seeking jobs choice. Hence, I believe that any country students school enrollment choices, they have close relationship to themselves country's economic scenario changes at the moment. Hence in behavioral economic view, it may explain why and how any country's economic environment can bring either positive or negative emotion influence to persuade or dissuade the student chooses to either continue further academic study or forgive continue further academic study.

So, behavioral economy theory is one kind of new economy and psychological science. Psychologists can apply this theory to research and explain and conclude how and why our social economy change can impact students, consumers, households, businessmen believe in order to make rational decision to earn more economic benefit and avoid economic loss. Also, behavioral economy theory also may help psychologists and economists to predict how and why our societies will ought to be changed to be better ot worse by which kind of factors accurately. So, it may help government leaders or businesses organizations decision makers to do more accurate decisions or strategies to solve any challenges in success.

- Can bchavioral psychologist apply vehicle owner individual driving times to measure or evaluate whether he/she has high income level or whether his/her income increases or decreases?

Can drivers' driving time reflect his/her general income level ? In general, whether private car owners , their driving times can be influenced by income changing level? It depends on different factors, e.g. the car driver does not want often spend 10 minutes to wait bus from home to working places or from working places to home two ways frequently.

I assume that, in general, private car owners do not want often drive themselves cars to go to anywhere, e.g. working people usually only like to drive themselves cars , when they need to work, even holiday leisure activity, they need to drive cars to arrive the leisure activity destination. So, it seems that any car owners , their cars purchase aims, they are either for working needs or leisure aims mainly. So, I bring this question: Suggesting that any countreis car owners, their cars purchase usually for leisure and working both intention. Can the car owner's per month driving times, it can reflect his/her income level whether it increases or decreases? It means that the car owner will increase driving car times, when his salary has increased or the car owner will decrease driving car times, when his salary has decreased? Can driving car times represent the car owner his/her general increasing or decreasing salary? Have they relationship between increasing or decreasing to car owner's driving times and his/her salary increasing or decreasing level?

Behhavioral economists can attempt to apply behavioral economic view to research general car owners their driving behaviors. In general, when can fuel price increases, it may influence car owners to reduce driving times because when they drive themselves cars frequently, their cars must need to use much fuel. Consequently, they will need to pay higher price to buuy another long driving time useful fuel. So, when any one car owner knows that car fuel prices are general increasing. They will be influenced to reduce to drive themselves cars to avoid more expenditure spending on car fuel aspect.

So, I assume car fuel price increases, it can influence general car users reduce themselves driving car times per day. They won't drive themselves to go to far destination, uness the destination is not too far. It means that general car owners like to drive cars to go to short distance destination only, if general car fuel price has increased significantly in local car fuel market. Hence, it seems that car fuel price whether rises up or falls down, it can influence many car owners avoid often drive themselves cars to go to long distance destination, in order to avoid frequent high fuel price expense. Also , it means that any car fuel seller ought not often rise fuel price in order to avoid many car owners reduce driving times behaviors. Consequently, car fuel and car purchase number will be influenced to reduce when the country has many car owners reduce driving times to go to long distance destination. It is driving car and using car fuel behavioral market principle, it means that when the car fuel price general increases, it influences general car owners reduce driving car want more times, because they do not want often buy new car fuel ar rising price level to avoid not essential economic loss on rising price of car fuel expenditure.

Hence, if this supposion to " general rising car fuel price level, " it will influence general car owners avoid to drive themselves cars to go to long distance destinations. It is reasonable and their driving car times will be influenced to reduce in society. Then, it explains that behavioral economists can attempt to gather general social car owner individual driving car times increases or decreases between last month and this month to evaluate whether it is direct car fuel price as well as whether it rises or falls down. This factor can judge whether what factor can cuse general car owner individual driving times increases or decreases in society. Also, it implies that we can depend on general car owner individual driving behavioral times to judge whether the car owner's salaary level had been increased or had been decreasing in the past. It is possibe that general social car owner individual driving time behavior is significantly increasing or decreasing, it may reflect whether the car owner has present salary , it has been increasing or has been decreasing. Because if the car owner whose salary has been decreasing significantly, the significant decresaing salary, it may influence the car owner reduces to spend long time to drive car to arrive another long distance far away destination frequently.

The reason is that he avoids to increase economic loss to use more car fuel for non essential driving use, when he feels that his income is significantly decreased.

Hence, any behavioral economists may attempt to gather household individual general expenditure data in order to conclude what factors influence the household changes his/her family behavioral consumption or consumption attitude. It means thay any household individual consumption attitude changes, it may be influenced by any product price changing factor, such as car fuel price case or the household overall rising or falling income level factor in household behavioral economic view.

Can market environment influence oil price change?

Market economy theory is an economic system and distribution are guide by the price signals created by the force of suppy and demand. So , the concept of market economy is an economic system in which economic decisions, and the pricing of goods and services are guided by the interactions of a country's individual citizens and businesses.

The both principles of market economy dicated that producers and sellers of goods and servces with offer tham at the highest possible price that consumers are willing to pay for goods and services . When the level of supply needs to level of demand a natural economic equilibrium is achieved. Hong Kong, Singapore, New Zealand, Switerland, United States , Ireland united Kingdom, these countries are applying market economy prinsiple to dominate themselves countries business activities. However, it is difficult to free market economy, because market economy depends on supply and demand regulate the economy, but a time free market economy is an economy in what all resources are owned by individuals.

The advantages of a market economy may include : Innovation, variety, and indidual choices, but it is distribution of wealth, poor work condition and environmental degradation. However, a pure market economy development is difficult because people will always have incentives to use to choose what kinds of product in preference. The characteristics of a market economy, they may include that it is unplanned free enterprise, private property, economic freedom, consumer competition incentive profit pursue, voluntary exchange,, limited government involvement, freedom of enterprise and choice, the role of self interest, market and price, the reliance on technology and capital goods, specialization, use of monetary ad to active, but limited role of government.

So, market economies work using the forces of supply and demand to determine the appropriate prices and quantities for most goods and services in the economy. Hence, one country needs to develop market economy, it needs have a good market environment, such as one commodity needs have advertisement to let consumers to know its existence, in economics, market does not refer why to a fixed location, on enough number balance of buyers and sellers, perfect competition, perfect competition, building good relationship between buyers and sellers, one price (no change) price to any product easily, sound monetary system. Then, when the country can have good market environment, it can develop or implement its market economy strategy more easily.

The free market economy may be the best economic strategy choice because it contributes to economic growth . It ensures competitive markets, supply and demand create competition, which also help ensure that this best goods or services are provided to consumers at a lower price (reasonable price). It can compare the best among perfect competition imperfect competition, oligopoly, monopoly. Hence, market economy encourages market force occurrence, e.g. when the price of crude oil increases, when there are shortages in the supply , when the shortages occur, they become market forces. The demand is more supply, which causes the prices to rise as the crude oil is less available and therefore consumers will be willing to pay more.

The market economy is decides, when the eants of the consumers and the profit motive of the producers will decide what will be produced and management (the owners) together will determine how goods will be produced in a market economy. So, such as oil sale case, when the country has many oil manufactures hope to tisee oil price, they won't manufacture more oil to supply to oil users, e.g. car drivers, public transport service organizations, the aim to bring oil shortage supply in order to rise oil price more easily.
So, free market economy may bring product unfair sale price to any consumers in the country. Because free market economy is too free for manufacturers / producers to make unreasonable product manufacturing decision whether their products manufacturing number (supply number) is more ore less in order to achieve the highest sale price.It

won't bring consumer benefit, when they need to pay high price to buy the product in long time. For oil product case example, when the country all oil suppliers, they make decision to manufacture less number oil product in order to reduce oil supply number. They aim to cause oil shortage crise, when the oil needers, e.g. when the country has many air planes need gas to private energy to fly frequently, but gas supply is less to airlines to pay higher gas price to buy, or the country has many people need to catch buses, but gas supply number is less. So, bus companies also need to pay higher gas price to buy even the country has many people own cars. They often need to drive cars to go to work or relax. So, many country car owners , they eed to pay higher gas price to drive themselves cars.

In fact, in the country implements free market economy strategy, so it causes many product manufacturers attempt to cooperate to reduce products manufacturing number. They aim to reduce produc supply , but when consumers number is still increasing. Their demand to the product increases, when the product's demand number is more than supply number, it will cause supply shortage crise. Consequently, the kind of product price may be reasonable to increase. Hence, in consumer behavior view, the country's consumers still accept to pay higher price to buy the product, because they believe the kind of product supply is decreasing.

Hence, it has relationship between how many product choice and consumer payment desire, if the market has many difficukt kinds of product to let consumers to choose, then the kind of product's price can not be increased easily. Such as oil product case, when the country has less number oil manufacturing number. Then, oil buyers feel there are not many oil suppliers to let them to choose and in general these several oil suppliers' oil prices are increasing together . So, oil consumers number will not be influenced to reduce easiy, because they have no many oil suppliers choice in the country.

What factors influence consumer purchase decision ?

Economic theory is based on the assumption that investors and consumers are rational and very efficient machines. They make the best choices for themselves. Laboratory tests reveal that investors' behaviors are much more complicated relative to the behavior assumes in most economic theories. Hence, economic theories is used by economists, they try to explain economic phenomena, to interpret why and how the economy behaves and what is the best to solution, how to influence or solve these economic phenomean. In principle, the approach to economic theory is divided into positive and normative.

The most popular economic theories include; Analyses of different market structures have yields economic theories that dominate the study of microeconomics. IN general, economic theory is applied to market organizations. They are perfect competition, monololistic competition, olgopolu, imperfect competition.

So, in any business environment, business on abve four type of economic organizations, they may attempt to apply economic theory to complex consumers behavior. Consumer behavior theory is the study of have people make decisions when they purchase, helping businesses and marketers capitalise on these behaviors by predicting how and when a consumer will make a purchase in economic environment organizational view.

In fact, in societies any economic factors may influence consumer behavior. Economic factors that influence consumer behaviors are : personal income, family income, income expectation, savings, liquid asset of consumer. So, it seems that personal income of a person is determinant of consumer individual buying behavior.

Hence, the role theory says that much of what we buy is to fulfill to characteristics of a role we see ourselves as playing. This can help us understand consumer behavior because people are more likely to buy things for what they mean not for what they do. So, the theory is consumer realistic because of consumers focus on a modest let of important goods and services, they may able to achieve societies is close to the theoretical optimum in term over utility.

● How economic theory explains our social consumer behavior causes?
For example, one product brand and advertisement strategy, if the product can develop good attractive advertisement and famous brand. Its campaigns may be a real asset in economic view to better meet the needs of its customers and increases sales (socio-economic classification).

If act, instead of economic factor can influence consumer behavior, other factors may also influence they include psychological, social , cultural personal factors, e.g. social class, role and status, personal age, occupation, life style, personality, motivation, past purchase experience. All of these are the consumer individual psychological factor. So, economic environment changes, it may influence consumers, how to decide to buy the kind of products, but this economic factor, it can not control or derminate overall consumer behavior in the overall consumption mrket (country) , in maco economic vie , the micro economic view, psychology factor to the consumer, it can also dominate or control the consumer behavior, e.g. product choice. For example, one lawyer, he had good lawyer job and high income to support him to pay one time expenditure to buy a new car, so he does not pay instalement to the car seller to buy the new car. So, in behavioral economic view, he won't have economic pressure to buy the new car, he does not need to pay installment and interest to own the new car after one year. Hence, when he gathers information concerns the new car technology development, he spends time to compare the new car different brands, price new car dealr choice, purchase timing and amount, after purchase repair service behavior. He makes the evaluation of alternative to different brands of new cars. Although, brand (A) is new car, its price is more expensive to compare other kinds of cars, because it has good design, large size, more seats, steel quality for driving safety reasons. He has enough money economic effort to choose to buy this brand (A) new car. But, when he compares it to another brand (B) new car. Although, its present car price is cheaper, but it does not represent tht its stell quality is worse, or not more driving safety and he also knows that the brand (B) new car will have another new car model to promote to car market, after three months. Moreover, brand (B) new car seller can build famous car brand image to same to brand (A) new car by its advertisement channel.

Hence, it seems that it is one perfect competition (fair competition) new car market in this country. Any new car sallers can dominate or control their new car sale price freely. So, this country new car market competition is serious, because this high income lawyer spends time to compare the both brand (A) and (B) new cars. He will be influenced to choose to buy brand (B) new car by its advertisement. So, this lawyer car purchaser will not feel that friends believe him have high income to influence him to choose to buy the brand (A) new car. He only consider whether which brand (A) and (B) nee car price is more reasonable factor to influence him to make the final new car purchase decision. So, the brand (B) new car's advertisement had persuaded him to choose to buy (A) last invention new car after 3 months. He chooses to delay time to buy brand (B) 's new invention car after 3 months, because he does not need to drive one new car immediately.

Hence, it seems that economic theory factor won't be the main factor to influence the lawyer to buy the brand (A) new car immediately, althought he has high stable income job. His psychological factor also influences his new car brand choice decision, e.g. he will feel that whether it can represent he has high social status or class when friends know he had owned one high price of new car, whether a high price of new car must represent he has high income of lawyer occupation, so, it seems that this high income lawyer must not choose to buy the high price of new car. he must neeed time to gather or research information to evaluate whether which brand of new car is valid to choose to buy.

Consequently, economic theory must not explain absolute right consumer behavior, it also depends on other factor, e.g. behavioral economic psychological factor, to assist it to conclude more accurate judgement why and how the consumer does his/her final purchase decision. So, psychologic economic theory can apply psychology and economic theory to conclude more clear understanding how and why the consumer chooses to do his/her final purchase decision in nowadays consumption market.

Whether what are the actual benefits , they may bring to influence our societies change better? I shall attempt to to explain above question. Economic is the social science that examines how individuals, businesses and entire societies manage scarce resources. Resources are by nature , limited. Only a finite amount of land exists, e.g. and people do not have unlimieted time to meet all of their needs and wants. So, if we can learn ho to apply behavioral economy theory to avoid resources waste, then our societies ought develop better.

Our society had changed from traditional economy to develop to nowadays knowledge economy. Traditional economy only produce and take what they need, so there is no waste or inefficiencies involved in produdig the goods required to survive as a society. However, traditional economy also have disadvantages, such as it isolates the people within that economt, large outside economies can win a traditional economy. It offers choices, these may be a lower overall quality of life, it creates specific health risk, unpredictability creates survival uncertainties.

Although, our socictics had been experiencing knowledge economy, but it also have disadvantage, knowledge economy means that our societies or business organizations need to learn how ro use knowledge management to keep business growth or social developing. Knowledge management is a systematic approach to capturing and making use of a organization collective expertise to create value. The potential advantages of effective knowledge management are significant , but as with most processes, advantages of knowledge management or knowledge econmic society may include:

Improved organizational or social productivities better and faster decision making, quicker problem solving, increased rate of innovation, supported employee/citizen growth and development within organizations or societies, sharing of specialiat expertise, better communication, improved business processes.

Hence if the organization or society can apply behavioral economic theory to learn knowledge management system , it can help the organization or society to develop better or more easier, e.g. create better products and services , develop better strategies, improve profitability or productivity, reuse existing skills and expertise, increase operational efficiency and staff productivity, recognise market trends early and gain on advantage over rivals make the most of organizations or social intellectual capital . Hence, it explains why when our organizations or societies can apply behavioral economy theory to learn how to apply knowledge management system to develop our organiztations or societies. Then, our societies or organizations will avoid to waste social resource organizational resource as well as achieve more productivities or service improvement, even gain profitability, it is the final aim of why our organizations or / and societies need to attempt to learn how to apply knowledge management system to achieve any objectives in behavioral economy view.

On conclusion, behavioral economic is the study of the effect that our societiesand organizations need to learn how psychological factors have on the economic decision making process of individuals. The importance of understanding behavioral economics for marketers is immeasurable as it follows for a better understanding of the human mind. So, behavioral economics plays a important role in our live and in the eocnomy. It helps governments and businesses learn on every day consumers activities and explains why we consume goods and services , the way we do, why we make certain choices, about ourselves or others and how we decide of action . Hence, behavioral economists need to examine each of these day -to -day choice resulting in progressive understanding of human behavior that combines both psychology and economy.

How do rules influence economic behavior?
Why are the rules of the economic system important? In our societies , our economic behavior occurs in a climate

of formal and informal rules. There sulres often act as incentives and influenced the choices people make, people choose to do jobs taht do not keep them fit, and now they have to make more time to stay healthy. So, our societies are experiencing behavioral economic rules made in order to let every one need to adapt how to change and influence to our lives. it is one actual knowledge economic society or knowledge economic social living mode that we need to learn how to adapt to live. We need to learn how to apply knowledge of economic changing behavior. UNderstanding behavioral economic and psychology for social impact our businesses can bring products , sale growth more easily or our societies can be improved to our living quality better.

The relationship between behavioral economy and our society , it may explain that if the result of economic scarcity in a society occurrence, due to that productive resources are limited, therefore, people can not have all the goods and services, they want, a result, they must choose some things and give up others , like individuals, governments and societies , experience scarcity because human wats exceed with can be made from all available resources.

Behavioral economic is the study of psychology as it relates to the economic decision making processes of individuals and organizations. Behavioral economy theory uses psychological experimentation to develop theories about human decision making and has identified a range of biases as a result of the way people think and feel. BE is trying to change the way economists think about people's perception of value and expressed preferences.

However, in our societies, we need have three basic economic problems. Economic systems is as a type social system must confront and solve the three quantities of goods shall be produced, how much and which of alternative tools and services shall be produced, how shall goods be produced what technology a well as for whom are the goods , or services produced who benefts?

All of these are our daily economic problems any organizations (societies) had been changing. We need new social science behavioral economy theory to help use to solve any one of social economic individual problems, for example, when a particular incident becomes cognitively available, it is became of social influence. Individuals are specially averse to losses, but how do we know whether we are facing a loss or instead of a foregone gain ? What is the status from which losses are measured ? how might social influence reduces or increase people's willingness to sacrifice their material sale-interest for the sake of fairness?

All of these matter, applying behavioral economic theory may attempt to explain the reason why the consequency occurs. Also, when some countries governments can apply behavioral economy theory to help them to do reasonable strategic decision in order to avoid any one of these social negative events occur, such as organizational crime, discrimination, environmental hazards, or threats to national security before any one country government decides to implement any strategic action, they may apply behavioral economic theory to weigh whether their decision may bring socity to earn more benefit or more loss, for example, if the country government permits the oil manufacturing firm continues to research the possible oil manufacturing elements at the oceans. Whether their oil research behavior on the ocean , it will bring how serious environmental hazard to cause global oceans have many fishes die per day, how much percentage successful chance oil discovery on anywhere in the oceans.

So, any country governments need to consider whether ocean land oil discovery chance is more important or reducing many fishes death number is more important when any country goverments continue to permit any one oil manufacturers continue to find oil land from oceans in order to manufacture more oil, during their ocean oil land manufacturing process, it may bring serious pollution to ocean water and causes many fishes drink the polluted oil water to be killed. For another exmaple, US government allows many local manfacturers set up factories in China, in order to let many US social manufacturers can pay cheap wages to employ China workers to help them to manufacture any products, e.g. mobiles, shoes, cloths, shirts, televisions etc. although US governmment can bring discrimination image to let China workers feel, they can have more job chance and to earn US manufacturer employers wages. In economic view, China can reduce workers unemployment ratio from US manufacturers' factories manufacture jobs chance. Also , US manufacturers can pay cheaper wages to Chinese workers to compare US domestic workers wages. But, US government neglects , it will also cause many US domestic factories manufacture workers had beed beginning to lose their factory manufacture jobs, because Chinese manfacture workers can replace them to do their Us social factory manufacture jobs more easily. Hence, in long term, US manfacturers choose to outsource local factory manufacture workers to them to do, it will cause US unemployed workers manufacture number increases., Hence , US government ought need to weigh long term high unemployment ratio social issue to US domestic factory manufacturing workers, whether US manufacturers cheap or low wages to Chinese factory manufacturing workers (low wage cost) is more important ot reducing US domestic factory manufacturing workers unemployed number social negative influence more important. If US government continue allows US manufacturers outsource domestic factory manufacturing workers to do, it must increase US local manufacturing workers unemployment number and it may cause US government needs to pay future more social welfare expenditure to these long time unemployment US manufacturing workers, even, social stealing crime may be influenced to increase . It implies that behavioral economy analysis can help our society to choose to make more reasonable decisions.

Can economic recession influence car buyers‘ purchases desire reduce? In macro economic view, it explains that economic recession means that the country has many people loss jobs, because economic recession, it causes many employers begain to reduce employees number to avoid salary expenditure increases, but clients number reduces. Hence, when one country is experiencing economic recession period, it will causes people reduces shopping expenditures, when many of people lose themselves jobs or some people feel that they will lose jobs as soon as possible . So, in societies, general consumers' consumption desires will be influenced to reduce, due to many of people had lost jobs or many of people feel that their employers will dismiss them due to they feel busineses are worse.

IN behavioral economic view, when one society has high unemployment ratio, e.g. graduate students can not find jobs easily, many of working people are losing present jobs, it implies that the country is experiencing economic recession .So, it will cause many products can not sell easily in the society, e.g. one Dell brand laptop price is average US$1,000. IN last year, the country US Dell brand laptop price was average US$1,000. IN common, Dell brand could sell this model laptop products 100,000 laptop numbers in last year. HOwever, in this year, Dell this model laptop price is not changed, it keeps US$1,000 average price, but Dell only sells 50,000 laptop number in US this year. So, it seems that US is experiencing recession, because there are many US people lose jobs, they can not find another jobs easily in short time. SO, in general, many US people begin to prepare some money in bank and they begin to reduce spend to buy any things easily. Also, because laptop is not essential product to anyone. It is only students, office employers and employees both customer target may be laptop product's main consumer groups. Another retired people, housewives, households they must feel need to buy laptop to use at homes. So, it explains that why US Dell brand laptop is significant decreasing laptop buyers (customers) number.Moreover, due to this US Dell brand laptop products average price are still kept to same to US$1,000 average price. It can not persuade laptop consumers to choose to buy Dell brand any laptop products easily when they may make price comparison to other similar kinds of laptop model products, e.g. Apple brand, Microsoft brand etc.

However, I assume that even Dell brand wil decide to reduce its different model of laptops average price to US $700 even $500 each piece. I believe that Dell brand computer seller is still difficult to sell its any model of laptop products easily in this year. The reason is because that when this year US is experiencing recession, in this high unemployment ratio US recession environment, many losing job American will avoid to spend to buy high price product, or the non essential product, such as laptop product it must not be essential product for any one and its price may be expensive to let the unemployed US people feel its price is too much to compare general non essential products, e.g. books, shoes, cloths etc. So, in ecojnomic recession environment, it may cause some general non essential products will be difficlut sold in the country's business market. It means that laptop is non essential product,.

So, when the country is encountering recession period, the country's laptop product consumer desire may be influenced to fall down. Although, some laptop sellers attempt to reduce their sale price in order to attract or persuade they choose to buy their any laptops. But, lower sale price , it is still difficult to help them to increase laptop sale number because general consumers will avoid to spend to buy non essential products, they will save much money in bank to prepare possible unemployment matters occur to them suddenly. So, when the country has many people feel that unemployment matter may occue to them suddenly, many people will choose to save more money in bank because they feel that they will be hard to find another jobs in short time easily, even graduate students or owning more year working experience people, they will plan to find another job to work in short time.

So, it explains that economic recession may influence consumer purchase desire to reduce, in special essential products purchase need to consumer will be influenced to reduce. Nut, essential products consumer purchase desire, they won't be influenced to reduce, otherwise their purchase desire may be influenced to rise when recession occurs, e.g. rice , vegetable, meat, pork, orange, banana, apple friuts common food. Why does essential products , such as foods their price may raise and food consumers purchase desire will not be influenced to reduce in recession. The reason is simple, when one country is experiencing recession, for example, COVID 19 disease occurrence, it can influence global people feel agraid, foods may be shortage to supply to their countries, e.g. China, there are many people feel fear that they can not buy rice, vegetable, meat foods from supermarket easily. Because COVID 19 disease influences many Chinese restaurants clients number decreaes, they are afraid to go to restaurants to contact the COVID 19 disease people to sit on the same table to eat together. So, restaurant clients decrease. COVID 19 disease occurrence influences many Chinese people choose to go to supermarkets to buy foods to cook at homes. So, supermarket foods purchase need number may be influenced to increase. Consequently, supermarket foods prices may be influenced to increase, because many Chinese people prefer to buy foods to cook from supermarkets to eat. So, in China present economic recession environment, COVID 19 disease encourages many Chinese household families choose to go to supermarkets to buy foods to cook at home, because food is essential to any one. So, Chinese supermarket food price may be influenced to increase by COVID 19 disease occurrence influence.

Organizational Behavioral economic management strategy

How organizations implement behavioral economy strategy ?

What does organizational behavioral economic strategy mean ? Behavioural economics aids marketing strategies by understanding how consumer decisions can be influenced. Behavioural economics is about understanding, not manipulating, consumers. Marketers can use these biases to craft ethical and informative campaigns that resonate with the target audience. The four elements of organizational behavior are people, structure, technology, and the external environment. By understanding how these elements interact with one another, improvements can be made. So, these four elements can help organizations how to implement behavioral economic strategy.. I shall explain as below:

Behavioral economics combines elements of economics and psychology to understand how and why people behave the way they do in the real world. It differs from neoclassical economics, which assumes that most people have well-defined preferences and make well-informed, self-interested decisions based on those preferences. Behavioral economy strategy can be applied to consumers or organizations both.

Organizations are also heavily influenced by economic factors. A market crash or a recession will directly impact the sales of an organization. When people are no longer able to afford a product or choose to spend their money elsewhere, companies are directly impacted.

According to the results, a majority of respondents said that the four C's—critical thinking, communication, collaboration and creativity—have been articulated within their organizations as priorities for employee development, talent management and succession planning. Strategic behaviour is basically decisions that take into account the possible reactions of others. For understanding strategic behaviour we use game theory. Economists have found that many examples of strategic behaviour can be understood by relying on the core concepts of incentives and information.

The most widely accepted model of OB consists of three interrelated levels: (1) micro (the individual level), (2) meso (the group level), and (3) macro (the organizational level). The behavioral sciences that make up the OB field contribute an element to each of these levels

Travel organizational behavioral economy strategy

How to determine future travel behavior from past travel experience and perceptions of risk and safety for the benefits to travel consumers?

How to determine future travel behavior from past travel experience and perceptions of risk and safety for the benefits to travel consumers? Why does individual traveler avoid certain destination(s) is(are) as relevant to tourist decision making as why who chooses to travel to others. Perceptions of risk and safety and travel experience are likely to influence travel decisions. If travel agents had efforts to predict future travel behavior to guess whether travelers will feel where is(are) risk and unsafe to cause who does not choose to go to the country to travel. Then, the travel agents will avoid to choose to spend much time to design the different traveling package to attract their potential travel consumers to choose to travel. The reason is because in the case of individual traveler's tourism experience, the traveler whose past disappointment travel experience (psychological risk) will be a serious threat to the traveler's health or life (health, physical or terrorism risk). The past safety or unhealthy risk to the country(countries) will influence the traveler decides to choose not to go to the countries(country) to travel again in the future.

What is push and pull factors to influence any traveler who chooses where is whose preferable travelling destination.

How to predict individual traveler's behavioral intention of choosing a travel destination. Understanding why people travel and what factors influence their behavioral intention of choosing a travel destination is beneficial to tourism planning and marketing. In general, an individual's choice of a travel destination into two forces. The first force is the push factor that pushes an individual away from home and attempt to develop a general desire to go somewhere, without specifying where that may be. The other force is the pull factor that pull an individual toward in destination, due to a region-specific or perceived attractiveness of a destination. The respective push and pull factors illustrate that people travel because who are pushed by whose internal motives and pulled by external forced of a destination. However, the decision making process leading to the choice of a travel destination is a very complex process. For example, a Taiwanese traveler who might either choose new travel destination of Hong Kong or another old travel Asia destinations again or who also might choose any one of Western country, as a new travel destination. The travel agents can predict where who will have intention to choose to travel from whose past behavior and attitude, subjective and perceived behavioral control model.

The factors influence where is the traveler choice, include personal safety, scenic beauty, cultural interest, climate changing, transportation tools, friendliness of local people, price of trip, trip package service in hotels and restaurants, quality and variety of food and shopping facilities and services etc. needs. So, whose factors will influence where is the individual travel's choice. It seems every traveler whose choice of travel process, will include past behavior. e.g. travelling experience, travelling habit, then to choose the best seasoned travelling action to satisfy whose travel needs. This process is the individual traveler's psychological choice process, who must need time to gather information to compare concerning of different travel packages, destination scene, climate change, transportation tools available to the destination, air ticket price etc. these factors, then to judge where is the best right destination to travel in the right time.

Why expectation, motivation and attitude factor can influence travelling behaviour.

Social psychology is concerned with gaining insight into the psychological of socially relevant behaviors and the processes. For instance, on a global level bad influence to global warming, it influences some countries extreme cold or hot bad climate changing occurrence, then it ought influence some travelers' behavioral decision to change their mind to choose some countries to go to travel at the moment which do not occur extreme hot or cold climate (temperature). e.g. above than 40 degree in summer or below than 0 degree in winter. Due to the extreme climate changing environment in the countries, it will cause them to feel uncomfortable to play during their trips. So, the global warming causes to climate changing factor will influence the numbers of travel consumption to be reduced possibly. This is global climate changing environment factor influences to bad or uncomfortable social psychological feeling to global travelers' mind of traveling decision. What is individual traveler expectation, motivation and attitude? Tourism sector includes inbound (domestic) tourism and outbound (overseas) tourism both incomes to any countries. According to recent article, a tourist behavior model has been developed, called the expectation, motivation and attitude (EMA) model (Hsu et al., 2010).

This model focuses on the pre-visit stage of tourists by modeling the behavioral process by incorporating expectation, motivation and attitude. Travel motivation is considered as an essential component of the behavioral process, which has been increasing attention from the travel; industry. The economic approach defines "tourism" is an identifiable nationally important industry. It includes the component activities of transportation, accommodation, recreation, food and related service. So, tourism behavioral consumption is concerned the individual tourist's usual habituate of the industry which responds to whose needs, and of the impacts that both the tourist and the tourism industry have on the socio-cultural, economic and physical environment.

However, travel motivation means how to understand and predict factors that influence travel decision making. According to Backman and others (1995, p.15), motivation is conceptually viewed as " a state of need, a condition that services as a driving force to display different kind of behavior toward certain types of activities, developing preferences, arriving at some expected satisfactory outcome." So, motivation and expectancy which has close relationship to any tourist before who decided to do any tourism of behavior. Some economists confirmed motivation and expectancy which has relations, such as expectation of visiting an outbound destination has a direct effect on motivation to visit the destination; motivation has a direct effect on attitude toward visiting the destination; expectation of visiting the outbound destination has a direct affect on attitude toward visiting the destination and motivation has a mediating effect on the relationship in between expectation and attitude.

Educational organizational behavioral economy strategy

Tutoring method factor

The tutoring method factor includes self-determined tutoring, academic advisor schedules tutoring, group tutoring, one-to-one tutoring, peer tutoring and professional tutoring. These different kinds of tutoring method can influence the final grades to any academic student. As the cognitive learning theory and humanistic theory both are for this study conceptual framework. The results of a one-way analysis of variance determined there were significant differences in final grades of students who received group tutoring compared to one-to-one tutoring and peer tutoring compared to professional tutoring.

In fact, many colleges and universities have had to provide tutoring to attend to the needs of all students' aims to teach them how to write assignments and how to exam to get higher grades. However, any methods of a tutoring will have benefits and weakness to any students. For example, students who attend group tutoring may have an advantage because other students may contribute additional information relevant to questions, whereas one-to-one tutoring will give the students the undivided attention of the tutor. In addition, students who attend tutoring provided by their peers rather than professonal tutors may feel more relaxed and relate to them differently then professional helpers. What methods do tutors use? Tutoring methods usually include self-determined, academic advisor, determined programs group, one-to-one, peer and professional tutoring. What is the relationship between final grades and tutoring programs. I suggested that academic programs, particularly professional tutoring are successful and may lead to increase student persistence in course completion. In fact, students who activity participated in the tutoring program had greater academic success compared to those who did not participate in the tutoring program. Further, no researchers had compared outcomes for students who received tutoring in a group setting rather than one-to-one settings.

In addition, no researchers had compared outcomes for students who receive tutoring from peer tutors rather than professional tutors. Also no research was found that outcomes were for students who were required to participate in tutoring services, but allowed to self-determine that schedules. However, research has shown that students who voluntary received tutoring service regularly most often received a passing grade in the course for which who received tutoring.

Reading habits among students and its effect on academic performance factor

Reading habits are well planned of study which has attained a form of consistency on the part of students towards understanding academic subjects and passing at examinations. Both reading and academic achievements are interrelated and dependent on each other. Reading habits involve personal investigation, self-study, self thinking and analysis to each bok's content. So, reading habit is the student himself/herself motivation, it is not motivated by teachers, who need to spend their leisure time in reading both English and literature. However, the problem most students have that contributes to their poor performance in tests and examinations is lack of proper reading habits. For an excellent performance, there is the need to the student to form good reading and study habits. Whether what are the reading habits among students? Has reading habit effect on academic performance? Is there a relationship between student's reading habits and academic performance? What kind of materials to students read when who visit the library? Why do students engage in reading? People read for different reasons and purposes, some of which include for pleasure, leisure, relaxation and for knowledge.

In student view point, reading is an essential tool for knowledge transfer and the habit of reading is academic activity that increases skills in reading strategies. It seems reading habit can help any student to raise knowledge and writing ability to prepare to write their assignments for those different subjects and examinations. It is possible that examination grades and study habit has close relationship.

Class attendance and academic performance factor

The major reasons are given by students for non-attendance which include external influences of assessment pressures, poor delivery of lecturers, timing of lectures and work commitments and financial constraints. Indeed, web-based learning approaches have become popular instead of some classroom attendance universities in our societies. So, it causes students who don't need to attend to classroom regularly. Although, some existing evidence points to a strong correlation between attendance and academic performance, no effect of the studies citied above demonstrate a causal affect. However, the levels of motivation, intelligence, prior learning and time-management skills is a major limiting factor to the utility of causal affect. However, these relationships are contingent upon a number of factors, such that it is nearly impossible to predict academic performance using socio-economic. To conclude, the non-attendance or attendance factor influences academic performance is difficult to measure, such as student motivation, socio-economic status and attendance is required to influence why the student choose to attend or not attend the classrooms.

The conclusion to drawn from this study is that gender, age, learning preference and entry qualifications did not cause any significant variation in the academic performance of students. Although, some students' academic performance were not significantly different from the rest of the students. It seems some talent students who don't need to attend any classrooms and their non-attendance behaviors won't influence their academic performance to be bad. Otherwise, some foolish students who need to attend classrooms to achieve passing grades.

Drinking and academic motivation factor

Whether academic motivation can be a mediator for achievement. It was hypothesized that heavy drinking decreases academic motivation, which subsequently also decreases academic achievement. The effects of drinking on univerity grades: Does academic motivation play a role? However, academic achievement can be influenced by a number of factors and the effect of alcohol consumption on achievement has been of particular interest to researcher. Heavy drinking habit of students, e.g. weekly drinking alcohol, and/or consumption six or more alcohol on each occasion of drinking, these heavy drinking alcohol behaviour can influence these drinking wine students whose grades to be gone down in possible. High drinking wine or alcohol habit can cause day time sleepiness, unhealthy behaviours, like unhealthy sleep patterns because they may be linked to behavioural consequences. Due to students who regularly drink alchohol, then whose drinking behaviours have interrupted sleep cycles: They go to bed late, wake up late and experience increased daytime sleepiness. All factors of which were found to be associated with decreased academic performance. It seems heavy drinking alcohol habit of intelligent students will get the bad academic performance also.

The link between sleep quantity and academic performance factor

Whether has it close relationship to link unhealthy sleep habits and academic performance. Such as current study examined the relationship between grade point average (GPA) and sleep, in terms of quality and quantity. In general, human need have four different aspects of sleep quantity. These aspect included number of nights spent with less than five hours of sleep during the past week, as well as during an average week, number of hours of sleep obtained in an average night, as well as the number of all nighter's the students. Results indicated a significant positive correlation between amount of sleep per night with GPA, and a significant negative correlation between average number of day per week that students obtained less than five hours of sleep and GPA.

Health sleep habits can defined , such as self-rated satisfaction with sleep, enough sleeping during the night non difficulty sleeping at night and non over sleeping. If students are unsatisfied with their quality of sleep, who will encounter studying problems, due to who lack nervous to attend any classrooms to listen any lecturers‘ speaking to remember any important contents of their different subjects every day. So, their non sleeping bad behaviour which will cause them to get the bad academic performance in possible finally.

The relationship between physical fitness and academic performance factor

Whether can lacking enough physical fitness sport cause students to get bad academic performance? In fact, human needs health physical ftness of life to carrying on working or studying. Physical movements of the body are vital for normal brain development to children or young adult. So if the child or young adult chooses to spend whose time to often play video games to watch television or occupies himself/herself on the computer on the weekends and after school, instead of any physical fitness sports in whose relax time to spend time to do. It will have chance to cause blood pressure, depression and other diseases to him or her. It seems any student ought have enough time to do physical fitness to keep him or her mental health benefit to prepare to have health body to learn. Otherwise, lacking physical activity will cause lower levels of self-esteem and lower levels of anxiety to cause lower academic performance in the classroom to any students. For example, the mathematics and science students who need have health body to go to classroom to study. So, enough physical sports activities are important to these students. Due to a more focused mindset on academic performance has hindered the quality and quantity of these mathematics and science students to learn in classroom everyday. So, physical fitness has close relationship to academic performance.

The relationship between student's learning style and academic performance factor

The student's personal factor, such as level of motivation, persistence, responsibility and need for structure, whether these factors can can influence whose academic performance. Which is learning style? It is the way a person processes, internalizes and studies new and challenging material. Student's performance may be related to learning preferences or styles as learners. Some experiments indicates that college students taught in their preferred learning styles scores higher on tests, fact knowledge, attitude and efficiency than those taught in instructional style. So mismatch of teaching styles and learning styles could give negative impaxt to students.

In the psychological view, due to students tend to be bored on inattentive in class, do poorly on tests, get discouraged about the course and may conclude that who are not good in the subject. As a result, students' success in classes may depend an understanding the learning style characteristics of students who enrol in the respective courses.

The relationship between time management and academic performance factor

Managing time is any student's responsibilities. Time management is a skill that every student should not only know, but also apply. A lot of university students complain about running out of time when who need to do a certain assignment or prepare examination. They get frustrated beause who are not able to finish it before the due date. On the other hand, they spend a lot of time to meet their friends or playing, so who have no enough time to enhance their learning of productivity in order to get low grades. For example, a subject assignment needs have a important due date to finish to submit because who lack time management skill to predict the size of assignment, who need how long time to finish. So they won't have enough time to finish the assignment to submit before the due date to cause to get fail grade of the assignment. In conclusion, any university students ought need to considerate these bad behaviours can influence their final grades. So, you ought to avoid to do these bad behaviours to reduce your bad grades risk occurrence.

CHAPTER SEVENTEEN

How Apple computer organizations apply behavioral economic strategies to improve service performance

Can Apple computer organization apply behavioral economic strategies to improve service performance ? If they can attempt , how they implement behavioral economic strategies to help them to improve service performance?

Behavior economics is crafted around many principles including framing, heuristics, loss aversion, and the sunk-cost fallacy. Companies use information from behavioral economics to price their goods, craft their commercials, and package their products.

For Apple computer ltd behavioral economic strategy case example:

Apple computer co had attempted to apply behavioral economic strategy to improve service performance. Choice architecture can greatly influence people's decisions. Apple retail stores use the following strategies to present choices for customers: 1) minimize the product choice selection; 2) provide a systematic way to evaluate attributes and make comparisons; and 3) utilizes intertemporal choice for payment options. Apple's method of communicating provides consumers' with trust, confidence, and a set of shared beliefs inspiring people to make a purchase from the company. The how refers to the actions a company takes to bring the beliefs into reality.

Business conduct is a set of principles designed to guide workers to conduct themselves with honesty and integrity in all actions representing a company. There are four main principles that guide Apple's business practices: honesty, respect, confidentiality and compliance. Macroeconomic factors affecting Apple Inc.'s stock performance. Macroeconomic factors play a crucial role in determining the performance of Apple's stock. Economic indicators such as GDP growth, inflation rates, and interest rates can significantly impact the overall sentiment of the stock market.

Apple builds Brand Loyalty through providing a superior customer experience, offering innovative products, and creating a strong brand identity.

Hence, Apple had implemented effective behavioral economic strategy to improve overall customer service performance. Apple conducts consumer behavior surveys to understand their preferences and launch products that can solve existing issues. Brand marketing is a powerful tool that oozes lifestyle, innovation, compassion, and style into the customer experience.

Socio-Psychological Impact of Apple's Brand Image

Apple, with its distinct brand image, creates a sense of belonging to the "Apple community." Consumers who identify with this group are more likely to conform to its preferences and behaviors.

Creating Brand Loyalty:

Product Ecosystem: Apple encourages customers to stay within its ecosystem by seamlessly integrating its devices and services. Once a consumer invests in one Apple product, they are more likely to continue purchasing others to maintain compatibility and enhance their overall experience.

Behavioral economics tells us that we can help people make wiser choices by changing the environment in which they are making decisions. This idea has wide applicability in financial and health decision-making, workplace productivity, and life happiness.

Research about behavioral economics—the study of how people make choices, drawing on insights from psychology and economics—can be extremely useful in designing and communicating employee health plans. Many health decisions that should be rational are not.

Honesty—Demonstrate honesty and high ethical standards in all business dealings. Respect—Treat customers, partners, suppliers, employees, and others with respect and courtesy. Confidentiality—Protect Apple's confidential information and the information of our customers, partners, suppliers, and employees.

At Apple, we approach everything we do with a deeper level of care and respect for your personal experience. You can sense it in our products, our stores, and also the ways we invest in our employees. It's a recognition of us all as individuals, who thrive when we have the resources that meet our own unique needs.

Productivity for everyone

Every iPhone, iPad, and Mac comes with powerful assistive features for vision, hearing, and motor skills. Apple devices let you write a text or email without seeing the screen. Live Listen lets you fine-tune your Made for iPhone hearing aids and AirPods to help you hear more clearly.

Apple is achieving this goal by using the rule of 3 S's, which is a simple three-step system to increase long-term productivity: streamline, systematize, and step back. Apple has taken advantage of economies of scope by producing a variety of products and services, such as computers, tablets, and phones. This has allowed them to reduce their costs, which has had a significant impact on their profitability.

The company has a dedicated team of customer support agents who are available 24/7 to help customers with any issues or concerns they may have. Apple also uses customer feedback to guide future product development, ensuring that new products and features meet the needs and preferences of its customers.

By positioning its products as high-end and aspirational, Apple creates a perception of desirability and prestige. The sleek and stylish design of Apple devices, coupled with their premium materials and craftsmanship, exude a sense of luxury that appeals to consumers who seek the best.

This type of segmentation is based on consumer's product knowledge, usage rate, loyalty status, and benefits sought. The loyalty that Apple commands amongst its users is legendary. Many users are dedicated followers of the brand and consistently upgrade to the latest models on release.

Apple measure's it's employee performance in to 3 categories: Teamwork, innovation and results. There are 3 levels of performance: Needs improvement, Met expectations, Exceeded expectations.

Current status: all Apple offices, stores, and data centers operate on 100% clean electricity and are carbon-neutral. Eliminating all plastic from packaging by the end of next year. 100% recycled aluminum used in MacBook, Apple TV, and Apple Watch enclosures. Phasing out leather in iPhone cases and Apple Watch bands.

Apple frequently gives every employee gifts ranging from the iPod shuffle to the iPhone. Even the storefront employees attend a considerable number of learning opportunities, team events, and activities, which allows them to keep their motivation high. Apple uses these events to reward and recognize its achievers. They believe in giving employees the freedom to decide how they want to work. This fosters a sense of ownership and enhances overall productivity. It comes as no surprise that an increasing number of customers are choosing Mac for the first time. At Apple, we work every day to put people first — by empowering them with accessible technology, being a force for equity and opportunity, creating an inclusive and diverse work environment, and respecting the human rights of everyone whose lives we touch.

Since Apple sells millions of iPhones each quarter, Apple can commit to component orders at significant volumes, with favorable negotiating leverage that results in volume-based supplier discounts.

Demand Forecasting

Apple leverages advanced analytics and data to predict consumer demand accurately. This predictive modeling helps Apple manage its supply chain efficiently, ensuring that products are available when and where customers want them. The iOS on iPhones is different from Google's Android, whereas the MacOS on the Mac computers is significantly different from Microsoft's Windows. The company also designs its own mobile processors in order to order to provide unmatched performance and better optimization with its own software.

Apple Inc.'s sustained competitive advantage can be attributed to its focus on user experience, continuous innovation, hardware, software, and services integration, branding excellence, ecosystem lock-in, effective supply chain management, strategic partnerships, and long-term vision. However, Apple also encounters new competitors.

Like many tech companies, Apple has suffered from a major consumer shift away from the pandemic-era focus on buying goods. At the height of the pandemic, hundreds of millions across the globe facing lockdowns replaced restaurant expenditures with couches, exercise bikes and tech products.

A detailed understanding of Apple's customers allowed the company to analyze consumer behavior more effectively. Apple uses this insight to tailor products and brand messages that resonate with the target audience making products that work better and are simple to use. When others are seen using Apple products, potential buyers interpret this as proof of the brand's quality and desirability. This type of social proof influences consumer behavior by reassuring them that they are making a wise choice.

How Apple Uses Psychology to Develop Outstanding Experiences

- They maintain Tribalism. ...
- Their retail experience encourages feelings of ownership.
- They Take Advantage of Social Proof. ...
- They also use the Availability Heuristic. ...
- They Maintain their Price Image. ...
- They use Heuristics. ...
- They have excellent attention to detail.

Apple's use of social media for product teasers and exclusive content drives consumer engagement and interest in its offerings. Apple's branding, advertising, and social media strategies have played instrumental roles in establishing the company as a global technology leader.

Apple uses five performance indicators as part of a holistic approach to its long-term performance plan. This includes customer satisfaction, core competencies, employee commitment and alignment (through a comprehensive employee survey), market share and shareholder value.

Every iPhone, iPad, and Mac comes with powerful assistive features for vision, hearing, and motor skills. Apple devices let you write a text or email without seeing the screen. Live Listen lets you fine-tune your Made for iPhone hearing aids and AirPods to help you hear more clearly.

Only Apple devices run iOS. By comparison, multiple manufacturers produce devices that use Google (GOOG 9.96%) (GOOGL 10.22%) Android. This means that if customers want to remain within Apple's ecosystem and keep their digital purchases, they must continue buying iOS devices.

Apple measure's it's employee performance in to 3 categories: Teamwork, innovation and results. There are 3 levels of performance: Needs improvement, Met expectations, Exceeded expectations. Apple gives employees weekly feedback so employees are always focused on achieving their goals. Apple uses a 360 process, illuminating new perspectives and uncovering creative strategies for improvement. Apple measures employee performance against three categories: teamwork, innovation, and results. Apple frequently gives every employee gifts ranging from the iPod shuffle to the iPhone. Even the storefront employees attend a considerable number of learning opportunities, team events, and activities, which allows them to keep their motivation high. Apple uses these events to reward and recognize its achievers. Apple's centralized NPS team uses customer feedback to better understand the reasons that turn customers into promoters or detractors. Furthermore, Apple's team does a daily standup, where employees review the NPS feedback received and discuss how to adjust their work accordingly.

Apple employs the decoy effect in its pricing strategy. By introducing three models of a product at different price points, they influence consumer choice towards the middle or higher-priced option, perceived as more valuable. The premium pricing strategy of Apple creates a perception of higher quality and exclusivity.

Hence, Apple had implemented effective behavioral economic strategy to improve overall customer service performance. Apple conducts consumer behavior surveys to understand their preferences and launch products that can solve existing issues. Brand marketing is a powerful tool that oozes lifestyle, innovation, compassion, and style into the customer experience.

Reference

Australian Bureau of Statistics (ABS), 2014. Australian National Accounts: National income, expenditure and product (cat. no. 5206.0). Accessed 2 February 2015. Australia from (abs.gov.au).

Beckerman, W., 1992. Economic growth and the environment: Whose growth? Whose environment? World development 20, 481-496.

Cornelia, B.F. (1999) Rural development news, the North Central Regional Center For Rural Development vol. no 24 , IOWA.

David J. Nowak & Gordon M. Melsler (2016) " Air quality effects of urban trees and parks." National recreation and park association, USA.

De Hollander, A. E. M., J.M. Melse, Elebret & P. G.N. Kramers (1999), " An Aggregate public health indicator to represent the impact of multiple environmental exposures" Epidemiology: 606-617.

Felce, D. and Perry, J. (1995). Quality of life: A contribution to its definition and measurement, vol. 16, no.1 pp: 51-74.

Grossman, G. M., and A.B. Krueger, 1991. Environment impacts of a North American free trade agreement. NBER working paper 3914. Cambridge, MA: National Bureau Of Economic Research.

Los Angeles Country Department Of public Health (2016), Country Health Ranking Model, Retrieved From www.countryhealthrankgings.org/our-approach. USA.

Melse, J.M. & A.E. M. De Hollander (2001). " Human Health And The Environment", background document for the OECD Environmental Outlook, OECD, Paris.

McGregor, S.L. T., & Goldsmith, E.B. (1998). Expanding our understanding of quality of life, standard of living and well-being. Journal of family and consumer science, 90(2), 2-6, 22.

McMichael, A.J. M. Mckee, J. Shkolnikov and T. Valkanen (2004), " Morality trends and setbacks, global convergence or divergence?", Lancet 363, 1155-1159.

Yale Center For Environmental Law And Policy (2006). Environmental Performance Index. Data available on-line at http://epi.yale.edu

Cone, J. D. and Hayes, S. C., (1980) Environmental Problems/Behavioral Solutions. Monterey, CA: Brooks/Cole.

Erekson, O.H., Loucks, O.L. Strafford, N.C. 1999.
The context of sustainability . In: Sustainability
perspectives for resources and business
USA, p. 3-21.

Daly, H.E. 1990, Towards some operational principles of sustainable development, ecological economics, 2(1), 1-6.

Guerts, M. D. (1986) "The 'bottle bill' effect on grocery stores' costs," International J ournal of Retailing, 1, 12-17.

Kirkby, J; O' Keefe P., Timberlake, L. (eds.) 1995. The earthscan reader in sustainable development. Earthscan Publications Ltd., London, 1-14p.

Hartwell, R.M. (1983). The origins of capitalism. A Methodological Eassy. in Pejovich (1983).

Needham, J. (1963), Poverties and Triumphs of the Chinese scientific tradition, in Crombie (1963).

Skinner, B. F. (1953) Science and Human Behavior, NY: Macmillan.

Winkler, R. C. and Winett, R. A. (1982) "Behavioral interventions in resource conservation: a systems approach based on behavioral economics," American Psychologist 37: 421-435.

Sustainable energy for ALL (SE4ALL) initiative, United Nations secretary. http://www.sustainableenergyforall.org

Towards a green economy pathways to sustainable development and poverty eradication. Unites Nations Environment program (UNEP), 2011 http://www.unep.org/greeneconomy

World energy outlook, executive summary, p.7 IEA , 2012

Australian Bureau of Statistics (ABS), 2014. Australian National Accounts: National income, expenditure and product (cat. no. 5206.0). Accessed 2 February 2015. Australia from (abs.gov.au).

Beckerman, W., 1992. Economic growth and the environment: Whose growth? Whose environment? World development 20, 481-496.

Grossman, G. M., and A.B. Krueger, 1991. Environment impacts of a North American free trade agreement. NBER working paper 3914. Cambridge, MA: National Bureau Of Economic Research.

www.ingramcontent.com/pod-product-compliance
Lightning Source LLC
LaVergne TN
LVHW070443061126
851858LV00011B/155
9798894982410